ORGANIZING
THE
SHIPYARDS

ORGANIZING
THE
Shipyards

UNION STRATEGY IN
THREE NORTHEAST PORTS,
1933–1945

DAVID PALMER

ILR Press an imprint of
Cornell University Press
Ithaca and London

CORNELL UNIVERSITY PRESS GRATEFULLY ACKNOWLEDGES A GRANT
FROM THE NEW JERSEY HISTORICAL COMMISSION THAT AIDED
IN BRINGING THIS BOOK TO PUBLICATION.

First published 1998 by Cornell University Press.

Printed in the United States of America

Library of Congress Cataloging-in-Publication Data

Palmer, David, b. 1949
Organizing the shipyards : union strategy in three
Northeast ports, 1933–1945 / David Palmer.
p.   cm.
Includes bibliographical references and index.
ISBN 0-8014-2734-7 (cloth : alk. paper)
1. Industrial Union of Marine and Shipbuilding Workers of America—History.
2. Trade-unions—Shipbuilding industry employees—Northeastern States—History.
3. Trade-unions—Organizing—United States—Case studies.   I. Title.
HD6515.S512I536   1998
331.88′12382′00974—dc21   98-26635

Cornell University Press strives to use environmentally responsible suppliers and materials
to the fullest extent possible in the publishing of its books. Such materials include
vegetable-based, low-VOC inks and acid-free papers that are recycled,
totally chlorine-free, or partly composed of nonwood fibers.

Cloth printing   10 9 8 7 6 5 4 3 2 1

To Don, Jim, and Fran Bollen; Arthur Boyson;
Lou Kaplan; Andy Reeder; and Phil Van Gelder

CONTENTS

ILLUSTRATIONS

TABLES

ACKNOWLEDGMENTS

Many individuals and organizations made this book possible. Retired shipyard trade unionists, workers, and their families provided invaluable assistance. In particular, I have drawn heavily on the experiences and knowledge of former IUMSWA staff organizers, officers, and rank-and-file elected officials, especially Don Bollen (and Muriel), Arthur Boyson (and Betty), Phil Van Gelder (and Miriam), Lou Kaplan (and June), Lucien Koch, and Andy Reeder (and Eva). Their work and life stories, as well as their analyses, provided through interviews, correspondence, and criticisms of earlier drafts, form the core of this organizing history of the Industrial Union of Marine and Shipbuilding Workers of America (IUMSWA). These individuals and their families, as well as others, welcomed me into their homes and spoke candidly about what they remembered. They also offered personal documents that form part of this study's "archival" research. They did not expect me to write an "official" history, but assumed that I would assess the events honestly based on my own interpretation.

Phil Van Gelder, the IUMSWA's first national secretary-treasurer, provided a remarkable overview of organizing in these ports from the perspective of the national office. He also gave me invaluable firsthand insights into John Green, the IUMSWA's founder, and major CIO leaders such as John L. Lewis and Sidney Hillman. Although I have criticized some of Van Gelder's policies and we differ in our assessments of IUMSWA leadership, it must be recognized that he made an outstanding contribution to the shipbuilding union movement and the CIO.

A number of individuals connected with the Fore River Shipyard and Quincy community helped me begin this project in 1982: Don, Jim, and Fran

Bollen; Steve Meacham, Jack Broder, and Elizabeth Sherman; and Arthur Boyson. Don Bollen gave me all my initial leads and became a good friend when we both lived in Lynn, Massachusetts. He later trained me as an organizer when we were both working for the Boston-area UE from 1984 to 1985, showing me in practice many of the CIO methods from the 1940s. Steve Meacham and Jack Broder were shipyard trade unionists and political activists of my generation; along with then graduate student Elizabeth Sherman, they encouraged me to write the local union's history. Arthur Boyson also became a close friend whom I interviewed many times during the 1980s. He was a true working-class New Englander, never afraid to criticize those he considered weak or opportunist but at the same time not wanting to prove himself any better than the next person. His lifetime spanned the twentieth century, from personal encounters with Eugene Debs and Joseph P. Kennedy through the triumphant era of John L. Lewis, the CIO, and FDR and then the McCarthy period, when some of his close workmates were persecuted, and finally to 1970s and 1980s, when a new group of radical trade union activists tried to reignite the shipbuilding union. Carl and Mary Carlson donated essential local union materials not available in archives. Others who spoke with me about the Fore River Shipyard and the Boston-area labor movement include Fred Bradley, Joe Buckman, Abe Cohen, Buster Cormier, Irving Coughlin, Zeke Frezetti, Vincent Hennebary, Lucien Koch, the Mitchelson family (Alex, Tom, and Agnes), Paul Mulkern, Ruth Parrish, Jack Pizer, and Frank Siegel. IUMSWA Local 5 secretary-treasurer Arthur Durand helped in arranging interviews at the union hall with several retirees.

Others told me the story of organizing New York Shipyard in Camden. Andy Reeder spent many inspiring hours with me over the last years of his life and taught me the meaning of "rank-and-file." He gave me originals or copies of virtually every union document, union-related photo, and news clipping he had. He also was the key organizer of the Camden "Welders' Reunions," where I met many of the New York Ship retirees interviewed here. Others connected directly or indirectly with New York Ship who helped were Horace Bevan, Jack Collins, Floria Coon-Teters, George "Chips" DeGirolamo, Edie and George Fishman, Janet Friedman, Thomas J. Gallagher (Tom Gallagher's son), Eleanor Gehoosky, Jessie Green Snyder (John Green's daughter), John A. Green (John Green's son), Charlie Harker, Leon "Reds" Johnson, Dora Katz, Arthur "Ott" Lynch, Bill McCann, George Snyder, Merville Willis, and the many other individuals who attended the New York Ship workers' reunions in Camden and Gloucester, New Jersey, between 1986 and 1988. Mike Merrill, an organizer of the first reunion, provided the names and contact numbers of many of these people.

For Federal Ship, Lou Kaplan provided me with most contacts. His trade union philosophy and organizing practice was the source for my conclusion that the IUMSWA's major organizing breakthroughs came from implementing the "rank-and-file" strategy (the term, however, is my own). His experience went far beyond Federal Ship and Fore River, although I have only briefly mentioned his other activities. His life story and accomplishments in the trade unions, however controversial, are at the very center of America's labor movement from the 1930s to the 1970s. Nat Levin's letters and telephone conversations were invaluable for helping me to understand the internal dynamics at the Federal yard. Although we were unable to meet in person, I learned much from him about Federal's core union leaders that I could never have discovered simply from the documents. Others who provided either interviews or correspondence, and in some cases union-related material, include Bill Chalmers, Terry Foy, Gabriel Kibildis, Charles Lawesson, Neil McMahon, Joe Peters, Al Petit-Clair, and Henry Tully.

Many librarians and archivists gave me invaluable assistance in locating crucial materials. At MIT's Hart Nautical Collection, director John Arrison led me to the extensive Fore River and Bethlehem collections, introduced me to the engineering side of steel shipbuilding, and offered critiques of my draft history of Fore River. Bethlehem Steel Corporation allowed me access to its papers at the Hart Nautical Collection. Hobart Holly, at the Quincy Historical Society, led me to important Fore River company sources and let me photocopy his personal copy of the Federal Shipbuilding ship list, acquired when he worked there as a naval architect and not to be found, as far as I know, in any libraries or archives. Appreciation is extended to the Quincy Historical Society, Massachusetts, for permission to reprint the Fore River Shipyard General Plan, in the Society's Bethlehem Fore River collection.

Lauren Brown and his staff provided superb help with the IUMSWA collection at the University of Maryland. I would like to thank the national officers of the IUMSWA (now merged with the IAM) for giving me access to the collection at the University of Maryland. Pete Hoefer, of the AFL-CIO Archives, discussed the project with me in its early stages and led me to Andy Reeder. Others who provided assistance are Richard Boyden, Jerry Hess, and Bill Creech at the National Archives in Washington, D.C., and Suitland; Claire Brown at Littauer Library, Harvard University; the Kearny Museum; the Kearny Public Library; the Newark Public Library's New Jersey Room; the Philadelphia Maritime Museum; the South Street Seaport Museum, New York City; the Wagner Archives, at Tamiment Library, New York University; David Zarowin at the Massachusetts Historical Commission; the Camden County Historical Society; Goldfarb Library at Brandeis University; Joe Doyle of the

American Labor Museum, Patterson, New Jersey; Christopher Baer of the Hagley Museum and Library; and Rosalind Libbey of the New Jersey Historical Society, Newark.

Community assistance came from Mary Campbell of Kearny; Joan Telfer of the Kearny Senior Citizens Center; and Lucy Parlee of the Quincy Senior Citizens Center. Historians who provided me with research leads and suggestions include Pat Cooper, Colin Davis, Nigel Hamilton, Bill Harvey, and Deborah Hirschfield. Among those who critiqued earlier versions of this history while I was at Brandeis University are John Demos, Carol Ely, Jim Green, Ralph Miliband, and June Namias. Jama Lazarow assisted in locating essential material related to Fore River while he was at MIT. James Kloppenberg, Nelson Lichtenstein, and Jacob Vander Meulen offered suggestions after reading the completed dissertation. Mary LeCaptain provided important suggestions and invaluable support while I was completing the initial study.

Morton Keller, my dissertation adviser, provided detailed and valued criticism as well as continuous encouragement. Alex Keyssar initially advised this project. He and Paul Faler made it possible for me to begin the study of labor history when I was making the transition from the trade union movement to the academic environment.

I received financial assistance from a Brandeis University Crown Fellowship, faculty research funds while at Harvard University's Social Studies program, and overseas conference funding and study leave from Flinders University of South Australia. I received a New Jersey Historical Commission research grant, and the dissertation was awarded the state's Driscoll Prize, which carried a publishing subvention; I would particularly like to thank Mary Murrin and Howard Green of the Commission.

Peter Agree, editor at Cornell University Press, remained encouraging throughout the long gestation of this book. Three anonymous readers for CUP provided critical and insightful suggestions. One reader in particular wrote extensive and detailed suggestions, especially regarding the problem of race and the shipyards, that made me rethink parts of the original manuscript in new ways. Grey Osterud did superb editing of the final manuscript.

I am grateful to Swallow Press, Chicago, and Thomas McGrath, Jr., for permission to reprint excerpts from page 143 of Thomas McGrath's *Letter to an Imaginary Friend, Parts I and II* (Chicago: Swallow Press, 1962, reprinted 1970). Joe Doyle initially told me of McGrath's connection to the Federal Shipyard, related in part in this long poem.

As the final manuscript was being prepared for publication, Greg Palmer, Jim Bollen, and Lou Kaplan helped me locate interviewees for permission to publish material from interviews and letters. To have done this solely from Australia would have been an extremely difficult, if not impossible, task.

Thanks also to Arthur Boyson, Jr., for giving permission to quote from those interviews with Arthur Boyson for which I did not have releases.

In Australia, Tom Sheridan of the University of Adelaide critiqued parts of the final manuscript and provided collegial support during critical times. At Flinders University, American Studies, appreciation is extended to Sue Hesch for comments and Sue Parkin for clerical assistance on early chapters. Finally, my thanks to Desiree Beasley for our many discussions of the larger issues and for critiquing the entire manuscript in its final form, and to Reuben and Nathan, who always made me realize there is a generation just beginning to discover the world.

DAVID PALMER

Adelaide, Australia

ORGANIZING
THE
SHIPYARDS

INTRODUCTION

The industrial union organizing drive of the 1930s was a movement for democracy. Talk to the mass production workers who took part in it, and they will tell you that what they wanted more than anything else was dignity. . . . Like democratic movements in America before and since, they believed that the human right to a job should take precedence over the property right to manage an enterprise as the employer sees fit.

> —Alice Lynd and Staughton Lynd, *Rank and File*

> The machines roar into life.
> The malignant
> Arcs of the welders sizzle across the darkness.
> The yard
> Groans and curses and shakes, tormented, as if to tear loose
> From the anchoring stone and mount toward heaven on its anquished song.

> —Thomas McGrath (poet), *Letter to an Imaginary Friend*, *Parts I and II*, describing work at Federal Shipyard during World War II

> Organizing fever was in the air.

> —Nat Levin, Federal Shipyard welder and union activist, from letter to David Palmer, March 31, 1988

"If we are to reverse the decline of the labor movement, organizing must be more than a slogan."[1] These words appeared in a late 1980s union pamphlet by the Communications Workers of America (CWA), one of the fastest-growing trade unions in the United States with some three-quarters of a million members. By 1995, the crisis in organizing became a rallying cry for John Sweeney's successful challenge to the long-complacent AFL-CIO of Lane Kirkland and Thomas Donahue. The problems confronting contemporary or-

---

[1] Communications Workers of America, "The CWA Triangle: Organizing, Representation, Community/Political Action" (Washington, D.C., c. 1990).

1

ganizers, however, were present when the CIO first took shape in the depths of the Great Depression. The current debate over how American trade unions can create viable organizing strategies stands to gain by better understanding the history of organizing.

This book relates how organizers in one union, the Industrial Union of Marine and Shipbuilding Workers of America (IUMSWA), developed strategy and tactics at the local level between 1933 and 1945, during the most critical organizing period for twentieth-century industrial unionism. The focus is on three huge shipbuilding complexes: New York Shipbuilding, Camden, New Jersey, in the port of Philadelphia; Fore River Shipbuilding, Quincy, Massachusetts, in the port of Boston; and Federal Shipbuilding, Kearny, New Jersey, in the port of New York. Two of the yards were owned by major steel corporations; Bethlehem Steel's shipbuilding division operated Fore River, while U.S. Steel controlled Federal Ship. New York Ship was acquired by Aviation Corporation, which later became AVCO.

While this study touches on rank-and-file workers' culture, workers' "consciousness," and the work process, it focuses mainly on how leadership helped shape workers' discontent and random resistance into a coordinated movement with an institutional, trade union framework. Many of the leaders in this history were rank-and-file workers. Some of them (Arthur Boyson) remained rank-and-file workers their entire lives. Some leaders were intellectuals (Phil Van Gelder) and some belonged to left-wing political organizations (Jim, Fran, and Don Bollen). I have tried, where possible, to provide a biographical framework for leaders' activities and their ideas on organizing and politics. In a sense, then, this book is a collective biography of union organizers at all levels within the IUMSWA of the Northeast.

Union organizers today need detailed information about workers and workplaces for successful organizing. The oral histories and union documents that form the basis of this history reveal that the early CIO organizers who were successful had the same frame of mind. This study therefore incorporates such detail, including precise chronologies, lists of departments and rank-and-file leaders' names, and, where possible, exact election results. Evidence on each shipyard's racial, ethnic, and gender makeup, however, is either fragmentary or not available.[2]

This book analyzes organizing failures as well as successes, especially in

---

[2] Company records of U.S. Steel, which owned Federal Shipbuilding, are closed to historians. Records of Bethlehem Shipbuilding are available only in limited form at Hart Nautical Museum, Massachusetts Institute of Technology; these documents do not include internal management records or personnel information (except for lists of aliens employed in the yard during World War I). New York Shipbuilding's records have disappeared, except for material on ships that is held by the Philadelphia Maritime Museum.

the case of Fore River, where the IUMSWA spent twelve years trying to organize. Understanding initial defeats is essential to any analysis of strategy, and reveals long-term trends and the shifting balance of forces between the union and management. Success, too, can only be measured against earlier problems; such a perspective reveals how those problems were overcome.

The development of strategy within the IUMSWA came about largely from the immediate experience of organizers in various locations. Planned strategies occasionally were put forward and tested, as when IUMSWA secretary-treasurer Phil Van Gelder attempted to engineer a national (or "general") shipbuilding strike in the spring of 1935 to accelerate organizing. More often, strategy was shaped by tactical successes and failures, which led to a high level of improvisation and uncertainty. The historical experience of AFL craft union failures in the shipbuilding industry, dating back to the end of World War I but extending into the early 1930s, was always on the minds of the IUMSWA national officers. At the same time, the historic successes of the United Mine Workers (UMW) and the Amalgamated Clothing Workers (ACW), along with the militant traditions of Scottish Clydeside shipbuilding unionism and the "direct action" tactics of the American, left-wing Industrial Workers of the World (IWW), influenced approaches to strategy.

Ultimately, it was organizers in the field working directly with rank-and-file leaders and workers, rather than full-time national officers, who devised successful organizing strategies. Some of these organizers later took their experience and organizing talents into other unions, where lessons from the shipyards could be applied to workers in different industries and conditions.

In twentieth-century America, shipbuilding has been geared overwhelmingly to military rather than commercial purposes. The United States was the world's largest producer of naval and merchant marine vessels during the two world wars. Furthermore, the naval side of the industry has always been concentrated in huge shipyards employing thousands of workers, some government-owned, but the majority operated by large corporations.[3]

---

[3] For histories of various aspects of the American steel shipbuilding industry during the twentieth century, see John Hutchins, *The American Maritime Industries and Public Policy, 1789–1914* (Cambridge, Mass.: Harvard University Press, 1941), pp. 441–81; Robert A. Kilmarx, ed., *America's Maritime Legacy: A History of the U.S. Merchant Marine and Shipbuilding Industry Since Colonial Times* (Boulder, Colorado: Westview Press, 1979); John G. Arrison, "Introduction of Steel into New England Shipbuilding," New England Section (Boston), The Society of Naval Architects and Marine Engineers, May 1986; Frederic C. Lane et al., *Ships for Victory: A History of Shipbuilding under the U.S. Maritime Commission in World War II* (Baltimore: Johns Hopkins University Press, 1951); Thomas J. Misa, "Science, Technology and Industrial Structure: Steelmaking in America, 1870–1920" (Ph.D. diss., University of Pennsylvania, 1987), especially "The Politics of Armour, 1880–1910"; and David A. Houn-

Most of the big private shipyards were built during the 1890s, when America gained international supremacy in a number of key industries. Shipbuilding expanded in response to the rise of American imperialism, which culminated in the Spanish-American War. By the early 1900s, major ship production was concentrated in four industrial complexes, which included Fore River, New York Ship, and Newport News. All were located on the East Coast and employed an average of at least 3,000 workers. (See Table 1.) In 1900, three shipyards were among the nation's thirty-one largest manufacturing plants (which had 3,000–10,000 workers each); only the steel and electrical equipment industries had more plants of this size.[4] Federal Shipbuilding, a new operation geared to World War I, joined the ranks of these giant yards by 1917. Unlike most of the wartime yards, however, Federal Ship did not disappear at the war's conclusion, but continued operating, becoming one of the "Big Five" by World War II.

---

shell, "Ford Eagle Boats and Mass Production during World War I," in Merritt Roe Smith, ed., *Military Enterprise and Technological Change* (Cambridge, Mass.: MIT Press, 1987). Histories of shipbuilding that concentrate on the concept of the military-industrial complex include Benjamin Franklin Cooling, *Gray Steel and Blue Water Navy: The Formative Years of America's Military-Industrial Complex, 1881–1917* (Hamden, Conn.: Archon Books, 1979); and Paul A. C. Koistinen, *The Military-Industrial Complex: A Historical Perspective* (New York: Praeger, 1980). On shipbuilding unionism and workers, see Bernard Mergen, "A History of the Industrial Union of Marine and Shipbuilding Workers of America, 1933–1951" (Ph.D. diss., University of Pennsylvania, 1968); Amy Kesselman, *Fleeting Opportunities: Women Shipyard Workers in Portland and Vancouver During World War II and Reconversion* (Albany: State University of New York Press, 1990); Deborah A. Hirschfield, "Rosie Also Welded: Women and Technology in Shipbuilding During World War II" (Ph.D. diss., University of California, Irvine, 1987); Bruce Nelson, "Organized Labor and the Struggle for Black Equality in Mobile During World War II," *Journal of American History* 80 (Dec. 1993) 952–88; Mary Martha Thomas, *Riveting and Rationing in Dixie: Alabama Women and the Second World War* (Tuscaloosa: University of Alabama Press, 1987); Merl E. Reed, "Black Workers, Defense Industries, and Federal Agencies in Pennsylvania, 1941–1945," *Labor History* 27 (Summer 1986) 356–84; Reed, "The FEPC, the Black Worker, and the Southern Shipyards," *South Atlantic Quarterly* 74 (Autumn 1975) 446–67; William H. Harris, "Federal Intervention in Union Discrimination: FEPC and West Coast Shipyards During World War II," *Labor History* 22 (1981) 325–47; Herbert Hill, *Black Labor and the American Legal System* (Madison: University of Wisconsin Press, 1985), esp. "The Shipbuilding Industry and the International Brotherhood of Boilermakers," pp. 185–208; Joshua B. Freeman and Steve Rosswurm, "The Education of an Anti-Communist: Father John F. Cronin and the Baltimore Labor Movement," *Labor History* 33 (Spring 1992) 217–47; and Karen Beck Skold, "The Job He Left Behind: American Women in Shipyards During World War II," in Carol R. Berkin and Clara M. Lovett, eds., *Women, War and Revolution* (New York: Holmes and Meier, 1980). Most of this literature focuses on the experiences of women and black workers in the South and on the West Coast during wartime, rather than on the union movement that was centered in the Northeast and began in the early 1930s.

[4] Daniel Nelson, *Managers and Workers: Origins of the New Factory System in the United States, 1880–1920* (Madison: University of Wisconsin Press, 1975), pp. 7–9.

Table I. Employment in Largest U.S. Coastal Shipyards, 1901–1916

Year	N.Y. Ship, Camden, N.J.	Fore River, Quincy, Mass.	Sparrows Pt., Md.	Union, San Francisco, Ca.	Newport News, Va.	Cramp, Philadelphia, Pa.
1901	4,000	*	2,500	4,000	7,000	7,000
1902	3,000	*	2,500	4,000	6,000	8,000
1903	4,200	4,000	2,000	*	6,500	8,000
1904	*					
1905	*					
1906	4,000	4,000	1,500	3,500	5,700	6,000
1907	4,700	4,000	1,500	3,500	5,700	5,000
1908	3,800	3,000	1,500	2,750	5,700	5,000
1909	4,000	4,000	1,500	1,250	5,000	*
1910	4,000	3,500	1,800	*	5,000	4,000
1911	4,000	3,300	1,500	*	5,000	3,500
1912	5,000	4,000	2,200	*	5,000	5,000
1913	5,000	*	2,000	1,750	5,000	4,500
1914	3,500	3,570	1,300	*	5,000	4,500
1915	4,500	4,200	2,300	1,600	5,500	5,000
1916	*	4,000	2,500	5,300	7,000	*

*No data available.
Employment at Harlan & Hollingsworth, Wilmington, Del., which ranked in size with these shipyards, was comparable to that at Sparrows Point.
Source: U.S. Dept. of Commerce, *Reports of the Commissioner of Navigation*, by year.

During the First World War, shipbuilding had become an integral part of America's early military-industrial complex. Organized labor, led by the AFL, played a prominent role in this war-based industry through its trade union leverage on production. Membership in AFL shipbuilding unions, which were organized by crafts, grew rapidly during the war, in part because of government support but even more from a massive strike wave initiated by workers themselves. Shipbuilding strikes accounted for 16.7 percent of all workers nationally who went on strike between April and October 1917, second only to all metal trades industries and ahead of coal mining.[5]

By early 1918, the government's Shipbuilding Labor Adjustment Board (SLAB) established wage awards by region, and the AFL's advance seemed quite solid. In early 1919, Bethlehem took the lead among national corpora-

[5] For a detailed account of shipbuilding unionism during and immediately after World War I, see David Palmer, "Organizing the Shipyards: Unionization at Fore River, New York Ship, and Federal Ship, 1898–1945" (Ph.D. diss., Brandeis University, 1990), pp. 136–256. Strike statistics from National Industrial Conference Board, *Strikes in American Industry in Wartime: April 6 to October 6, 1917* (Boston: NICB, March 1918), p. 7.

tions in the industry by signing an agreement with the thirteen AFL Metal Trades unions in shipbuilding. Although the agreement appeared to recognize these unions, it had more resemblance to a loose memorandum of understanding. It did not mention wages or establish concrete improvements in working conditions. It did seek to link the AFL unions with local shop committees, or "works councils," which the SLAB had authorized, but it did not grant exclusive recognition to the AFL. Bethlehem used these schemes for public relations, but continued to ignore the SLAB award of increased wage rates. That same year, the corporation began setting up its own Employee Representation Plans (ERPs), which were nothing more than company unions designed to undercut the AFL.

AFL union officials mistakenly believed that the SLAB award and the agreement with Bethlehem were opening a new progressive era for shipyard workers. Joseph Flynn, a top Boilermakers Union officer in charge of organizing, blindly asserted in 1919 that the AFL-Bethlehem agreement "will no doubt lead to the complete organization of all of the employees of this company." Bethlehem management, however, saw the arrangement as temporary, while viewing its ERP company union arrangement as permanent. Bethlehem Steel president Eugene Grace made his real intentions clear in 1920 when he stated: "I firmly believe that any character of relations or association, to support and protect the open shop principle . . . in this country is a good thing."[6]

Workers in the shipyards disregarded their national union officers' call for labor peace and followed their local leadership instead. They went on strike in response to company intransigence, not only at Bethlehem yards, but at New York Ship, Federal Ship, and many other locations. They did so along craft lines, through individual unions and at different times, rather than as a single, unified industrial action. Bethlehem and companies like it defeated the AFL unions one by one. By the time of the 1922 railroad shop strike (led by the IAM), the shipyard divisions of the craft unions were totally destroyed as viable organizations. With a reactionary, anti-labor Republican administration holding power in Washington, the AFL shipbuilding union locals lost their last leverage point and collapsed. Only individual activists remained, if they were lucky enough not to lose their jobs in the "shipbuilding depression" of the early 1920s.

The feeling of betrayal among the rank-and-file ran deep and lasted a generation. In 1935, IUMSWA national secretary-treasurer Phil Van Gelder summarized this anger in his *Book of Facts for Shipyard Workers.*

---

[6] *Boilermakers' and Iron Ship Builders' Journal*, Feb. 1919, p. 105; Eugene Grace testimony to Lockwood Committee (1920), as quoted in NLRB, First Region, "Bethlehem Shipbuilding v. IUMSWA Local 5," Case nos. I-C-25 and I-C-536, Intermediate Report, Aug. 23, 1938, p. 9, National Archives (hereafter cited as NA), RG 25, Box 1669.

The craft unions were licked one at a time. . . . They lost money on strikes, and members were thrown out of work so they couldn't pay dues. Some of the union officials and business agents ran away with the treasuries, and some grafted, and some got good jobs for themselves at the expense of the rank and file membership. . . . The International Association of Machinists . . . and the Boilermakers . . . were the leading A. F. of L. unions in the shipyards, and they became so weak that the big corporations no longer took them seriously.[7]

Behind Van Gelder's charge was the most serious accusation of all: that the rank-and-file had been denied a voice, had been cheated, and had been misled through division and weakness. The IUMSWA, Van Gelder assured them, was a very different type of union.

Founded in 1933 at New York Shipbuilding in Camden, New Jersey, the IUMSWA was the first industrial union of the 1930s to originate outside the AFL and survive the decade intact. The IUMSWA's main distinction was its industrial form of organization, with all crafts and skill levels under one union. The United Electrical Workers Union (UE), also a new non-AFL industrial union, was not established until 1936, some three years later. The IUMSWA was able to organize in part because of the persistence of trade union identity among shipyard workers, which had carried over from the turbulent World War I years. The combination of high skill levels, which induced strong pride in shipbuilding as a unique industry, with difficult working conditions and harsh yard-level management contributed to shipyard workers' openness to industrial unionism. The establishment of the IUMSWA was a pioneering organizational achievement.

The IUMSWA played a major role in the labor movement during World War II as well. In 1943, the peak year for war production, the industry that employed the most workers was not steel, aircraft, or motor transport (cars, trucks, and tanks), but shipbuilding. New shipyards alone employed over half a million workers. By 1943, the number of workers employed in all private shipyards reached some 1,400,000, and navy yards employed over 300,000. In April 1933, only 49,000 had worked in the shipyards, and even in June 1940 the number had risen to just 168,000. For the ascendant CIO, shipbuilding became one of the labor movement's most critical organizing targets during World War II.[8]

[7] Phil Van Gelder, *Book of Facts for Shipyard Workers* (Camden, N.J.: IUMSWA, 1935), p. 3.

[8] Paul R. Porter, "Labor in the Shipbuilding Industry," in Colston E. Warne, Warren B. Catlin, et al., eds., *Yearbook of American Labor*, vol. 1: *War Labor Policies* (New York: Philosophical Library, 1945), pp. 345–46; U.S. Department of Labor, "Wartime Employment, Production, and Conditions of Work in Shipyards," *Bureau of Labor Statistics Bulletin* No. 824 (Washington, D.C.: Government Printing Office 1945), pp. 1–3. For general histories of labor

Officially, the IUMSWA claimed close to half a million members by 1944 and 1945. The actual membership figures, however, were far lower. In 1944, the peak year for the IUMSWA, membership stood at 208,800; a year earlier, at the highest point of shipbuilding employment during the war, the IUMSWA had only 135,600 members. What accounts for this discrepancy between ship-building's huge employment numbers and the far lower totals of IUMSWA members? How could this occur at a time when government agencies, such as the National War Labor Board, looked favorably on unions as part of the tripartite industrial relations process and provided "automatic" mechanisms, such as maintenance-of-membership provisions, that should have enhanced union growth?[9]

The reasons for the IUMSWA's initial success at New York Ship in 1933 and its later, wartime difficulties in organizing at a number of critical locations, especially Fore River, can be found in large part by understanding local organizing history. Favorable economic and political conditions alone did not then, and do not now, guarantee union growth.

The historical evidence, when examined in detail first at the local level and then at the national level, points to the importance of both conditions and the role of union leadership and institutions. The long-range planning and organization that leaders devise for institution- and movement-building can be designated as strategy. Tactics are short-term actions that are taken within various phases of this strategy. Union organizing strategy involves several phases. The key ones are preparation, initial organizing, and consolidation. A critical turning point for American unions has historically been union recognition by management. From 1937, recognition hinged on an election authorized by the National Labor Relations Board (NLRB), and was usually followed by the negotiation and signing of an agreement between the union and management. Organizing at New York Ship and Federal Ship, however, did not follow this

---

during World War II, see Joel Seidman, *American Labor from Defense to Reconversion* (Chicago: University of Chicago Press, 1953); and Nelson Lichtenstein, *Labor's War at Home: The CIO in World War II* (Cambridge: Cambridge University Press, 1982). Both of these seminal works mention the IUMSWA, but give far more attention to the Steelworkers, Miners, and Auto Workers.

[9] The IUMSWA claimed various membership totals at different times during World War II. By 1944 they hovered near the half-million mark. The Labor Research Association's *Labor Fact Book 7* (New York: International Publishers, 1945), p. 63, gave a figure of 400,000. As late as April 11, 1945, *The New England Shipbuilder* (which was used in the 1945 Fore River campaign) claimed that IUMSWA president John Green was the "leader of 500,000 shipyard workers." The most persuasive IUMSWA membership figures, which are based on per capita receipt calculations, come from Leo Troy, "Trade Union Membership, 1897–1962," Occasional Paper 92, National Bureau of Economic Research (New York: Columbia University Press, 1965), table A-2.

pattern, because formal NLRB operations that functioned effectively and with proper authority had not yet been firmly established. Even after 1937, organizing entailed more than specific legal arrangements between the union and management. Most decisive, this book argues, was the level of local union membership and involvement and the existence of local leadership that could mobilize these members into an active movement.

This book raises a number of historical problems related to union-building and organizing: issues of internal union organization, bureaucracy, centralization, and the limits of local democracy and autonomy; labor law, government institutions, and local and national politics; management, production, and industrial relations policies, as well as counter-strategies to unionization; and the social base for unionism and union support.

Throughout this book I have, wherever possible, provided detail on the racial, ethnic, and gender composition of the workplace and community. There are severe limitations, however, in existing data on these workplaces. No documentation of specific numbers of workers by ethnicity or race exists for these three yards, except for Fore River Shipyard's "Alien Reports" for 1917 and 1919 that list non-citizen workers by country of origin. For the 1930s and 1940s, it is possible to get some sense of the ethnic and racial composition of these yards by piecing together anecdotal evidence from oral histories and IUMSWA, company, government, and newspaper sources. At various points, I use census data to provide a racial and ethnic profile of the surrounding communities. Aggregate data on shipyard workers by region for World War II is generally misleading for companies like Bethlehem Shipbuilding in Massachusetts, New York Ship, and Federal Ship, which hired women and blacks for the most part only into the temporary, auxiliary yards (at Hingham for Fore River and at Newark for Federal). Newspaper figures, too, are unreliable because the local press tended to inflate employment at yards within its immediate circulation range. Some hiring of blacks and women did occur at New York Ship and Federal during World War II (at least more than at Fore River), but this history (in the phase of consolidation rather than initial organizing) is beyond the scope of the present study.[10]

The IUMSWA's local organizing history in the Northeast ports reveals some of the limitations of CIO unionism. Too often the new unions neglected the larger social context, which encompassed community and other social movements involving women and blacks. Shipbuilding employers generally pre-

---

[10] "Alien Reports," glass photos, Negative Box 18, "Yard History Misc.," Bethlehem Collection, Hart Nautical Museum, MIT. For Federal Shipbuilding during World War II, see Palmer, "Organizing the Shipyards," pp. 676–788.

ferred "white" labor for skilled jobs, and they hired workers from Southern and Eastern European backgrounds for semi-skilled and unskilled positions where enough native-born or Northern European immigrant workers could not be found. Although the IUMSWA constitution opposed ethnic, racial, religious, and political discrimination (but not discrimination by sex), the union did not commonly challenge discriminatory employer practices. The IUMSWA maintained one seniority list for all workers, in contrast to the Boilermakers and other conservative AFL unions that had separate black and white lists, but the IUMSWA did not take the initiative to bring black workers into the Northeast yards.

The IUMSWA can be viewed not only as a union institution but also as a part of a social movement beyond the parameters of formal structures. Many current trade union activists seeking to reform and transform American unions take a similar perspective, and often use the terms "social unionism" or "community unionism." But during the 1930s, this "movement" in shipbuilding was usually confined to the workplace, with the "community" (including women, blacks, and others) playing only a supportive role.[11]

For the CIO organizing era, a company-specific framework is especially appropriate. This study draws on a wide range of government, company, and union documents, as well as local newspapers and other publications. Oral histories are essential to this workplace-based approach. Combined with extensive archival sources, these narratives make it possible to reconstruct much of what occurred at a local level, whether at the workplace or in the community.[12] To this end, I conducted personal interviews with over fifty people during an eight-year period. Most were shipyard workers who were active in the IUMSWA, a number were staff organizers or union officers, and a few were family members or spouses of workers. In some cases I interviewed groups, such as the Mitchelson family in Quincy and the retired welders in the Cam-

---

[11] Alain Touraine, "Unionism as a Social Movement," in Seymour Martin Lipset, ed., *Unions in Transition* (San Francisco: ISC Press, 1986), pp. 151–73, provides an excellent summation of this "movement-institution" dichotomy from a theoretical perspective. For its application to American trade unionism, see Kim Moody, *An Injury to All: The Decline of American Unionism* (New York: Verso Press, 1988), esp. pp. xiii–xxi, 331–50; and Jeremy Brecher and Tim Costello, eds., *Building Bridges: The Emerging Grassroots Coalition of Labor and Community* (New York: Monthly Review Press, 1990). For the international implications of this problem, see Alain Touraine et al., *Solidarity: Poland 1980–81* (Cambridge: Cambridge University Press, 1984); and Alain Touraine et al., *The Workers' Movement* (Cambridge: Cambridge University Press, 1987).

[12] In taking this company-specific approach, which relies heavily on oral histories, I was especially influenced by Peter Friedlander, *The Emergence of a UAW Local, 1936–1939: A Study in Class and Culture* (Pittsburgh: University of Pittsburgh Press, 1975); and Ronald W. Schatz, *The Electrical Workers: A History of Labor at General Electric and Westinghouse, 1923–60* (Urbana: University of Illinois Press, 1983).

den area. I interviewed a few of the most important individuals connected with the national union and the three yards' locals a number of times and established written correspondence where possible. When I completed drafts of chapters, I asked for criticisms and corrections from some of these former officers and organizers, including Phil Van Gelder, Lou Kaplan, Lucien Koch, Jim and Don Bollen, and Andy Reeder.

For many retired union activists, recording their history became an affirmation of their contribution to the trade union movement and a summation of their life's work. When people see their history retold after traditions have been forgotten, it can have a powerful effect on them. Andy Reeder, who had worked as a welder at Federal Ship, offered these comments in response to my chapter on organizing there. "Some of these men that fought the company unions and the company were so great and what fine men they were. No one can ever know the sacrifices made. They were men who stood up to be counted. The first two times I read your paper, I was frightened as it turned the clock back for me. I was there—how we ever did it, I just don't know." [13] Many workers I interviewed had a similar response and recognized for the first time that their lives had historical, not just personal, meaning.

This book is divided into three sections, each covering the critical organizing years at one of the three yards. Part I deals with organizing at New York Ship from 1932 to 1935, along with the establishment of the IUMSWA. Chapter 1 focuses on the initial organizing and the new union's key leaders, all of whom were shipyard workers, and describes the dynamics of organizing inside a huge steel shipbuilding complex. Chapter 2 relates how and under what conditions IUMSWA Local 1 waged its first strike and won a contract in 1934. Chapter 3 focuses on the long 1935 strike, which forced the IUMSWA to concentrate its organizing in Camden. Recognition had not been adequately secured the year before, so the union not only had to mobilize workers and the community but also needed to gain the support of officials and politicians in Washington, D.C., including President Franklin D. Roosevelt. By this time, IUMSWA president John Green and the national union had moved from the socialist ideals of workers' control of the early 1933 union to more nationally acceptable social democratic politics of the left wing of FDR's New Deal administration.

Part II focuses on organizing Federal Ship from 1934 to 1938, and also covers critical organizing developments at private yards in New York harbor. Chapter 4 describes the initial organizing efforts, which began separately in different yards, and relates how the IUMSWA implemented an imaginative

---

[13] Andy Reeder letter to David Palmer, Aug. 4, 1986.

but, for the time, customary strategy at Federal Ship: takeover of the company union followed by a massive, though brief, strike for recognition. Chapter 5 deals with organizing at Federal Ship after the union won its first contract but had only limited power and a weak membership base. This struggle took place in the larger context of a general strike in the port of New York that almost destroyed the IUMSWA. Continued organizing at Federal Ship required direct-action tactics that created sharp differences between local trade unionists and the national officers, especially IUMSWA national president John Green, over how much local democracy the national union would allow. The initial organizing phase at Federal did not end until the 1940 NLRB election, but this legal landmark hardly resolved the growing and complex divisions within the IUMSWA.

Part III covers Fore River from the 1920s to 1945. This yard was the last of the three to be organized, and it is the failures of the IUMSWA's Fore River campaigns before 1945 in particular that illuminate the local-national tension within the union. Two main themes throughout this history are, first, the continued dominance of Bethlehem management over its workers through company unionism and its promotion of the fear that the IUMSWA was run by communists and "outsiders," and, second, the failure of the IUMSWA national officers, until 1945, either to find capable local leadership or to allow talented staff and local people to pursue organizing suited to conditions in Quincy and the greater Boston region.

Chapter 6 surveys the 1920s and 1930s, from the inception of Bethlehem's ERPs following the AFL unions' collapse to the numerous challenges and setbacks the IUMSWA encountered during the Great Depression, when the corporation outmaneuvered the IUMSWA in numerous legal battles and managed to hold workers' loyalty. Chapter 7 details the 1941 organizing drive and election, which became a microcosm of the struggle between local "democrats" and national office "centralists," and the emergence of open anticommunism at the upper levels of the IUMSWA. The eventual takeover of the campaign by the CIO and the eclipse of local union activists presents a remarkable parallel with recent problems in the American labor movement. Chapter 8 concludes by explaining how Fore River organizers developed a highly effective rank-and-file–based organizing strategy, which actually recalled the IUMSWA's perspective in its first years in Camden. The road to success in 1945 was a difficult one, revealing deep divisions in the IUMSWA that could not be healed in the postwar era.

This history is as much the story of the organizers and workers who waged these union campaigns as it is of three giant shipyards organized by the IUMSWA during its formative years. The development of trade union strategy and tactics was not merely a historical "trend" or "social force," but was a conscious process undertaken by individuals working daily in the ship-yards and communities. These shipyards and even the union itself have disap-peared, and many of those interviewed have now passed from the scene. It is my hope, however, that the collective experience of these workers and orga-nizers can provide not just a historical but also a living perspective for those today facing a similar crisis in their workplaces and unions.

PART I

INDUSTRIAL UNIONISM COMES TO THE YARDS: NEW YORK SHIP, 1933–1935

CHAPTER 1

"Joining in One Strong Union" Founding the IUMSWA at New York Ship, 1933

The New York Shipbuilding Corporation, located in Camden, New Jersey, was at the heart of the United States naval construction program and military-industrial complex for over half a century. It began as a speculative venture capitalized by Andrew Mellon and other financiers in 1899, during the first steel shipbuilding boom in the wake of the Spanish-American War. From its inception, the yard was conceived as a giant production complex. The founder and first president, Henry Morse, deliberately designed it with massive shipways and adjoining shops to handle the efficient building of ships. The yard came to specialize in battleships and destroyers by World War I, but it could easily build ocean liners and virtually any other type of vessel.[1]

Located on the banks of the Delaware River in the port of Philadelphia, New York Ship could draw on the country's most skilled shipyard craftsmen. At the turn of the century, the company employed over 4,000 workers and ranked as one America's 100 largest industrial plants. By the First World War, shipyards in the United States employed over half a million workers, giving the American Federation of Labor (AFL) Metal Trades unions unprecedented opportunities to organize. Shipyard workers, including those at New York Ship, joined by the thousands and won wage increases under regional agreements guaranteed by the government's Shipbuilding Labor Adjustment Board. With the end

---

[1] *Fifty Years: New York Shipbuilding* (Camden, N.J.: New York Shipbuilding Corp., 1949), pp. 11–19. For Andrew Mellon's financial connections to New York Shipbuilding, see U.S. Cong., Senate, Special Committee Investigating the Munitions Industry, *Hearings*, 74th Cong., 1st sess. 1935 (Washington, D.C.: Government Printing Office, 1936) (hereafter cited as "Munitions Industry Hearings," 1935), "Naval Shipbuilding—New York Shipbuilding Corporation." (U.S. Government Printing Office hereafter cited as GPO.)

of the war, however, federal support for such agreements ended, naval cut-
backs decimated shipbuilding employment, and the AFL unions collapsed in
a wave of desperate and futile localized strikes.[2]

By 1933 the nation's shipyard union movement reemerged at New York
Ship in a very different form from the discredited AFL's craft unions. The
Camden shipyard union activists built an entirely new organization, independent of the AFL: the Industrial Union of Marine and Shipbuilding Workers of
America (IUMSWA). The revitalization of trade unionism at New York Ship
during the early 1930s depended, for the most part, on four critical factors: the
advantage provided by management's poor strategy and tactics; the regional
advantage of the vibrant Philadelphia-South Jersey union environment around
Camden, which contributed to a major organizing upsurge in the area; the dramatic shift in federal government policy brought about by the administration
of President Franklin D. Roosevelt and its supporters in Congress; and, perhaps most decisive, the development of new union leadership within the yard.

The New York Shipbuilding Corporation, along with a few other major construction yards, maintained a small number of very lucrative contracts in 1932
and 1933, despite the Depression's devastation of the economy. In 1932, the
cruiser *Tuscaloosa* and the ocean liner *Manhattan* were under construction at
New York Ship, and yard employment, though not always steady, averaged
about 2,000. As one of the three major private shipyards in the nation, New
York Ship was not in danger of closing its doors, despite its public claims to
the contrary.[3]

Nevertheless, earnings and working conditions for the average shipyard
worker deteriorated substantially with the onset of the Depression. There had
never been security in shipbuilding employment, except through the good
graces of a friendly foreman. Declining shipyard production and employment
during the Depression only increased workers' vulnerability, even though construction yard workers, unlike those who worked in the repair yard, were not
subject to the hiring shape-up. New York Ship, like all large shipyards in the
early 1930s, had a totally male production workforce. Layoffs came arbitrarily, with no warning. Single men were generally the first to go, regardless of
their seniority. Even skilled tradesmen could be shuttled to any job when

---

[2] U.S. Dept. of Commerce, *Reports of the Commissioner of Navigation* (Washington, D.C.:
GPO, 1901). For information on the largest industrial plants in 1900, see Daniel Nelson, *Man-
agers and Workers: Origins of the New Factory System in the United States, 1880–1920*
(Madison: University of Wisconsin Press), pp. 4–9.

[3] "Munitions Industry Hearings," 1935, Parts 1 and 18–24, and Senate Report No. 944,
Part 1; "Vessels Constructed by New York Ship," 1900–1967, New York Shipbuilding Corporation, Camden, N.J., in Philadelphia Maritime Museum.

needed. These practices were especially demeaning for shipyard workers, a skilled and proud group of men.[4]

Shipbuilding corporations maintained great inequities in pay as well. The big yards set base rate wages for some 29 occupations, but the specific rates for these classifications were different in every yard. Wages also varied within many of these classifications, because most yards had piece rate and bonus systems that added pay onto the base rates. Promotion to the top of a classification depended on a foreman's subjective evaluation of a worker's productivity and attitude. This chaotic wage system became a common feature of the non-union shipbuilding environment in the 1920s and remained a major source of discontent in East Coast yards during the 1930s.[5]

Shipyard workers' earnings plummeted from 1929 on, as employers cut weekly hours. Even the "Big Three"—Fore River, New York Ship, and Newport News—put many workers on short time. Minor increases in hourly wage rates hardly amounted to an adjusted compensation. At New York Ship, the cut in the company's total expenditure for wages between 1929 and 1933 was 22.7 percent, about average for the industry. This decline occurred at the same time as the overall drop in earnings experienced by most workers during the Depression. Shipbuilding companies sought to sustain their profits, even with the lag in major government contracts, partly through such cuts. New York Ship's president Clinton Bardo publicly stated that the company was losing money, but in private boasted to the board of directors that it made a net profit of over $6 million between 1926 and 1934.[6]

Nationally, both workers and employers at first favored shorter hours as a way to prevent layoffs and retain essential workers. President Herbert Hoover promoted the "share-the-work movement" already under way in many indus-

---

[4] Group interview with New York Ship retirees, Aug. 16, 1987, Gloucester, N.J.: Ben Maiatico, George Snyder, Charlie Harker, Arthur "Ott" Lynch, Andy Reeder, Bill McCann, Horace Bevan, Jack Collins, and Leon "Reds" Johnson; Andy Reeder interview (with Lou Kaplan), Sept. 3, 1986, Wilmington, Del.

[5] "Relative Weekly Earnings for Shipyard Trades in September 1933 and in 1929 . . . ," by National Council of American Shipbuilders, October 10, 1933, for the NRA Shipbuilding Code Authority, NA, RG 9, Box 5257. Wage inequities were worse on the East Coast than in the Pacific Coast yards, which may have helped to fuel this discontent. For the persistence of this pattern during World War II in merchant ship construction, see Frederic C. Lane et al., *Ships for Victory: A History of Shipbuilding under the U.S. Maritime Commission in World War II* (Baltimore: Johns Hopkins University Press, 1951), pp. 411–27.

[6] "Relative Weekly Earnings for Shipyard Trades in September 1933 and in 1929 . . . ," National Council of American Shipbuilders; "Munitions Industry Hearings," 1935, Part 19, Exhibit No. 1535, C. L. Bardo to Board of Directors of New York Shipbuilding, Oct. 18, 1934, pp. 5257–58; Van Gelder report, July 27, 1939, IUMSWA Archives, Series V, Box 1, Special Collections, University of Maryland at College Park Libraries.

tries as a way of dealing with unemployment, but this temporary remedy hardly solved the problem. When Franklin D. Roosevelt replaced Hoover in 1933, workers' hopes began to rise again. That year New York Ship workers learned that the company would get new government contracts; many assumed that this would bring improved pay and an end to layoffs.[7]

Within this volatile environment, New York Ship's management gave workers an advantage not present at either Fore River or Federal Ship. Led by President Bardo, the company had an unusually passive attitude toward the new union movement. The owners installed a company union in 1919, but during the 1920s it lapsed. New York Shipbuilding management's lack of a comprehensive labor relations system or policy reflected its isolation within the corporate world and a failure to respond to new and rapidly changing conditions. In contrast to Fore River, New York Ship did not belong to a chain of shipyards, nor did it have any direct management ties to a major steel company. Labor relations policy at New York Ship originated entirely within the yard itself. The Camden-based plant attempted to diversify during a brief period of outside ownership by the American Brown-Broveri Corporation from 1925 to 1931, but its approach to employees did not change.[8]

By 1932, New York Ship put in place a loose committee system, which workers and foremen called the "employee shop committee." In contrast, Fore River instituted a more sophisticated employee-elected Employee Representation Plan (ERP), with an elaborate plant-wide committee structure. While Fore River's system offered various employee benefits, such as social activities and a nominal health and safety program, New York Ship's company union offered employees nothing except occasional conversations between handpicked worker representatives and foremen, while management itself distributed a booklet of "safety rules and instructions" for new workers. New York Ship's management selected one representative per department who would meet individually with foremen over "grievances," making the "committee" little more than a paper organization. As New York Ship union activist Ben Maiatico recalled, "it was a committee of one."[9]

---

[7] Arthur Boyson interviews, Oct. 4, 1982, and Sept. 12, 1986, Quincy, Mass.; Bardo to Hugh Johnson, Aug. 8, 1933, NA, RG 9, Box 5252; Irving Bernstein, *The Lean Years: A History of the American Worker, 1920–1933* (New York: Da Capo Press, 1960), pp. 306–7, 312–21.

[8] Clinton Bardo to Walter Teagle (chairman, Industrial Advisory Board of the NRA), Sept. 1, 1933, NA, RG 9, Box 5253; Maiatico interview, Aug. 16, 1987; "A Brief History of the New York Shipbuilding Corporation," Sept. 1, 1964, typed manuscript, Camden County Historical Society (hereafter cited as CCHS).

[9] Maiatico interview, Aug. 16, 1987; Boyson interviews, Oct. 4, 1982, and Sept. 12, 1986; Alex, Tom, and Agnes Mitchelson interview, May 8, 1987, Quincy, Mass.; Bardo and William Mullin (Chairman, General Shop Committee) to Shipbuilding and Ship Repairing Industries

The second factor explaining the rise of unionism at New York Ship related to its location: the unusual regional concentration of industry in the Philadelphia area and of shipbuilding along the Delaware River generated a virbrant labor movement. This region had a long history of labor activity, rivaling that of New York City but without the intense political factionalism that divided left- and right-wing union activists in New York. Camden in particular had a more cohesive working-class culture with an organized political presence, reflecting the larger scene in Philadelphia and its environs, although African Americans were generally excluded from the labor movement. Socialists, New Dealers, and independent AFL unionists tended to work together, in contrast to the bitter divisions among various communist, socialist, and traditional AFL advocates that characterized early 1930s New York City trade unionism.

Both Camden and Philadelphia had workers' neighborhoods on a smaller scale than New York and North Jersey. Camden, like Philadelphia, had deep racial divisions, and blacks were generally excluded by the city's major employers. During the 1930s, African Americans comprised about ten percent of Camden's residents. By 1940, during the production buildup to World War II, there were only 34 blacks out of 3,203 workers employed in the city's shipbuilding industry, which was concentrated almost entirely at New York Ship. This exclusionist employment environment helped fuel racism within the shipyard, but not all workers went along with the prevailing ideology.[10]

Among white workers, there was less distance between immigrants and the native-born, in both the workplace and social life, than was the case in North Jersey, which had substantial Eastern and Southern European ethnic enclaves. European immigrants comprised about ten percent of Camden's population; the largest groups came from Italy, Poland, Ireland and the British Isles, Rus-

---

Committees, and NRA Labor Committee, Aug. 31, 1933, NA, RG 9, Box 5253. "Information for Employees," New York Shipbuilding Corp. (Camden, 1919), and "Safety Rules and Instructions of the New York Shipbuilding Corp.," New York Shipbuilding Corp. (Camden, Jan. 1932); both in New York Shipbuilding files, CCHS. On the formation of company unions as a response to the NRA, see Irving Bernstein, *The Turbulent Years: A History of the American Worker, 1933–1941* (Boston: Houghton Mifflin, 1969), pp. 39–41.

[10] U.S. Dept. of Commerce, Bureau of the Census, *Sixteenth Census of the United States: 1940, Population*, Vol. 2, *Characteristics of the Population*, Part 4, New Jersey, Tables 34, A-37, A-40, A-41, and A-43, and Vol. 3, *The Labor Force*, Part 4, New Jersey, Table 17 (Washington, D.C.: GPO, 1943). Andy Reeder and Jack Collins reflected the contrast—and paradox—in the outlook that white shipyard workers held toward blacks. Reeder was personally quite racist, although progressive on industrial union policy where race was not a factor, while Collins advocated equality for blacks in the workplace and personally trained black welders, even though he was an active anticommunist. Observations on community and ethnicity in Camden are drawn from my own comparison of interviews with New York Ship retirees and Federal Ship retirees. Collins interview, Sept. 13, 1987, Gloucester, N.J.; Reeder interviews, 1987–88.

sia, and Germany.[11] In contrast to African Americans, European immigrants were represented in the New York Ship workforce; workers from Ireland and the British Isles and from Germany were especially numerous. Camden's local political system was responsive to workers' concerns and was democratic, in contrast to North Jersey, where such places as Jersey City were dominated politically by entrenched urban bosses.

Within this relatively favorable regional environment, the new union leaders at New York Ship developed a focused, practical program that was reinforced by contact with other vital unions and labor movement resources in the Philadelphia area. Their strategic focus stood in marked contrast to the confusion exhibited by New York Ship's management.

By 1932, Philadelphia had become a center for the AFL's left wing, which had close relations with the left wing of the Socialist Party (SP). The relatively conservative AFL metal trades and building trades divisions had virtually no influence among New York Ship workers. Shipyard unionists in Camden also had a regional advantage over their New York Port brothers, who faced corruption in the maritime shape-up system and political schisms between Communist industrial union advocates and conservative AFL craft union supporters. Nor did Camden activists encounter the profoundly conservative New England culture of small-town Quincy that confronted Fore River organizers.

In 1933 the American labor movement began to reassert itself after a decade of decline. The first major strike wave since the end of World War I hit the nation in July. It came a month after the passage of the National Industrial Recovery Act (NIRA), which indirectly encouraged union organizing and collective bargaining. Some 94,000 of the 125,000 strikers worked in two industries concentrated in the Northeast: clothing workers, primarily in New York and other metropolitan areas; and textile workers, predominantly in eastern Pennsylvania hosiery factories.[12]

The importance of this revitalized union activity in New York, Philadelphia, and eastern Pennsylvania should not be underestimated. Philadelphia and New York City witnessed major organizing campaigns by the Amalgamated Clothing Workers Union (ACW), which were conducted on a scale unmatched in any other cities. In 1914 the ACW had been organized on an industrial rather than craft basis, and it gained admission to the AFL in late 1933. The United

---

[11] *Sixteenth Census of the United States: 1940, Population*, Vol. 2, *Characteristics of the Population*, Part 4, New Jersey, Tables A-40 and A-41.

[12] U.S. Dept. of Labor, Bureau of Labor Statistics, *Handbook of Labor Statistics* (Washington, D.C.: GPO, 1976), p. 508; Lewis L. Lorwin and Arthur Wubnig, *Labor Relations Boards, The Regulation of Collective Bargaining under the National Recovery Act* (Washington, D.C.: Brookings Institution, 1935), pp. 88–89.

Mine Workers of America (UMW) also had an industrial form of organization, adopted at its founding in 1890. The UMW was the other major AFL union that laid the groundwork for the new union movement of the 1930s. It wielded considerable influence in Pennsylvania, both in local trade unions and state politics.[13]

Some workers at New York Ship, such as union activist John McAlack, had worked in the coal mines; they looked to the UMW as a model for the future and to its president, John L. Lewis, as the leader of industrial unionism. At the same time, some of the young left-wing organizers with the ACW who became active in organizing the shipbuilders union used the Socialist Party's network to establish links with trade unionists beyond the clothing industry. In 1933 and 1934, these younger activists sharply criticized the National Recovery Administration (NRA) of the early New Deal as an arm of big business and the conservative AFL. Other aspects of the Roosevelt administration's new labor policies, however, had a moderating influence on their long-term organizing strategies. At New York Ship between 1933 and 1935, labor organizers such as John Green and Phil Van Gelder combined tough industrial union tactics common to the Philadelphia-Camden region with a more moderate social democratic strategic outlook that was required when approaching New Deal officials in Washington.

This changed political context was the third major factor contributing to the growth of New York Ship's union movement. In the spring and summer of 1933, the stage was set for a union resurgence among shipyard workers. President Roosevelt introduced sweeping legislation for economic recovery, including major subsidies for naval shipbuilding contracts. The President had long been an advocate of a stronger United States Navy and now was able to achieve his objective under the guise of funding shipbuilding production and employment.

The National Industrial Recovery Act had a significant impact on labor-management relations at New York Ship in 1933. Section 7(a) guaranteed shipyard workers the right to organize unions. The Act also gave the government the means for subsidizing Navy construction contracts, which were dubbed public works projects, thus enabling shipbuilding manufacturers to hire more workers. Finally, the NIRA promised that the industry's NRA code board in Washington would include representatives of shipyard labor as well as of business and the government.[14]

---

[13] Bernstein, *Turbulent Years*, pp. 89–91.

[14] On the connection between the NIRA and naval contracts, see, for example, "Contract for the Construction of Torpedo-Boat Destroyer No. 356" (for New York Shipbuilding Corpora-

NRA code hearings on the shipbuilding industry, which began in July, examined shipyard production and working conditions in order to ascertain how to regulate wages and hours. The proponents of the NRA hoped to stimulate production through placing a ceiling on hours while setting minimum wages that would improve workers' living standards. To handle labor relations, the NRA Shipbuilding Board established an Industrial Relations Committee (IRC) to investigate and mediate labor disputes. As was typical of the first New Deal's unwieldy bureaucracy, the Shipbuilding IRC did not become fully operational until late 1934. Its members included top officers from the AFL Metal Trades unions, shipbuilding corporation executives, and public representatives from the government. The IRC's objectives and jurisdiction conflicted with another new government agency, the National Labor Board (NLB), established August 5, 1933, to handle labor disputes in all industries. This confusion within the New Deal bureaucracy plagued New York Ship union organizers for another three years.[15]

As early as summer 1933, New York Ship trade unionists learned that they could not rely on either the NRA's IRC or the NLB to help them win their demands. The NRA failed to change the harsh reality of shipyard life. Section 7(a) contained no enforcement provisions, forcing workers to rely on their own devices to obtain union recognition. Despite the rise in employment during the summer of 1933, which was due to NIRA-funded naval contracts, shipbuilding managers were able to cut workers' wages because of the government-mandated reduction of working hours. As for the promise of a voice for workers in Washington, only AFL Metal Trades union representatives served on the Shipbuilding Code Board. These officials expressed a general concern for the average shipyard worker, but adamantly opposed the industrial unionists' independent activity, which the AFL condemned as "unauthorized" and "dual unionist."[16]

Despite these emerging obstacles, faith in President Roosevelt and the infusion of government money into the shipyards boosted the expectations of New York Ship workers. For the first time in a decade, they became convinced that working conditions could change for the better. In many respects, the moment

---

tion, NIRA approved June 16, 1933, contract signed August 3, 1933), NA, RG 9, Box 5257. Identical contracts were issued to the other major East Coast shipyards, including Bethlehem Fore River and Federal Shipbuilding, on the same dates.

[15] "Transcript of Proceedings, Shipbuilding Code Hearing, First Day, July 19, 1933," NA, RG 9, Box 5249; Lorwin and Wubnig, *Labor Relations Boards*, pp. 45–88, 442–43.

[16] "Transcript of Proceedings, Shipbuilding Code Hearing, First Day, July 19, 1933," NA, RG 9, Box 5249; Lorwin and Wubnig, *Labor Relations Boards*, pp. 45–88, 442–43; Phil Van Gelder interviews, Oct. 25, 1982, Newark, Del., and Jan. 6, 1983, Catonsville, Md.

resembled the summer of 1917, when thousands of workers had openly challenged shipyard management's autocratic rule because they thought that a new era for labor had begun.[17]

The fourth factor contributing to the new movement was union leadership. Favorable conditions alone would not create a new union; effective leadership played a decisive role. Shipyard activists at Camden initiated a very different strategy than AFL organizers in the port of New York did. They concentrated their organizing within a single shipyard at first, and moved out to other locations later. They tried to draw all of the yard's workers into their union, regardless of skill level, department, or pay grade, and they pushed for a single union agreement with the company, specifying wages, working conditions, and workers' rights on the job. Most important at this stage, the entire leadership worked inside the shipyard.

The IUMSWA's organizing strategy at New York Ship evolved in stages, with each requiring some form of direct action. The last two stages involved mass strikes. The leaders of New York Ship's union did not decide upon this strategy in advance, but created it in the midst of the struggle. They utilized old and new tactics, always considering changes in conditions and the various groups (management, government, community, other unions) involved. These leaders made remarkable innovations, as did their counterparts in other industrial sectors who also were organizing on the principle of "one union in one industry."

From 1933 to 1935, union leadership at New York Ship developed on three levels. The first level consisted of the top leaders who were the initial organizers. They were the main devisors of strategy and eventually became the national union's first elected officers. The second level was comprised of those in major divisions within the yard (shops and ways) who were recognized as leaders by their immediate peers. They carried out the plans and often contributed to tactical decisions. Many later became elected officers of the local Camden union. The third level encompassed those who were active mainly in their own departments and crafts. In the beginning they acted as the "foot soldiers" who mobilized the rank-and-file in their immediate area. Once the local was established at New York Ship, they became department stewards.

John Green was the central leadership figure by the fall of 1933. Around him was a diverse group of highly motivated men committed to creating a new union. Most important was Tom Gallagher. Other key figures included John

---

[17] For a detailed discussion of the shipyard strike wave of 1917, see Palmer, "Organizing the Shipyards," pp. 136–84.

McAlack, a veteran unionist who, like Green, was a socialist; J. William Mullin, who moved from heading the company union to serving as president of IUMSWA Local 1; and future staff organizers Charlie Purkis, Francis "Pat" McCann, and Francis Hunter, who were native-born, working-class men of Northern European ancestry. This core leadership expanded to include others over the next two years. By late 1933, Gallagher emerged as the union's second leading figure; he remained Green's closest ally for two decades. In the eyes of many workers, both men had "solid" working class credentials. They had little formal schooling, like virtually all workers at New York Ship, but they were self-educated and articulate, which added to their credibility.[18]

In many respects Green and Gallagher represented two wings of the labor movement at New York Ship. Green spoke and acted from the left-wing trade union perspective of the American Socialist Party and Scottish Clydeside syndicalism, while Gallagher epitomized the liberal Democratic union leader of the 1930s who was loyal to the Democratic Party and President Roosevelt. Workers were drawn to Green because of his leadership ability and militant, highly effective tactics. Gallagher made them feel at home in the new union movement because of his progressive but moderate politics, his Catholic background, and his American roots. The fusion of these diverse cultural and political elements within the core leadership helped create a vitality and vision that New York Ship's unimaginative management could not match.

In 1916, when he was only twenty years old, Green led a strike in a major Clydeside shipyard, for which he had to stand trial under Britain's Defense of the Realm Act. This strike occurred in the midst of the militant shop stewards' upheaval in England and Scotland, which had a highly politicized, antiwar outlook. Green's pride, both as a tradesman and a unionist, is evident in his claim that he not only "served his time as an apprentice seven years on the River Clyde" but also "never worked in any other but a closed shop on the other side." He remained a member of Lodge No. 183, United Society of Boilermakers and Iron and Steel Shipbuilders, until his departure for America.[19]

---

[18] J. William Mullin et al. (IUMSWA Local 1) to William Davis (NRA), Oct. 13, 1933, NA, RG 9, Box 5253; Maiatico interviews, Aug. 16, 1987, and Sept. 13, 1987; Van Gelder interview, June 6, 1983; Eleanor Gehoosky (John McAlack's daughter) interview by Janet Friedman, 1988, Trenton, N.J. Green, like many shipyard craftsmen, educated himself by reading books on his own each night; Jessie Green Snyder interview, handwritten notes, Sept. 13, 1987, Cherry Hill, N.J.

[19] *The Shipbuilder*, Feb. 28, 1957, pp. 1–2; "Re: John Green, Man No. 23110" (unsigned report, probably done by New York Shipbuilding Corporation detective, c. 1934), NA, RG 9, Box 5243, "Case D-13"; Union dues book of John Green, United Society of Boilermakers and Iron and Steel Shipbuilders of Great Britain and Ireland, Branch Whiteinch No. 2, Lodge No. 183, book 1 (Jan. and Feb. 1922) and book 2 (no year), in personal possession of John Green's son, John A. Green, Collingswood, N.J. For discussion of the shop stewards' movement, as well as

Green emigrated from Clydebank, Scotland, in 1923 and arrived in Philadelphia on July 2, just in time for the celebration of Independence Day, which held symbolic significance for him throughout his life. Although he was a socialist and a critic of capitalism, he quickly developed a strong bond with his adopted land and its democratic traditions. Green seemed, at least through the early 1930s, to find no contradiction between the two, perhaps because his socialism during these years was directed more at business than at American political institutions. During that time he advocated a socialism that had syndicalist strands, stressing radical industrial trade unionism and workers' control rather than relying primarily on mainstream political participation and action, but he did not reject party politics entirely. His activism in the Socialist Party shifted after several years to strong support for President Roosevelt and the new Democratic Party coalition of the mid-1930s. Green probably left Scotland because of layoffs in the country's declining shipbuilding industry. He discovered that the same conditions existed in America when he tried, without success, to obtain employment in the shipyards around Philadelphia. Even though he had always been a sheet metal worker, or "tinsmith," he was hired at the Atwater Kent Radio Company, where he stayed for three and one-half years. In 1926 he finally managed to get a job at the Cramp Shipyard in Philadelphia, but after a year and a half was laid off.[20]

In 1931, at the age of thirty-five, Green took a job at New York Ship. He brought to his new position a wealth of trade union and political experience. He had established roots in Philadelphia and had become good friends with a wide range of trade unionists and political radicals, especially those active in the Socialist Party's left wing. By 1934 he became treasurer of the party's North Philadelphia Branch, where he met Phil Van Gelder, a young organizer for the ACW, and Moshe H. Goldstein (known as "M. H."), a lawyer who championed progressive causes. Others in this local party branch included Franz Daniel, who became a leader in the Textile Workers Organizing Committee; Alice Hanson (Cook), who became a professor of industrial relations at Cornell University; Paul Porter, who served as head of the World War II–

Clydeside unionism and politics, see Iain McLean, *The Legend of Red Clydeside* (Edinburgh: Donald, 1983); James Hinton, *The First Shop Stewards' Movement* (London: George Allen and Unwin, 1973); William Gallacher, *Revolt on the Clyde, An Autobiography* (New York: International Publishers, 1937); Joseph Melling, "Whatever Happened to Red Clydeside? Industrial Conflict and the Politics of Skill in the First World War," *International Review of Social History* 35 (1980) 3–33; John Foster, "Strike Action and Working-Class Politics on Clydeside 1914–1919," *International Review of Social History* 35 (1980) 34–70.

[20] "Re: John Green, Man No. 23110"; "Statement by John Green," quoted in typed memo originally from *The Citizen*, Jan. 25, 1935 (city unknown), NA, RG 9, Box 5254; Jessie Green Snyder interview.

era Shipbuilding Stabilization Commission; and SP Central Committee member Wesley Cook.[21]

The group of young socialists with which Green associated belonged to a left-wing faction of the Socialist Party known as the Revolutionary Policy Committee (RPC), which had originated in response to the party's rightward drift a decade earlier. In the late 1920s, the membership of the Socialist Party was centered in New York City, where for the most part it consisted of devoted followers of Morris Hillquit and other older leaders. This "old guard" had become conservative by socialist standards, and was protective of its power. Younger, more radical members blamed the party's decline during the 1920s on this old guard and were proud that they generally did not come from New York but from other parts of the country, which they considered more representative of the American people.[22]

By the early 1930s, some of these young party members had moved to the left of Norman Thomas, the original challenger to Hillquit, to form the RPC. Philadelphia, where some party members were heavily involved in trade union organizing, became an important center for the RPC. Although Green's comrades in the North Philadelphia Socialist Party branch belonged to the RPC faction, the personal ties they developed proved more important than their common political ideology in determining their future careers. In later years they played significant roles in the labor movement and became Democratic Party loyalists who followed the lead of Sidney Hillman.[23]

When Green began working at New York Ship, he developed close ties with union-oriented workers such as Tom Gallagher and Francis Hunter, who were not part of the political left. Green's ability to live comfortably in both political and cultural worlds is evident from his public identification with "An Appeal to the Membership of the Socialist Party," a pamphlet published in April 1934 by the SP's RPC faction, when he was head of New York Ship's IUMSWA Local 1. In addition to Green, Van Gelder and eighty others signed it, including future CIO leaders Franz Daniel and Roy Reuther. The RPC criticized the NRA as "a gigantic attempt to use methods of planning—state capitalism—in the interest of the most powerful financial and industrial mag-

[21] "Re: John Green, Man No. 23110"; "Statement by John Green"; Van Gelder interview, June 11, 1987.

[22] Daniel Bell, *Marxian Socialism in the United States* (Princeton: Princeton University Press, 1967), pp. 157–60. Bell notes that "behind some of the attacks on Hillquit was an attitude characteristic of typical Mid-western provincialisms that 'New York is not America'" (p. 160).

[23] Bell, *Marxian Socialism in the United States*, pp. 157–78; Revolutionary Policy Committee (RPC), *An Appeal to the Membership of the Socialist Party*, April 1934 (2nd ed.), in personal possession of Van Gelder; conversations with Van Gelder, 1986–88. Phil Van Gelder met his wife, Miriam, at a house where some of the RPC socialist members lived.

nates." It called for a socialist "Workers' Republic," "a united front of all working class organizations," opposition to fascism and war, an end to racial discrimination, and recognition of the Soviet Union. While the RPC opposed the moderate policies of the Socialist Party leadership, it also castigated the "disruptive" tactics of the Communist Party (CP). The RPC did not advocate the violent overthrow of the U.S. government, but instead called for the socialist "possession of the state machinery by the mandate of the workers." Of particular relevance for those party members who worked in the labor movement was the RPC's support for industrial unionism, which the RPC held should remain within the framework of the AFL.[24]

For the most part, the ties between socialists and more conventional trade unionists were built on a practical basis, which had a profound impact on the IUMSWA's early development. This process brought Green, Van Gelder, and Goldstein into a working relationship around organizing, and it facilitated broader alliances between the IUMSWA and the emerging CIO union movement. At the same time, it distanced Green and the shipbuilders' union from the Communist Party, which at that time was attacking the Socialist Party as "social fascist." Nonetheless, in his first years at New York Ship Green had contact with individual working-class Communists in Camden and, like many shipyard workers, probably read the *Daily Worker*. Like many large industrial plants during the 1930s, New York Ship became a virtual melting pot for the working-class left wing. Even with his contacts among various labor-left activists, however, Green focused on the practical side of trade unionism.[25]

Tom Gallagher was more representative of the average American-born shipyard worker. Unlike Green, he had no prior trade union background. He was, at least nominally, a Catholic, and he was basically a hands-on man, preferring pragmatic Democratic Party politics to the "class struggle" political philosophies of the day. Born in Philadelphia in 1900, Gallagher was a third-generation American of Irish and German stock. He did not attend school further than the fourth grade; as the oldest son, he had to work on the family's South Jersey farm. Despite his educational disadvantage, Gallagher proved himself an articulate and competent trade unionist when he directed the 1935 union negotiating committee. Tom and his brother Pat learned carpentry from their father while working at construction sites. He also picked up blueprint

[24] Conversations with Van Gelder, 1986–88; Thomas J. Gallagher (Tom Gallagher's son) interview, Aug. 15, 1987, Stratford, N.J.; RPC, *Appeal to the Membership of the Socialist Party*.

[25] Conversations with Van Gelder, 1986–88; "Re: John Green, Man No. 23110"; George "Chips" De Girolamo interview, June 14, 1987, Marlton, N.J.; George Snyder interview (with New York Ship retirees), Aug. 16, 1987, Gloucester, N.J.; Conversations with Jim and Don Bollen, 1982–88, concerning *Daily Worker* distribution at Fore River Shipyard; Abe Cohen interview, Feb. 19, 1987, Quincy, Mass.

drawing through correspondence school. However, he was unable to use these skills when he got hired as a rigger at New York Ship in 1918, a job that required no special education or training.[26]

Gallagher was laid off at various times during the 1920s, but from 1930 on he worked continuously at the yard. During the 1930s he developed a passion for unionism. He quickly became a respected leader and excelled as Green's assistant. His son, Thomas J. Gallagher, describes what he was like in these years:

> Unions were his life. He didn't do anything or know anything except union. I can still recall he never took a vacation. Everybody else got . . . two weeks after ten years. When he was in the union he never took a vacation, except one year. We were living in Westfield Acres, a low rent development in East Camden. I played on a baseball team there. I was in the second year of high school [1938] and can still remember him sitting in the grandstand, all by himself, watching me practice. One day. Then he went back to work, that was enough vacation for him.

Another revealing incident occurred when the family bought a tape recorder. Gallagher's sister sang a song, but he gave a talk on the union, which was his idea of entertainment. When he became a full-time union official at New York Ship, he spent every evening at union meetings with workers and afterward went to the bars with the men to socialize and talk shop. He was close to his family, but during the week he only saw them at supper time, at precisely the same hour each day.[27]

The other socialist in the initial 1933 organizing leadership besides John Green was John McAlack. He entered New York Ship as a teenager around the turn of the century when the yard first opened, starting as an apprentice electrician and eventually attaining the highly skilled position of mechanical telegrapher. His trade union philosophy had been shaped before he came to New York Ship. During six months in the Pennsylvania coal mines, he saw terrible conditions. Many of the workers were Russians, Poles, and other Eastern European immigrants who had almost no knowledge of English. The victim-

---

[26] Gallagher interview; "Minutes, a meeting between a Committee from [IUMSWA Local 1] . . . and representatives of [New York Ship]," Camden, April 8, 1935, NA, RG 9, Box 5254; *Camden Courier Post*, July 30, 1935, p. 3. "To be a rigger or hitcher on outside work a man needs no special education, but should have good health and strength and be able and willing to work out of doors"; Bureau of Vocation Guidance, Division of Education, Harvard University, *Shipyard Employment, A Place for Men to Help Win the War* (Washington, D.C.: U.S. Shipping Board, 1918), p. 40.

[27] Gallagher interview.

ization of these immigrant workers shocked him, and as a second-generation Pole he identified with their plight. The "company store" system soon drove him into debt. When he finally managed to pay off what he owed, he returned to Philadelphia, only to find that he had no money for the Delaware River ferry to Camden. He had to ask a stranger for the five-cent fare to get home.[28]

The experience taught him firsthand the necessity of union protection. During World War I, after almost two decades at New York Ship, McAlack became active in an AFL craft union. In 1918 he represented New York Ship workers in Washington, presumably when the Shipbuilding Labor Adjustment Board was preparing its standardized wage decision for the Delaware River District.[29]

McAlack had an acute awareness of discrimination against Eastern Europeans, whom employers and others often labeled ignorant "square-heads." To get hired at New York Ship, he changed his name from the Polish spelling, Michaleck, to an Irish-looking McAlack, but he retained the original pronunciation. Like Gallagher and Green, McAlack was largely self-educated. He became active in the Camden branch of the Socialist Party and even ran for mayor once, receiving a respectable vote from the Polish and other immigrant neighborhoods. He frequented Socialist Party meetings and picnics in Camden with his family, but was tolerant of viewpoints that differed from his own. McAlack never lost sight of his Polish roots; he spoke fluent Russian and Polish and could understand Yiddish and Italian, which was valuable for organizing. His role in building the IUMSWA was brief, for he died of cancer on the eve of the 1934 strike. Although it is difficult to make a full assessment of his activities and influence, he appears to have been an important link between the older men from the World War I era, who remembered the AFL in its militant days, and the younger generation, who came of age during the 1920s, when the open shop reigned, and during the early 1930s, when industrial unionism was on the horizon.[30]

Green had close ties with a number of leaders at the secondary level who shared his Scottish experience (whether they were born in Scotland or immi-

[28] Gehoosky interview; Hunter et al. to Davis, Oct. 13, 1933. McAlack signed this letter to NRA official William Davis, along with Green, Hunter, Gallagher, Mullin, Purkis, and James Turnbull, indicating that he was in the initial core of the union.

[29] Gehoosky interview. Eleanor Gehoosky does not recall the name of McAlack's union from the World War I years. Ben Maiatico told me that there were many men at New York Ship in 1933 who had been members of the Boilermakers Union during World War I. McAlack most likely was in the IBEW because of his trade, but he may have been in the Boilermakers.

[30] Gehoosky interview; Hunter (on IUMSWA stationary) to John McAlack, April 18, 1934, in personal possession of Janet Friedman. Hunter's letter to McAlack states in part: "I was sorry to hear of your illness for I would like you to be with us at this time as I am sure your experience of the past would help us greatly." McAlack died on May 13, 1934.

grated to the Clyde shipyards from Ireland). This group included machinist Mike Smith, who became one of the IUMSWA's best staff organizers; maintenance electrician John "Scottie" Knowles, a Local 1 trustee for two decades; and welder Jimmy McKissock, a department steward for many years and IUMSWA Local 1 president under the regime of local secretary-treasurer Tommy "Driftpin" Saul, the dominant figure at New York Ship in the late 1940s. The large number of Scots in the IUMSWA leadership stemmed from their predominance in the highest skilled jobs, such as shipfitting and sheet metal. Many of the Scots who came to America had shipyard and trade union experience from the Clydeside, giving them an advantage over other groups such as Italians or Poles. The Scots also were acculturated more quickly into American working-class culture and experienced less ethnic discrimination than other immigrants because they were English speakers, which allowed them to advance rapidly within the new union movement.[31]

The majority of New York Ship's IUMSWA leaders at all levels were American-born, as were most of the yard's workers. Francis Hunter, Charlie Purkis, and Francis "Pat" McCann were representative of the first generation of IUMSWA Local 1 leaders, who would never attain national leadership status but who rose beyond the level of department representative. This local leadership provided the vital link between the top leaders and the shop stewards who dealt with rank-and-file union members. Hunter, who became IUMSWA Local 1's first executive secretary, subsequently held a number of other local elective IUMSWA posts, after failing as a staff organizer.[32]

Charlie Purkis had worked in the yard for some years. He was a pipe fitter in his forties by 1932. He never held an administrative post, but played a critical role as an organizer and trouble-shooter. Ben Maiatico, who worked as Purkis's helper, recalled that "Charlie was one of these kind of guys that like to pat you on the back, to get you going." Purkis directed the picket lines during the 1934 and 1935 New York Ship strikes. In 1935, he became the first IUMSWA staff organizer recruited from inside a shipyard. Later in the decade, he had difficulties with the national office regarding his organizing activity and returned to his old pipefitting job at New York Ship, an embittered man.[33]

Pat McCann was in his thirties when the organizing drive began. A family man with three children, he had lived in Camden since 1909. When not at the shipyard, he made extra income as a Justice of the Peace. He was proud of

[31] Maiatico interview, Aug. 16, 1987; *Shipyard Worker*, 1935–1939.

[32] Maiatico interview, Aug. 16, 1987; Hunter, "Unionism at Work," IUMSWA Local 1 Education Committee (Camden, 1943). This assessment of Hunter's staff organizing is my own.

[33] Maiatico interviews, Aug. 16 and Sept. 13, 1987; Van Gelder, "Report of the Executive Secretary to 2nd National Convention," Aug. 21, 1936, IUMSWA Archives, Series I, Subseries 4, Box 11.

being a registered Democrat. Like Purkis and Hunter, he also became a staff organizer in the mid-1930s, but for a much shorter period, with assignments confined to the Delaware River yards, especially Sun Ship. He may not have had good luck in this position, or he simply may have preferred a stable job, because he returned to New York Ship, where he remained active in department-level union positions through the 1940s.[34]

Even after he was back at his old job, McCann continued to be one of the best "volunteer" organizers assisting staff on other Delaware River campaigns. He also carried more political clout among New York Ship workers than Purkis or Hunter did. In many ways, however, he represented the independent-minded unionists in the yard whom Green could not control in later years. While Gallagher became Green's assistant and right-hand man, McCann went his own way by the 1940s. In this respect, he was representative of the increasing number of shipyard trade unionists who preferred local union autonomy. This trend helped create and sustain rank-and-file workers' commitment to industrial unionism, but it also became a problem for the national union officers, who found such independent-minded workers hard to control. McCann supported Local 1's breakaway from the IUMSWA and its reaffiliation with the AFL's Boilermakers in the late 1940s, despite his dislike for local demagogue Tommy "Driftpin" Saul, who led the secession movement.[35]

From the beginning of the organizing drive in 1933, Green had volunteer organizers in virtually every part of the yard. Individuals in this group, the third level of leadership, could operate out of each department partly because of the company's "shop committee" setup. The older system of representation retained a certain craft identity, having been established near the end of World War I when the AFL Metal Trades unions at New York Ship were on the verge of collapse. New York Ship's "departments" often were simply craft divisions, such as riveting, sheet metal, or inside machining. By 1933, volunteer organizers for the new independent union could build on a fusion of craft and industrial union values, promoting trade pride while advocating the inclusion of all New York Ship workers.[36]

As a tinsmith (sheet metal worker), Green easily maintained communication with these department organizers. Many workers regularly passed through

[34] *Camden Courier Post*, July 30, 1935, p. 3; New York Ship retirees interview, Aug. 16, 1987.

[35] Reeder interview, May 30, 1987, Wilmington, Del.; Maiatico interview, Sept. 13, 1987; "Shop Officers—1949, Local No. 1—IUMSWA," IUMSWA Archives, Series V, Box 7.

[36] Maiatico interview, Aug. 16, 1987; De Girolamo interview. Maiatico's understanding of how yard activists maintained contacts and established inside networks through their ability to walk from department to department proved invaluable for this analysis.

the sheet metal shop, located at the center of the North Yard (the original section of the shipyard) directly adjacent to Piers 1 and 2. Purkis was based in the pipe shop, directly behind the sheet metal shop. Gallagher was assigned to the riggers shop along Pier 1, just north of the sheet metal shop, but probably did most of his work in the assembly areas. These three leaders readily maintained contact. Gallagher and Purkis had the opportunity to circulate around the yard, providing the union with easy access to shops and shipways.[37]

Many other volunteer organizers were active in this "nucleus," as workers themselves called the core group. The most valuable of these organizers circulated throughout the yard, especially along the shipways where the majority of workers could be found. Arthur "Gummy" Rogers, who organized in the electrical department, probably spent most of his time, both on the job and for the union, out on the ships. Bob Rulon worked as a painter, which also required movement between the shops and the ways. Ed Baker, a ship carpenter, most likely did finished work in the shop and then went onto the ships to install what he had built. "Scottie" Knowles roamed through the shops and ways as a maintenance electrician. Pat McCann, of the pipe covering department, probably spent most of his time on the ships, even though he was based in a shop. Eugene Madeline made his contacts through his job in the central tool room, located in the very middle of the plant complex behind Ways 1 through 10 (the Destroyer Yard built during World War I).[38]

Three out of some twenty primary and secondary leaders were shipfitters: Rich Benson, Charles "Hook" Danner, and Charles Mitchell. This trade had long been critical to organizing on the shipways. The 1933 organizing took place before the standardization of production welding, so these shipfitters probably dealt most often with riveters and those in related crafts, including tack welders.[39]

When welding began to replace riveting in the mid-1930s, tack welders were the first ones to learn the job. John Brown became the most important welding organizer in 1934. He was an Austrian immigrant who was probably a member of the Communist Party, but he knew how to translate his radical ideas into the pragmatic, yet militant, language and style of industrial union-

[37] Maiatico interviews, esp. Aug. 16, 1987; Van Gelder interview, Oct. 11, 1987; Hunter et al. to Davis, Oct. 13, 1933; Hunter to Davis, Feb. 6, 1934; "Minutes," Local 1 and New York Ship negotiations, April 1934.

[38] Maiatico interviews, esp. Aug. 16, 1987; Van Gelder interview, Oct. 11, 1987; Hunter et al. to Davis, Oct. 13, 1933; Hunter to Davis, Feb. 6, 1934; "Minutes," Local 1 and New York Ship negotiations, April 1934.

[39] Maiatico interviews, esp. Aug. 16, 1987; Van Gelder interview, Oct. 11, 1987; Hunter et al. to Davis, Oct. 13, 1933; Hunter to Davis, Feb. 6, 1934; "Minutes," Local 1 and New York Ship negotiations, April 1934.

ism. Under him, a whole generation of young welders received their education in trade unionism; his protégés included future Local 1 leaders "Chips" De Girolamo and Andy Reeder. In 1933, however, most of the new union's leadership came from skilled shop trades such as sheet metal, pipefitting, and electrical, while few came from the "steel trade" jobs, such as drillers and reamers, riveters, or welders. Welder John Brown, the most prominent of the "steel trade" group, was not visibly active until 1934.[40]

The first significant organizing at New York Ship began in the spring of 1933. The AFL had been discredited for many years, and its presence was confined to a small group of coppersmiths, one of the highest-paid jobs in shipbuilding. The initial impetus for change came from pipefitter Charlie Purkis, who had become bitterly dissatisfied with yard conditions after a 15 percent pay cut and a major layoff in 1932. Shipbuilding owners instituted this cut on an industry-wide basis in East Coast yards, claiming that Depression conditions required it. Although Purkis kept his job, tinsmith John Green, who had been hired on November 4, 1931, was laid off.[41]

In June 1933 Congress had just passed the National Industrial Recovery Act. Purkis felt the time was right to launch a drive for a genuine election in his department to replace the pro-company representative on the "employee shop committee." He was chosen by pipefitting department workers, which gave him the chance not only to handle immediate departmental grievances but also to organize the rest of the yard. Maiatico, who worked as his helper, described how Purkis did this. "He would be gone for long periods of time. Of course, I would continue on with the job, so that there was nothing lost . . . so far as his productivity was concerned. Then next thing I knew I wouldn't see Purkis for almost all day. . . . He'd come back and tell me, 'Boy, you're doing a great job—I'll see that you're taken care of.' . . . It was fine with me." Other organizers apparently followed his lead. Within a month, a number of men

[40] Maiatico interviews; De Girolamo interview; Reeder interviews, 1986–1988. John Brown should not to be confused with John W. Brown, a GEB member and organizer from Maine. Chips De Girolamo, a colleague of John Brown's in the early 1930s, read the *Daily Worker* with him, though the two disagreed politically. Andy Reeder remembered Brown as a militant trade unionist who taught him how to be level-headed. Reeder also believed that John Brown was unfairly red-baited. Both Brown and Reeder were active in the Progressive Caucus, the group that backed Phil Van Gelder for national secretary-treasurer during the 1946 split in the IUMSWA.

[41] Maiatico interviews; Typed notes on wages and hours situation at New York Ship (1931–1933), no date or signature, NA, RG 9, Box 5252, (file) "16. *Labor* (N)"; "Re: John Green, Man No. 23110"; U.S. Congress, House, Subcommittee of the Committee on Labor, *Hearings Relating to Labor Practices of Employers of Labor in the Shipbuilding Industry*, 74th Cong., 1st Sess. (Washington, D.C.: GPO, 1935) (hereafter cited as "Hearings, Labor Practices in Shipbuilding," 1935), John Green testimony, p. 16.

who advocated an independent union had made inroads into the company union structure.[42]

John Green, who had been rehired in 1932, was laid off again on April 13, 1933. Although he missed the early months of organizing, he was rehired on July 11, just as the efforts of Purkis and other independent-minded shop committee representatives reached a peak. They urged Green to become a shop committee representative, but he refused. He was convinced that the committee had failed to make any headway in compelling the NRA to restore the wages that had been cut in 1932. Other workers who were disenchanted with the company union gravitated toward Green. Even though Green opposed the company union, he apparently maintained ties with Purkis and other shop committee representatives, which effectively united those operating within the company structure with worker activists outside of it.[43]

Green was assisted in his organizing by Paul Porter, a fellow member of the Socialist Party's North Philadelphia Branch. Although Porter did not work in the yard, he helped Green with strategy and in writing the union's first constitution. The explicitly anticapitalist preamble combined American syndicalist views, especially Eugene Debs's fusion of IWW and Socialist Party ideals, with Green's Clydeside working-class socialism, also syndicalist in character. It borrowed words from the American Declaration of Independence emphasizing basic citizens' rights. The preamble stressed the need for trade union unity, without regard to nationality, race, or religion:

> We, Marine and Shipbuilding Workers of America, believing in the solidarity of all workers, irrespective of race, color, creed or national origin, hereby declare our purpose of joining in one strong union to win our just demands for a fuller life, liberty and the pursuit of happiness. These rights are today denied us. Experience of the past has taught us that rights are not won without struggle. Through our Union we prepare ourselves for the Workers' struggle, not merely to win concessions of higher wages and shorter hours, but to abolish forever the system of exploitation that compels us to support with our labor an idle owning class.[44]

[42] Maiatico interview, Aug. 16, 1987; "Re: John Green, Man No. 23110." D. A. Williams ("Chairman Shop Committee") and Bardo to Franklin Roosevelt, July 21, 1933; Bardo and Mullin to Shipbuilding and Ship Repairing Industries Committee and NRA Labor Committee, with additional "Employees' Position" by Mullin, Aug. 31, 1933; both NA, RG 9, Box 5253.

[43] "Re: John Green, Man No. 23110"; Joseph A. Raffaele, "The Rise of Industrial Unionism in the American Shipbuilding Industry" (MA thesis, Temple University, 1948), p. 36; "Hearings, Labor Practices in Shipbuilding," 1935, Green testimony, p. 16.

[44] Van Gelder interview, Oct. 11, 1987; First IUMSWA Constitution, Preamble, NA, RG 9, Box 5243, (file) "Compliance" (in April 1935 section).

This philosophy seems to have guided the organizing during the summer of 1933, even though the constitution was not written until at least October. While Green's activity inside the yard appears to have been solely union-oriented, the preamble indicates that he was motivated by a social vision. For the time being, at least, he sought to build a movement that would empower workers inside the shipyards and eventually enable them to take control of the companies. The "exploiting class" was not the government but the capitalists who ran the corporations.

New York Ship's shop committee was so weak that many workers did not even know it met as a body and voted on issues. Management told the NRA that the shop committee met regularly and had functioned as an elected representative structure since 1919. But in fact the shop committee appears to have been little more than a makeshift operation, which only began to meet regularly around June 1933.[45]

By July, controversy developed over NRA code provisions in the industry. New York Ship president Clinton Bardo spent considerable time attacking the NRA Shipbuilding Code Board's proposed regulation that would prohibit private companies from operating on a forty-hour week, and he tried to use the shop committee to advance this goal. Bardo, along with other shipbuilding executives, claimed that Navy yards would have an unfair advantage over private yards because they were to be exempt from the NRA code and its hours restrictions.[46]

On July 25 the AFL, which advocated a thirty-hour limit as a way to create jobs, and the shipbuilding owners, who wanted to retain the forty-hour week to maximize production, agreed to the compromise of thirty-two hours proposed by NRA chief Hugh Johnson. President Roosevelt approved the code the following day, but neither labor nor management was satisfied with this solution, despite their administrative concurrence. Owners continued to object on the basis that the shorter hours reduced productivity and raised costs, while labor came to view the decision as a deliberate pay cut.[47]

Nevertheless, acceptance of the NRA Shipbuilding Code by New York Ship and other shipbuilders cleared the way for Navy contracts, the companies' main concern. New York Ship, one of the top beneficiaries, received contracts

[45] Maiatico interview, Aug. 16, 1987; Hearings on Shipbuilding Code, Bardo testimony, July 19, 1933.

[46] Hearings on Shipbuilding Code, Bardo testimony, July 19, 1933; Williams and Bardo to Roosevelt, July 21, 1933; Bardo to Johnson, Aug. 8, 1933; William A. Davis Memorandum on New York Shipbuilding, Sept. 9, 1933, NA, RG 9, Box 5253; *New York Times*, July 13, 1933, pp. 20–23, 25.

[47] *New York Times*, July 25, 28, 1933; Bardo and Mullin to NRA Labor Committee, Aug. 31, 1933.

for two light cruisers and four destroyers. At the same time, organizing activity in the yard came to a head. On August 4, 150 workers signed a petition protesting the Navy's projected centralization of ship design in the industry and the expected lack of work for New York Ship draftsmen. John Green and John McAlack were among the signatories, even though they were blue-collar craft workers. Their action in support of the draftsmen indicates that they took seriously the effort to unite every wage earner into their union movement, regardless of occupational status.[48]

The organizers' best opportunity came two days later, on August 6, when Bardo again cut wages. In July, the shop committee had agreed to Bardo's proposal to increase pay rates effective July 23. This raise brought wages back to the levels prevailing prior to the 1933 cut. On August 6, however, the Shipbuilding Code's thirty-two-hour week took effect, which allowed Bardo to reduce total wages paid per week by 15 percent, returning wages to the 1933 level. Addressing NRA officials, Bardo defended his actions by claiming that he had actually raised *hourly* wages relative to those paid during the previous month; that he was following accepted NRA industry policy; and that he therefore had not reduced wages. Technically he may have been correct, but the workers only saw history repeating itself: reduced hours without retention of existing *weekly* wages received under the forty-hour week effectively meant another 15 percent pay cut like the one in 1932.[49]

At this point Bardo no longer had control of the situation in the yard. William Mullin, an independent, became the new chairman of the shop committee, replacing former chairman D. A. Williams, who had sided with Bardo when dealing with the NRA. Williams later became part of management, and by the late 1940s rose to plant manager and then company vice president. When Bardo posted the notice of the new pay scale on August 6, protests broke out immediately, led by Green. According to Ben Maiatico, "the movement was on. . . . That triggered off the whole organizing campaign. Everything just seemed to fall into place. Everybody felt, well, we got to organize, we have to organize, otherwise we don't know where we're going to go with these wage cuts. Wages were bad enough as they were, and 15 percent was just too much. And everybody started to sign up." Green and his colleagues now began openly to organize workers, although they took precautions to avoid get-

[48] New York Ship Marine Draftsmen to Hugh Johnson (letter and petition), Aug. 4, 1933, Box 5252; Contracts for Destroyers and other Naval vessels (NIRA approved June 16, 1933), Aug. 3, 1933; "Note 1" attached to John Frey to William Davis, Oct. 27, 1933, Box 5256; all NA, RG 9.

[49] Bardo to Johnson, Aug. 8, 1933; Bardo to Johnson, Aug. 11, 1933; Mullin to NLB, Aug. 31, 1933; Bardo and Mullin to NRA Labor Committee, with "Employees' Position" by Mullin, Aug. 31, 1933; "Hearings, Labor Practices in Shipbuilding," 1935, Green testimony, p. 16.

ting fired. "It was still a bit underground . . . to get guys signed up," Maiatico recalled, but "they got plenty signed up."[50]

On August 7, Bardo managed to get the shop committee to endorse the demand for a return to forty hours. The vote was 23 to 2 to back Bardo, with 2 abstentions. Green and his group refused to go along with the committee, forcing shop representatives to take an informal poll in their departments. To Bardo's surprise, a staggering majority—1,340 to 159—opposed his plan to increase hours as a way to raise wages artificially. Nevertheless, he refused to rescind the wage reduction created by the thirty-two-hour week, claiming he was paying above NRA minimum rates for the shipbuilding industry.[51]

Treading a moderate line, Mullin turned to the National Labor Board for direct intervention. On August 31 he requested that the Board nullify the Shipbuilding Code "in its present form" and raise pay "to the level prevailing before cuts in wages and working hours were instituted late in the depression." Mullin and the new movement were beginning to be heard in Washington, it seemed, when NRA Deputy Administrator William Davis commented that he saw no evidence of widespread worker support for the forty-hour week advocated by Bardo and other shipbuilding executives.[52]

Bardo knew he faced a serious problem, but he still clung to the illusion that his goals were the same as the workers'. On September 1, he wrote to the chairman of the NRA Industrial Advisory Board in New York City that the workers' "mental attitude is being harassed and disturbed by the organizations and agitators and their viewpoint. . . . This whole situation can be no better expressed than in the protest which they have filed against the 32-hour week."[53]

Green and the other organizers focused on using a series of mass meetings in August and September to establish the union on a sound footing. Two hundred workers attended the first gathering at the Camden Elks Club. Some wanted separate organizations by craft, undoubtedly with AFL Metal Trades affiliations. Green and other leaders instead proposed a single charter for the entire yard. The craft spokesmen then asked if they could break away into separate unions if such a charter were adopted. The group reached no final decision at this time. At the following meeting, those attending agreed that the new

---

[50] Williams and Bardo to Johnson, July 21, 1933; Bardo and Mullin to NRA Labor Committee, Aug. 31, 1933; Mullin to NLB, Aug. 31, 1933; "Agreement between New York Shipbuilding Corp. and IUMSWA Local 1," June 23, 1950, IUMSWA Archives, Series V, Box 7; Maiatico interview, Aug. 16, 1987.

[51] Bardo and Mullin to NRA Labor Committee, Aug. 31, 1933; Mullin to NLB, Aug. 31, 1933; Davis Memorandum on New York Shipbuilding, Aug. 31, 1933.

[52] Bardo and Mullin to NRA Labor Committee, Aug. 31, 1933; Mullin to NLB, Aug. 31, 1933; Davis Memorandum on New York Shipbuilding, Aug. 31, 1933.

[53] Bardo to Walter Teagle, Sept. 1, 1933, NA, RG 9, Box 5253.

union would remain independent of the AFL. Green and the rest of the leadership issued application cards, and those present established a membership fee of 50 cents. In subsequent meetings at the Democratic Club of Camden, the debate over craft versus industrial unionism continued. At one point, an AFL representative appeared as a guest speaker and gave the Federation's position on craft organization. Green's industrial union views remained those of the majority, however, and on October 3 those attending the organizing meeting founded the Industrial Union of Marine and Shipbuilding Workers of America (IUMSWA), independent of the AFL. The new union members adopted by-laws and elected officers, including William Mullin (who was still chairman of the company union) as president, John Green as vice president, and Francis Hunter as executive secretary. Although based only at New York Ship, the IUMSWA referred to itself as IUMSWA Local 1, because it planned to expand into a national industrial union for all shipyard workers.[54]

At the same time, the new union maintained contact with the government and dealt with Bardo's company union. IUMSWA Local 1 informed the NRA that workers had voted 1,819 to 142 to form the independent union, refuting Bardo's claim that the company union spoke for the workers. By this time, Mullin and Purkis had led the move to dissolve the company's shop committee, thereby making the independent union's officers "the only official representatives of the employees of the New York Shipbuilding Corporation."[55]

Six days after the founding of the IUMSWA, union attorney M. H. Goldstein filed a complaint with the National Labor Board demanding immediate action on wage improvements at New York Ship. Although he was a socialist like Green, Goldstein became one of the main proponents for a legal-oriented, moderate course within the IUMSWA. He provided critical assistance in the union's relations with the New Deal bureaucracy during the 1930s and remained the union's attorney for his entire career. He never became a union officer, but exerted tremendous influence at the highest levels of the organization. Goldstein's role indicates that legal tactics were taken seriously by the industrial union movement from the very beginning, even if they were not the main tactics used. Militant job action, socialist-oriented trade union leadership, and ordinary legal maneuvers coexisted within the IUMSWA.[56]

Union members met on October 20 for a strike vote on the wage cut, but decided against a walkout. The members may have thought it best to wait for the

[54] Raffaele, "The Rise of Industrial Unionism in the American Shipbuilding Industry," pp. 36–37.

[55] Hunter et al. to Davis, Oct. 13, 1933.

[56] Maiatico interview, Sept. 13, 1987; Hunter et al. to Davis, Oct. 13, 1933; "Reply from Mr. C. L. Bardo to the Members of the Committee . . . March 23, 1934," NA, RG 9, Box 5254.

NLB to take up their case, and they probably realized that their union did not have the strength to win a strike at this time. Over the next five months, the union tried to use various legal channels to resolve the wage dispute, but made no headway. This deadlock was due in part to the dozens of strikes elsewhere that were being dealt with by the NLB. Disputes not involving job actions, such as the one at New York Ship, were a low priority for the Board.[57]

In addition, the AFL had a vested interest in many of these walkouts that it did not have at New York Ship, where workers had chosen the unaffiliated IUMSWA as their representative. While the AFL had the ability to exert pressure in Washington to get action on its own cases, the IUMSWA had no powerful contacts within the federal government in 1933, much less a voice in any NRA bodies. For the IUMSWA to advance, Green and the other leaders had to consider alternative tactics focused on the shipyard itself. The union local at New York Ship first had to go through some process of negotiation with management to achieve full legitimacy among the workers.

By late 1933, John Green and his colleagues succeeded in building a union movement at New York Ship. The IUMSWA had an elementary structure and a popular following. An alliance of moderates, former company unionists, and socialists had been forged and had won the support of the majority of rank-and-file workers.

Clinton Bardo ran New York Ship until late 1934. His presence gave the union an unusual advantage, because he was a far less sophisticated or ruthless adversary than other shipbuilding executives at places like Fore River, Federal Ship, Newport News, or Sun Ship. Union recognition at New York Ship, however, would not come without a struggle. In early 1934 it became evident that the industrial union movement in the shipyards first had to secure a base in a single yard, which would require winning a recognition strike in Camden.

---

[57] Hunter et al. to Davis, Oct. 13, 1933.

CHAPTER 2

Organizing for a First Contract:
The 1934 Strike at New York Ship

The second phase of organizing at New York Ship required full mobilization of the IUMSWA's membership base to win both recognition and a union contract from management. IUMSWA leaders continued to focus on internal organizing, and challenged the company on critical job-related issues. They also began to draw the community and local government into the struggle, as the union confronted a possible strike situation. Despite its small size, the IUMSWA had an unusual advantage over many other developing industrial unions of the early 1930s. It could exert leverage with the federal government because, in the eyes of officials, the high concentration of naval production in the American shipbuilding industry made it desirable to maintain a stable labor relations environment for defense interests. At New York Ship alone, naval contracts totalled over $52 million by mid-1935.[1] Ultimately, the IUMSWA had to persuade the federal government to intervene on its behalf in Camden. The need to appeal to the federal government reshaped the union's political outlook and shifted its strategic objectives away from workers' control of industry toward a more pragmatic and limited industrial trade unionism compatible with the emerging New Deal political economy.

Immediately after the IUMSWA's founding in October 1933, Local 1 Vice-President John Green, Secretary Francis Hunter, and other leaders attempted to spark organizing in other major shipyards on the Delaware River. They wanted to make the IUMSWA more than just a local institution and envisioned

---

[1] *Philadelphia Record*, May 10, 1935.

building it into a national industrial union. The IUMSWA leaders first established links with Sun Ship in Chester, about forty miles south of Philadelphia. Charles Renner, the union's primary inside contact, organized Local 2 among a small group of men. With two locals nominally in place at Camden and Chester, the organizers decided to form a "Central Body" within the IUMSWA consisting of representatives from each yard, with Renner as secretary. This initial expansion reflected undue optimism. The IUMSWA did not succeed in organizing Sun Ship until eleven years later because of management's harsh policies. Most infamous was its company union, complete with thugs outfitted in brown uniforms and "SS" (Sun Ship) emblems, who routinely threatened and used physical violence against union organizers. Although the IUMSWA also developed contacts at Pusey Jones, a smaller yard in Wilmington, Delaware, workers there did not form Local 3 until early 1934. The IUMSWA found it impossible to expand into the Philadelphia Navy Yard because a number of workers retained their allegiance to AFL Metal Trades unions.[2]

The IUMSWA operated as an organization based at New York Ship from late 1933 through 1934, even though it had two new locals and a "Central Body." Local 1 held meetings in Camden during November and December, 1933, and began regularly to collect dues and pass out union buttons, but organizing was still conducted mainly by word of mouth. On January 19, 1934, a sparsely attended union meeting passed a resolution that Local 1 apply for a charter and seal from the IUMSWA's Central Body. At least on paper, the IUMSWA became a regional labor organization, not one restricted to just a single company. Despite these aspirations, New York Ship management still refused publicly to recognize the union, even though Clinton Bardo and his staff dealt with its representatives on an informal basis. A larger national shipbuilding union could not be built until this immediate obstacle was overcome.[3]

The union decided to test its strength in March, when it submitted demands to the company and then met with Bardo to discuss the issue of a full contract. Local 1 focused on a wage increase and union recognition, but after two labor-management conferences it became obvious that Bardo would not move on these points. Bardo expressed doubts that the union represented a majority

[2] Phil Van Gelder interviews, Jan. 6, 1983, and June 11, 1987; Francis Hunter to Charles Renner, Jan. 26, 1934, IUMSWA Archives, Series V, Box 12, Special Collections, University of Maryland at College Park Libraries; Andy Reeder and Lou Kaplan interview, Sept. 3, 1986; *Shipyard Worker*, Dec. 18, 1936.

[3] Ben Maiatico interview, Aug. 16, 1987; Joseph A. Raffaelle, "The Rise of Industrial Unionism in the American Shipbuilding Industry" (MA thesis, Temple University, 1948), pp. 36–37; "Hearings, Labor Practices in Shipbuilding," 1935, John Green testimony, p. 16; George "Chips" De Girolamo interview; Hunter to Renner, Jan. 26, 1934; Van Gelder interview, June 11, 1987.

of yard workers and requested that the union negotiating committee provide him with "a certified statement of bona fide membership of yard workers in your Union." He also refused officially to recognize elected representatives in grievances, stating that only his old joint "general committee" system, with management appointing its own representatives, would be acceptable. The IUMSWA naturally rejected his proposal to bring back the company union.[4]

When Bardo again raised the issue of returning to the forty-hour week, the union came out unequivocally in support of the NRA Code's shipbuilding standard of thirty-two hours. Bardo's resistance led Green to modify his blanket condemnation of the NRA. From this point on, Green skillfully drew on pro-labor federal policies to buttress the IUMSWA's position.[5]

New York Ship's most important building contracts were with the U.S. Navy for four destroyers and two light cruisers. Although the Navy Department administered the contracts, funds for these capital ships came not from the Navy but from the Public Works Administration (PWA) of the NRA. To further complicate matters, the Department of Labor, led by Secretary Frances Perkins, had a keen interest in promoting the New Deal's emerging collective bargaining philosophy and the fair settlement of strikes, and it maintained a close watch on shipyard labor relations. Thus three different bodies within the Roosevelt administration had an interest in what happened at New York Ship. All three—the Navy, the NRA Shipbuilding Code Authority, and the Labor Department—had direct contacts at the yard, which led to conflicting policy positions and jurisdictional claims regarding the situation in Camden. Both management and the IUMSWA vied for support within this New Deal labyrinth.

Local 1's negotiating committee agreed to outside arbitration when talks reached a deadlock, but the union opposed giving jurisdiction of the case to the Industrial Relation Committee (IRC), recently formed by the NRA Shipbuilding Code Authority, because it believed that IRC Chairman (and Shipbuilding Code Deputy Administrator) J. B. Weaver sided with management. H. Gerrish Smith, spokesman for the major shipbuilding corporations and a former Fore River Shipyard manager, also had significant influence within the IRC and the Shipbuilding Code Authority. Furthermore, the AFL Metal Trades, which considered the IUMSWA a dual-unionist organization, controlled labor representation on the IRC. If the government were to intervene, the IUMSWA preferred an agency with relative independence from business and AFL inter-

---

[4] "Request as Submitted to the Committee on Friday, March 16th, 1934 . . . Discussed . . . on Thursday, March 22nd, 1934—Conditions and Terms of Employment Desired by Industrial Union of Marine and Shipworkers, Camden Local No. 1"; Clinton Bardo to Hugh Johnson, March 28, 1934; "Reply from Mr. C. L. Bardo to . . . the Committee . . . Friday, March 23, 1934"; "To All Employees" statement by Bardo, March 26, 1934; all NA, RG 9, Box 5254.

[5] "Reply from . . . Bardo to the Committee . . . March 23, 1934."

ests, such as the Labor Department or the newly created National Labor Board (NLB).[6]

IUMSWA leadership made careful preparations for the strike. Despite the apparent low turnout at the initial March 24 union meeting, the organizers canvassed a majority of the yard's workers. In Green's words, they asked them "whether they were willing to submit to arbitration by the newly-created Industrial Relations Board for the shipbuilding and ship repairing industry [NRA], the question of the increase of wages. . . . To a man, those consulted expressed themselves as unalterably opposed to any such step." After weeks of negotiations, Local 1 members concluded that they had no alternative but to strike. When the union held a strike vote, a majority officially backed the leadership and endorsed a walkout. Three days later, after Bardo refused the union's demands, another strike vote was taken, and again a majority backed the strike action. "The following morning, Tuesday, March 27th," Van Gelder recounted, "the whole yard walked out on strike, even to [those in the job of] leaders," who worked in the highest job classification eligible for union membership. "The plant was shut down 100 per cent."[7]

The company alleged that only 125 workers at the first union meeting voted to strike. The union, on the other hand, claimed that 2,605 out of 3,315 yard workers were members and that the strike had widespread support. Union leadership effectively mobilized 2,500 or so workers with an allegiance to Local 1, which gave legitimacy to the union's contention that a majority backed the walkout. Every morning and afternoon at the shift changes, thousands of workers marched in an orderly mass picket along the street adjacent to the shipyard's main entrance. Van Gelder recalled: "As soon as the men saw the Union meant to fight, they rushed in to pay up their back dues. Even with all this money coming in there was only a few thousand dollars in the treasury— not much to spread amongst 3000 men." To survive a strike, the IUMSWA had to reach beyond the men in the shipyard to people in the community.[8]

During the first week of the strike, Green's Socialist Party colleagues came to Camden to assist the picket line. They were led by Phil Van Gelder, and in-

[6] Bardo to IUMSWA Negotiating Committee, March 27, 1934; Bardo to Johnson, March 28, 1934; Weaver to K. M. Simpson, c. March 1934; J. B. Woodward (IRC Secretary) to Weaver, April 3, 1934; Weaver to IRC, April 3, 1934; H. Gerrish Smith (Code Authority Chairman and head of National Council of American Shipbuilders) to Robert F. Wagner (Senator, NLB), April 24, 1934; Smith to Woodward, April 24, 1934; Bardo to Smith, April 24, 1934; all NA, RG 9, Box 5254. Bardo to Weaver, April 3, 1934; Weaver to Bardo, April 6, 1934; both NA, RG 9, Box 5252. The Shipbuilding IRC did not take its final form until the NRA administration order of November 7, 1934, even though it functioned as early as April 1934.

[7] Bardo to Johnson, March 28, 1934 (with John Green press statement quoted directly); Phil Van Gelder, *Book of Facts for Shipyard Workers* (Camden, N.J.: IUMSWA, 1935), p. 7.

[8] Bardo to Johnson, March 28, 1934; Van Gelder, *Book of Facts for Shipyard Workers*, p. 7.

cluded Franz Daniel, Alice Hanson (Cook), Newman Jeffrey, and John Deare, who filmed the mass picket lines. Although Green first became acquainted with Van Gelder through the North Philadelphia Branch of the Socialist Party, he did not bring Van Gelder into the IUMSWA until the eve of the 1934 strike. Not a shipyard worker, Van Gelder came from a very different background from Green. His father had been an electrical engineer at GE and Westinghouse in New Jersey and later became head city engineer for the Philadelphia subway system. Although the senior Van Gelder was an "old-fashioned Republican," his progressive leanings made him sympathetic to his son's concern for social justice. At the onset of the Great Depression, Phil Van Gelder finished a college degree and taught briefly as a philosophy instructor at Brown University.[9]

Deciding to join the political left and the labor movement, Van Gelder returned to Philadelphia, where he quickly developed a knack for union organizing. He spent several months organizing with the Amalgamated Clothing Workers during the 1934 Philadelphia strikes, which put him on good terms with ACW president Sidney Hillman. Van Gelder also helped Philadelphia drivers waging a city-wide taxi strike, where he learned many of the street-oriented organizing tactics used in later shipyard union drives. When he began to work exclusively with Green and the IUMSWA as an outside organizer, Van Gelder continued to draw his salary as a paid organizer from the Socialist Party, a definite financial advantage for Local 1. As a socialist, Van Gelder was influenced by Norman Thomas's political works, but it was the terrible Depression conditions confronting workers, more than theory, that led him to a career as a union organizer. Nevertheless, many former shipyard workers thought of Van Gelder as the union's "philosopher" because of his background and interest in left-wing ideas. Together, Van Gelder and Green became the core national IUMSWA leaders during the 1930s.[10]

Support for the New York Ship walkout soon spread throughout the community. In Van Gelder's words, "the other unions, local merchants, and friends of the workingmen came to our support. We ran the strike economically, borrowed and chiselled, and made every dollar do the work of two or three." Much of the public seems to have wanted a settlement benefiting "both sides," as one letter published in the *Camden Courier Post* indicated: "The willingness

---

[9] Van Gelder interview, Oct. 11, 1987; Van Gelder interview, June 11, 1987.

[10] Van Gelder interviews, Oct. 11, 1987, and June 11, 1987; Amalgamated Clothing Workers of America, *Report of the General Executive Board and Proceedings of the Tenth Biennial Convention*, Rochester, N.Y., May 14–19, 1934, pp. 51–53, 112–15. For assessments of Van Gelder's leadership and role as IUMSWA "philosopher" (all generally positive), see: Lou Kaplan interview, Jan. 8, 1983, Collingswood, N.J.; Andy Reeder interview, May 30, 1987; De Girolamo interview.

of both sides to discuss the matter peacefully and without prejudice proves that both labor and capital are learning that to reason is better than to fight. Much unanticipated good may result from this strike." [11]

The New York Ship strike apparently had a broad impact on other Camden workers, contributing to a strike wave in the city. A week after the shipyard workers walked out, employees at the city's large Campbell's Soup plant went on strike, which became a bitter conflict with frequent clashes on the picket lines. These workers were organized by Canners' Industrial Union Local No. 1 and led by Frank Manning, who also was education director of Camden's Socialist Party. Then, on April 5, some 600 out of 800 workers at the Radio Condenser Corporation walked off the job, led by the Radio Workers Industrial Union (RWIU) Local No. 2. Workers at Camden's large RCA plant, where the fledgling RWIU Local No. 1 was located, supported the Radio Condenser workers but did not walk out. Both of these disputes were settled before the end of the New York Ship strike. [12]

The strike at New York Ship was the largest in Camden, and it quickly brought calls for immediate federal mediation from many in the community, including the pro-labor *Camden Courier Post*. Within days, Secretary of Labor Francis Perkins dispatched Philip Chappell, the Labor Department's Conciliation Commissioner, to mediate in Camden. Both Bardo and Green welcomed his assistance, but Green made it clear that the union's cooperation did not mean that it would abandon the strike without gains. The 3,000 workers who marched two abreast outside the shipyard gates when Chappell and Bardo conferred for the first time on April 7 remained disciplined and fully committed to their cause. [13]

Under federal mediation and Chappell's influence, negotiations began to make some progress. After three days, Bardo raised his wage offer to 10 percent, while the union came down from 37.5 percent to 25 percent, which Green claimed matched the Philadelphia Navy Yard's rates. Bardo still refused to agree to a union shop, but stated that he would "recognize" the union. The IUMSWA replied that this was unacceptable, but pressed on with the wages issue. To hammer home the union's position, some 3,000 workers at a mass meeting thundered a resounding "No" when John Green asked for a vote on Bardo's wage offer. By this time, Green had taken over as acting president of Local 1 in place of Mullin, consolidating his leadership of the IUMSWA. [14]

In the second week of April, Bardo became anxious to settle the strike, ap-

---

[11] Van Gelder, *Book of Facts for Shipyard Workers*, p. 7; Letter from "An Observer," *Camden Courier Post*, April 3, 1934.

[12] *Camden Courier Post*, April 1–7, 9–11, 13, 20, 21, 24, 25, 28, May 3, 4, 1934.

[13] Ibid., April 1–7, 1934.

[14] *Camden Courier Post*, April 10, 11, 1934; Van Gelder interview, June 11, 1987.

parently because of rumors that the U.S. Navy planned to remove the cruiser *Tuscaloosa* if production did not resume. His bargaining power, however, was severely limited by the need to have his actions approved by the company's board of directors. Subsequently, some key figures in the corporation who were connected with majority stockholder Errett Lobban Cord, a young speculator who had just gained control of Aviation Corporation (later AVCO), began to sit in on the negotiations. Bardo now found himself on the defensive and did his best to reach a settlement satisfactory to both the union and the Cord interests. Pressure to moderate also came from some middle managers, who supported a negotiated settlement but were not currently employed by the company. Former New York Shipbuilding personnel supervisor O. L. Preble, for example, informed the *Courier Post* that "the workmen should not be condemned for feeling as they do, for while the property loss has been very great and so many employers are now and have been for a long time 'in the red,' workmen and their families have in many cases not had enough to eat, let alone any real comforts of life. . . . It is so much easier to find some answer to the controversy in a friendly atmosphere, than it is in an antagonistic atmosphere." Bardo shifted to this more conciliatory approach and continued to negotiate, though he publicly stated on a number of occasions that he was finished talking. He did not engage in open red-baiting, nor did he advocate using force against the strikers. Later he discovered that other leading shipbuilding executives, who had long advocated the open shop, did not approve of his style.[15]

Bardo's shift toward moderation allowed Green to take the initiative. On April 16 Green opened a major lobbying campaign on behalf of the strike and led a delegation of twenty-six worker representatives to Washington. The delegation tried unsuccessfully to see President Roosevelt, but was able to meet with Secretary of Labor Frances Perkins. She was sympathetic to the workers' cause and, through Labor Department Solicitor Thomas Eliot, contacted the Navy, the Shipbuilding Code Authority of the NRA, the NLB, and the PWA, all in an effort to resolve the strike. Perkins raised the issue of the NRA's stipulation that all PWA-funded projects "shall contain a clause 'to insure . . . that all employees shall be paid just and reasonable wages'." She made it clear that the New York Ship strikers had legitimate wage demands and that a "mutual agreement" was the only proper type of settlement. It soon became apparent, however, that the Navy rather than other government agencies held the real power to pressure Bardo. The IUMSWA called on the Navy to readjust New

---

[15] *Camden Courier Post*, April 10, 11, 12, 18, 1934; Thomas Eliot to Frances Perkins, May 8, 1934, NA, RG 174, Box 37; Jacob Vander Meulen, *The Politics of Aircraft: Building an American Military Industry* (Lawrence: University of Kansas Press, 1991), pp. 93, 95–96 (for background on Cord and AVCO).

York Ship's contracts, worth $52 million, as an answer to Bardo's claim that a wage increase was impossible under the contracts' existing provisions. Bardo angrily demanded that the IUMSWA end its lobbying and declared that he no longer would negotiate over wages because the whole matter of contract payments now was uncertain, but DOL Conciliation Commissioner Chappell managed to get both sides back to the bargaining table after a few days.[16]

The IUMSWA focused its Washington efforts on influencing President Roosevelt to intervene. Three representatives—Phil Van Gelder, David Cole, and Pat McCann—lobbied in the national capital for the duration of the strike. With the help of NRA Labor Advisory Board member Matthew Boyd, Van Gelder and the others presented their case to officials controlling New York Ship's NRA public works funds. Bardo's latest refusal to continue negotiating helped persuade these officials that the IUMSWA's demands had merit. The IUMSWA representatives also lobbied members of Congress, including Senator Robert Wagner, who spoke with President Roosevelt about settling the strike.[17]

In response, Bardo tried to get the IRC to endorse his objectives. Through the IRC he continued to lobby the NRA for the forty-hour week, believing that raising weekly working hours would make it appear that he was granting higher wages. His attempts proved partially successful when his ally, IRC chairman and Shipbuilding Code Deputy Administrator J. B. Weaver, managed to raise the NRA shipbuilding code from thirty-two to thirty-six hours. Bardo also wanted either the Regional Labor Board or the IRC to be the sole mediator in order to exclude the Labor Department, but he seriously underestimated the Labor Department's influence on some IRC representatives. One such Labor Department official was A. J. Doyle, who had an AFL background but did not necessarily follow the IRC's Metal Trades representatives. He had opposed the transfer of jurisdiction to the IRC since April 26 because of what Conciliation Commissioner Chappell had told him about the case. Doyle explained to his IRC colleagues, "if Mr. Bardo could be given to understand that neither this Committee [IRC] nor any Governmental Agency would intervene,

---

[16] *Camden Courier Post*, April 16–19, 23, 1934; Perkins (with Eliot) to Henry Roosevelt, April 25, 1934, and Perkins (with Eliot) to Congressman Charles Wolverton, April 25, 1934, both NA, RG 174, Box 37.

[17] *Camden Courier Post*, April 18, 19, 25, 1934; Matthew Boyd (Labor Advisory Board) to Harry Slattery (Assistant Secretary, Department of the Interior), introducing Van Gelder (organizer) and the New York Ship Local 1 Union Negotiating Committee, April 17, 1934, NA, RG 9, Box 5253. This document is the first one from the NRA collection to mention Van Gelder's name. Van Gelder did not recall the exact date when he started working with IUMSWA Local 1, but thought that it was during or just before the 1934 strike; Van Gelder interview, June 11, 1987.

and that [the] solution rested solely with him . . . the matter might yet be adjusted."[18]

In Washington, the union continued to pressure Bardo. On April 25, Van Gelder's committee attempted to see Secretary of the Navy Claude Swanson, but instead met with Assistant Secretary Henry Roosevelt, the real power in the Department. Back in Camden, Green accused Bardo of "feeding at the trough filled with public funds—taxpayers' funds," and charged that the IRC was nothing more than a "boss-dominated board." Authority rested not with the IRC but with conciliator Chappell, who was "a personal representative" of Labor Secretary Perkins and President Roosevelt. "As far as we are concerned," Green declared, the strike "will be settled between the strikers' representatives, Bardo and this mediator."[19]

Meanwhile, community leaders sent the President hundreds of telegrams supporting the union, and picket captain Charlie Purkis collected petitions with 15,000 signatures calling for federal intervention on behalf of the workers.[20]

Bardo had lost the initiative in Washington as well as in Camden. Government jurisdiction in the case remained with those loyal to Roosevelt and the popular character of New Deal policy, rather than business interests within the NRA bureaucracy. On April 25, the President and the Cabinet discussed the New York Ship strike and concluded that the dispute had to be settled immediately to avoid jeopardizing the Navy's reconstruction program. One critical factor in the decision may have been that the Camden strike had created a bottleneck in the design end of the Navy's entire building effort, because New York Ship draftsmen had responsibility for a number of plans used at other major yards, including Newport News and Fore River.[21]

Following President Roosevelt's decision that a resolution had to be found, IRC chairman J. B. Weaver suddenly reentered the picture. He told the union on May 2 that Bardo was making his final offer: a 13 percent wage increase. But he also told Green that the Navy planned to remove the *Tuscaloosa* if the strike did not end quickly. Green charged coercion, even though the union stood to gain more from these developments than did the company. The threat was real, and five days later Secretary of the Navy Swanson made it official: the yard had to resume work by May 14 or the *Tuscaloosa* would be transferred to the Philadelphia Navy Yard. Pressure seemed to be building against

[18] *Camden Courier Post*, April 24, 1934. Bardo to Weaver, April 3, 1934; H. G. Smith to Wagner, April 24, 1934; Smith to Woodward, April 24, 1934; Bardo to Smith, April 24, 1934; Bardo to Weaver, May 8, 1934; all NA, RG 9, Box 5252. A. J. Doyle Memorandum to IRC staff, April 26, 1934, NA, RG 9, Box 5254.

[19] *Camden Courier Post*, April 25, 1934.

[20] Ibid., April 27, 1933.

[21] Ibid., April 26, 1934.

the union, as thugs tried to disrupt the picket line and negotiating committee member Ed Baker was threatened at gunpoint. Aside from these incidents, no other violence occurred and the pickets remained as strong as before.[22]

In fact, the pressure that the Navy, NRA authority, and Department of Labor put on Bardo to settle was far more intense than anything the union experienced. Green and the IUMSWA, for all their militancy, had always sought to negotiate, while Bardo became, in the eyes of Washington agencies and officials, the real intransigent. Labor Solicitor Eliot noted in his final report to Secretary Perkins: "When Bardo refused to come to terms here in Washington last week, and under pressure from the Navy announced that he would open Monday, the workers staged an impressive demonstration, gaining much public support." The government's threat against Bardo finally made him capitulate, because he realized that "if he remained adamant, the wage question would probably be taken out of his hands altogether."

In negotiations on May 11, Bardo once again increased his offer, to a 14.6 percent raise in wages. This time the union accepted his offer and declared victory.[23]

The strike had been solid, with virtually no workers entering the yard. The union won a contract, and it also built a loyal following in Camden. Despite the heated words exchanged by Green and Bardo, the community was not seriously divided by the conflict. As the *Camden Courier Post* noted in its editorial, "Full Speed Ahead": "The New York Shipyard strike will go down as one of the most unusual on record. There was no violence. Although 3300 men were involved, there was not a single arrest. . . . The settlement was a fair compromise."[24]

In many respects, IUMSWA Local 1 won a model contract that was a milestone achievement for the early 1930s. The wage increase amounted to a restoration of what had been cut in 1932 and brought New York Ship wages up to levels comparable to other Delaware River yards. In addition, the local won the right to preferential hiring for union members and a signed, one-year agreement, which amounted to union recognition. The grievance procedure involved stewards and a business agent, as well as guaranteeing the right to binding arbitration, and had no specific prohibition against strikes or job actions. The company acceded to a recall system based on previous employment in the shipyard. Although not strictly a seniority clause, this provision indi-

[22] Ibid., May 5, 7, 9, 12, 1934; Howard Sloan to Weaver, May 11, 1934, NA, RG 9, Box 5254.
[23] Eliot to Perkins, May 14, 1934, NA, RG 174, Box 37; *Camden Courier Post*, May 12, 1934.
[24] *Camden Courier Post*, May 14, 1934.

rectly protected workers from arbitrary layoffs. The company also agreed to extra shift pay, holiday pay, and a shorter probation period.[25]

Perhaps most significant of all, the workers who attended the contract ratification meeting viewed the settlement as a hard-fought victory. As the *Camden Courier Post* reported, "Green introduced Chappell on the platform as 'the man who has done more than any other person to bring about this settlement.' At these words, the entire crowd leaped to its feet and cheered itself hoarse for the government mediator." Virtually every striker attended the standing-room-only meeting, which was held exclusively for union members. After the negotiating committee members and Chappell spoke, IUMSWA attorney M. H. Goldstein read through the entire contract. "Time after time . . . the men interrupted with enthusiastic cheering." The union had ballots ready for a secret vote, but "when Goldstein had finished, one of the men got up and made a motion from the floor that the vote be taken by acclamation. There was a unanimous response to this motion, and then Green called for the vote. The answer was deafening, in favor of acceptance."[26] A critical stage of the organizing process had been accomplished. Workers saw the new industrial union as their own.

Looking back forty-eight years later, Van Gelder recalled the advantage that management had given the IUMSWA in this first strike. "It was a fairly simple strike. Everybody went out. The company didn't try to operate the yard because they had nobody to do it with, and Bardo didn't know how to fight the union. . . . He made the mistake of offering a little more every week, so the longer they stayed out the more they got. . . . He had no preparation."[27]

The New York Ship walkout occurred at the onset of the national strike wave of 1934, which undoubtedly contributed to IUMSWA Local 1's momentum. The IUMSWA's victory in Camden was one of the few success stories for labor during that year. Harry Bridges's Longshoremen won in San Francisco, as did militant Teamsters in Minneapolis. But the largest strike of the year, involving hundreds of thousands of textile operatives led by the United Textile Workers, ended in disaster. Similarly, in the automobile industry, the AFL's Federal Local 18384 was defeated in the spectacular Toledo Auto-Lite strike.[28]

The New York Ship walkout was far smaller than those strikes, and differed from them in several respects. Although Socialist Party members Green and Van Gelder led the strike, the SP's role was minimal, compared to the Com-

[25] Ibid., May 12, 1934.
[26] Ibid.
[27] Van Gelder interview, Oct. 25, 1982.
[28] For a detailed overview of these 1934 strikes, see Irving Bernstein, *The Turbulent Years: A History of the American Worker, 1933–1941* (Boston: Houghton Mifflin, 1969), pp. 217–317.

munist Party's role among San Francisco's longshoremen or the Trotskyists' role among the Minneapolis Teamsters. While these other strikes were led by AFL affiliates, at New York Ship the IUMSWA established an industrial union completely independent of the AFL. Obtaining a signed contract signified recognition, which almost no independent unions had won to date. The tactics of the strike were militant, relying on a mass picket line of 2,000 to 3,000 shipyard workers. In contrast to strikes elsewhere in 1934, no violence occurred at New York Ship, and the walkout had attracted widespread community support, from local merchants to police and city officials.

Despite its small scale, the 1934 strike at New York Ship served as an important symbol for the American labor movement. It established the IUMSWA as an independent industrial union that had to be reckoned with and positioned New York Ship workers at the center of this small but critically important shipyard movement. The other independent unions active in Camden that year failed to develop the power that the IUMSWA did. The Canners' union soon disappeared. The small, Camden-based Radio Workers Industrial Union eventually joined James Carey's union group based in Philadelphia, which then merged into the United Electrical Workers Union (UE) by 1936.[29]

Green's ability to outmaneuver Bardo tactically, both in Camden and Washington, laid a solid foundation for the IUMSWA. At the same time, Green and Van Gelder were pulled away from socialist politics and into the pragmatic world of mass trade unionism. Although they remained at odds with the AFL and craft unionists, they began to identify more with New Deal officials and the Roosevelt wing of the Democratic Party, political allies who had helped the IUMSWA win its first contract. In taking on Bardo and New York Ship management both locally and in the nation's capital, Green and Van Gelder carried the fight beyond the experience of their adversary. Management simply had not expected such a wave of support for the new union. The 1934 strike taught the IUMSWA's leadership the critical importance of federal government intervention for shipyard organizing. Even with government assistance, however, worker mobilization remained the starting point for every phase of organizing, and building the national union remained the overall objective. Gaining a local contract and official recognition at New York Ship were initial steps in that process.

The model for the IUMSWA's subsequent shipyard organizing emerged from the tactics activists learned in building the union internally during 1933 and in a more public way during the 1934 strike. These early experiences at New York Ship set the stage for organizing on a broader regional and then

[29] Van Gelder letter to David Palmer, Nov. 22, 1986 (on the UE and the support that IUMSWA Local 1 gave the 1936 Camden RCA strikers, who belonged to the UE); Bernstein, *Turbulent Years*, pp. 603–15.

national scale, but the problem of developing a viable national organizing strategy remained. IUMSWA Local 1 discovered that the 1934 walkout was only a dress rehearsal for the bitter and protracted New York Ship strike of 1935. This conflict became the real test of whether the IUMSWA would survive, and it determined the union's direction for years to come.

CHAPTER 3

"It Will Have to Come from Washington" The 1935 New York Ship Strike and the Fight for Full Recognition

Workers had to wage a second strike in 1935 in order to consolidate the IUMSWA at New York Ship, but this strike had far broader implications than the first one. The walkout stemmed from a breakdown of the accord that Local 1 had won from New York Ship's president, Clinton Bardo, and it tested the limits of the union leadership's ability to remain militant yet disciplined. Workers became more involved in running the strike on a tactical level than in 1934, raising the level of participation and sense of democracy in the union. At the same time, John Green moved to centralize strategic decisions, first at the negotiating table and then on the picket lines. This strike also compelled Green and Van Gelder to abandon much of their anti-capitalist program and rhetoric and to adopt a tactically militant trade unionism that could welcome the intervention of the Roosevelt administration and follow a strategy of political moderation. In 1934 these leaders accepted federal intervention, but by 1935 they saw government action as essential to any solution, a conclusion that was confirmed after two months of picketing and stalled negotiations.

In order to secure recognition through a strike, the union had to build its support among the yard's workers, their families, the Camden community, and the area's trade union movement. Mobilizing this broad base of support became the precondition for the new political relationship between the IUMSWA and the federal government. The IUMSWA had tried to expand beyond Camden from late 1933 to early 1935, but met with little success. The second New York Ship strike forced the union to retreat from its organizing in other locations in order to concentrate on Camden.

The victory that IUMSWA Local 1 had won with the signing of the first contract in May 1934 became uncertain by early 1935. The union had to contend

Table 2. IUMSWA Locals Chartered by 1935

Local	City	Company/Group	Charter Date
1	Camden, N.J.	*New York Ship	10-03-33
2	Chester, Penn.	*Sun Ship	09-29-34
3	Wilmington, Del.	*Dravo; *Pusey & Jones	09-29-34
4	Bath, Maine	*Bath Iron Works	09-29-34
5	Quincy, Mass.	*Bethlehem Fore River	09-29-34
6	New London, Conn.	Electric Boat	09-29-34
7	San Francisco, Calif.	Union Iron Works	01-07-35
8	Newport News, Va.	Newport News	04-12-35
9	San Pedro, Calif.	*Repair Yards	05-01-35
10	Seattle, Wash.	Repair Yards	05-11-35
11	Oakland, Calif.	Repair Yards	07-15-35

*Signed IUMSWA contract won prior to 1950. None of these locals was recognized by management at the time of charter.

Sources: Phil Van Gelder, *Book of Facts for Shipyard Workers* (Camden, N.J.: IUMSWA, 1935); Bernard Mergen, "A History of the Industrial Union of Marine and Shipbuilding Workers of America, 1933–1951" (Ph.D. diss., University of Pennsylvania, 1968), pp. 1, 249–53; *Shipyard Worker*, 1936–1949.

not only with opposition from New York Ship's management but also with the hostility of the AFL craft unions that claimed to represent shipyard workers. The IUMSWA publicly asserted that it was making limited gains organizing in new locations and established seven locals on the Atlantic Coast and four on the West Coast, but none of these except for New York Ship had a sizable membership (Table 2). Only five of these early locals ever won signed union-management agreements, and all but one of these five were on the East Coast. The IUMSWA's weakness on the West Coast was due mainly to AFL dominance there.[1]

When IUMSWA leaders established their union as an organization independent of the AFL, they wanted a united membership that was not broken up into separate craft units. They therefore made the largest East Coast construction yards their primary organizing target. The IUMSWA held its first national convention in September 1934 in Quincy, Massachusetts, both as a sign of the union's growth beyond Camden and because the union attached great importance to organizing Quincy's huge Bethlehem Fore River Shipyard. The gathering was a modest affair, but it had historical import for the emerging industrial union movement of the 1930s. Fifty-four delegates arrived in Quincy by bus, with the largest groups from Camden, Wilmington, and Chester. As Phil Van Gelder recalled: "The bus left us off at Quincy Square, and we walked

[1] Phil Van Gelder, *Book of Facts for Shipyard Workers* (Camden, N.J.: IUMSWA, 1935), pp. 7–8.

to Quincy Point [the shipyard neighborhood], a couple of miles, the whole bus load. . . . We couldn't pay any more." The convention established a national executive board with representatives from the six locals; elected a general executive board (GEB) to direct the union; and adopted a constitution that Van Gelder wrote, which was based mainly on that of the Amalgamated Clothing Workers Union. The delegates also authorized publication of the *Shipyard Worker*, the IUMSWA's national newspaper.[2]

By spring 1935, however, the IUMSWA retained only minimal influence among workers at the other big shipyards in the Northeast. Efforts to organize the Fore River Shipyard stalled, while the union ran into even greater difficulties at the giant Newport News, Virginia, yard. When Van Gelder and IUMSWA organizer Charlie Purkis tried to initiate a high-profile union drive at Newport News in early April 1935, management fired thirty supporters and easily won the three-week-long strike that followed, which destroyed the local.[3]

After the successful 1934 strike at New York Ship and the founding of the national union, Green and Van Gelder sought affiliation with the American Federation of Labor as a way to strengthen their organizing status in the industry and to augment their union resources. On February 15, 1935, the AFL rejected the IUMSWA's request for a charter, despite interest from UMW president John L. Lewis, who was still within the Federation's ranks. Conservative AFL leaders charged that the IUMSWA threatened the Federation's existing craft jurisdictions in shipbuilding and was therefore "dual unionist." The AFL also continued to block the IUMSWA's attempt to gain representation on the Industrial Relations Commission (IRC) of the NRA Shipbuilding Code Board. In the months that followed the AFL's rejection of the IUMSWA's bid for affiliation, Green and Van Gelder were not surprised to learn that AFL members on the IRC and the New York Ship management were working together against the IUMSWA.[4]

The New York Shipbuilding Corporation changed ownership after the 1934 strike. When Clinton Bardo resigned as president, the makeshift labor relations policy that had allowed the IUMSWA to gain a foothold in the yard

---

[2] Van Gelder interview, Oct. 25, 1982; IUMSWA, *Proceedings, 1st National Convention,* Sept. 28–30, 1934.

[3] Van Gelder, *Book of Facts for Shipyard Workers,* p. 8.

[4] John W. Brown (for IUMSWA GEB) to John L. Lewis, Sept. 9, 1934; Lewis to Brown, Sept. 15, 1934; Brown to Lewis (with IUMSWA GEB's application for AFL affiliation), Jan. 12, 1935; Lewis to Brown, Jan. 14, 1935; all in *The CIO Files of John L. Lewis,* part 1, reel 7 (University Publications of America microfilm). Irving Bernstein, *The Turbulent Years: A History of the American Worker, 1933–1941* (Boston: Houghton Mifflin, 1969), p. 384. Brown, a friend of Lewis from his days as an organizer with the UMW, introduced Lewis to newcomers Green and Van Gelder.

changed as well. Bardo's successor, John F. Metten, adhered to the firm anti-union style of other executives then running major shipyards, but because of Local 1's broad following among rank-and-file workers he could not simply fire Green and other union leaders.

In late 1934, entrepreneur and New York Ship shareholder Errett Lobban Cord bought the shipyard from American Brown-Broveri Electrical Corporation, which had owned it since 1925. Under Cord, New York Ship became a subsidiary of the Aviation Corporation, later known as AVCO. As part of an effort to reorganize managerial policies, Cord and his board of directors allowed Metten to hire new upper-level managers to run the yard.[5]

Metten had come up from the ranks, starting in the shipbuilding industry at sixteen as a machinist's apprentice sometime in the early 1890s. He boasted that he had never been a member of any union. After working at a number of trades in various yards, including Newport News, he finally was promoted to foreman at New York Ship. In the 1920s, he became (in his own words) "connected with the design and the managing ends of the business." Then in October 1934, L. B. Manning, the new chairman of the board, persuaded Metten to become president of the shipyard in order to "try to straighten it out." Metten was unmarried and had no children, but proudly stated, "I'm married to shipbuilding!" He equated his role as New York Ship's president with that of the captain of a ship, and thought of the yard's workers and staff as his "crew." He regarded the union, with its "radical" leaders, as a threat to the discipline required for shipbuilding and believed that it sought to destroy the company through its unpatriotic, "communistic" goals.[6]

Metten brought in Carl M. Kaltwasser as executive vice president. A newcomer to the Camden area, Kaltwasser had only worked for New York Ship for a year. He had a degree in mechanical engineering and experience in the utility business. Many workers saw Kaltwasser as a cold, cerebral technocrat with no ties to either shipbuilding or the city.[7]

---

[5] "A Brief History of the New York Shipbuilding Corporation" (no author or publisher), Sept. 1, 1964, CCHS; Letter by Clinton Bardo to Board of Directors of New York Shipbuilding Corp., Oct. 27, 1934, as quoted in U.S. Congress, House, Subcommittee on Labor, *Hearings Relating to Labor Practices of Employers of Labor in the Shipbuilding Industry*, 74th Cong., 1st sess. (Washington, D.C.: GPO, 1935), hereafter cited as "Hearings, Labor Practices in Shipbuilding," 1935, pp. 9–11.

[6] "Hearings, Labor Practices in Shipbuilding," testimony of John Metten, July 29, 1935, pp. 79–95; "Announcement by the New York Shipbuilding Corp.," biographical notice published by New York Shipbuilding on Metten, Kaltwasser, and Campbell, Nov. 1934, CCHS (exclamation in original).

[7] "Announcement of the New York Shipbuilding Corp."; "Minutes," IUMSWA Local 1 and New York Shipbuilding contract negotiations transcript, May 21, 1935, comments by Green, NA, RG 9, Box 5243.

Roy S. Campbell, the new general manager, also became a key player in 1935. Like Metten, he had begun his career as a rank-and-file worker, moving from mold loft apprentice to master mechanic and finally to superintendent. He also had experience in government construction, having just returned from a leading position in the Boulder Dam project. Most other management replacements came from within New York Shipbuilding.[8]

Bardo's 1934 settlement with the union, in which he had conceded a substantial wage raise at the last minute, evoked criticism from the company's board of directors, who clearly wanted a change. Unlike Bardo, Metten delegated responsibility for handling labor relations to his immediate subordinates, while he took overall responsibility for the business. He left the details of yard production to others, which gave him more time to deal directly with the top government officials who were the link to new naval contracts. When management began negotiations for a new agreement with the union in the spring of 1935, General Manager Campbell and the head of personnel took charge. This time management's major objective was to erode and then to eradicate the independent union from the shipyard, rather than to accommodate it as Bardo had.[9]

IUMSWA Local 1 faced a range of obstacles after the 1934 strike agreement. Late that year, the union found it impossible to bring a number of unresolved grievances to arbitration because the company refused to agree on a third, neutral arbitrator for the disputes. The AFL Metal Trades also obstructed Local 1's progress as an independent union. They claimed dues-paying members among the coppersmiths and the sheet metal workers, even though these craft unions had only a handful of followers in the yard.[10]

Relations between the NRA Shipbuilding Code Authority and the IUMSWA had been poor since 1933. They worsened after the IRC rejected the IUMSWA's request for representation on the government body in June 1934. By early 1935, the IUMSWA's frustration with the NRA, particularly its "labor"

[8] "Announcement of the New York Shipbuilding Corp."; "Hearings, Labor Practices in Shipbuilding," Metten testimony, July 29, 1935, p. 88.

[9] "Minutes," IUMSWA Local 1 and New York Shipbuilding contract negotiations transcript, April 8, 1935, Box 5254; R. S. Campbell to Gallagher et al., April 9, 1935, Box 5243; "Minutes," IUMSWA Local 1 and New York Shipbuilding contract negotiations transcript, May 21, 1935; all NA, RG 9.

[10] Kaltwasser to IRC, Feb. 28, 1935; Arthur Koehler, Local No. 82, Coppersmiths' Union, AFL (Philadelphia) to IRC, Feb. 14, 1935; W. M. O'Brian, Sheet Metal Workers' International Association, AFL, Washington, D.C., to Doyle, Feb. 15, 1935; H. Newton Whittelsey to New York Shipbuilding, Feb. 21, 1935; all NA, RG 9, Box 5243. Van Gelder interview, Oct. 25, 1982; Ben Maiatico interview, Aug. 16, 1987; George "Chips" De Girolamo interview; Charles Harker interview.

committees, reached the breaking point when the IRC refused to assist the IUMSWA at New York Ship or to honor requests for representation elections at New London, Connecticut, and San Francisco-area yards. In protest, Van Gelder wrote to the National Industrial Recovery Board that "the Industrial Relations Committee . . . was set up without consulting the majority of ship-yard workers, and they have no representation on it." The IRC's failure "to fa-cilitate the orderly settlement of labor disputes, and to protect the rights of the workingmen in the shipyards" left the IUMSWA with "no other recourse but to prepare for strike action." [11]

The union at New York Ship elected a negotiating committee in April that included leaders from the 1933 and 1934 struggles, as well as some new men. Tom Gallagher, Green's key ally, chaired the committee, giving it stability and balancing Green's dynamic though often volatile style. Welding steward Chips De Girolamo recalled that Gallagher "was a very good diplomat. [He] was the guy that would quiet [Green] down. Green would walk in with a chip on his shoulder." Green remained the chief strategist. He was now Local 1's ex-ecutive secretary, the most powerful local union officer, and was also national president of the IUMSWA. Green, Gallagher, Francis "Pat" McCann, and Ed Baker were committee veterans from the previous year, as was the committee's secretary, David Cole. Lewis Vennell, John Diehl, Charles Mitchell, and Lo-cal 1's vice president, William Pommerer, were new faces. William Mullin, Local 1 president and a founder of the union, also served on the negotiating committee. [12]

On April 8, 1935, the union submitted its proposal to the company, and three days later it gave notification that it wanted to terminate the old contract. A deadlock quickly developed over three main demands: the preferential union shop (which management insisted on calling, incorrectly, the "closed shop"), elimination of the incentive system (based on both piecework and bonus), and a 15 percent wage raise. The negotiating committee also sought to refine the classification system. This objective revealed the extent to which the IUMSWA combined craft and industrial unionism, even though it claimed to be solely "industrial" in outlook. New York Ship and the other major yards had at least twenty-four different trades, ranging from unskilled laborers to highly

[11] Van Gelder to Robert Wagner, June 13, 1934; B. M. Stern (NLB) to Van Gelder, June 19, 1934; both NA, RG 9, Box 5239. Van Gelder to Whittelsey, Aug. 17, 1934, NA, RG 9, Box 5250. Green and Van Gelder to NRA, Jan. 15, 1935; Whittelsey to Vaughn, IRC memos, Jan. 19 and 24, 1935; Van Gelder to Doyle, Feb. 1, 1935; Van Gelder to National Industrial Re-covery Board, Feb. 2, 1935; Whittelsey to Van Gelder, Feb. 7, 1935; all NA, RG 9, Box 5242.

[12] "Conditions and Terms of Employments Desired by . . . Local No. 1," March 22, 1934, NA, RG 9, Box 5254; De Girolamo interview; "Minutes," IUMSWA Local 1 and New York Shipbuilding contract negotiations transcript, April 8, 1935.

skilled shipfitters and draftsmen, which produced a bewildering set of wage rates. The 1934 agreement established a simple three-level rate system based on the categories of skilled, semi-skilled, and unskilled, which applied equally to each trade classification and reduced the number of different rates from 77 to 12. The union wanted an equitable rate system for all workers in the yard, but also sought to maintain standard rates for the higher trades. The union claimed that the company abused even this modified system by misclassifying skilled workers, paying them less than they earned on nonshipyard jobs elsewhere, which eroded morale. As a result, highly skilled workers were motivated to participate in the union. It was no coincidence that all the negotiating committee members, with the exception of Gallagher, held highly skilled jobs. While these men advocated industrial unionism, they had not abandoned a strong sense of craft pride. As the talks became more polarized, however, the classification demand receded, while the wage demand and the demand for union recognition based on the "preferential union shop" came to the fore.[13]

Management and the IRC, with AFL assistance, began to work together behind the scenes to block a strike vote and prevent the mobilization of yard workers by Local 1. On April 19, the IRC authorized a subcommittee to investigate the situation in Camden. Assistant Deputy Administrator H. Newton Whittelsey of the NRA Equipment Division, who served as an IRC member, asked IRC Chairman Arthur Wharton to take this initiative. Wharton was the national president of the AFL-affiliated International Association of Machinists, which had substantial shipyard membership during World War I. The two IRC members assigned to the subcommittee by Wharton were Joseph W. Hart, a management employee of New York Shipbuilding, and John J. Lane, the "expert" on the committee. For the next month, Hart and Lane traveled back and forth between Washington and Camden to report on the discussions they had with both parties. They were joined at various times by IRC labor representative W. A. Calvin, president of the Boilermakers and Iron Shipbuilders Union and secretary-treasurer of the AFL's Metal Trades Department. Calvin had been hand-picked for the IRC position by John Frey, national president of the ultra-conservative Molders' Union and head of the Metal Trades Department. Some in the Navy Department sought to block a IUMSWA strike at New York Ship. Captain Henry Williams, who attended IRC meetings as NRA liaison

---

[13] Agreement between New York Shipbuilding Corp. and IUMSWA Local 1, May 11, 1934, point 5, as quoted (in full) in *Camden Courier Post*, May 12, 1934; Green et al. to New York Shipbuilding Corp., April 11, 1935, NA, RG 9, Box 5243; "Relative Weekly Earnings for Shipyard Trades in Sept. 1933 and in 1929 . . . for Five Private Shipyards," NA, RG 9, Box 5257, (file) "23. *Statistics*, Misc., Folder #1"; "Minutes," IUMSWA Local 1 and New York Shipbuilding contract negotiations transcript, April 8, 1935; De Girolamo interview; Andy Reeder interview, May 30, 1987; Jack Collins interview, Sept. 13, 1987, Gloucester, N.J.

officer, encouraged Whittelsey's request for IRC intervention in the dispute. According to IRC executive secretary A. J. Doyle, Williams believed that the breakdown in negotiations at New York Ship required the IRC to "take some action, preferably action looking toward making this vote of the Union a secret ballot. If this were done [Williams] felt a majority would not vote for a strike." Doyle adamantly opposed such intrusion into a union's internal affairs, as he had in 1934, but was overruled by Whittelsey, with the support of Captain Williams.[14]

When the subcommittee presented its initial findings on the situation in Camden to a full IRC meeting, the IUMSWA's demand for a "preferential shop" became a special target. Whittelsey and Williams persuaded the other representatives that it was illegal. The AFL concurred, claiming that the rights of AFL union members at New York Ship would be violated because they would be forced to hold memberships in two separate unions. The following day, Whittelsey wrote to the company and the union stating the IRC's position that the "preferential shop" proposal was illegal and warning that its adoption "would be liable to the charge of violation of the Code of Fair Competition for the Shipbuilding and Shiprepairing Industry and Section 7(a) of the National Industrial Recovery Act, and therefore, place your Navy contracts in jeopardy." This action hardened the IUMSWA leadership's antagonism toward the IRC, compelling it to turn to other officials and agencies in Washington to outmaneuver New York Shipbuilding management. The union's offensive began with a scathing response from negotiating committee chairman Tom Gallagher, who refocused the entire struggle on one critical issue: full recognition by New York Ship of IUMSWA Local 1 as exclusive collective bargaining agent, based on the fact that a majority of workers supported the union. The question at hand was whether a government official had the authority to destroy what was a "perfectly legal" right. Furthermore, Gallagher charged, "we have come to the . . . conclusion that your letter . . . was not written upon your own initiative, but at the request, and for the benefit of the New York Shipbuilding Corporation [as it] has posted copies of your letter throughout its yard, on N.R.A. letterheads."[15]

When IRC subcommittee members returned to Camden, the union refused to talk with them, but New York Shipbuilding management and the AFL-run Camden Central Labor Union did. Local 1's suspicion that New York Ship was

[14] Whittelsey to Barton Murray (Division Administrator, Equipment Division, NRA), May 6, 1935, NA, RG 9, Box 5254; Doyle memo on Williams discussion, April 19, 1935, NA, RG 9, Box 5243.

[15] Doyle memo on Williams discussion, April 19, 1935; Whittelsey memo to Murray, May 6, 1935; Whittelsey to Campbell (New York Shipbuilding) and IUMSWA, April 24, 1935, NA, RG 9, Box 5243; Gallagher to Whittelsey, April 25, 1935, NA, RG 9, Box 5254.

bargaining in bad faith appeared to be justified. On April 29, management resumed negotiations with the union, but on the same day it also met with Hart and Lane to determine how to block a strike vote. Late that afternoon, Lane wired Doyle from his hotel in Philadelphia that the company was "circularizing employees exhorting them to seriously consider dangers of strike." Lane believed that "if a secret ballot was taken employees would vote against [a] strike," giving hope "that [a] strike will be averted."[16]

The IRC's attack on the demand for a preferential shop prompted Green and Gallagher to increase the level of IUMSWA activity in Washington. On April 30, the two union leaders met in the capital with Sidney Hillman, a key NRA Board member and president of the Amalgamated Clothing Workers Union, who then mobilized the other members of the national NRA Board while refusing to talk to Whittelsey. IUMSWA national secretary Van Gelder's ties with the Amalgamated helped Local 1 make this crucial connection with Hillman. The following day NRA executive secretary Leon C. Marshall officially informed the New York Shipbuilding Corporation that Whittelsey's April 24 communication "was unwarranted and hereby disavowed." Marshall directed the company to post his statement in the yard and also released it to the press, further eroding management's position. The IRC, however, refused to modify its anti-IUMSWA stance. Defending Whittelsey's letter, the IRC subcommittee proposed a "solution" to the labor problem that reflected the AFL's position. Before any agreement between labor and management could be reached, it contended, "an election by crafts should be held under proper governmental supervision in order that all employees might be afforded the opportunity of exercising their rights under the law." Conducting a union election by crafts, however, was completely out of touch with workers' sentiments in the yard. The workers had voted overwhelmingly in 1933 for an independent industrial union and against the AFL craft organizations, and by 1935 their agenda focused on better wages and working conditions, not another union election.[17]

Metten tried to use the NRA to his advantage, but he underestimated the growing pro-labor sentiment among many officials and representatives in Washington. The IUMSWA benefited from this political shift and sought sup-

---

[16] "Report of the Industrial Relations Subcommittee," May 6, 1935; Lane to Doyle, April 29, 1935; both NA, RG 9, Box 5243.

[17] Whittelsey to Murray, May 6, 1935; L. C. Marshall to New York Shipbuilding, May 1, 1935; Francis Biddle press release (NLRB), May 2, 1935; all NA, RG 9, Box 5243. *Philadelphia Record*, May 2, 3, 1935; "Report of the Industrial Relations Subcommittee," May 6, 1935. For FDR's inclusion of labor, and Hillman, on the reconstituted National Industrial Recovery Board, see Ellis W. Hawley, *The New Deal and the Problem of Monopoly* (Princeton: Princeton University Press, 1969), pp. 106–7.

port from Congress. An ongoing Senate investigation of profiteering in ship-building and other defense industries, under liberal Republican Gerald Nye, made the shipyard workers appear to be victims of disreputable practices by New York Ship and other companies. Senator Nye openly criticized the Whit-telsey letter declaring the "preferential shop" illegal and used the incident as an opportunity to attack the NRA. "This affair is astounding. A minor official of the NRA calmly arrogated to himself the power to lay down a labor policy of the most sweeping implications and against organized labor. The incident adds further proof to the great mass already on hand of incompetence and un-desirability of the NRA as a recovery agency." The IUMSWA's strongest sup-port came from Camden Congressman Charles Wolverton, who successfully pushed for a House investigation of the labor situation at New York Ship. New York City Congressman Vito Marcantonio, popularly known as the "Red Re-publican" and an ally of Mayor Fiorello La Guardia, also took a special inter-est in the New York Shipyard workers.[18]

The decision whether or not to strike was made on Saturday, May 4, when more than 4,000 union members met at Camden's Convention Hall. After some debate, the members agreed to a secret ballot. Instead of counting the ballots on the spot, Local 1 president Mullin took the ballot boxes, with the votes uncounted, to the union hall. They were kept there until the next day, when Gallagher announced to the press that union members had voted 5 to 1 to go on strike if no progress was made in negotiations. The company claimed that the vote was fraudulent because of the union's questionable handling of the ballots. This event would come back to haunt Mullin. Over the next few months, however, it was proven beyond doubt that workers solidly supported the union and the strike.[19]

With negotiations deadlocked in the days before the strike deadline, the La-bor Department made a final attempt to work out a settlement, entering as me-diator at the union's request. The Department sent in veteran Conciliation Commissioner Philip W. Chappell, who had settled the strike the previous year. The union had earlier proposed to the company that its members would work for a year under the old contract and submit the dispute to arbitration, but the company refused the offer. Now the union made a more specific proposal to Chappell, suggesting that the men return to work under the old contract, without discrimination, pending settlement through arbitration by a board

---

[18] "Munitions Industry Hearings," Parts 18 and 19, "Naval Shipbuilding, New York Ship-building Corporation," Jan. 21 to Feb. 11, 1935; "Extension of Remarks of Hon. Charles A. Wolverton," *Congressional Record*, Appendix, Sept. 10, 1935, pp. 15282–86; "Hearings, La-bor Practices in Shipbuilding," July–Aug., 1935; *Philadelphia Record*, May 3, 1935.

[19] *Philadelphia Record*, May 5, 8, 1935; "Report of the Industrial Relations Subcommittee," May 6, 1935; Doyle to Wharton and Calvin, May 8, 1935, NA, RG 9, Box 5243.

appointed by the Labor Department. The *Camden Courier Post* reported that Chappell put this proposal to the company, although he denied doing so. This union proposal was later taken up by Secretary Perkins as her own, and Chappell advocated it in Camden.[20]

As the first shift approached early on Monday morning, May 13, shipyard workers began mass picketing. By 6:45 a.m., over 3,000 strikers lined Broadway Street, which ran for about a quarter of a mile past the entrance gates along the eastern side of the yard. At 7:45 the work whistle blew, but none of the yard's production workers entered the open gates. Only supervisors, maintenance workers, clerical workers, and a handful of apprentices passed through the lines. Production stopped completely. Union members walked the picket line until 8 a.m., a pattern repeated daily. Ben Maiatico recalled: "After every mass picket in the mornings we would all march to Walnut Hall. Of course, they would go there to eat, get a cup of coffee. . . . Our kitchen was there. . . . [Then] there would be some well known person who would get up and give a speech to keep the morale of the people going during the strike. . . . We usually had mostly our own people who got up to speak."[21]

In the afternoon, the strikers returned for a second mass picket to cover the shift change. A majority of the yard's workers repeated this disciplined picketing each day. According to Phil Van Gelder, the strike was "solid" for its entire duration, and "very, very few people . . . had any idea of going into that shipyard while that strike was on." Besides the daily mass picketing, a team of pickets led by Pat McCann kept a twenty-four-hour watch on all access points to the shipyard. Some twenty to fifty strikers stood at each of the street entrances around the clock. On the Delaware River side of the plant, a "marine" picket of boats blocked approaches to the ways and docks.[22]

The mobilization of union members went beyond picketing and mass meetings. Workers participated in a wide range of committees that often served as a training ground for future leadership of the local union. Some dealt with internal union matters, others reached out to the community, and delegations led by negotiating committee members made regular lobbying trips to Washington. Van Gelder recalled that the local "had committees that went around and

[20] *Philadelphia Record*, May 8, 11, 1935. Kaltwasser to Doyle, May 9, 1935; Doyle to IRC members, May 13, 1935; both NA, RG 9, Box 5243; "Remarks of Wolverton," *Congressional Record*, Appendix, Sept. 10, 1935. "Hearings, Labor Practices in Shipbuilding," July 19, 1935, Green testimony, p. 18; P. W. Chappell to H. L. Kerwin, "Strike at the New York Shipbuilding Corp. . . . ," Aug. 1, 1935, NA, RG 174, Box 37; *Camden Courier Post*, May 11, 1935.

[21] Doyle to IRC members, May 13, 1935; "Hearings, Labor Practices in Shipbuilding," Aug. 20, 1935, Green testimony, p. 157, and July 29, 1935, Metten testimony, p. 82; *Camden Courier Post*, May 13, July 6, 1935; *Philadelphia Record*, May 14, 1935; Maiatico interview, Aug. 16, 1987.

[22] Van Gelder speech at New York Ship IUMSWA Local 1 Reunion.

collected food," while another committee spoke "to the chief real estate agent in Fairview where a lot of people—workers—lived . . . and they all paid rent. Very few of the workers there, at that time, owned their homes." The agent agreed not to evict the strikers on the promise that they would pay the back rent when work resumed.[23]

Strikers also solved the problem of providing food by relying on cooperative efforts. According to Tom J. Gallagher, the son of the negotiating committee chairman, union members took their trucks to South Jersey "and the farmers would give them produce—fruits and vegetables. Then they would bring it back and share it with the rest of the people." Camden merchants also assisted the strikers by extending credit to buy groceries. "When all those people were on strike, the guy [in the store] would let it ride—until something good happened." These relationships reflected the close-knit character of the community and the breadth of local support for the strike. New York Ship workers formed the backbone of the blue-collar communities of Camden and neighboring Gloucester. Local businesses and politicians knew that the area's economy depended on the money shipyard workers earned. Support from the families of shipyard workers proved most critical to sustaining the strikers on a day-to-day basis. Although only men worked in the shipyard at this time, women, especially the wives of the workers, helped maintain unity and morale. Women ran a union kitchen twenty-four hours a day for the pickets, and as the strike progressed they extended their support beyond these domestically oriented activities.[24]

IUMSWA Local 1 also received support from local Camden politicians. The Depression made Camden County Republican Party officials, who controlled the area's politics, more liberal and responsive to the needs of their working-class constituents. Republicans faced strong opposition from a group of Democrats who called themselves the New Deal Non-Partisans. Additional pressure not to oppose the shipyard union and its workers came from third-party groups, including the Independent Group, the Good Government League, the Socialist Party, and the Communist Party. Almost every political party had at least one candidate with a working-class background.[25]

Shipyard trade unionists could be more certain of support from local politicians than from Washington officials. At a Camden Republican Party rally on May 12, the day before the strike began, city commission candidate Frederick von Nieda introduced a resolution supporting the strike, which was passed

[23] Ibid.
[24] Thomas J. Gallagher interview, Aug. 15, 1987, Stratford, N.J.; Maiatico interview, Aug. 16, 1987.
[25] *Camden Courier Post*, May 13, 1935.

unanimously by the 3,500 people attending. Outgoing Camden Mayor Stewart, along with other local officials, endorsed the strike, ensuring substantial community opposition to the company. After von Nieda won election as a new city commissioner and became Camden's mayor, he declared at a mass union meeting of 2,500 strikers: "Your cause is my cause." He warned that he would not tolerate the importation of strikebreakers into the city and would give full authorization for the police to enforce this prohibition. City Commissioner George Brunner, of the New Deal Non-Partisan League, also pledged his full support for "an amicable settlement," proclaimed the "fundamental, natural, as well as legal right . . . to peacefully picket," and called on the police "to maintain a neutral attitude." Mayor von Nieda, wanting to be fair to both sides, attempted to confer with New York Shipbuilding management the following week, but Vice President Kaltwasser left word with the mayor's secretary that "there would be little use of holding a conference."[26]

A further advantage for the union was the very favorable local press coverage it received. A May 23 editorial in the city's leading newspaper, the *Camden Courier Post*, criticized the shipyard management for not negotiating in a reasonable way. The *Courier Post* provided detailed and generally sympathetic coverage of the strike. A balanced selection of letters to the editor also gave the workers a public voice.[27]

The support gained from local small business and political leaders during the first weeks of the strike helped broaden the base of community support. Ben Maiatico believed that "all the business people supported us. All the politicians supported us—the mayor and the members of the commission. . . . The police department supported us. . . . They closed their eyes to a lot of things. . . . So we had the support from all areas of the community."[28]

More than such daily concerns as maintaining the picket line, providing for strikers' families, and mobilizing community support determined the strategy and tactics of the strike. The political outlook of the workers and the union leadership had an influence, especially in determining how to deal with the federal government. Green and Van Gelder retained their skeptical view of the government in 1935, but they found a new ally in the Department of Labor. This sentiment seems to have been shared for the most part by the other IUMSWA leaders and the yard workers. The majority of workers appear to have been New Deal trade union liberals (some Democrats and some "inde-

---

[26] Ibid., May 13, 14, 24, 25, 29, 1935.
[27] Ibid., May 23, 1935.
[28] Maiatico interview, Aug. 16, 1987. The Chamber of Commerce sided with New York Shipbuilding management; it was representative of large employers in the city, all of whom appear to have been anti-union.

pendents"), but there were also a fair number of Republicans, some socialists, and a small group of communists. When it came to shipyard jobs, however, these political views became secondary, because the federal government subsidized virtually all New York Ship's contracts. The union had no choice but to deal with members of Congress, the Department of Labor, the Department of the Navy, and President Roosevelt.[29]

Green and Van Gelder invited a wide range of speakers to Local 1 meetings during the strike, including a number of left-wing political leaders whom they considered friends of labor. Among these were Socialist Party head Norman Thomas and Communist Party leader Robert Minor. Management used these associations to exaggerate the influence of left-wing politics on the IUMSWA and paint the union as a "Communist conspiracy." In fact, the union leaders took a strong position against uninvited Communist Party intrusion into internal union affairs, in contrast to the welcome they extended to selected Communist Party speakers. When CP members distributed a "special strike edition" of its New York Ship shop paper, *The Shipyard Workers' Voice*, Green protested their presence to police near the yard. He also declared publicly that the workers would run their own strike and that they "don't want any outside interference." Despite this evidence, New York Ship's president Metten claimed in testimony before the House Subcommittee on July 29 that distribution of this Communist paper was part of union policy and proved that the IUMSWA itself was Communist.[30]

Although the IUMSWA's leaders kept a clear distance from the Communist Party, they did not single out party activists and other radicals for ridicule, a practice known in the union movement as "red-baiting." According to Van Gelder, the CP was hardly a threat to Local 1's leadership, for it played virtually no role in the New York Ship strike. Nonetheless, a number of New York

[29] State government played virtually no role in the strike at New York Ship, in contrast to other major strikes of the 1930s, because of the initial involvement of the federal government through Navy ship contracts and Department of Labor mediation. For the ambivalent attitudes of other 1930s industrial unionists, who were similar in ethnic makeup and skill levels to those in the IUMSWA, toward New Deal politics and the government, see Steve Babson, *Building the Union: Skilled Workers and Anglo-Gaelic Immigrants in the Rise of the UAW* (New Brunswick, N.J.: Rutgers University Press, 1991); Joshua B. Freeman, *In Transit: The Transport Workers Union in New York City, 1933–1966* (Cambridge: Cambridge University Press, 1989); and Ronald W. Schatz, *The Electrical Workers: A History of Labor at General Electric and Westinghouse, 1933–60* (Urbana: University of Illinois Press, 1983).

[30] Van Gelder interview, June 11, 1987; "Hearings, Labor Practices in Shipbuilding," July 29, 1935, Metten testimony; *Camden Courier Post*, June 3, 1935; *Philadelphia Record*, May 16, 1935; *The Shipyard Workers' Voice*, "Special Strike Edition," vol. 1, no. 2 (May 1935), NA, RG 9, Box 5254.

Ship workers read *The Daily Worker* and argued over its politics, even if they disagreed with the party.[31]

Communist Party activists could be vocal, so they often gave the appearance of being stronger than they actually were. The party's policy at this point was to criticize the IUMSWA leadership for not electing a "broad strike committee representative of every department in the yards." The Communists also attacked the leadership's dealings with government officials. *The Shipyard Workers' Voice* declared: "WE SHOULD STATE RIGHT NOW THAT NO ARBITRATION BOARDS, GOVERNMENT OR OTHERWISE, shall enter into the settlement of this strike, and that conciliators, be they government agents, preachers, or any other so-called 'outside' peacemakers, are OUT . . . and that any terms for settlement must have the approval of our membership expressed by a majority vote."[32]

The Communists incorrectly assumed that the overall direction of the strike came from the Socialist Party, because both Green and Van Gelder were well-known members. They claimed to have sent a committee to meet with the Socialist Party to discuss their proposal for electing a joint strike committee, and alleged that this offer had been turned down. Green and Van Gelder clearly had no interest in bargaining of this type. There is no evidence of workers who belonged or were sympathetic to the Communist Party pursuing what amounted to a "no arbitration board" plan after this incident. From this point on, the Communists seem to have supported the overall campaign. In late July, Communist Party activists tried once more to distribute literature at the gates, but again they were driven away by the union leadership.[33]

The party's momentary bid for influence in the strike was part of its national trade union policy, which was still in the ultra-left phase that preceded the Popular Front. In the late 1920s, the CPUSA had abandoned its policy of "boring from within" existing AFL unions and sought to organize left-wing "industrial unions" independently through the party's Trade Union Unity League (TUUL). All of these CP-led unions eventually collapsed or merged with CIO-based unions by the mid-1930s. The failure of the TUUL's approach led many local CP activists to work within existing labor organizations, including newly developing ones like the IUMSWA, despite the CP's officially sanctioned sectarianism. Many local CP activists who sought a practical level of unity were operating contrary to party policy, at least until the Comintern officially

---

[31] Van Gelder interview, June 11, 1987; De Girolamo interview.
[32] *The Shipyard Workers' Voice*, May 1935 (emphasis in original).
[33] *The Shipyard Workers' Voice*, May 1935; *Camden Courier Post*, "But Arbitration Isn't A Communist Idea!" (editorial), July 30, 1935.

adopted the Popular Front strategy in August 1935 and the CPUSA followed suit. Van Gelder remembered being called a "social fascist" by the Communist Party in these years, despite the efforts that he and other Socialist Party members made to establish a cooperative relationship. In later years, Communist influence grew at New York Ship, but at no point did the CP have a significant following among the yard's workers. If workers at the yard were open to any kind of radicalism at this time, it had an economic rather than political character.[34]

The industrial unionism developing at New York Ship was not the syndicalist type of the Industrial Workers of the World (IWW) either, although the IWW's tradition of direct action on the shop floor had considerable appeal. Some leading shipyard activists were influenced by IWW tactics, such as slow-downs, but they did not belong to the IWW and rejected its broader strategic outlook. The early objective of IUMSWA leaders at New York Ship was to build a shipyard workers' union, not "One Big Union" of all workers or even a general union of maritime workers. Unlike the radical and anti-political IWW of the 1910s, the IUMSWA from the beginning saw lobbying as essential to its success. In this sense, the social democratic values of Van Gelder and his mentor, Sidney Hillman, predominated. By 1935, Green and Van Gelder had learned to act as realists, and they had little use for the utopian side of syndicalism or for the revolutionary outlook of the Communist Party.[35]

The emerging political philosophy of the IUMSWA can best be seen in the IUMSWA leaders' regular contact with the federal government throughout the

[34] The relationship of the CPUSA and rank-and-file CP union activists with the 1930s trade union movement is a complex one. For an overview of the shift from the TUUL period to the Popular Front, see Fraser M. Ottanelli, *The Communist Party of the United States: From the Depression to World War II* (New Brunswick, N.J.: Rutgers University Press, 1991). For a positive assessment of Popular Front policies from the 1930s to World War II, see Maurice Isserman, *Which Side Were You On?—The American Communist Party During the Second World War* (Middletown, Conn.: Wesleyan University Press, 1982), pp. 1–17. For highly critical views, see Harvey Klehr, *The Heyday of American Communism, The Depression Decade* (New York: Basic Books, 1984); and Bert Cochran, *Labor and Communism: The Conflict That Shaped American Unions* (Princeton: Princeton University Press, 1977). Van Gelder's comments on the CPUSA are from the June 11, 1987, interview.

[35] A debate on whether there should be one union for all maritime workers (shipyard workers, seamen, and longshoremen) took place in the IUMSWA's *Shipyard Worker* in the fall of 1936. The position of "One Big Union" for maritime workers was defended in a letter from a New York Harbor shipyard worker. In its reply, the IUMSWA defended its own position: an industrial union for shipyard workers based on the emerging CIO model. Commentary on the IWW is drawn from the Reeder, Kaplan, and De Girolamo interviews. For an example of IWW activity in the port of Philadelphia, see Lisa McGirr, "Black and White Longshoremen in the IWW: A History of the Philadelphia Marine Transport Workers Industrial Union Local 8," *Labor History* 37 (Summer 1995) 377–402.

strike and in the union's inability to extend its militancy beyond Camden during 1935. After union members voted to walk out, a delegation made up of Van Gelder, Cole, and Diehl headed for Washington to meet with officials from the Labor Department and the Navy and with leaders in Congress. When they returned to Camden, Van Gelder proposed that the union organize a general walkout in the big East Coast yards where the IUMSWA had some following. In this way the strike at New York Ship could be turned into a broader organizing tool. Van Gelder and Green called a General Executive Board meeting of delegates from locals at New York Ship, Fore River, Bath Iron Works, Sun Ship, Pusey Jones (in Wilmington), Newport News, and Electric Boat (in New London), but the delegates rejected the general strike plan. Such an approach was highly unrealistic; none of the other locals had a signed contract, and the IUMSWA had no representation in the two key New York Port yards, Federal Shipbuilding (in Kearny) and Staten Island Shipbuilding. This flawed plan revealed the national leadership's inability to devise a national strategy at the time, which compelled it to increase its advocacy in Washington, and made it even more evident that the IUMSWA's base in Camden had to be secured before organizing could be developed elsewhere.[36]

Union-management negotiations in Camden were underway on May 21 as workers continued their mass picket outside the yard. The bargaining session in the company's offices was particularly stormy that day. The union decided to extend mass picketing throughout the day so that when the talks started at 10 a.m. thousands of workers on Broadway Street were visible from the office window. At the bargaining table, Green attacked Metten and Kaltwasser for trying to divide the top union leadership from the members. Gallagher acted as the diplomat, while Green, the firebrand, told the company representatives: "The meeting was opened this morning and my name was brought into it. . . . I understand this insidious propaganda to come from the New York Shipbuilding Corporation." General manager Campbell replied: "What insidious propaganda?" Green shot back:

Such as, if Green was out of the way and so forth and so on, both parties could come to some kind of an agreement. I want to keep personalities out of it but I can reiterate just this same kind of stuff as G—damned skunk Cameron and G—damned skunk Campbell, and ice water, cold water Kaltwasser, and stuff

---

[36] "Report of the Executive Secretary," by Van Gelder to 2nd National IUMSWA Convention, Aug. 21, 1936, IUMSWA Archives, Series I, Subseries 4, Box 11, Special Collections, University of Maryland at College Park Libraries; *Philadelphia Record*, May 19, 1935; *Camden Courier Post*, May 20, 1935.

like that. That's all a part of the game. But listen, this corporation has 4600 men in the street and this committee is willing to meet you half way all the time.[37]

Discussion returned repeatedly to the question of union recognition, specifically the preferential shop. The company continued to hold the position that having one union as exclusive bargaining agent was illegal, despite the NRA's statement to the contrary. Then the company raised the argument that IUMSWA Local 1 did not represent a majority of New York Ship workers and that only a small number of workers actually wanted to strike. At this point Green tore into Campbell:

> Green: Now, just a minute. In the first place, do you really think we represent the majority of the men in the yard? Do you have any doubts?
>
> Campbell: Well, I don't know. . . . We are perfectly willing to accept the fact that you represent enough people so that I can sit down and discuss our problems with you. As far as your authority to represent every individual in the yard I have nothing to show that it is true. In fact, I strongly suspect that it is entirely the opposite.
>
> Green: (looking out the window) Isn't those gates closed?
>
> Campbell: Yes.
>
> Green: Isn't the men in the street?
>
> Campbell: Right.
>
> Green: Isn't that enough to satisfy you?
>
> Campbell: That doesn't indicate to me necessarily that the majority of the people want to go on strike.[38]

There were, in fact, around 3,000 "men in the street," but for management this simply represented union coercion of its employees.

The other union representatives adopted Green's style. McCann and Pommerer had angry words for general manager Campbell and personnel manager George W. Cameron. Even Mullin, who was usually quite subdued, became combative. The most bitter exchange revolved around the issue of "rights," which the union and management defined in very different ways.

> McCann: I think as an American citizen I have the right to discuss with you and say whether I shall work piece work.

---

[37] "Minutes," IUMSWA Local 1 and New York Shipbuilding contract negotiations transcript, May 21, 1935.

[38] Ibid. (parenthetical comment in original, grammar as in original).

Campbell: No, that shall be a matter of employment. You don't have to work here if you don't want to.

Pommerer: Isn't that the same thing as joining the Union—you have the right to join it or stay out?

Cameron: Yes, but the management is running the plant.

Pommerer: It is our muscles that built that damned plant before you ever thought of Camden. I have dropped many hours of sweat in there as a kid. We built it—not these executives.

Campbell: Are you through? . . .

Green: These men have banded themselves into an organization and I think they have a right to sell their labor and say under what conditions they shall work. Don't you think that is their prerogative as a free American citizen? . . .

Campbell: You don't have to work here. . . .

Gallagher: You won't give the union man preference. . . . You are still not giving the American citizen his rights. . . .

Green: I say [it is the] sweat of the brow that operated that plant and made it what it is today; and although you can't realize it [to] the men in the City of Camden, this place is their home and they are not going to allow themselves to be turned out in the streets by a few sharks.[39]

The talks went nowhere that day. As Gallagher put it, "I believe, if we sum this up right, we stand the same way as when we came in." The IUMSWA's early focus on "capital versus labor" can be seen in these negotiations. The rhetoric of class conflict was something that Green knew well and that workers liked to hear. The main concern of the union leaders at this stage, however, was to have workers' job rights respected by the company, not with how labor could eliminate capital. They took for granted New York Shipbuilding Corporation's right to exist as an employer, but believed that management ignored workers' "rights" as American citizens in the workplace. Above all, they wanted union members to have the best possible wages and working conditions, as well as an independent voice on the job—in one union negotiator's words, to have a fair "part of the business." The union leaders believed that it was labor, not capital, that really made New York Ship what it was.[40]

After two months of concentrating on mobilizing its members through mass picketing and gaining strong backing from the community, the IUMSWA ac-

---

[39] Ibid.

[40] "Minutes," Local 1 and New York Shipbuilding negotiations, May 21, 1935; *Camden Courier Post*, July 9, 1935.

celerated its activity in Washington. The union's shift in focus coincided with a momentous change in the direction of the New Deal and American labor law. On May 27, 1935, the Supreme Court ruled that the NRA, including its Section 7(a) labor provision, was unconstitutional. New York Ship's ability to use the NRA's IRC as an alternative to the Labor Department abruptly ended. The decision also eliminated the AFL's IRC representatives from the New York Ship dispute. The death of the NRA, which was viewed by many liberals at the time as a blow to labor, actually benefited IUMSWA Local 1's strike and freed the new union from pro-business government officials connected with the Shipbuilding Code Authority. Congress passed the National Labor Relations Act on June 26, and President Roosevelt signed it into law on July 7. The new law did not directly affect the situation at New York Ship, because the NLRA and the new Labor Board had not reached an operational stage by the summer of 1935. This legal dilemma created an impasse, which the Labor Department sought to overcome, and it increased the confusion over how the federal government should intervene. In late May, IUMSWA leaders had pushed for a full Congressional investigation into the causes of the strike and management's intransigence, which was one way to compel the government to act on the union's behalf. The union also directly petitioned President Roosevelt to intervene and posted Baker and Diehl on a full-time basis in Washington so that every possible opportunity to gain support could be utilized.[41]

The company also went on the attack, using anticommunism as its main weapon. New York Ship president Metten wrote Congressman D. Lane Powers of Trenton that "we are sure that over 85 percent of our people are satisfied with their working conditions and would be glad to come back to work if the fear of reprisal by a militant Communistic minority were removed." On behalf of the IUMSWA, Gallagher forcefully refuted this charge "as nothing other than the old subterfuge used by greedy, oppressive employers . . . to confuse the public, and if possible, cause dissension among the strikers." Management knew that the union had no ties with the CP and "that none of its officers, leaders, or active members are Communists."[42]

To counter the company's red-baiting, the union began to distance itself from its radical past. In a discussion with Senator A. Harry Moore of New Jersey, Green and McCann dismissed the document that Metten cited as evidence of the union's "Communism": the preamble to the IUMSWA's original 1933 constitution, which was undoubtedly inspired by Clydeside syndicalism and American left-wing socialism. They observed, "some years ago a previ-

---

[41] "Minutes," IUMSWA Local 1 and New York Shipbuilding contract negotiations transcript, May 21, 1935; *Camden Courier Post*, May 24, 28–30, June 1, 5, 1935.

[42] *Camden Courier Post*, June 3, 4, 1935.

ous constitution [1933] may have contained such an indication but . . . the present [1934] constitution does nothing of the kind." The IUMSWA had deleted the call to "abolish forever the system of exploitation that compels us to support with our labor an idle owning class." Instead, the new preamble advocated "militant industrial unionism" and "the united front of all workers in the Industry . . . base[d] . . . upon the principle of rank and file control [of the union], unrestricted trade union democracy, and . . . an aggressive struggle for an ever higher standard of living." Better wages and working conditions, not the abolition of the capitalist system, had become the IUMSWA's goal. Green pointed out to Senator Moore that the union stood for a strong national defense and that the company impeded this government program by holding back a settlement.[43]

This official shift by the IUMSWA away from advocating worker ownership and the abolition of capitalism was actually set in motion, without any major debate, at the First IUMSWA Convention in September 1934. Mike Smith, of Local 1, submitted a resolution supporting government ownership of all "munitions and war supply industries." John Mitchell, also of Local 1, put forward a resolution supporting the building of a labor party "for the purpose of gaining control of the State and establishing collective ownership of the financial institutions and . . . basic industries." Both men were socialists, and both motions were defeated, presumably with the support of socialists Green and Van Gelder, whose presence dominated the convention. Two years later, at the Second IUMSWA Convention, it was Smith who recommended concurrence with the modified preamble in its more moderate, non-socialist form. The convention did not endorse FDR for reelection because it was divided on whether to support the Democratic Party, which Smith and Van Gelder labeled "the bureaucratic party." Green concluded the convention, however, with rousing socialist rhetoric: "We must go further for the eventual solution. When the day comes when industry will say it can not longer produce for a profit, then we must be in a position to take over industry and run it for ourselves. There is the solution. And that program requires organization and then more organization." Nevertheless, the 1936 convention revealed a strong shift, which was evident throughout 1935 in the union's practice, toward limited industrial union goals and a program in line with the emerging Second New Deal. By

[43] Ibid., June 5, 1935; Preamble to 1st IUMSWA Constitution, 1933, quoted (in full) in Metten testimony, "Hearings, Labor Practices in Shipbuilding," July 29, 1935, p. 80; Whittelsey to Barton Murray, May 6, 1935, NA, RG 9, Box 5254 (for text of first IUMSWA Constitution); *Shipyard Worker*, July 9, 1937, p. 1; *Constitution of the IUMSWA*, as amended Aug. 22, 1936, Preamble. The IUMSWA's national newspaper, which began publishing in early 1936, first used this new preamble on its masthead on August 22, 1936, after it was officially approved by the second convention. The revision was done after the September 1934 convention in Quincy.

mid-1935 Green and Van Gelder had set aside their left-wing political ideology when engaged in union affairs, while they built alliances with New Deal Democrats to further the cause in Camden. The IUMSWA's political shift from a radical to a liberal outlook had a strong social democratic character, with roots in Sydney Hillman's advocacy of a welfare state favorable to labor and similar to the one promised under the New Deal.[44]

By June 1935 the union came to realize, as it had in 1934, that the Department of the Navy held the balance of power in Washington because the Navy could grant or withdraw shipbuilding contracts. In reply to letters and visits from both sides involved in the Camden dispute, however, the Navy stated that it did not have jurisdiction in the case and viewed the strike as the Labor Department's concern. Navy Secretary Claude Swanson and Chief of Naval Construction Rear Admiral Emory S. Land held that it was "not relevant" to compare wage scales in private yards with those in Navy yards, where hours differed and the government regulated labor conditions directly. New York Ship's wages, they further noted, were higher than those in other private yards. By mid-June, the Navy's refusal to get involved led to a bipartisan public outcry in Camden for federal intervention to settle the strike.[45]

The turning point for the second New York Ship strike and for IUMSWA Local 1's final organizing campaign came in July, as the opposing sides headed for a major confrontation. On July 1, a Monday morning, eighteen men carrying large briefcases stepped quickly from cabs, walked through the picket line, and entered the company offices. The union leadership understood that the company had finally begun its long-expected "back-to-work" campaign. Local 1 immediately issued a call for more pickets, and by 10:30 a.m. several thousand lined the street in front of the gates. The newcomers had arrived at New York Ship to conduct a "survey" among the workers; they were directed by Major Henry F. Holthausen, a New York City attorney with connections to the advertising firm of N. W. Ayer and a former assistant attorney general under Attorney General Harlan F. Stone. The Major also hired some 200 inter-

---

[44] IUMSWA, *Proceedings, 1st National Convention*, Quincy, Mass., Sept. 28–30, 1934, p. 7; IUMSWA, *Proceedings, 2nd National Convention*, Camden, N.J., Aug. 20–23, 1936, pp. 16, 31, 43, 44; Van Gelder interview, June 11, 1987. On the collapse of the Socialist Party during the 1930s, see Daniel Bell, *Marxian Socialism in the United States* (Princeton: Princeton University Press, 1967), pp. 157–93. John Green left the Socialist Party after the organization's 1938 convention. For a superb discussion of Sidney Hillman's social democratic and corporatist philosophy and practice in the labor movement and how these related to Hillman's connection with the Roosevelt administration, see Steven Fraser, *Labor Will Rule: Sydney Hillman and the Rise of American Labor* (New York: Free Press, 1991), pp. 259–372.

[45] *Camden Courier Post*, June 10, 12, 13, 1935.

viewers, mostly college students from Philadelphia, to conduct the poll. The only questions in the survey dealing with the strike asked if the employee wanted to return to work under the old wage schedule and preferred to work forty hours instead of thirty-six, "thereby increasing your earning capacity by 11.1 percent."[46]

The Major did not suspect that the ranks of the interviewers would be infiltrated by union activists, including the IUMSWA's young national secretary-treasurer, Phil Van Gelder, who vividly remembered the company project.

> I was young and full of beans at that time, and I decided I'd be one of the young college boys. So I got hired by them. . . . We had a list of strikers we were supposed to contact, and get "their idea" that they'd like to go back to work. . . . So I . . . excused myself for a minute. I went into a store and I telephoned the union office downtown, and they sent out a car with Bill Pommerer [Local 1 vice president], "Hammer" Powell, and a couple other hefty looking guys. They found us and . . . Hammer Powell says, "I don't think you really want to make a survey here. . . . I think the best thing for you to do is turn that car around and go back to Philadelphia where you came from and tell them that we're running the strike over here, and we don't need any help from N. W. Ayer or anybody else."

The union delegation scared the students, who then returned to Philadelphia where all the survey teams met at a hotel. The advertising agent in charge of the operation told everyone: "Now I want you all to fill out your questionnaires, and tell us who you saw and how many want to go back to work." Van Gelder then stood up and said: "Now look . . . don't sign anything, because you're involved here with a strikebreaking operation. I wouldn't advise you to get involved in any way, shape, or form." The agent jumped up and cried, "Who are you?!" Van Gelder responded, "I'm secretary of the union." The agent then threatened to have Van Gelder arrested, but Van Gelder replied that he had taken no money, so he couldn't be charged with anything. "He rushed out to get the police. I advised everybody to leave and I left. The whole thing was in the *Philadelphia Record* the next day, and they were laughed out of court."[47]

Van Gelder's ability to mobilize the IUMSWA against the company's plan on such short notice suggests how well organized the union had become and demonstrates the company's failure to win support from the community, much less from the workers. The Camden police arrested one canvasser for not hav-

---

[46] Ibid., July 2–3, 5, 1935; Van Gelder speech, Oct. 25, 1986.
[47] Van Gelder speech, Oct. 25, 1986.

ing a permit to distribute literature and did not bother any of the strikers who "encouraged" the students to leave the city. Clearly, Camden was still shipyard workers' territory and not a company town.[48]

As Major Holthausen attempted to get the back-to-work campaign off the ground, the union increased the tempo of the strike. More than 1,500 strikers rallied at the ball park on Broadway and Everett Streets, where they heard Socialist Party leader and presidential candidate Norman Thomas. He told the enthusiastic crowd that their "fight against the corporation to ultimate victory [will] bolster the morale of organized labor throughout the country." Workers and their supporters then marched to the shipyard, with Thomas at the head, where they formed a mass picket.[49]

Women played a critical role in supporting the union and the strike. Wives, mothers, and daughters of shipyard workers were decisive in influencing the men in their families, and many sought to do more than just provide kitchen assistance. The experience of living through the Great Depression strengthened their ability to adapt to hardship and take risks equal to those of the men. As Ben Maiatico observed:

> It should be pretty strongly emphasized that women—the wives of the men who worked in that yard during the strikes—they were very, very supportive. Both strikes. They used to come out every morning. . . . The pickets would be on the yard side, and these women would be on the opposite side of Broadway . . . by the hundreds. The mere fact that they supported their husbands in the strike was enough to win those strikes. You know, the saying is that strikes are won or lost in the kitchen. And there's a lot of truth to that because they put up with a lot of adversity in those days.[50]

Holthausen realized the importance of these women and targeted strikers' wives for his propaganda, but the IUMSWA countered him wherever it could. Letters began to appear on a regular basis in the *Courier Post* that were supposedly written by strikers' wives and mothers who wanted an end to the dispute and an end to the union. One of these, signed by "Dumb Bell," asked: "Will someone please answer a few questions for a dumb-bell? . . . I really don't know much about [the strike], since I am only a striker's wife. . . . Is there any law which says a man can't go to work as long as he is satisfied with his work? . . . I agree [the union] is strong, in fact it is rank." In contrast, pro-union women spoke with a firm and positive voice, indicating the extent to which the

---

[48] *Camden Courier Post*, July 5, 9, 12, 15, 1935.
[49] Ibid., July 6, 1935.
[50] Maiatico interview, Sept. 13, 1987; *Camden Courier Post*, July 18, 1935.

IUMSWA had organized workers' families and the community at large. "Kate" responded to "Dumb Bell" by asking:

> Why will some women be dumbbells and then have the nerve to admit it? I am a striker's wife and proud of it. I attend every ladies' night meeting that I am able and my chest just swells with pride, and even though my feet near break with blisters I dance right on. . . . So come on "Dumbbell," attend a few of our meetings at the hall. . . . My husband and his Dad do their duty every day on the picket line and at the hall. See that your husband does the same.[51]

Holthausen continued his "survey" campaign by crafting a post-card ballot asking employees if they wanted "to get back to work . . . under the company's agreement." Green urged all Local 1 members to check "yes," rendering the questionnaire useless. Management, again at Holthausen's initiative, then sought a poll through the auspices of the American Legion, a conservative ally. When the Legion announced that it would hold a secret ballot vote at its headquarters, the scheme ignited a storm of protest not just from the union but from many local branches of veterans' organizations whose members included workers. Within a day the Legion was forced to withdraw its proposal.[52]

As the company escalated its anti-union campaign, stress from the strike and problems of deciding tactics produced rifts within the union negotiating committee. By early July, two key committee members who were also Local 1 officers had come to believe that the public side of the fight had gone too far. On July 15 (the day the American Legion poll was announced), William Mullin told the press that he was resigning as Local 1 president and from the negotiating committee; he was stepping down for a number of reasons, he said, "but primarily I am tired of having the strike fought in the newspapers instead of down here" at the shipyard. Since May, Mullin had been defending himself from company attacks in the press regarding his questionable actions in May's strike vote balloting. Local 1 vice president William Pommerer, an outspoken Green loyalist and a trade unionist unafraid of offending people, replaced Mullin as the local's president.[53]

The resignation of negotiating committee secretary Ed Baker revealed far deeper divisions. On July 19, Mayor von Nieda issued a statement calling on

---

[51] *Camden Courier Post*, July 15, 20, 1935. For a discussion of the importance of women in the labor movement during the 1930s in totally male workplace settings and the impact of community- versus workplace-focused organizing on women and trade unionism of the era, see Elizabeth Faue, *Community of Suffering and Struggle: Women, Men, and the Labor Movement in Minneapolis, 1915–1945* (Chapel Hill: University of North Carolina Press, 1991).

[52] *Camden Courier Post*, July 12, 15, 16, 17, 19, 1935.

[53] Ibid.

both sides to "scrap all contracts and agreements," return to work, and hold an election. This action outraged the union leaders. They asked Baker, an active Republican like the mayor, to persuade von Nieda to change his mind, but on the day of Baker's visit the *Camden Courier Post* published a public statement by David Cole, speaking for the negotiating committee, that criticized the mayor and called on him to change his position. Baker did not learn of the statement until the newspaper was on the streets. In protest at what he felt was a premature attack on the mayor, Baker angrily quit all of his leadership positions in Local 1. Baker, like Mullin, retained his union membership.[54]

Baker's public letter of resignation revealed the extent to which strike leadership had become centralized. He had been an activist since 1933 and was unafraid to take public stands. As late as July 14 he had made a speech in New York City's Times Square to publicize the cause of the strike. He had no permit, but several hundred spectators prevented him from being arrested until after he had finished. Baker found the internal dynamics of the 1935 negotiating committee shockingly autocratic compared to his earlier organizing years at New York Ship, which he believed was a more democratic time for the union. In his letter he recalled that he "was one of the few men who, along with John Green, Richard Benson, Austin B. Geist, Purkis, Mullin and others, started this union. . . . This was to be a rank and file union. Today it is far from that." He had brought numerous concerns before the strike committee that he believed should be put to the members, but "each time I was overruled. . . . Instead of working together as a committee, two or three members do things on their own accord."[55]

The pace of events precluded the possibility of such direct rank-and-file participation in decision-making. Maintaining the momentum of the strike required disciplined and centralized decisions on virtually an hour-by-hour basis. Strike leaders Green, Van Gelder, and Gallagher understood that the workers overwhelmingly opposed Mayor von Nieda's plan to reopen the yard and would support decisive action against it. Baker, however, accurately predicted the erosion of rank-and-file union democracy in the IUMSWA, an issue that gained increasing importance in the union over the next decade.

On July 20, New York Ship announced that it would reopen the yard in three days regardless of the picket line, which brought the strike to a new crisis level. Since Mayor von Nieda's plan coincided with the company's back-to-work campaign, New York Ship president Metten endorsed it and quoted excerpts in a letter he sent to all employees announcing the yard's reopening. At this point Secretary of Labor Frances Perkins intervened directly by publicly

[54] Ibid., July 15–17, 19, 22, 1935.
[55] Ibid.

proposing her own plan: all strikers would return to work without discrimination, the old 1934 contract would be renewed for one year, and all issues would be subject to arbitration under a board selected by the Secretaries of the Labor and Navy Departments. Perkins's proposal had its origins in the union's initial offer to conciliator Chappell in May. Metten rejected the Secretary of Labor's plan, stating that "it would spell the ruination of the yard . . . would result in more strikes . . . and eventually would close the yard for good."[56]

The day before the company's planned reopening, the picket lines grew larger, as over 3,000 workers refuted Metten's claim that 75 percent wanted to return to work. Almost 100 women stood on the opposite side of Broadway, cheering the long lines of strikers in front of the yard, as Green directed the pickets and delegated responsibilities to committeemen. That evening, 2,200 union members voted overwhelmingly to accept a modified version of Secretary Perkins's proposal. The only major change the union wanted concerned the selection of the arbitration board: one member would be chosen by the company, one by the union, and the third by both parties. (The Departments of Labor and the Navy would make this selection in case of a deadlock). New Jersey Governor Harold Hoffman announced that he would not send in the state police unless he received word from local authorities that they could not control the situation, and Mayor von Nieda reiterated that he would not allow police to aid strikebreakers. The real question had become whether or not a substantial number of workers would cross the picket lines.[57]

In the early morning of July 23, the main shipyard gate stood open waiting for workers to return, but by 5 a.m. the union picket line stretched two deep for half a mile along Broadway. When the mayor arrived at 7:15, he was immediately drawn into a heated argument already under way between Green and General Manager Campbell. Green turned to von Nieda and said, "Mr. Mayor, we have been double-crossed. . . . You said you would have no extra police here." When von Nieda asked the officer in charge why police had come to the picket lines, the officer replied that he thought they were needed. In fact, only forty-five patrolmen and seven motorcycle police were present, a small number of law enforcement officers compared to other strikes of this size during the 1930s. Green again pushed the mayor, charging that "the company is trying to intimidate us into creating disorders. We want to go along in an orderly fashion . . . but if the company persists in having their foremen take men in, police or no police, I'm going to order the main gate picketed and blocked."

[56] Ibid., July 20, 22, 1935; Metten letters to New York Shipbuilding Employees, July 19 and 21, 1935, NA, RG 9, Box 5254.

[57] *Camden Courier Post*, July 20, 22, 23, 1935.

He momentarily convinced von Nieda, who angrily told the officer in charge: "Lieutenant, I don't care who the policeman is, from the chief down, if they escort any strikebreaker or any man into that yard, I'm going to fire him on the spot." After speaking with Green and the police, von Nieda walked into the yard to talk with company officials. When Green followed him through the gate, Vice President Kaltwasser ordered Green to stay out and shoved him. Green did not push back, but he later filed charges of assault and battery against Kaltwasser. The court soon issued a warrant for Kaltwasser's arrest, handing the union some superb publicity and increasing Green's public stature.[58]

Although von Nieda failed to keep his word and police escorted strikebreakers into the yard, the amount of police coercion used against the strikers was comparatively small in the context of the volatile 1930s. The scabs did have to run a gauntlet of union pickets. In one incident, ten strikebreakers were led to the gate by the copper shop foreman, but first they had to pass in front of a crowd of angry women across the street. The women shouted at these men, and a dozen or so "broke loose and charged at the marching group . . . beating them over the heads and backs." The strikebreakers did not try to defend themselves, and walked as quickly as they could into the yard. This outburst occurred after union leaders discovered that none of these men had previously worked at New York Ship. When Mayor von Nieda later ordered police to disperse the huge crowd of women and men opposite the yard, it took police more than an hour to clear the area.[59]

Throughout the day the situation was extremely tense. Strikers at the gate tried to block the path of entering cars, but the police formed a "flying wedge" that forced the strikers apart. Union men then ran down to cross-streets that fed into Broadway to stop cars there. Even with this pressure, the union maintained remarkable control. Green walked up and down the picket line enforcing order and counseling against violence, telling strikers to "lock arms" if anyone tried to enter.[60]

Five hundred pickets stayed at the gates throughout the day until 3 p.m., when mass picketing resumed. By this hour most of the strikebreakers had already gone home. City commissioners Mary Kobus and George Brunner came to the shipyard gate to talk with workers on the afternoon picket line and were greeted with cheers. The strikers' anger soon gave way to festivity as

[58] Ibid., July 23, 1935; *Philadelphia Record*, July 24, 1935.

[59] *Camden Courier Post*, July 23, 1935; *Philadelphia Record*, July 24, 1935. Accounts of the strike in the Philadelphia and Camden press and in archival sources give no further detail on the identity (including racial background) of strikebreakers beyond what is presented here.

[60] *Camden Courier Post*, July 23, 1935.

they celebrated their successful shut-down of the plant. The *Courier Post* reported that

> Salaried employees were permitted to pass out in silence. The others [strike-breakers] were "razzed" lengthily. The boos reached their loudest when Mayor Ernest Richie of Gloucester, a timekeeper at the plant, drove out. The pickets marched under a hot afternoon sun. Trucks hired by the union kept them supplied with water. The area took on a carnival atmosphere in contrast to the grimness of the morning, with purveyors of cold drinks doing a land office business.

The union claimed that a majority of workers had walked the picket line that day. According to Green, of the 320 people who entered the yard that morning, only 47 were hourly employees: 22 strikers who had given up, and 25 who were new employees.[61]

Mayor von Nieda, as mercurial as ever, was shaken by the confrontation between the strikers and management, and telephoned Secretary Perkins to criticize her for not getting involved at an earlier date. When Perkins spoke to the press, however, she made it clear who she thought was to blame for the deadlock.

> I don't think the Mayor is speaking by the book when he says I have been interested only the last few days. The department has been in touch with both the union and the management ever since the strike started, and with the union even before the walkout. The attitude of the company ends any possibility of arbitration. I intend, however, to keep Conciliator P. W. Chappell and Howard Colvin working on the matter.

Although the company claimed otherwise, Perkins stated that she was "convinced that the union represents an 'overwhelming majority' of the shipyard workers."[62]

On July 24, the second day of the company's attempt to reopen the yard, the number of pickets grew. The women's ranks on the opposite side of the street also increased. The *Camden Courier Post* reported: "More than 200 wives and sympathizers of the strikers were in line under the leadership of Mrs. Sadie Whalen . . . who carried a large American flag. Many others also carried flags. . . . Three carried babies."[63]

That evening, violence erupted away from the picket lines, as the strikers'

---

[61] Ibid.
[62] *Philadelphia Record*, July 24, 1935; *Camden Courier Post*, July 23, 1935.
[63] *Camden Courier Post*, July 24, 1935.

patience reached the breaking point. While Green and other union leaders maintained an image of strict non-violence, accounts by those who remembered the events of July 24 indicate that workers used violence behind the scenes to discourage strikebreaking. Gallagher's son Tom, who was a high school student at the time, recalled that the scabs "would go in in the morning and then when they came out the cops would only take them so far [in] their cars. And the strikers used to catch them by the railroad on Morgan Street, and beat the hell out of them, turn over the cars and everything else." Phil Van Gelder, who was one of the leaders on the picket line that day, remembered the company having "a bunch of goons they hired down in South Philadelphia. They brought them over and they got some of them in the yard alright. But when they came out that night it was really something. . . . Our guys were chasing them up and down Broadway right into City Hall . . . and they beat them up . . . right there."[64]

After a crowd of forty or fifty men had broken every window in tool-keeper George Bossler's car at the corner of Morgan and Broadway, he vowed, "I won't go back to that yard tomorrow. I know when I'm licked!" They also stoned other vehicles in the caravan of strikebreakers' cars. Police rushed to the scene and broke up the crowd. Management knew that the strikebreakers were vastly outnumbered and that the pressure to stay away from work was becoming too intense to expect these men to return. Bossler related that inside the shipyard the strikebreakers "got a free lunch [and] one of the bosses addressed the crowd." He "told us he knew how we must feel because of the heckling we were getting and said he wouldn't blame any of us who don't return tomorrow."[65]

Those directly involved in the fighting found the violence more serious than it appeared to be in the newspapers. George "Chips" De Girolamo, who ran the "chiseling" committee which was responsible for soliciting food from local merchants during the 1935 strike, decades later recalled what he had experienced personally. "Twenty-seven stitches, right?" He held up his right arm and pointed to a scar about two and one-half inches long. "The strikebreaker came to me with a knife, right? And we took real good care of him. I'm bleeding like a stuck pig. . . . Oh yea, they had strikebreakers in there."[66]

Minor attacks by both sides spread to the neighborhoods. Union sympathizers threw yellow paint through the window of one strikebreaker's home. Vandals on the other side targeted John Green's house by throwing red lead paint inside it, but curiously the union did not mention this incident to the

[64] Thomas J. Gallagher interview; Van Gelder speech, Oct. 25, 1986.
[65] *Camden Courier Post*, July 25, 1935.
[66] De Girolamo interview.

press. Green's daughter Jessie remembered that "the union set up guards, to watch, at each end of the street where we lived. Bill Harker, who would remain a staunch Green loyalist his entire life, was in charge."[67]

Over the next two days, the company placed notices in area newspapers offering up to $5000 reward for information leading to the arrest and conviction of anyone involved in the interference or injury of employees "returning" to work. Under the banner "Mob Violence Will Not Open the Shipyard," the company severely criticized not only the union but also city commissioners Brunner and Kobus, who supported the strike. The company also sought to incite racial antagonism among strikers and their supporters. It claimed that outsiders were packing the picket line because "70 colored men" were present, even though "between Jan. 1, 1935 and May 11, 1935, only 16 colored men" were employed in the yard. These tactics backfired, increasing the unity among strikers, the community, and local elected officials.[68]

Green claimed a "complete victory" for the union on July 25, the third day of the attempted reopening, after the company announced that it would close down the main power plant. Gallagher confirmed this assessment and confidently told the press, "men who have been inside informed us that all they did was to sit around and smoke cigarettes." Organizer Charlie Purkis declared that not a single strikebreaker crossed the picket line that day. As for the outbreak of violence on July 24, the community saw it as a product of New York Shipbuilding's belligerence toward the union. Even conciliator Philip Chappell, supposedly a neutral party in the dispute, wired his superior in Washington that the violence had been provoked by the company.[69]

The IUMSWA also stopped New York Shipbuilding actions in the courts. The company sought a sweeping restraining order against the strike that would have barred picketing, "verbal coercion" at people's homes, and other pro-union activities in the Camden area. Despite the sporadic violence on July 24, the judge concluded that the strike was a matter for the local police to handle. He did require the union to show cause why an injunction should not be granted and ordered a continuance, but the union managed to get the case

[67] Jessie Green Snyder interview, Sept. 13, 1987, Cherry Hill, N.J.

[68] *Camden Courier Post*, July 25, 26, 1935. Although the IUMSWA opposed racial discrimination in its constitution, it did not promote hiring of black workers at the shipyard. But with some substantial support from blacks in the community—if the *Camden Courier Post* and the company are to be believed—the IUMSWA appears to have taken a more progressive stance on the issue of inclusion than management did. This glimmer of racial non-discrimination by Local 1, evidence for which is anecdotal at best, soon disappeared until the advent of World War II.

[69] *Camden Courier Post*, July 25, 26, 1935; "Hearings, Labor Practices in Shipbuilding," July 29, 1935, Rep. Griswold quoting telegram from Chappell to Kerwin, July 25, 1935, p. 89.

transferred to federal court. Van Gelder recalled that with this further delay the case "just got lost," which in effect prevented an injunction.[70]

These tactical victories at the local level, combined with the state and federal governments' refusal to commit troops, meant that New York Shipbuilding Corporation could not possibly break the strike by using force. Now it could only hope to starve the strikers back to work through a prolonged refusal to bargain seriously or to arbitrate. But as the conflict shifted from Camden to Washington, Metten and other New York Shipbuilding executives lost their last government ally, the Department of the Navy.

By late July the focus of the strike moved to Washington, while between 2,000 and 3,000 workers and supporters picketed daily at the shipyard gates. Although mass picketing had stopped production at New York Ship for over two months, virtually no progress had been made in negotiations. John Green told Congress: "Up to the present time we have been unable to move that firm from its original position. We feel that the New York [Shipbuilding] company has got to be moved, and if that is done *it will have to come from Washington.*" Gallagher confirmed Green's assessment, speaking to the Camden press after the union's victory over New York Ship's attempt to reopen the yard: "It is now up to Washington. The obligation of the federal government is clear. It must force this corporation to come to terms with the union or else let somebody else step in who knows how to manage a shipyard."[71]

Regardless of the growing turmoil in Camden, the Navy, and in particular Assistant Secretary of the Navy Henry Roosevelt, firmly reiterated that the Department would not get involved. This situation led the union leadership to believe that a breakthrough would occur only if President Roosevelt directly intervened, but it did not seem likely that the President would act unless the union's government allies pushed him to take a stand. The IUMSWA's most steadfast supporters were Congressional representatives on the special investigative subcommittee, especially the outspoken representative from New York City, Vito Marcantonio, and the Labor Department directed by Secretary Frances Perkins. Marcantonio did not intend to concede anything to the company, while Perkins proved far more flexible. In the end, however, these two figures played critical roles in Local 1's survival.[72]

New York Ship's attempt to reopen the yard with strikebreakers led the

[70] *Camden Courier Post*, July 24–26, 1935; *Philadelphia Record*, July 29, 1935; Van Gelder interview, Feb. 20, 1988.

[71] "Hearings, Labor Practices in Shipbuilding," July 19, 1935, Green testimony, p. 18 (emphasis added); *Camden Courier Post*, July 23, 1935.

[72] *Camden Courier Post*, July 11, 1935; "Hearings, Labor Practices in Shipbuilding," July 26, 1935, pp. 57–58, 67.

House Committee on Labor to create the special investigative subcommittee that effectively put New York Ship's management on trial. It looked into alleged collusion between the Navy and the company, and put new pressure on the Labor Department and the President to intervene more directly on behalf of the workers. In defense of the union, some in Congress, particularly Representative Marcantonio, challenged management's charges that IUMSWA Local 1 was a communist organization and did not represent a majority of workers.

New York Shipbuilding's blundering press propaganda and its inept responses in the Congressional hearings spurred community support for the strikers. Camden City Commissioner George Brunner and City Solicitor Edmund Bleakly testified before the subcommittee on the urgency of ending the strike, declaring that the economic well-being of Camden and the surrounding area was at stake. After Brunner placed the blame squarely on management, the company attacked him and City Commissioner Mary Kobus for talking with picketing strikers. Brunner and Bleakly represented the interests of small businessmen as much as they did Camden's blue-collar voters. Brunner ran a plumbing business, although originally he had been a union plumber. He responded that New York Ship's attack on him as "stupid" and a liar was "slanderous, venomous, vindictive." Kobus replied in her own defense that she "was born and raised in Camden and taught respect for the American flag and the Constitution" as a public school teacher. "If mingling with one's fellow citizens and workingmen of all classes is a violation of office; if obtaining first-hand information in the course of my duties and of the facts concerning this serious situation is a violation of law and order, I am willing to accept the indictment."[73]

When Metten failed to appear for his scheduled testimony on July 25, J. W. Hart, the former industry member of the NRA Industrial Relations Committee who now represented the National Council of American Shipbuilders, appeared in his place. Hart informed the subcommittee that "it was being sadly misinformed on the facts of the case." Chairman Glenn Griswold of Indiana angrily replied that Metten's failure to appear and his "high-handed attitude seem . . . to be typical of everything the company has done throughout this controversy."[74]

The investigation gave the IUMSWA an excellent forum for its case, but the company fared badly. Subcommittee members Marcantonio and George Schneider (Wisconsin) firmly defended the strikers and the cause of labor in

[73] "Hearings, Labor Practices in Shipbuilding," July 25, 1935, Edmund Bleakly testimony, pp. 33–36, George Brunner testimony, p. 37; *Camden Courier Post*, May 13, July 27, 1935.

[74] *Philadelphia Record*, July 26, 1935.

general, while the others, who were relatively neutral, appeared impressed by the testimony of John Green and Phil Van Gelder. Green revealed that the company had saved 15 percent on the actual cost of labor and materials for three cruisers built between 1927 and 1934, which totaled $3,620,000, and that the 1934 contract settlement was two cents below the top hourly rate at non-union Sun Shipbuilding just twenty miles away and one cent per hour below the New York Harbor rates. This information contradicted the claim by Metten and Kaltwasser that New York Ship had the best rates in the Philadelphia area.[75]

Metten decided to testify on July 29 in order to make one last, desperate stand against the union. The words he chose in his defense were direct and uncomplicated: "The first issue in the Camden shipyard strike . . . is Communism versus Americanism." The strike was a Communist plot to obstruct and destroy America's defense industry, and the IUMSWA was led by radicals and communists. Metten's evidence included a Socialist Party article, which he claimed was written by Local 1 secretary-treasurer Francis Hunter; quotations from the Communist Party's shop paper, *Shipyard Workers' Voice*; the 1933 preamble to the IUMSWA constitution; a detective's report that Green had Communist contacts; and the fact that men on the picket line were wearing red buttons and were singing the union song "Solidarity," which Metten understood "to be some kind of a Communist song."[76]

Francis Hunter was anything but a socialist. Metten may have confused him with Frank Hunter, who was a leader in the Camden branch of the Socialist Party and no relation to Francis. As for Communist Party literature, the IUMSWA leadership had prohibited its distribution on the picket lines, including the issue that Metten quoted. The charge regarding the 1933 preamble had no foundation; the union had replaced it with a more moderate one in 1934, and in any case it was hardly "communist." As for Green's contacts, in these years he talked with any pro-labor group or person, regardless of political affiliation, who might aid the strike. The buttons that Metten attacked as communist were IUMSWA dues buttons, and red was the color for July. When the congressmen turned to the bargaining issues of the strike, Metten replied that management had to be in full command and that disputes with the union could not be arbitrated.[77]

---

[75] "Hearings, Labor Practices in Shipbuilding," July 19, Aug. 13, 16, 1935, Green and Van Gelder testimony; Bardo to Board of Directors (NYS), Oct. 27, 1934, as quoted in testimony, pp. 9–11; Bardo to Board of Directors, May 14, 1934, as quoted in testimony, pp. 22–23; Metten and Kaltwasser testimony, July 29, 1935.

[76] "Hearings, Labor Practices in Shipbuilding," July 29, 1935, Metten testimony, pp. 79–84.

[77] Van Gelder interview, Oct. 11, 1987; Van Gelder speech, Oct. 25, 1986; "Hearings, Labor Practices in Shipbuilding," July 29, 1935, Metten testimony, pp. 85, 87, 91.

Labor Secretary Perkins also issued a statement disagreeing with New York Ship management: an investigation by the Department had found no evidence of communism in the union. The *Camden Courier Post* reported that the city's top officials, including the mayor and the chief of police, saw no connection between the union and any "Communist" activity. In an editorial entitled "BUT ARBITRATION ISN'T A COMMUNIST IDEA!" the newspaper derided the company's charge, defending the IUMSWA's "Americanism." "It is quite obvious that the only reason Mr. Metten calls them [the union] Communists now is because he'd rather talk about Moscow than discuss the REAL ISSUES OF THE STRIKE. . . . Then why not settle this strike on American Principles? . . . They don't have arbitration in Moscow. It's an American institution." [78]

The confrontation at the shipyard gates on July 23 and 24 and the Congressional investigation that followed brought enormous national publicity to Local 1, particularly in the labor movement. The strikers were chronically short of funds, and the leadership was aware that this problem could break the union, especially at this stage. When the IUMSWA aggressively sought financial assistance from other unions, it received an overwhelmingly positive response. According to Van Gelder, the IUMSWA "sent committees up to New York, and to Philadelphia, to Chester and Wilmington [and] got donations from other unions all over the country." Most of these were affiliated with the AFL. A total of seventy-three union organizations (especially locals) and six IUMSWA locals contributed strike funds. Core support came from future member unions of the CIO, while the most conservative AFL craft unions in shipbuilding—the Boilermakers, Molders, International Brotherhood of Electrical Workers, and Patternmakers—gave nothing. [79]

The most important support came John L. Lewis's Mineworkers (UMW). The UMW president did not intend to have his union's donation taken as charity. Rather, it was an investment in a potentially powerful ally for the new industrial union movement that Lewis planned to build. Van Gelder and David Cole met with Lewis on July 29 at the UMW's headquarters in Washington. Lewis "knew about the strike," according to Van Gelder; "he read about it in the papers." Lewis authorized Philip Murray, who was there with him, to give the IUMSWA delegation a contribution of $2,500. Lewis was especially in-

---

[78] *Camden Courier Post*, July 30, 1935 (emphasis in original).

[79] Van Gelder speech, Oct. 25, 1986; Van Gelder, *Book of Facts for Shipyard Workers*, Appendix. Fifty-five different unions gave donations to the 1935 strike. Most of them were local unions belonging to the AFL, but a number of independent left-wing unions also gave support. Aside from the UMW, the most supportive locals were affiliated with the ACW, the International Ladies Garment Workers, and the Hosiery Workers. Even the AFL-dominated Camden Central Labor Union gave a donation.

terested in the use of mass picketing at the New York Shipyard "because he'd seen pictures of this picket line . . . a half a mile long." The UMW contribution in particular "helped our food kitchen and our food supply." Although Local 1 already operated a makeshift kitchen, David Cole told the press that these funds were needed "to establish a commissary to supplement the inadequate relief being received by the men on strike. . . . We declared that we felt a contribution from such a source would help the morale of the men." [80]

Behind the scenes, President Franklin D. Roosevelt maintained an interest in the developments at New York Ship. Normally the President did not intervene in a labor dispute unless he believed all other government channels were deadlocked and the national defense or economy were endangered. In this case, the President had a capable team acting on his behalf, led by Labor Secretary Perkins, his long-time associate from New York, and Assistant Secretary of the Navy Henry Roosevelt, his cousin, who had responsibility for the naval construction program. The President's primary concern regarding New York Ship was to maintain the pace of the Navy's building program rather than simply to promote better industrial relations. [81]

Among top-level Washington officials, Labor Secretary Perkins had taken the lead in May when she authorized Philip Chappell, of the Department's Conciliation and Mediation Service, to deal directly with both union and management. Perkins also became the main link between the union and the federal government, as she channeled Chappell's longer reports on the strike directly to FDR. By July 18, almost a week before the company attempted to reopen the yard, Perkins had lost patience with the company's refusal to arbitrate, and she drafted a memo for her department and the Navy calling for naval takeover of the government-contracted shipbuilding if management persisted in its noncooperation. After reading Perkins's thoughts, FDR telephoned Assistant Secretary of the Navy Henry Roosevelt to confirm his approval of this approach. [82]

The next day Perkins sent identical letters to the union and company calling for an end to the strike and a renewal of the old contract pending an arbitrated settlement covering all issues under dispute. In this proposal she made no

[80] Van Gelder speech, Oct. 25, 1986; photocopy of UMW check signed by Lewis and UMW secretary-treasurer Thomas Kennedy in Van Gelder, *Book of Facts for Shipyard Workers*, Appendix; *Camden Courier Post*, July 31, 1935.

[81] Government records indicate that President Roosevelt was far more involved in the settlement process of major labor disputes than either he or Perkins was willing publicly to admit. For Perkins's later contention that FDR remained aloof, see Francis Perkins, *The Roosevelt I Knew* (New York: Harper and Row, 1946), pp. 302–27.

[82] Perkins (unsigned) to President Roosevelt, Aug. 1, 1935; "Strike at New York Shipbuilding . . . ," Chappell's Labor Department report to Kerwin, Aug. 1, 1935; Perkins to Metten, July 18, 1935; Perkins memorandum (unsigned) and handwritten comment, July 18, 1935; all NA, RG 174, Box 37.

mention of a representation election as a point for arbitration. Metten rejected her offer, but 2,200 IUMSWA members in Camden unanimously voted support, with the proviso that the selection process for the arbitration board be modified. At the same time, union members unanimously rejected the company's proposal to return to work and hold a new representation election.[83]

Negotiations now shifted to a tripartite approach, involving the Labor and Navy Departments, management, and the union. This process did not involve direct negotiations between management and the union, but rather a bilateral arrangement whereby the Labor Department dealt with the union and the Navy negotiated with management. Department of Labor officials and the Navy stayed in regular contact to assess overall developments. On July 25, after two days of confrontation between pickets and strikebreakers at New York Ship, President Roosevelt discussed the strike with Labor Secretary Perkins and Assistant Secretary of the Navy Henry Roosevelt at a cabinet meeting to assess what progress, if any, had been made in negotiations. Subsequently the President sent a handwritten memo to Henry Roosevelt and Perkins conveying his deep concern that they deal firmly with New York Shipbuilding management's intransigence:

I think you had better tell the N.Y. Shipbuilding Co. that:

(1) They must arbitrate

(2) They must meet their employees

(3) They will not get allowance for loss of time under Navy Contract from now on if they don't.

(4) They will not be allowed to bid on new ships if they don't settle.

When asked about the New York Ship strike at a press conference several days later, the President replied, "I hope to get something started the next few days. It is about time that it is settled."[84]

Previously Roosevelt had stressed that he was not involved in efforts to settle the dispute. His new position, that the Navy Department should push New York Ship to agree to arbitration by threatening to terminate the company's contracts, represented an important policy shift. His approach essen-

---

[83] Labor Department press release (with quotation from Perkins letter), July 19, 1935; Metten to Perkins, July 20, 1935; Chappell to Kerwin, July 23, 1935; all NA, RG 174, Box 37.

[84] Franklin D. Roosevelt memorandum (photo) on 1935 New York Shipbuilding strike to Perkins and H. Roosevelt, in Franklin D. Roosevelt, *F.D.R.: His Personal Letters, 1928–1945*, vol. 1, ed. Elliot Roosevelt and Joseph P. Lash (New York: Duell, Sloan and Pearce, 1950), between pp. 428 and 429 (punctuation as in original); President Franklin Roosevelt, White House press conference transcript, July 26, 1935; *Camden Courier Post*, July 27, 1935. For other comments on the New York Ship strike by President Roosevelt, see White House press conference transcripts, May 17, July 5, Aug. 2, 7, 9, 14, 21, 1935.

tially replayed the one he took toward the 1934 New York Ship strike. This time Roosevelt privately expressed far more alarm, perhaps because of the length of the strike, but he still delegated Perkins and Henry Roosevelt to assume direct responsibility through their respective departments.[85]

Prior to the July 25th cabinet meeting, the Navy Department had taken the position that it could not take sides in the dispute. At lower levels of the bureaucracy, however, the Navy actively opposed the strike and frequently met on an informal basis with Metten and other managers from New York Shipbuilding. After the President became more directly involved, Assistant Secretary of the Navy Henry Roosevelt turned the department's policy, both official and unofficial, in the opposite direction. He informed Metten on July 27, in line with FDR's memorandum, that it had "become imperative that construction work on these vessels shall proceed. Unless the Corporation can resume operations without further delay it will become necessary for the Navy Department to take over these vessels in their present state and to build them to completion." The Navy Department expected New York Ship to resume work at the yard by settling the dispute "through arbitration." He gave Metten a deadline of no later than 12 noon on July 31 to reply in the affirmative. Henry Roosevelt's exact proposal to Metten on how arbitration should proceed, which was contained in this letter, was not publicly disclosed, even though the Assistant Secretary presented the letter's broad outlines to the Congressional subcommittee investigating the strike.[86]

In his ultimatum to Metten, Henry Roosevelt essentially repeated the plan that Labor Secretary Perkins had previously submitted to the union, but with one significant difference. He listed the first of six "main points to be submitted [for] arbitration" as "determination of the employees' proper representatives for the purpose of collective bargaining, as contemplated by the Wagner Act," which in essence left the IUMSWA's status at New York Ship in doubt. When he consulted with Perkins, she objected to this alteration of her original proposal, claiming it would "make it possible for further delay," because workers already had chosen IUMSWA Local 1 as their representative. But Henry Roosevelt kept to his position, which had been the Navy's outlook from the beginning of the dispute. Furthermore, FDR himself had seen Henry Roosevelt's letter and offered no criticism, so the Assistant Secretary appeared to be standing on firm ground. This apparently minor change led to serious problems. It brought to the fore one of the decade's most important trade union issues, which was a fundamental though controversial part of the Wagner Act:

[85] Franklin D. Roosevelt memorandum (photo); White House press conference transcript, July 26, 1935; *Camden Courier Post*, July 27, 1935.

[86] "Hearings, Labor Practices in Shipbuilding," Aug. 6, 1935, p. 111; Henry Roosevelt to Metten, July 27, 1935, NA, RG 174, Box 37.

the right of a union to exclusive representation in a workplace provided a majority of employees select it.[87]

The company continued to stall, initially replying that it would accept arbitration only if a number of "conditions" were met. Assistant Secretary Roosevelt rejected Metten's equivocation and reiterated that the government would take over production if New York Ship did not agree to an unconditional arbitration board appointed by the President. He gave Metten an extension of one week to decide, indicating that President Roosevelt now had a strong personal interest in the matter.[88]

A week *after* the deadline, on August 8, New York Ship's management finally agreed to arbitration on Assistant Secretary Henry Roosevelt's conditions, this time with the proviso that the Navy choose the board and that the arbitrators themselves be Naval officers. When Labor Secretary Perkins notified Gallagher, the head of the IUMSWA negotiating committee, on August 9 that the company had agreed to arbitrate, she included Henry Roosevelt's point regarding "determination of . . . employee representatives." Union leaders interpreted her revised position as a capitulation to New York Ship's conditions on arbitration, which included a new union representation election as its most important point. Because Perkins's letter did not mention the IUMSWA by name, they feared that she no longer backed recognition of the union as the yard's sole bargaining agent for workers and that striking union members would have no protection against company reprisals once they returned to work.[89]

Despite New York Shipbuilding management's equivocation, the Navy Department was pleased with Metten's response, but it would not make his letter of "acceptance" public. To the IUMSWA and its allies, a possible settlement seemed to be unraveling. Representative Vito Marcantonio accused the Assistant Secretary of the Navy of backing down on the ultimatum. Speaking for the union, Gallagher expressed his "disappointment" at the secrecy surrounding the exchange and said that the union only had authority to support Perkins's original plan of July 22.[90]

---

[87] Henry Roosevelt to Metten, July 27, 1935; Perkins to Henry Roosevelt, July 29, 1935; Henry Roosevelt to Perkins, July 29, 1935; all NA, RG 174, Box 37.

[88] "Hearings, Labor Practices in Shipbuilding," Aug. 6, 1935, pp. 111–13 (includes Metten letter to Henry Roosevelt, July 30, 1935, as quoted in H. Roosevelt's testimony of Aug. 6, 1935, and Henry Roosevelt letter to Metten, Aug. 1, 1935); *Philadelphia Record*, Aug. 8, 1935.

[89] Metten to Henry Roosevelt, Aug. 7, 1935; Kerwin to Chappell, Aug. 8, 1935; Henry Roosevelt to President Roosevelt, Aug. 8, 1935; Perkins to Gallagher, Aug. 9, 1935; Chappell to Kerwin and Perkins, Aug. 9, 1935; Chappell memorandum, Aug. 10, 1935; all NA, RG 174, Box 37.

[90] *Philadelphia Record*, Aug. 9, 1935; Chappell memorandum, Aug. 12, 1935, NA, RG 174, Box 37.

The IUMSWA leadership turned down Perkins's newest offer, assuming that it was only the company's proposal to the Navy. When Perkins informed Gallagher on August 12 that this proposal was in fact a *government* offer, union members voted 1600 to 400 at a special meeting to reject it and booed when the names of Henry Roosevelt and Perkins were mentioned. Only Labor Department conciliator Chappell retained any credibility with the strikers at this point.[91]

Once again, Congress provided a national forum for the IUMSWA strikers. Representative Marcantonio became the union's most visible defender in Washington and vocally challenged the Roosevelt administration to take tougher action against delays by New York Ship's management. He helped guarantee a decent settlement for the IUMSWA by reconvening the subcommittee hearings and allowing Van Gelder and Green to give their side of the story. The union leaders, as before, were relatively restrained in their testimony. Marcantonio, however, harshly criticized Perkins for allowing the company "to cover itself legally . . . by simply using the word 'arbitrate'." He had "never seen a more disgraceful trick pulled on a group of workers. . . . It is an outrage. . . . The letter of August 9, 1935, by Secretary Perkins, is a complete surrender and capitulation on the part of the Department of Labor to the New York Shipbuilding Corporation."[92]

The actual record of what Perkins was doing behind the scenes to advance the union's cause refutes Marcantonio's allegation. Her handling of this crisis reveals that she was not the stereotypical "social worker," as some have claimed, who was more interested in social policy and legislation than assisting the trade union movement. Her practice inside the bureaucratic maze of the Roosevelt administration shows that she acted as a committed ally of the IUMSWA and was its most effective advocate in getting FDR to intervene on the union's behalf.[93]

The company had already lost its last ally in Washington. Metten made one futile final maneuver, pleading with Henry Roosevelt for "protection" (that is,

---

[91] Gallagher to Perkins, Aug. 10, 1935; Perkins to Gallagher, Aug. 12, 1935; Chappell to Kerwin, Aug. 14, 1935; Gallagher to Perkins, Aug. 14, 1935; all NA, RG 174, Box 37.

[92] "Hearings, Labor Practices in Shipbuilding," Aug. 13, 1935, pp. 123, 129–30; Aug. 20, 1935, p. 155.

[93] For a reassessment of Frances Perkins's role as Secretary of Labor similar to my own, see Winifred D. Wandersee, "'I'd Rather Pass a Law than Organize a Union': Frances Perkins and the Reformist Approach to Organized Labor," *Labor History* 34 (Winter 1993) 5–32. For the standard interpretation of Perkins playing only a background part in New Deal labor relations, in contrast to her central role in helping to formulate social policies, see Murray Edelman, "New Deal Sensitivity to Labor Interests," in Milton Derber and Edwin Young, eds., *Labor and the New Deal* (Madison: University of Wisconsin Press, 1957), pp. 161–63; and Bernstein, *The Turbulent Years*, pp. 172–205, 318–51.

New York Shipyard, aerial view of covered ways section of the plant, looking away from Philadelphia, 1940s. In the foreground is the Delaware River. Directly behind the shipyard is Camden, and in the upper right is Gloucester. *Source: Fifty Years: New York Shipbuilding* (Camden, N.J.: New York Shipbuilding Corp., 1949).

Second New York Shipyard strike, women supporters on the picket line, 1935. Although women were excluded from (non-clerical) shipyard employment, they actively supported the IUMSWA and the strikes of 1934 and 1935. According to Ben Maiatico, without them the strikes could not have been won. Employment at New York Ship did not become open to women until World War II was well under way. *Source: Philadelphia Record*, July 25, 1935.

Ship launch at New York Shipyard, the covered ways, late 1930s or World War II era. Unlike the exposed shipways common to most shipyards, these covered ways at New York Ship made it possible to work year round in any type of weather. *Source: Fifty Years: New York Shipbuilding* (Camden, N.J.: New York Shipbuilding Corp., 1949).

Delegates to Second National IUMSWA Convention, Camden, N.J., 1936. Seated starting fourth from right: Tom Gallagher, Phil Van Gelder, and John Green. William Pommerer is the large man seated fourth from the left. John "Scotty" Knowles is sixth from the left, row two. John W. Brown (from Maine) is at the left end of row three. Photo reprinted courtesy of Phil Van Gelder.

New York Shipyard meeting of union and management with Local 1 executive secretary Ben Maiatico (left rear) and Local 1 recording secretary (and later president) Andy Reeder (seated right) recognizing the subforemen's department of IUMSWA Local 1, 1943. Reeder, having moved from jobs at Federal Shipyard to New York Ship, became the leader of the campaign to unionize the subforemen. Others present were (top row, from left) Harry Parker, industrial relations manager; Thomas "Driftpin" Saul, chairman of Local 1 negotiating committee and later leader of the secessionist movement into the AFL Boilermakers; (seated, from left) M. H. Goldstein, national attorney for the IUMSWA; Wilford Moses, president of Local 1; and Colonel Gardiner, attorney for New York Shipbuilding. Photo reprinted courtesy of Andy Reeder and Eva Reeder.

troops) to open the shipyard. By this time the Assistant Secretary had no intention of honoring such a request. In response to rumors that the Marines
might be called in, Lieutenant Commander C. G. Moore, Navy press chief,
stated that "it would be entirely unprecedented in navy history, and, anyway,
that's the last thing in the world we would think of doing." Clearly, no government officials—local, state, or federal—wanted to use force to stop the
mass picket, still numbering over 3,000 each day.[94]

In a final effort to break the deadlock, Perkins appealed directly to FDR. In
a lengthy private memorandum of August 20, she identified the one practical
issue that could resolve the strike: abandoning the company's insistence on
"determination of representatives" in exchange for dropping the IUMSWA's
demand for a "closed shop." FDR already supported eliminating the latter,
which was advocated by New York Ship and the Navy, but he had not understood the full import of the union's opposition to a representation election.
Perkins framed her argument on behalf of the union in terms of the "true
meaning of the Wagner Act," which had been passed just two months earlier.
Perkins's communication to FDR was a very personal appeal and reveals her
true sentiments toward this new industrial union and others like it:

> On the whole, I am convinced that the union is right in objecting to arbitration
> of this issue of whether or not it represents the men. . . . . The Government *never*
> in the past has arbitrated the question of whether a union represents the men,
> when the evidence is so plain . . . and the employer has so often dealt on a foot-
> ing which plainly shows that he appreciates that the majority of his men belong
> to the union. And I am persuaded that the only reason why in this case the New
> York Shipbuilding Company wants the issue arbitrated is either (1) because the
> company objects to the particular men whom the union has put on its negotiat-
> ing committee or (2) because the company wishes to make it appear the Gov-
> ernment is hostile to the union. Whichever is the motive, we cannot countenance
> it, for in this country, (unlike the situation in Fascist countries) the workers are
> entitled to self-organization, and neither the company or the Government has
> anything to do with the result of their voluntary choice.

Her rationale for defending the right to self-organization, however, was based
on how power was exercised morally through persuasion, not just legally on
technical, contractual grounds:

> I realize that the *legal* power of the Government over the New York Shipbuild-
> ing Company, by reason of the naval contracts is less than is sometimes sup-

---

[94] Metten to Henry Roosevelt, Aug. 16, 1935, NA, RG 174, Box 37; *Philadelphia Record*,
Aug. 19, 21, 1935.

posed. But the *moral* power is very great, and I believe that it might lead to an end of the strike if you asked the Secretary of the Navy to use the prestige of his high office and his persuasive powers to have the company agree to an arbitration in which the question of union representation or recognition was not involved.

This appeal on behalf of the Camden strikers was very much like Perkins's encouraging words to pro-union workers when she visited the Homestead steel complex in 1933, but her role in this particular chapter of New Deal-era labor relations remained hidden, even to the IUMSWA leaders.[95]

President Roosevelt followed Perkins's advice, and on August 22 company and union officials, under government guidance, finally reached an acceptable agreement on the arbitration process. Secretary Perkins's low-key negotiating role and invisible influence on the President were more instrumental in pressuring New York Ship's management to move than were Representative Marcantonio's fiery, pro-union public attacks. The President issued an executive order that authorized a Camden Board of Arbitration, named its three members, and detailed the matters to be arbitrated. Most important, the union agreed to drop the demand for a preferential shop in exchange for explicit recognition of IUMSWA Local 1 by New York Ship's management.[96]

Formal ratification by both parties took place on August 26. Approximately 2,600 Local 1 union members voted, with only three or four in opposition, to ratify the President's arbitration proposal. According to the *Philadelphia Record*, "the [union] hall rang with cheers when leaders declared the strike resulted in recognition of the union." Leadership immediately recalled the remaining twenty-five pickets under John Diehl from the gates, and the twenty-four-hour picket line that had been maintained for over fifteen weeks disbanded. New York Ship's board of directors accepted the plan hours later, at 2:25 in the morning. The directors met for over eight hours, and when they signed the agreement to arbitrate, they "broke up without issuing a statement." It was clear who had won.[97]

Workers returned to their jobs on August 29 as production at the shipyard resumed. The old contract continued for almost two months, while the union and the company bargained under the Camden Board of Arbitration's direc-

---

[95] Perkins to President Roosevelt, Aug. 20, 1935, NA, RG 174, Box 37 (emphasis in original). For Perkins's 1933 visit to Homestead, see Perkins, *The Roosevelt I Knew*, pp. 217–21.

[96] Charles Wolverton, "Extension of Remarks in the House of Representatives, Aug. 23, 1935," *Congressional Record*, Appendix, Sept. 10, 1935, pp. 15282–86, which includes the complete text of President Roosevelt's Aug. 24 "Executive Order Creating the Camden Board of Arbitration," as well as correspondence between Representative Wolverton and the President.

[97] *Philadelphia Record*, Aug. 28, 1935.

tion. Finally, on October 12, the Board issued its decision in the form of a contract. Although it was modest compared with the union's original demands, the agreement awarded IUMSWA Local 1 important gains. Piecework and incentive pay, which the union originally opposed, were retained, but the rate of pay for such work was increased by 5 percent. Workers were granted a general wage increase of 5 percent, as well as a cost-of-living provision and a number of other improvements in benefits. The work week was kept at thirty-six hours. The probation period was reduced to four weeks, thereby strengthening job (and union) security. The right to arbitration and a grievance procedure with departmental stewards were guaranteed once again, but this time a permanent arbitration board was established for the yard. The no-discrimination clause, which covered union activity, also was renewed.[98]

For the first time, a New York Ship union agreement contained a stipulation that "there shall be no stoppage of work," as a way to prevent "direct action" over grievances. This "no-strike" provision was almost impossible to enforce. Wildcat strikes would be a way of life at New York Ship for the next twenty years. Differences over classification rates were not settled in this contract and remained a volatile issue in Camden and every shipyard the IUMSWA organized during the 1930s.[99]

The "preferential shop" that the union initially proposed had, of course, been dropped as an arbitration point. Union stewards continued to sign up members and collect dues on an individual basis, without interference from management. Local 1 used this process as an organizing tool. By the late 1930s, workers took great pride if their departments were "100 percent" signed up. Rivalry between departments for the highest membership rate became a catalyst for union consolidation and participation.[100]

The conclusion of the 1935 strike culminated a three-year effort to organize the union at New York Ship. The organizing in 1934 and 1935 was a process of "consolidation," a term commonly used by union organizers for the organizing stage that followed company recognition. This second stage turned out to be as important as the initial 1933 effort to build a core leadership group and

[98] "The Camden Board of Arbitration Award," Oct. 12, 1935, NA, RG 9, Box 5254; IUMSWA Local 1 Education Committee, *Unionism at Work* (Camden, 1943), pp. 18–19; Van Gelder, *Book of Facts for Shipyard Workers*, pp. 11–12.

[99] "The Camden Board of Arbitration Award"; New York Ship group interview, Aug. 16, 1987.

[100] "The Camden Board of Arbitration Award"; New York Ship group interview, Aug. 16, 1987. New York Shipbuilding did not institute a modified union shop provision until World War II. For discussions of dues collection, membership levels, and their relationship to worker involvement in the union at New York Ship, see Reeder and Maiatico interviews, and *Shipyard Worker*, 1936–1945.

a union local. Most industrial unions of the early 1930s did not survive in their original form, making the IUMSWA almost unique. At the local level, however, the IUMSWA went through a long process of organizing that was common to all unions in these years.

By 1935, the union had been transformed. It no longer regarded the New Deal bureaucracy as the enemy, but treated the Roosevelt administration as the friend of shipyard labor. In the course of the 1935 strike, Green and Van Gelder exchanged their militant socialist and syndicalist outlook for a social democratic trade unionism that allowed them to work comfortably with liberal Democratic Party politicians and officials. They continued to use militant trade union tactics, but now balanced these with arbitration and lobbying.

Most rank-and-file workers readily accepted the union leadership's new perspective. John Green was right when he concluded that if New York Ship was to be moved, "it will have to come from Washington." This analysis had profound implications for IUMSWA organizing over the next ten years. The key issues became to what extent organizing should resort to legal and government channels for assistance and maintain a national, rather than local, focus. The IUMSWA's particular advantage in gaining government support was its position within a strategically important defense industry: privately based naval shipbuilding.

The other critical way in which the IUMSWA was transformed during the 1935 strike was the drift toward centralizing power within the union, especially that held by John Green, the IUMSWA's national president. This centralization was balanced by a broadening of practical democracy at lower levels, especially on the shop floor. Rank-and-file workers, stewards, and committees played critical roles in the strike and contributed to building a stronger trade union organization at New York Ship.

Workers' groups at lower levels of the union had limited or no power regarding broader decision-making on union strategy, finances, staff hiring and firing, and government connections. While some "shop floor" union democracy furthered union growth, the strike provided Green with a rationale to increase central control at the top. This trend accelerated over the next five years. By World War II, Green had virtually total control over the national union through his loyalists in the national office and in key union locals. Paradoxically, the seeds of trade union bureaucracy and autocratic control were sown during one of the IUMSWA's most democratic and participatory periods, when there was some balance between democracy and centralization.

With Camden's Local 1 consolidated by late 1935, the IUMSWA could effectively devote its energy to organizing in other locations. In the remaining years of the 1930s, the IUMSWA continued the strategy of concentrating its organizing drives in specific yards, a painful lesson still only partially learned.

Simultaneously it was able to move toward a broader regional approach. Not until World War II did the union's resources allow it to challenge the shipbuilding companies on a national level.

The greatest proof that concentration of forces could lead to victory was the drive that now began in the port of New York. While Camden's New York Ship was the first company to become solidly unionized under the IUMSWA, the adjacent yards along the Delaware River remained difficult places to organize. In the next two years the union turned much of its attention to organizing yards around New York Harbor and North Jersey, including the region's biggest private operation: Federal Shipbuilding in Kearny.

PART II

BUILDING NEW LOCALS:
FEDERAL SHIP, 1934–1938

CHAPTER 4

Building a New Base: New York Harbor
and Federal Ship, 1934–1937

The IUMSWA turned to organizing in other locations after the 1935 victory at New York Ship. Initial organizing efforts went slowly because of the financial drain of the second Camden strike. While continuing to organize in New England and on the West Coast, the union focused its efforts on the yards in the port of New York, including those in North Jersey. Its ultimate target was Federal Shipbuilding in Kearny, New Jersey, a yard that grew from about 600 workers in the depths of the Depression to over 3,000 by 1936 and rivaled the "Big Three" (New York Ship, Fore River, and Newport News). Once it was organized, Federal Ship became the IUMSWA's second most important local and a critical source for new union leadership.[1]

Federal Shipyard workers were at the center of one of the nation's most vibrant labor environments during the mid-1930s. The IUMSWA soon gained a reputation in the port of New York as a militant industrial union, in contrast to the corruption and failures associated with the AFL craft unions in shipbuilding. Other important industrial unions developed and expanded rapidly in New York City and North Jersey during the late 1930s. Some older organizations, mainly in the needle trades, had been founded before the First World War and had become AFL affiliates. New industrial unions, including the Transport Workers Union (TWU), the National Maritime Union (NMU), and

---

[1] "Approximate Employment Figures by Various Districts," in H. G. Smith to Whittelsey, May 31, 1934, NA, RG 9, Box 5257. The report listed 655 workers employed at Federal in 1933, less than 10 percent of shipyard workers in the New York area; the Robins and Staten Island yards each employed three times as many workers.

the United Electrical Workers Union (UE), became affiliated with the CIO. These three new unions in particular had left-wing leaders at the top who were aligned with the Communist Party, and by World War II all three New York-based organizations achieved significant power within the CIO. Shipyard trade unionists had many contacts in the NMU and the UE, because companies where these unions had members often had manufacturing and commercial connections with the region's shipbuilding industry. The NMU was the IUMSWA's main ally on the docks and in the repair yards, while the UE had strong ties with inside organizers at the construction yards, particularly Federal Ship. For shipyard organizers, these were ties among equals, because IUMSWA organizing in the port of New York either preceded or coincided with the rise of local UE and NMU organizing.[2]

A number of factors made it easier to develop local union leadership at Federal Ship: the yard's unique industrial setting; the diverse ethnic makeup and generally pro-union stance of its labor force; its relatively unsophisticated upper-level managerial policy, combined with bad yard-level supervision that created discontent; a weak company union; and a generally pro-union regional environment. These favorable conditions alone did not produce a union movement at Federal Ship. The drive to organize had to be solidly based among workers within the yard. Former union activist Nat Levin felt that the repair yards in the New York port had little influence on Federal workers, as contact with them was minimal. The two major private construction yards at Staten Island and Hoboken did have an impact, however; union activists from those yards were brought in to organize, "especially from Hoboken," Levin stated. But "there is no question in my mind that the union was organized *mostly* from the inside, with N.Y. Ship–IUMSWA help." Most important to Levin, in 1937 "organizing fever was in the air."[3] As the IUMSWA's New York Harbor–North Jersey regional campaign gained momentum in 1936 and 1937, it seemed that almost every yard in the region would soon be organized. At this time the union's organizing strategy still continued to focus on the dynamics within each yard and the development of rank-and-file leadership. It was not

---

[2] Irving Bernstein, *The Turbulent Years: A History of the American Worker, 1933–1941* (Boston: Houghton Mifflin, 1969), pp. 424–31, 584–85, 606; Joshua B. Freeman, "Catholics, Communists, and Republicans: Irish Workers and the Organization of the Transport Workers Union," in Michael H. Frisch and Daniel J. Walkowitz, eds., *Working-Class America: Essays on Labor, Community, and American Society* (Urbana: University of Illinois Press, 1983), pp. 265–75; Phil Van Gelder letter to David Palmer, Nov. 22, 1986. The UE was formed in March 21, 1936, and affiliated with the CIO in November 1936, the same date as the IUMSWA; Bernstein, *Turbulent Years*, pp. 426, 606.

[3] Nat Levin letter to David Palmer, March 31, 1988 (emphasis in original).

until the summer of 1937 that these local struggles merged into a broader ship-yard union movement.

The IUMSWA initially targeted United Shipyard's Staten Island Shipyard, which had been the center of a general strike in the port in 1933 encompass-ing both longshore and shipyard workers. The yard again became a flash point in September 1934, when 100 welders among the yard's 1,000 workers struck unsuccessfully for union recognition. The welders affiliated as a craft unit with the independent International Association of Mechanical Welders, Local 13, but faced opposition from the AFL's discredited Marine Workers Metal Trades District Council as well as from United's management. On Staten Is-land, as elsewhere in the industry, the AFL continued to prefer no union to one that it did not control, and therefore refused to back the strike.[4]

In mid-October 1934, Phil Van Gelder sent organizer Charlie Purkis to the yard to see if the IUMSWA could recruit members, but Purkis made little headway. Layoffs after the defeat of the welders' strike added to the IUMSWA's difficulties, and in January 1935 Van Gelder transferred Purkis to Newport News. As the IUMSWA's only national organizers, Van Gelder and Purkis covered the entire East Coast from New England to Virginia. When New York Ship headed into its second strike in the spring of 1935, their lim-ited organizing activity tapered off; full-scale organizing in the port of New York resumed only in late 1935.[5]

The AFL had not won much of a membership base among shipyard work-ers in the port of New York. Its Boilermakers Union had a substantial follow-ing in Seattle and San Francisco, where unions managed to survive the open shop drive of the 1920s. In New York, the building trades unions fragmented any effort to organize the shipyards, which were far larger in the mid-1930s than those on the West Coast. Van Gelder recalled that craft unions in the New York City area did a great deal of non-shipbuilding construction work, which he believed gave them little incentive to pursue shipyard organizing as ag-gressively as their West Coast counterparts. Many building craftsmen in East

---

[4] "Exhibit 'g'," "United Dry Docks Inc. and International Association of Mechanic Welders, Local No. 13, Marine Workers Metal Trades District Council of the Port of New York, intervening," Case No. 190, NLRB, Nov. 6, 1934, NRA Shipbuilding Code IRC Hear-ing, Jan. 24, 1935, NA, RG 9, Box 5253. For a detailed account of the 1933 general New York port strike, see David Palmer, "Organizing the Shipyards: Unionization at Fore River, New York Ship, and Federal Ship, 1898–1945" (Ph.D. diss., Brandeis University, 1990), pp. 258–99.

[5] IUMSWA, *Proceedings, 2nd National Convention*, Report of Secretary-Treasurer Phil Van Gelder, Aug. 1936, p. 7.

Coast cities considered shipbuilding degrading and preferred to have their own separate locals.[6]

The AFL failed to recognize the emergence of a new system of shipbuilding production, which created new, skilled jobs in the industry. Even though the 1934 Staten Island welders' strike met defeat, it marked the beginning of an important trend: the rise in militancy of shipyard welders, who replaced riveters as the most vocal union activists. This trend resulted from the gradual decline of riveting and the growth of production welding. The spread of the new technology of production welding meant that acetylene welders could easily enter the ranks of electric welders, thereby attaining higher status in the hierarchy of shipyard labor. By 1936, this shipbuilding trade was growing faster than any other in the industry. Workers learned this new skill in independent trade schools, at welding schools inside the yards, or on the job. Few welders had any allegiance to the AFL because welding was not a traditional building trade with an elaborate apprenticeship system. They got their jobs through the companies just as unskilled workers did, rather than through the good graces of a craft union. These young men knew that their skills were in demand and usually had little patience with the shoddy treatment commonly accorded yard workers.[7]

The welders played a particularly important role in naval construction. Companies did not yet build ships on the module basis, to which welding was essential, but construction trends were moving in this direction. Welders generally had more independence and a greater spirit of egalitarianism than riveting gangs. Although organized into production teams, welders worked individually along a line of plate or a butt (metal joint); their output could be measured and, in many yards, they were paid piece rates. Welders had equal status within their production team, in contrast to the rivet gang, with its hierarchy of riveter, holder-on, passer, and heater boy. Although the mid-sections of ships, especially warships, still had to be riveted, hundreds and later thousands of welders gradually displaced the rivet gangs as the main production workers on the ways. They soon predominated in shop areas off the ways as well, where production was increasingly done in subassembly areas.[8]

[6] Van Gelder interviews, 1987–88; Arthur Boyson interviews, 1982–87 (for similar patterns in the port of Boston).

[7] Andy Reeder interviews, Sept. 3, 1986; May 30, 1987; May 21, 1988. Reeder believed that the youthful, independent spirit of the new type of welders was the key to their militant trade union activities. Interviews with other welders, particularly from New York Ship and Federal, corroborate this perspective. Jack Collins interview, Sept. 13, 1987; George "Chips" De Girolamo interview; New York Ship IUMSWA Local 1 Reunion, Oct. 25, 1986; First Annual Welders' Reunion (New York Ship), May 31, 1987, Gloucester, N.J.; Second Annual Welders' Reunion (New York Ship), May 1988, Gloucester, N.J.

[8] Boyson interviews; Terry Foy interviews, May 20, 1988, Union, N.J., and April 6, 1988,

After the second New York Ship union agreement was signed in October 1935, the IUMSWA obtained a $1,000 loan from the United Mine Workers to send organizer Charlie Purkis to the port of New York and organizer John W. Brown, the UMW veteran and friend of John L. Lewis, to Fore River. The union needed this assistance, according to Van Gelder, because the Camden strike had "very much depleted" the union's treasury. That month, Purkis returned to the Staten Island Shipyard, making it his major target in the port. The fall was the busy season for repair yard work but a slack time for construction yard jobs. Although Staten Island had both construction and repair sections, the IUMSWA decided to single out the construction yard, because its lower turnover rate made it easier to organize. The campaign began slowly, but gained momentum after Van Gelder arrived to assist Purkis. The union enrolled enough shipyard workers to charter Local 12 on February 11, 1936, and by May 12 the union local had become strong enough to make contract demands on the company.[9]

United's management initially refused Local 12's proposals. After a week the union responded by authorizing a strike, but it did not take immediate action. A major obstacle was the company's claim that it could not recognize the IUMSWA as the workers' sole representative because a number of employees belonged to rival AFL craft unions. The AFL's Marine Workers Metal Trades Council was, in fact, making the same contract demands as the IUMSWA. The dispute ended when a poll was held in June; the IUMSWA decisively defeated the AFL by 1,399 to 84 votes. The yard election was conducted by an impartial board agreed to by the company, rather than a government board, and it gave the IUMSWA clear legitimacy.[10]

By the end of June, after several rounds of hard bargaining, Staten Island management granted Local 12 recognition and a signed contract that included a five percent wage increase. Van Gelder believed this agreement represented only a partial victory because it did not cover the yard's repairmen. The persistence of this non-union environment in the repair yards became the catalyst for a year-long organizing drive in the port under Purkis's leadership. This campaign coincided with the national sit-down strike wave of late 1936 and early 1937, which created excellent organizing conditions for shipyard trade unionists in the port.[11]

Union, N.J. (with Lou Kaplan). Foy was helpful in explaining how rivet gangs operated during World War II; Boyson, who started on a Fore River rivet gang in 1917, provided similar background for World War I.

[9] IUMSWA, *Proceedings, 2nd National Convention*, Van Gelder Report, Aug. 1936, p. 8.

[10] *New York Times*, May 21, 26, June 6, 1936; Van Gelder to John L. Lewis, June 6, 1936, *The CIO Files of John L. Lewis*, part 1, reel 7 (University Publications of America microfilm).

[11] IUMSWA, *Proceedings, 2nd National Convention*, Van Gelder Report, Aug. 1936, p. 8;

Although the first Staten Island union contract had limitations, it represented a major step forward for the IUMSWA. This was only the second time since the IUMSWA's founding some three years earlier that a major shipbuilding company had signed a written union agreement covering all production workers, rather than just selected crafts. The IUMSWA now had signed contracts with two yards critical to the industry in the ports of Philadelphia and New York, making it the most important shipbuilding union in the country despite its relatively small size.

The IUMSWA's expansion into this key New York port yard came on the eve of the November 1936 split in the AFL between the CIO, led by John L. Lewis, and the traditional wing, led by William Green. While AFL Metal Trades officials tried to sabotage the 1935 New York Shipyard strike and Federation leaders barred the IUMSWA from AFL affiliation, CIO chairman Lewis became a strong supporter of the new shipyard union, recognizing it as a valuable new ally. Van Gelder solidified the new alliance when he wrote to Lewis after the Staten Island victory. The agreement with United Shipyards, accomplished without a strike, represented "a notable gain for our organization, and should result in the organization of the entire Port of New York into the Industrial Union." Overall, the agreement "is even better than our Camden contract." Van Gelder added, "we are watching with great interest your campaign in the steel industry, and also developments in the A F of L." He concluded by saying that he and Green hoped to visit Lewis in Washington to "discuss these and other matters of importance." [12]

Van Gelder realized that he and Purkis could not possibly cover so large a territory as the port of New York on their own, especially if North Jersey were included. Although North Jersey was physically connected to the port, it seemed a remote and forbidding place for industrial unionists in early 1936. Van Gelder referred to it as the "wilds of North Jersey where unionism (except for the A F of L type) was taboo." [13] Entrenched urban political machines and bosses, especially Jersey City's anti-union Mayor Frank ("I am the law") Hague, made union work difficult and dangerous. Organizing these shipyards required veteran activists and a strategy that targeted one or two yards at a time.

In July, Van Gelder again turned to John L. Lewis for financial assistance.

IUMSWA, *Proceedings, 3rd National Convention*, Van Gelder Report on Organizing, Sept. 1937, p. 16.

[12] Van Gelder to Lewis, June 30, 1936, IUMSWA Archives, Series V, Box 1, Special Collections, University of Maryland at College Park Libraries.

[13] IUMSWA, *Proceedings, 3rd National Convention*, Van Gelder Report, Sept. 1937, p. 15.

This time he emphasized the connection between the giant shipyards and the big steel companies, where Lewis was conducting a major union organizing campaign. He told Lewis that the IUMSWA lacked funds "to capitalize on this advantageous situation" in the New York port and shipyards generally. The union could afford only three organizers: Charles Renner, at Sun Ship; Purkis in New York; and Van Gelder, who had "to spend a certain amount of time in the Camden office." Van Gelder continued:

> If we are going to take advantage of the present situation we must have at least two more organizers, one for Quincy (Bethlehem plant) and one for Kearny (U.S. Steel's Federal yard). These two yards are among the five most important in the country and employ 7 or 8 thousand men between them. The fact that they are owned by steel corporations also makes it important that we start work on them at this time.

Van Gelder asked for "two or three organizers" from the CIO, or at least a loan of $2,000 so that the IUMSWA could hire its own. He reiterated his admiration for Lewis's role in promoting the new industrial unionism, noting that "our members look upon the U.M.W. as sort of a guardian angel of our Union, and in our three years of struggle to organize the shipyard workers on an industrial union basis, your support has been of incalculable value. We have succeeded where the craft unions have failed." The UMW immediately lent $2,000 to the IUMSWA, knowing that it would be put to good use.[14]

Van Gelder's correspondence with Lewis revealed his basic organizing strategy for the coming year: to concentrate heavily on the New York port area (including North Jersey); to latch on to the momentum building in the CIO's steel industry organizing drive, especially at U.S. Steel and Bethlehem, which both owned large shipyards; and to ally with the increasingly separatist industrial unions in the AFL. Lewis had congratulated Van Gelder and the

---

[14] Van Gelder to Lewis, July 17, 1936, IUMSWA Archives, Series V, Box 1; IUMSWA, *Proceedings, 2nd National Convention*, Auditor's report on the union's financial status, Aug. 1936, p. 23. When considering whether Lewis or Hillman had been a greater influence on him, Van Gelder replied that it was Lewis without a doubt, because Lewis could reach down to average workers and move them; Van Gelder interviews, 1982–1989. Van Gelder also saw Lewis alone as the founder of modern industrial unionism. Van Gelder's July 17, 1936, letter reflected his identification with Lewis's populist industrial unionism of the early CIO years, in contrast to Hillman's more staid, social democratic liberalism. While Van Gelder swung between these two points at various times in his long labor career, he usually returned to the perspective advocated (publicly) by Lewis. Van Gelder's primary identification with Hillman lasted only from 1940 to 1945, when Lewis challenged initial American involvement in World War II and then went on to oppose the no-strike pledge.

IUMSWA on their success at Staten Island and provided minimal but critically important funds, but the IUMSWA staff and workers inside the yards did their own organizing. Local shipyard trade unionists preferred this way of operating, and it proved to be the most successful.[15]

The funds provided by the UMW to the IUMSWA put a new organizer, Mike Smith, on the staff by the end of August, allowing Purkis to concentrate on signing up shipyard workers in Brooklyn. Smith came from the machine shop at New York Ship and was a founding member of Local 1. He had been a delegate to both of the IUMSWA's national conventions and was elected to its first national executive board. His main assignment was to organize U.S. Steel's Federal Shipbuilding, but he also had the task of organizing in other parts of North Jersey, especially Hoboken.

The Federal Shipyard assignment appeared to be a difficult one. The yard had never had a union contract (or so John Green claimed) since its opening during World War I, even though the AFL and the IWW had been active there. Smith also had to deal with the management of United States Steel, notorious for its long anti-union record. The destruction of the older AFL unions by Andrew Carnegie during the 1892 Homestead strike had allowed his steel company and its successor, U.S. Steel (merged by J. P. Morgan with numerous other steel producers by 1901), to keep unions out for almost half a century. Although trade unionists mounted a major strike in 1919 to organize steel workers along industrial lines, they were decisively defeated by a management counteroffensive led by U.S. Steel. The late 1930s were far more promising times for industrial unionism, however. If Van Gelder was correct, the organizing groundswell in the New York yards spearheaded by Staten Island soon would spread to North Jersey. The union could then build a new base in the heart of the shipbuilding industry, even if it ultimately had to confront a major subsidiary of U.S. Steel.[16]

Nationally, U.S. Steel had moderated its labor relations approach under its new chief executive officer, Myron Taylor. From mid-1936 to early 1937, the CIO's Steel Workers Organizing Committee (SWOC), led by Philip Murray under John L. Lewis's guiding hand, secured significant leadership positions in U.S. Steel's company unions. Taylor knew that he had to compromise or face a bitter, potentially violent strike. His background was in banking, not

---

[15] Lewis to Van Gelder, July 7, 1936, IUMSWA Archives, Series V, Box 1.

[16] For background on U.S. Steel and setbacks for AFL union organizing before the 1930s, see David Brody, *Steelworkers in America: The Nonunion Era* (New York: Harper, 1969); and John A. Garraty, "The United States Steel Corporation versus Labor: The Early Years," *Labor History* 1 (Winter 1969) 3–38.

steel-making, which apparently gave him a more detached and less adversarial outlook on labor relations than other top executives in the industry. He had no intention of letting an explosive labor upheaval drive the corporation into the ground, having pulled it out of a long-term slump by the mid-1930s. Since 1933, U.S. Steel and the UMW had had collective bargaining agreements in the company's "captive mines." This arrangement made Taylor confident that he could deal with Lewis on a reasonable basis, which contributed to his recognizing the SWOC rather than forcing a strike.[17]

As a subsidiary of U.S. Steel, Federal Shipbuilding had a distinctive managerial environment. Its labor policies fell somewhere between those of New York Ship and Bethlehem Fore River. Federal Ship did not fire union organizers, as was routinely done at Fore River, unless it was provoked by strike actions. During the peak of the 1937 Federal Ship organizing campaign, a revived company union represented a substantial threat to the IUMSWA's activities. Federal's company union, like Fore River's, was known as an Employee Representation Plan (ERP), with a Works Council as its central body. It had been meeting regularly with management for four years, making company unionism more firmly entrenched at Federal than at New York Ship. Unlike Fore River, however, Federal's company union did not have extensive employee participation or numerous committees.

Myron Taylor's promotion of "flexibility" in U.S. Steel's negotiations with top union officials never carried over to Federal Shipbuilding and does not appear to have affected yard-level management. Terrible working conditions at Federal Ship created opportunities for organizing. Widespread harsh treatment by shop-level supervisors (known as "snappers") and the danger of shipyard work at Federal tended to unite workers from all skill levels and ethnic backgrounds. Welder Nat Levin, one of the yard's original inside organizers, was "shocked" by "the hazardous working conditions" when he started in 1936. "We pulled welding cable under very dim lights on single plank scaffolding 40 feet in the air in the main cargo tanks of oil tankers (*Esso*, and *Texaco*), and a few foul mouthed snappers told us we had to be tough to work there."[18]

Federal's rapid employment growth from new naval contracts gave Smith another organizing advantage, as younger shipyard workers tended to be more open to the union. In 1934, the Navy awarded contracts to Federal Shipbuilding for the construction of four destroyers. Additional naval commissions followed, which led to a steady increase in the number of yard workers. Em-

---

[17] Bernstein, *Turbulent Years*, pp. 46–9, 448–72.
[18] Levin letter to Palmer, March 11, 1988.

ployment climbed to 2,500 in May 1937 and 5,700 in March 1940. By August 1941, on the eve of World War II, the yard had over 12,000 workers and was building more destroyers than any other shipyard in the United States.[19]

The government's promotion of standard ship designs led to major changes in shipbuilding methods and employment and to the ascendancy of an industrial over craft outlook in the yards. By 1937 the trend toward welded hulls was proceeding at a rapid pace. Welder Nat Levin held that the rise in employment and a new openness to industrial unionism was related to this shift in shipbuilding technology, which included electric welding and fabrication of large sections of ships. To meet production demands, Federal's management had to hire workers wherever it could find them. By the mid- to late 1930s, experienced shipbuilders, especially welders, were in great demand. As Federal Ship had one of the lowest wage rates on the East Coast, numerous skilled workers who had been forced out of jobs elsewhere because of their union activity were able to get jobs at the yard. According to Levin, many of IUMSWA Local 16's early leaders at Federal Ship were "younger men—mostly welders and new shipyard workers, from [the] Delaware Bay area—New York Ship and Sun Ship, but some from the south—Newport News, especially." Organizer Mike Smith easily got men into the yard who were willing to organize for the IUMSWA, including Mike Shapiro (pronounced "Sha-py-ro" by workers), a welder who became Smith's key man for this recruiting operation.[20]

Levin was an important "volunteer organizer" among the welders, and he established close friendships with Smith and Shapiro. He originally followed his father's trade of carpentry, where he developed a positive outlook toward unions, an egalitarian philosophy, and a sense of solidarity across ethnic differences. "[As a carpenter] I worked with a scaffold man helping to build very solid and safe working areas for masons, plasterers and helpers. The men were all Union members—many old country English, Irish, Scotch, Italian, and everyone seemed to show respect for one another." Levin was able to translate these ideals into action when he began organizing Federal Shipyard welders for the IUMSWA. As a result of their youth and their lack of prejudice against the unskilled, the welders gave the organizing drive unusual vitality and unity.[21]

Growing dissent within the company union provided another edge for the IUMSWA. In January 1935, worker representatives on the Works Council

---

[19] *Shipyard Worker*, May 21, 1937; March 8, 1940; August 8, 15, 22, 29, 1941.

[20] Collins interview, Sept. 13, 1987; George Snyder interview; Reeder interviews, May 30, 1987, and May 21, 1988; Levin letter to Palmer, March 31, 1988.

[21] Levin letters to Palmer, March 11 and Nov. 18, 1988. Mike Shapiro and his wife were witnesses at Levin's wedding in 1939, an indication of the closeness of their friendship.

called for equitable wage increases, but they were rebuffed by Federal Ship-building president Lynn Korndorff, who countered "that individual merit would be rewarded." By late 1936, many workers had lost confidence in the company union and wanted an alternative organization to represent them.[22]

Finally, Smith's personal style and commitment to the average shipyard worker were well received by men at the Federal yard. He effectively articu-lated their everyday concerns and seems to have tapped into a groundswell of rebellion in the yard, directing it in a positive way. The strong personal ties that Federal Shipyard workers felt with Smith went beyond admiration for his trade union abilities. Levin recalled, "Mike Smith was the ideal person for these early organizing activities. He was Scotch-Irish, Roman Catholic (couldn't be red-baited), experienced as an organizer (compared to most of us), very pa-tient, absolutely no conceit, honest and a very warm human being."[23]

The layout of the Federal yard proved particularly favorable for Smith's approach to organizing. At New York Ship, many of the skilled trades shops were situated at the entrances to the shipways, making organization of the craft workers there essential. At Federal, however, a long plate shop ran along the rear of the ways, while the skilled trades shops were behind the plate shop and completely separate from the ways. Federal Ship's particular yard configura-tion meant that organizing could be centered in the plate shop and then radi-ate out to the other shops and the ways, making shipfitters and other "steel trades" (based in the plate shop) essential to any drive. While highly skilled workers were among the leadership at Federal, more came from the steel trades, such as welding or chipping and caulking, than had been the case at New York Ship. This contrast reflected differences between the two yards' types of production and ships, not just their shop setups. New York Ship had been designed for building elaborate vessels, such as ocean liners and battle-ships, which required extensive outfitting by diversified skilled trades and shops. Federal Ship, on the other hand, built smaller scale merchant ships dur-ing World War I and specialized in destroyers after 1933; it also built many tankers. All marine engineering was subcontracted, making the hull, or ship-ways, division by far the largest employment area. Although New York Ship and Fore River also had their highest concentrations of workers in the hull di-vision, the numbers in Federal's hull division exceeded theirs. By the late 1930s, Federal Ship became a leader in hull construction innovation, such as subassembly and prefabricated production. Furthermore, the layout of the Federal yard reflected the fact that it was built during World War I, almost two

[22] Works Council Minutes (Federal Shipbuilding), Jan. 25, 1936, IUMSWA Archives, Se-ries V, Box 50; *Shipyard Worker*, Nov. 6, 1936.

[23] Levin letter to Palmer, March 11, 1988.

decades after New York Ship and Fore River, when engineers could incorporate more advanced production flow techniques.[24]

Smith began the Federal Shipyard drive with the usual methods. With help from Purkis, he established inside contacts. Probably the most important of these men was Alex Turoczy, who, according to Van Gelder, oversaw the campaign. Although Turoczy was a chipper and caulker based in Department 32, the plate shop, he worked mainly on the ways. According to Levin, Turoczy was "a very hard worker . . . on the job and for the union, made to order for Mike Smith, with his . . . Slavic, Roman Catholic background." Turoczy became Federal Shipyard Local 16's first financial secretary and later joined the IUMSWA national staff to organize Sun Ship and Fore River. With a core of "volunteer organizers" in the plate department, the drive could operate out of the hub of the shipyard.[25]

Another chipper and caulker critical to the early union was Dan Deans, from Department 43 where the riveters were based. Deans became the local's first president and remained active in the union through World War II. Like Turoczy, he was one of the "older men with [a] strong craft background," according to Levin; he was honest, providing a "very strong, powerful influence." From the shipfitters (Department 35) came George Redpath. The machine shop (Department 66) was a relatively conservative area, as in most shipyards, and had the highest number of skilled workers of any department. The union's voice in the machine shop was Karl Neugebauer, who later became shop steward. Abe Rothery, of Department 40, represented the drillers and reamers. He was an "old-timer," a black worker in a department that had some of the toughest, least desirable jobs and a number of Eastern European and black workers. Black workers had been hired at Federal Ship during World War I, but most were laid off during the 1920s "shipyard depression." The few black workers who remained were confined to the drilling and reaming department and to cleaning jobs around the yard. Levin recalled that "Abe Rothery was a wonderful guy . . . absolutely incorruptible, and a first-rate example, especially for the young black workers." Of the older leaders, these

[24] See ship lists for Federal Shipbuilding (in personal possession of Hobart Holly, Quincy, Mass.), New York Shipbuilding (Philadelphia Maritime Museum), and Fore River Shipyard (Hart Nautical Museum). For background on shipyard design, see Frederic C. Lane et al., *Ships for Victory: A History of Shipbuilding under the U.S. Maritime Commission in World War II* (Baltimore: Johns Hopkins University Press, 1951), pp. 202–35; *Fifty Years: New York Shipbuilding Corporation* (Camden: New York Shipbuilding Corp., 1949); and Harry E. Gould, "History of Bethlehem's Fore River Yard," *SNAME, Historical Transactions, 1893–1943* (1945), pp. 202–7. Lou Kaplan in particular emphasized the importance of the plate shop for organizing at the Federal Shipyard.

[25] Levin letters to Palmer, March 11, 1988 and Jan. 8, 1989; Van Gelder interviews, 1988.

were among the most important. Most of them, according to Levin, were from the "old country, especially English, Irish, Scotch, [with] shipyard union training. . . . Mike Smith made canny use of them."[26]

Smith relied mainly on Mike Shapiro to organize the welders. Shapiro brought in a number of union men from New York Ship. He later became a staff organizer, assisting at Sun Ship, and then a regional director in the South. Levin, who went from a tack welder in 1936 to a production welder on the night shift in 1937, remembered Shapiro as one of the "spark plugs for us." Together, the younger workers, who were primarily welders, and the older, craft-oriented men formed a solid organizing committee. Levin noted that "all our early activity had to be under cover," even after the union won recognition.[27]

To reach as many workers as possible, Smith openly distributed the *Shipyard Worker* every week and, according to Van Gelder, "worked quietly and painstakingly with [a] small group of key individuals." Articles in the national union paper attacking intolerable working conditions at Federal Ship appeared within a month of Smith's arrival. One told the story of the "death ship" tanker *Pan Maine*, which "will go to sea with the bloodstains from workers' mangled bodies obliterated from its sleek sides by many coats of glistening paint. . . . Two men in Kearny had their lives crushed out, five others had their bodies horribly crippled as a lifelong reminder of the speedup in the Federal Shipyard to hurry the *Pan Maine*'s riding down the ways." Speedup was a volatile issue, especially among riveters and welders, for it was a major cause of fatigue and accidents.[28]

Open hostilities between workers and foremen commonly erupted in the yard, as the *Shipyard Worker* reported. In one case a carpenter "crossed a hard right to the foreman's jaw and hit the street for his action." Smith warned that while this worker's action may have been justified, "individual resentment of the kind is suicidal." One month later a number of inside machinists, most of whom were Scottish, threatened to quit over abusive treatment by a foreman.

---

[26] Levin letters to Palmer, March 31 and Nov. 18, 1988; Henry Tully interview, April 4, 1988, New York City. Department numbers and names of leaders are cross-referenced from Levin's letters to Palmer, IUMSWA Local 16 documents, and the *Shipyard Worker* from 1937 to 1940. For background on black workers at Federal Ship, see the *Federal Shipbuilder*, 1918–1921; and Tully interview. Local 16 papers in the IUMSWA Archives have virtually no references to black workers, revealing the weakness of the IUMSWA in actually implementing the principle in its constitution barring racial discrimination.

[27] Levin letters to Palmer, March 11 and Nov. 18, 1988. For a positive assessment of Shapiro's organizing at Sun Ship, see Kaplan interviews, 1982–89. For a highly critical evaluation of his role in race relations in Mobile, Alabama, see Bruce Nelson, "Organized Labor and the Struggle for Black Equality in Mobile during World War II," *Journal of American History* 80 (Dec. 1993), pp. 982–88.

[28] IUMSWA, *Proceedings, 3rd National Convention*, Van Gelder Report, Sept. 1937, p. 16; *Shipyard Worker*, Oct. 16, 1936.

Speaking as a fellow Scotsman and machinist, Smith urged them to "bide awee.... The solution is not in running away from conditions ... [but depends on] lining up with the Industrial Union."[29]

The organizing at Federal Ship stood on secure ground when Smith called the first open meeting in February 1937. By this time a large number of Federal Shipyard workers had signed up, and the union was assured of a big turnout. Furthermore, the IUMSWA was gaining a reputation around New York and North Jersey as a rapidly growing union. Only three months earlier Purkis had set up Local 13 in Brooklyn, made up of a half-dozen repair yards. And nationally the IUMSWA no longer appeared to be a struggling and isolated union, because it was now connected with the CIO. In November 1936, John L. Lewis brought the IUMSWA and the UE—both independent unions—into the CIO, thus adding to the stature of the shipyard union. This move helped to "seal the split in the labor movement," according to the historian Irving Bernstein. In the first months of 1937, moreover, the CIO conducted major national campaigns in auto and steel, which indirectly gave IUMSWA organizing at Federal Ship a big morale boost.[30]

Over 500 Federal Shipyard workers came to the February 26 mass meeting at Jersey City's Ukrainian Hall. In a "fiery" address, John Green reported on a sit-down strike then in progress at the Electric Boat yard in New London, Connecticut. He attacked Jersey City mayor Frank Hague for his opposition to labor and for siding with the "company stooges." As for charges by local politicians and Federal Shipyard management that he was a communist, Green sarcastically replied, "if what I am telling you is Communist, then I guess I'm a Communist." He went on to relay greetings from Lewis, who hoped that the yard would be organized within a month, in time for negotiations with U.S. Steel. (Lewis and U.S. Steel's Myron Taylor had been meeting privately throughout January and February.) About 100 workers openly signed membership cards immediately after the meeting, even though Mayor Hague had ten Jersey City detectives inside the hall. Although some 70 percent of Federal's 2,000 workers still had not joined the union, those attending the meeting constituted about one-fourth of the workforce. In the following weeks, the union held other organizing meetings at CIO headquarters in Newark in order to reach workers from Kearny, Newark, and Harrison, all towns within Federal Ship's vicinity.[31]

[29] *Shipyard Worker*, Jan. 22, Feb. 26, 1937.

[30] *Shipyard Worker*, Nov. 13, 1936, Feb. 19, March 5, 1937; Bernstein, *Turbulent Years*, p. 426.

[31] IUMSWA, *Proceedings, 3rd National Convention*, Van Gelder Report, Sept. 1937, p. 16; News clipping, newspaper and date unknown, IUMSWA Archives, Series V, Box 50; *Shipyard Worker*, March 5, 1937.

Benjamin Fairless, president of U.S. Steel's Carnegie-Illinois Steel Company, and Philip Murray, head of the CIO's Steel Workers' Organizing Committee (SWOC), signed a preliminary union agreement on March 2 that opened the way for the unionization of U.S. Steel's mills. The IUMSWA's Federal Shipyard drive now began to gain full momentum, riding on the heels of the SWOC's victory. Just a month earlier, the UAW had won its sit-down strike against General Motors in Michigan. Nationally, the union movement had reached a peak, providing ideal organizing conditions at Federal. Shipyard workers began to see their activities as part of this larger movement, with the growth of their own union day by day around the New York port. By March 12, Local 15 at Fletcher Dry Dock and Tietjen-Lang in Hoboken was chartered, establishing the first IUMSWA local on the Jersey side.[32]

In the last months of the Federal Ship campaign, Smith targeted several key groups at the yard. Riveters received the greatest attention in the *Shipyard Worker*, undoubtedly because they were so numerous and were particularly angry over the company's refusal to grant a wage increase. Smith probably considered the riveters a critical group to organize on the ways, because the welders already were solidly with the union. He also focused on shipfitters, chippers and caulkers, and carpenters. The shipfitters had the highest status among shipbuilders, and many, including union activist Frank Mason, were Clydeside veterans. They worked closely with workers from other trades out on the ways and had special responsibilities for the proper placing of plate prior to riveting or electric welding. Shipfitters had to be experienced and highly reliable. Workers of this type proved invaluable to the campaign. In the shops, Mike Smith personally tried to organize the machinists, many of whom were Scottish like him, but he did not make much headway, primarily because the machine shop had become an enclave for the company union. Smith also brought more welders into the yard as volunteer organizers. John Green would send word that welders were available, most likely from New York Ship. Smith met them in Jersey City in the evening, undoubtedly to familiarize them with the organizing situation in the yard, before they were hired by the company at the gate the following morning.[33]

Within a month, a groundswell had developed for the union. At a March 15 meeting attended by some 1,000 workers, Federal Shipyard Local 16 was

[32] Bernstein, *Turbulent Years*, pp. 472–74; Levin letter to Palmer, March 11, 1988; *Shipyard Worker*, Feb. 19, March 12, 1937.

[33] Kaplan interview, Jan. 8, 1983; *Shipyard Worker*, Jan. 22, March 26, 1937; Van Gelder to Mike Smith, April 14, 1937, IUMSWA Archives, Series V, Box 50. In contrast to recent practices, most CIO volunteer inside organizers began promoting the union almost immediately after they were hired, as Andy Reeder (Sun Ship and Federal), Don Bollen (Fore River), and Al Petit-Clair and Lou Kaplan (Federal) confirmed.

chartered and local officers were elected, including Deans as president and Turoczy as financial secretary (the two top positions). Within a week, the union claimed that 2,000 of the yard's 2,500 workers had joined. Neither the intimidation of Jersey City's Mayor Hague nor the Kearny town government's efforts to ban leafleting at the shipyard gates could stop the drive. In March, Hague's police simply stood at a distance while workers paid organizers a penny a piece for leaflets, thereby circumventing the Kearny anti-solicitation ordinance. Smith made organizing easier in April by setting up a second temporary union office in Newark, in addition to the regular one in Jersey City. While union meetings for Local 15, Hoboken, had to be held in neighboring Union City because of police harassment, Local 16 met in Jersey City for the most part and did not seem to have these problems, perhaps because so many workers from the Federal yard attended union functions.[34]

On April 8, when John Green asked SWOC chairman Philip Murray for assistance, the IUMSWA was ready for the showdown with Federal Shipbuilding president Lynn Korndorff. In reply, Murray told Green that he should deal directly with Federal's management, underscoring the independence of the IUMSWA's campaign at Federal from SWOC's steel industry drive. A week later, Green told Korndorff that a majority of the employees now belonged to Local 16 and requested a meeting at the earliest possible date. Korndorff agreed to talk with the union.[35]

At this point the union had everything in place. A large majority of the workforce had signed up as members, and volunteer organizers had jobs inside the yard—especially among the young firebrand welders. The union was holding regular membership meetings, members had elected a local union executive board as well as shop stewards in key departments, and these departments were beginning to have their own shop meetings. Workers also openly wore their union buttons at work. Most important, the union was ready to take over the company union, the Employee Representation Plan, from the inside. The SWOC used this tactic extensively in steel during late 1936, but the IUMSWA had pioneered the approach three years earlier, when Mullin and Purkis commandeered New York Ship's company union for Green's new, independent union. At Federal Ship the workers overwhelmingly backed the IUMSWA, so the union could safely use this tactic once again. On April 21, Van Gelder

[34] *Shipyard Worker*, March 26, April 16, 1937; M. H. Goldstein to Samuel L. Rothbard, April 3, 1937, IUMSWA Archives, Series V, Box 50.

[35] Green to Philip Murray, April 8, 1937; Murray to Green, April 10, 1937; Van Gelder to Green, April 15, 1937; Green to Korndorff, c. April 1937; Korndorff to Green, April 20, 1937; all IUMSWA Archives, Series V, Box 50.

wired Smith to "go ahead with the company union plan." When the company union held elections for representatives a few days later, IUMSWA candidates won all vacant posts, giving them a majority in the leadership. The IUMSWA even defeated the president of the company union.[36]

Korndorff and Industrial Relations Manager James H. Love met on April 26 with Local 16 negotiating representatives Deans, Turoczy, and Strainga and national staff representatives Van Gelder and Smith. Simultaneously, the Works Council, the governing body of the ERP, held a special meeting. Pro IUMSWA Works Council representatives offered two resolutions, both carefully prepared by the union attorney, M. H. Goldstein. The first declared the company union illegal for bargaining purposes, because the "Industrial Union" represented the majority of Federal Ship workers. The second stated that the company union was dissolved "immediately and for all time." The motions passed by a vote of eight to two. "Mass resignations" from the company union then followed, and the Works Council's chairman notified management of these actions. Admitting defeat, Korndorff posted yard notices the next day announcing that the Works Council would no longer be funded by the company and that no more elections would be held.[37]

At the separate April 26 meeting with Korndorff, the union presented three preliminary demands: recognition of IUMSWA Local 16 as the sole collective bargaining agent for the shipyard; negotiations over wages, hours, and working conditions to begin within seven days; and agreement to a written contract. Korndorff turned down the first point categorically, stating that *exclusive* recognition "would deny the rights of employees who may belong to other organizations, and of individual employees." Although this issue was not resolved until an NLRB election three years later, Korndorff did start to negotiate.[38]

By May 6, Local 16 had submitted a list of 15 contract demands, with recognition as sole bargaining agent at the top. For two weeks the talks made little progress. Local 16 members finally decided to stage a two-hour sit-down on May 17 as a show of strength. The strike began on the ways, where four naval vessels were under construction, and then spread throughout the yard. The

[36] *Shipyard Worker*, April 2, 16, 23, 1937; Bernstein, *Turbulent Years*, pp. 455–57; Van Gelder to Smith, April 21, 1937, IUMSWA Archives, Series V, Box 50.

[37] *Shipyard Worker*, April 30, 1937. Chairman of Federal Shipbuilding Employee Representation Plan to Korndorff, April 26, 1937; Local 16 resolutions for April 26, 1937, meeting written by Goldstein; Van Gelder to Smith, April 15, 1937; Green to Smith, April 19, 1937; Van Gelder to Smith, April 21, 1937; Korndorff to Van Gelder, April 26, 1937; Goldstein to Van Gelder, April 29, 1937; all IUMSWA Archives, Series V, Box 50.

[38] *Shipyard Worker*, April 30, 1937. Korndorff to Van Gelder, April 26; Van Gelder to Korndorff, April 27; Goldstein to Van Gelder, April 29, 1937; all IUMSWA Archives, Series V, Box 50.

only open resistance to the action came from some inside machinists in Department 66, who claimed to be members of the Shipyard Employees Association (SEA). This new company union had been formed after workers disbanded the ERP.[39]

On the following morning, the company fired truck driver and Local 16 member Frank O'Brien, igniting a second sit-down. Management responded by closing the plant. Angry workers then marched over to the machine shop to deal directly with the anti-union SEA men. Smith and Local 16 officers, who were in negotiations and had heard the yard's closing whistle, got word of this action. They entered the plant and persuaded the workers to march out of the yard en masse, thus avoiding a potentially serious confrontation at the machine shop. Management then shut off the yard's power and closed for the day.[40]

At a special union meeting in Jersey City that afternoon, some 1,900 workers of many nationalities, and including black as well as white workers, voted to strike. Van Gelder was present at the vote and gave immediate strike authorization from the national union. Local 16 leaders then set up a mass picket of almost 2,000 men during the shift changes and some 200 during work hours. As in Camden two years earlier, a marine picket guarded port entrances, in this case along the Hackensack River.[41]

When organizer John W. Brown arrived in Kearny to help with the strike, he was amazed at the fighting spirit of Federal Shipyard workers compared to the oppressive resignation of those at Bath Ironworks Shipyard in Maine, which unfortunately was characteristic of much of New England. To Brown, the Federal strike mirrored the political promise of the American Revolution and was proof of the unifying power of industrial unionism's egalitarianism. Once again the IUMSWA's industrial union organizing was characterized as an "American" struggle of "citizens" for their rights. In Brown's words,

> It took just three and one-half working days, with a solidified united front; not a Judas in the ranks nor a scab in the rear, in which 2500 men stood as one man, and compelled this subsidiary of the mammoth United [States] Steel Corporation to agree to the ideals and principles of the Industrial Union of Marine and Shipbuilding Workers of America.
>
> There were no boisterous remarks, no vile or vulgar language, and no disorder. Men of a dozen different nationalities, black men and white men, first-class mechanics, helpers, handymen, apprentices and unskilled laborers

---

[39] *Shipyard Worker*, May 7, 21, 1937; *New York Times*, May 19, 1937, p. 14.
[40] *Shipyard Worker*, May 7, 21, 1937; *New York Times*, May 19, 1937, p. 14.
[41] *Shipyard Worker*, May 7, 21, 1937; *New York Times*, May 19, 1937, p. 14.

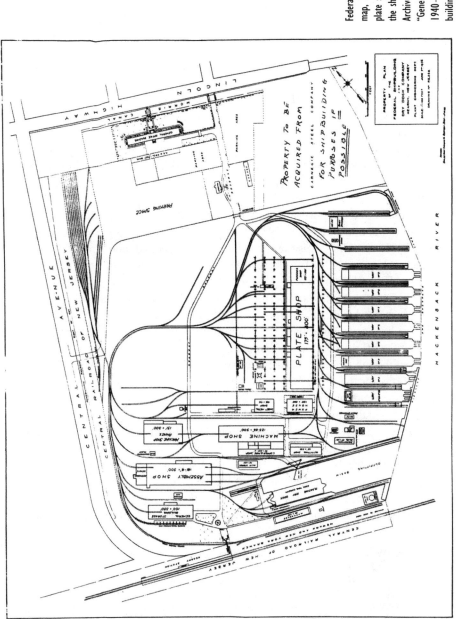

Federal Shipyard plant layout map, 1936. Note how the plate shop is adjacent to all of the shipways. *Source:* National Archives, RG 19, Box 452, "General Correspondence, 1940–1945," "Federal Shipbuilding and Dry Dock Co."

marched shoulder to shoulder in orderly lawful procession in the exercise of their sovereign rights as citizens of the United States . . . [E]very man put his heels down and with head erect and soul serene, with eyes beaming in a new light and conscious of the justness of their cause they marched back and forth, back and forth, like Washington's sentinels at Valley Forge when the great American republic was yet in the making.[42]

After three days, the mass pressure succeeded, and on May 22, Korndorff signed a contract with Local 16. He did not accept a union shop, but he verbally agreed to let the IUMSWA be the exclusive bargaining agent, a promise workers soon discovered was meaningless. Although the union failed to win a general wage increase, the company did establish a minimum wage and a grievance procedure. Overall, the agreement resembled the model contract the SWOC had signed with U.S. Steel's Carnegie-Illinois Company. For a first contract it was a sizable victory.[43]

In yards around the port of New York, the IUMSWA signed contracts at the rate of about one a month in 1937, with Federal Ship the biggest victory. Nationally, Federal Ship was the second largest and second most important yard organized by the IUMSWA during the 1930s, after New York Ship. Employment at Federal Ship grew rapidly, with over 1,000 new workers hired during the 1937 campaign; at various times in the late 1930s, employment at Federal even surpassed that at New York Ship. With the IUMSWA victory at Federal Ship, a new organizing base had been built in New York–North Jersey that rivaled the original success in Camden.[44]

Even though the national strike wave of 1937 had created highly favorable conditions for the drive, IUMSWA Secretary-Treasurer Van Gelder believed that Mike Smith deserved major credit for his leadership of the campaign. At the union's national convention in the fall, he declared that "Smith's work in building up Local 16 was as good a piece of single handed organizing work as has ever been done in this Union; and it should also be noted that insofar as North Jersey has been opened up for unionism, the IUMSWA did it, for we staged the first general distribution of literature there, and conducted the first mass picket line in the history of Hague's back yard."[45]

Although the national officers and Local 16 recognized Smith as an out-

---

[42] John W. Brown, "Workers Should Know—Asses Could become Lions," *Shipyard Worker*, May 20, 1937.

[43] *Shipyard Worker*, May 28, 1937; Agreement between Federal Shipbuilding Corp. and IUMSWA Local 16, May 22, 1937, IUMSWA Archives, Series V, Box 50.

[44] IUMSWA, *Proceedings, 3rd National Convention*, Van Gelder Report, Sept. 1937, p. 16.

[45] Ibid.

standing organizer, Green now assumed primary responsibility for enforcing the contract at Federal Ship, because the yard had become a critical power bloc within the IUMSWA. He soon discovered that workers felt a greater loyalty to Smith than to the national office, and as a consequence, a power struggle developed between the local and national levels, with Smith caught in the middle. By the end of May 1937, Local 16 was ready for the next organizing stage: increasing the union's membership, building a stable local organization, and implementing the first contract. The way that Local 16 workers carried this out created a major rift over the course of organizing strategy taken by the national union.

CHAPTER 5

Direct Action and the Limits
of Local Union Democracy:
Organizing Federal Ship, 1937–1938

Although IUMSWA Local 16 had won its first contract at the Federal Ship-yard, union-building at Kearny, New Jersey, had not yet gone beyond the second phase, complete organization of the yard. Trade unionists confronted an "endless daily fight for Union recognition and respect," former welding steward Nat Levin recalled. While the company recognized the union on paper, it maintained an anti-union policy that was only aggravated further by "the arrogance of L[ynn] H. Korndorff, president of Federal." Under such conditions, union activists relied on direct action to force the company to bargain in good faith. Over the next three years, workers waged what amounted to a continuous guerrilla war for their rights on the job.[1]

This stage of union organizing was shaped by the dynamics of a growing struggle for power between Local 16 and the national office. The heart of the controversy centered on the national officers' efforts to centralize IUMSWA leadership and policy. Many in Local 16, however, favored an emphasis on autonomy and membership democracy. They believed that contract enforcement depended not just on formal, contractual mechanisms but also on direct action. Local leaders had to mobilize workers, not merely represent them, if Federal Ship was to be fully organized. Activists relied on the grievance procedure whenever possible, but they turned to sit-downs, slow-downs, and even sabotage when they had exhausted the legal remedies available to them. At virtually every turn, those who led the ongoing skirmishes with management encountered opposition to direct action tactics from the IUMSWA's national

---

[1] Nat Levin letter to David Palmer, March 11, 1988.

officers, particularly President John Green. These shop-level leaders took risks and succeeded in winning substantial gains for workers in the process. As a result of their efforts, IUMSWA Local 16 remained viable through these difficult years.

The 1935 strike at New York Ship had been instrumental for consolidating the organization of IUMSWA Local 1. Kearny Local 16 won its first contract through an equally massive, but very short and peaceful, strike. While thousands of workers were mobilized, the strike at Federal Ship did not last long enough to allow organizers to educate workers or to develop a disciplined internal union structure comparable to the one that had emerged at New York Ship during the long strike of 1935. Nevertheless, the Kearny organizers could afford to be somewhat methodical in establishing Local 16's leadership, for they enjoyed substantial outside assistance from the national IUMSWA, as well as the moral backing of the CIO and a revived labor movement. Many of Kearny's new leaders were workers who led job actions ("direct actions," as the activists called them) *after* the signing of the May contract.

The CIO strike movement had a significant influence on Federal Shipyard trade unionists in 1937. Not only were there hundreds of sit-down strikes around the country, but shipyard workers in the New York harbor area staged a huge, port-wide strike. New York City had some of the nation's most militant left-led industrial unions, including the Transport Workers Union, the National Maritime Union, and the United Electrical Workers, all of which had a powerful influence in the surrounding area. The New York City–North Jersey region was perhaps the most important industrial-commercial concentration in the United States in 1937, especially in terms of industrial diversity, volume of trade, population, and number of trade union members. As late as the 1980s, it still was the most unionized region in the nation. The Federal shipyard in Kearny was located at the hub of this huge industrial-commercial network.[2]

Events during the summer of 1937 proved to be a watershed for John Green and the IUMSWA, as the shipyard union president turned toward a modern variant of business unionism while encountering problems with rebellious local unionists at the Federal yard and elsewhere.[3] Although Green saw advan-

---

[2] For union density between the 1930s and 1980s, see Leo Troy, "The Rise and Fall of American Trade Unions: The Labor Movement from FDR to RR," in Seymour M. Lipset, ed., *Unions in Transition* (San Francisco: ISC Press, 1986), pp. 75–109, esp. 84–85.

[3] For a discussion of American business unionism in its earlier AFL form, see the favorable assessment by Philip Taft, "On the Origins of Business Unionism," *Industrial and Labor Relations Review* 17 (Oct. 1963) 20–33, and the highly critical evaluation by Philip Foner in *History of the Labor Movement in the United States*, vol. 3, *The Politics and Practices of the American Federation of Labor, 1900–1909* (New York: International Publishers, 1964).

tages in utilizing new government labor relations bodies and laws on the IUMSWA's behalf, the National Labor Relations Board (NLRB) was not the main mechanism on which the IUMSWA national office relied for organizing, consolidation, and dispute resolution during 1937. Green increasingly relied on private-sector–based union-management conferences, arbitration, and negotiated settlements, believing them more effective than strikes and job actions. Rank-and-file activists grew impatient with this strategy. Although the Supreme Court had ruled that the Wagner Act was constitutional, administrative enforcement of the Act in the field involved a protracted legal struggle and often did little in the short term to advance broad-based local organizing. Private-sector alternatives also had their limitations, which pushed local activists to take matters into their own hands. The driving force for local organizing and consolidation in the shipyards of New York harbor came not from the newly evolving legal code and jurisdiction of the NLRA and NLRB but from the actions of workers in the yards who created their own enforcement mechanism. The IUMSWA's national office, led by Green, believed that these rank-and-file–based, direct action tactics jeopardized the union's standing.[4]

The strike of 15,000 shipyard workers that engulfed the New York port during the third week of June marked the initial turning point, forcing national officers Green and Van Gelder to take a tougher stand on central direction of the union. Green and Van Gelder assumed full direction of the strike only after it had spread throughout the harbor region and created a crisis situation for the union. At the same time, they faced other serious problems. More wildcat strikes erupted in the Kearny yard, even though workers had a union contract and were not part of the general strike.[5]

A major campaign to organize repair yards in the port of New York, led by staff organizers Charlie Purkis and Mike Smith, took shape during 1937, beginning at United's Staten Island shipyard, where the IUMSWA had a year-old agreement. Repairmen there had not joined the union, even though all work-

---

[4] This analysis is influenced by social movement theory that emphasizes the centrality of local activity for organizing. See, for example, Aldon Morris, *The Origins of the Civil Rights Movement: Black Communities Organizing for Change* (New York: Free Press, 1985). In contrast to those writing on civil rights and other movements, labor historians have tended to interpret the CIO and the movement around it within institutional, legal, or cultural frameworks rather than through the perspectives taken by union organizers. See, for example, Howell Harris, *The Right to Manage: Industrial Relations Policies of American Business in the 1940s* (Madison: University of Wisconsin Press, 1982); David Brody, "The Emergence of Mass-Production Unionism," in Brody, *Workers in Industrial America* (New York: Oxford University Press, 1980), pp. 82–119.

[5] *Shipyard Worker*, June 18, 1937.

Table 3. IUMSWA Locals Organized in the Port of New York, Feb. 1936–May 1937

Local	Location	Company	Charter Date	Type
12	Staten Island	Staten Island Shipbuilding †	02-11-36	c, r
13	Brooklyn	Robins ‡ and others	11-11-36	r
15	Hoboken, N.J.	Tietjen-Lang ‡, Fletcher †, others	03-12-37	r
16	Kearny, N.J.	Federal Shipbuilding	03-19-37	c
20	Weehawken, N.J.	misc. small repair yards	05-12-37	r
21	Brooklyn	Navy Yard	05-19-37	c, r
22	Chelsea, N.Y.C.	shore gangs	05-26-37	l

Type of yard or job site (main production):
  r repair yard
  c construction yard
  l laborers' work cleaning docked ships (non-shipbuilding)
Ownership:
  † owned by United
  ‡ owned by Todd
Sources: IUMSWA, *Proceedings, 3rd National Convention,* Sept. 1937, p. 8; IUMSWA, *Proceedings, 2nd National Convention,* Report of Secretary Phil Van Gelder, Aug. 1936, p. 8.

ers technically were covered by the agreement. The IUMSWA decided to organize them into a single unit so their specific needs could be addressed, and from there the drive spread to other repair yards.[6]

By the end of May 1937, the IUMSWA had reached new strength, with seven locals chartered in the New York harbor area (Table 3). The union then sought to bargain for a single agreement covering all private shipyards in the port. The overwhelming majority of these yards did dry dock (repair) work. Local 12 at Staten Island became the de facto leader of port-wide negotiation efforts in June because the companies where the new locals were situated did not recognize the IUMSWA. When United unilaterally raised wage rates at the Staten Island yard to an average of 98 cents an hour, other yards immediately did the same. Talks at Staten Island reached an impasse when local IUMSWA leaders continued to demand $1.25, precipitating the strike. On June 10, Staten Island workers walked out. The yard's local leadership called the strike without authorization from the union's national office, but Van Gelder gave his approval when he heard what had occurred.[7]

---

[6] IUMSWA, *Proceedings, 3rd National Convention,* Sept. 1937, National Officers' Organization Report, pp. 16–18, undoubtedly written by Van Gelder. Agreement between United Shipyards, Inc. [Staten Island only] and IUMSWA, June 4, 1936, in possession of Van Gelder.

[7] IUMSWA, *Proceedings, 3rd National Convention,* pp. 16–18.

Arriving from Camden, Van Gelder took personal charge of the situation and immediately notified Purkis that United's other yards in Brooklyn and Hoboken (but *only* this company's yards) should join the strike. Unexpectedly, Hoboken Local 15 voted to strike Todd's Tietjen-Lang yard as well. Two days later, Brooklyn Local 13 followed suit, voting to strike Todd as well as United. This development made the situation unusually difficult for the IUMSWA, because Todd and United could now join forces to combat the strike. By June 14 the walkout had spread to almost every port yard, including many of the smaller, independent ones. Van Gelder had hoped to confine the strike to the yards of one company, but by mid-June he had to deal with a general shipbuilding strike in the port. While United at least sat down at the negotiating table, Todd would not even talk to the union. It was as ambitious for organizers to contest Todd, the nation's leading ship repair company, as it was to challenge Bethlehem Shipbuilding in the construction yards, where no breakthroughs had been made. Nevertheless, Van Gelder was optimistic that the union would prevail and recognized the importance of the struggle there. As he stated to the IUMSWA convention "the Todd Corporation is the largest factor in the repair industry nationally, and New York is the key spot."[8]

Van Gelder and Green took personal charge of the strikes in Brooklyn after Purkis became ill, while Smith handled those in Hoboken. The "general strike" strategy for the port, which was smaller in scale than Van Gelder's failed 1935 idea for a national "general strike" in shipbuilding, now appeared viable to both local leaders and the IUMSWA's national officers. Van Gelder promoted this strategy as late as the fifth week of the strike, when he told other IUMSWA locals

> We have tied up the port as it has never been tied before and there are only three yards where a few strikebreakers are going in. . . . The New York strike will be of tremendous consequence to this Union throughout the country as there are more shipyards in this port than in any other single place throughout the United States. We have a hard fight on our hands there and we must all get behind it and make it a victory, because whatever is won in New York will react to the benefit of all other Locals.

He saw the port strike as a "history making fight" and expected that "a victory in New York will give us a strangle hold on the key point of the whole industry."[9]

---

[8] Ibid., pp. 16–20.

[9] Ibid., p. 17; Van Gelder to Local 1, Camden, July 12, 1937, IUMSWA Archives, Series V, Box 1, Special Collections, University of Maryland at College Park Libraries.

Van Gelder soon discovered that there were serious flaws in how the strike was being conducted. The first problem was the lack of adequate preparation. Local IUMSWA leaders had not tried to negotiate with the Todd yards until *after* the general strike was already underway. Bad timing also hurt the strike; the walkout occurred at the beginning of the slack season for repair yards. A third weakness was the lack of central leadership for the strike. The national officers tried to take charge after the fact, but events overwhelmed them. By the time Van Gelder stepped into the picture, area locals were demanding that all yards stay out until every yard had a signed agreement. Van Gelder and Green wanted to settle wherever possible, but they failed to develop a consensus for this position among local leaders. Sharp differences emerged between the national officers and a new staff organizer from a local repair yard, which soon turned a number of local leaders and union members against the two national officers.[10]

The most serious weaknesses were the absence of solid trade union organization and leadership, insufficient strike funds, and an underestimation of the ruthlessness of the big shipbuilding companies. According to Van Gelder, the Robins yard in particular "was less than half organized, and nobody knew it." Furthermore, "in all three Locals there was a lack of secondary leadership; that is, competent or experienced members for the food committees, relief committees, legal defense, finances, etc." Poor leadership, he believed, was a grave danger to the union and honest union members. "A considerable number of the choices for these vital posts later turned out to be scabs, stool pigeons, professional finks, dishonest self-seekers, or plain incompetents, and they seriously hampered the efforts of the good and conscientious workers who were trying to win the strike."[11]

By early July, management organized a powerful back-to-work movement, first at Todd and then at United. Todd's Robins plant reopened under heavy police protection, despite mass picketing. A week later United did the same at the Staten Island yard. Throughout July, 12,000 workers remained on strike at twenty-five yards in the port region. Van Gelder observed, "the police department was completely at the disposal of the employers, and nobody saw it." Local governments' support for employers in the New York port made the situation quite different from that in Camden two years earlier. Police repression became fierce, while the union's financial resources dwindled to almost nothing.[12]

By this time the national staff was stretched to the breaking point. The union

[10] IUMSWA, *Proceedings, 3rd National Convention*, pp. 17–18, 22–23.
[11] Ibid., pp. 22–23.
[12] Ibid., pp. 18, 22; *New York Times*, July 9, 11, 13, 14, 1936.

had assigned five staff organizers to the strike. They were joined by Green, Van Gelder, and attorney Goldstein, who worked virtually full-time around New York. To finance this operation, the CIO (through the UMW) provided two loans totaling $10,000, and the Camden local made substantial contributions. Van Gelder estimated that the strike was costing the union about $1,000 a day. Over 100 workers had been arrested, and many had to pay a high bail to be released. Police violence escalated dramatically in response to the large groups of pickets who stoned scabs and their police escorts at the shipyard gates. On July 16, Brooklyn police arrested two workers on the picket line at the Robins yard, took them to another location, and then brutally beat them. These tactics undoubtedly instilled fear in many workers. From this point on, support for the strike gradually eroded.[13]

Four days before the beating of the two Robins yard workers, a New York supreme court justice issued an injunction against IUMSWA picketing. Ongoing hearings before the regional NLRB did nothing to improve the situation for the union. Local political leaders offered no assistance, despite the progressive reputation of such city officials as Mayor Fiorello La Guardia. Many of the workers in the New York port's repair yards were transient, unlike shipyard workers in Camden, and they lacked the strong community ties that might have influenced local politicians. On the other hand, the management at Todd and United, the largest repair yard companies in the harbor, appear to have had significant influence on local government officials.[14]

By August, Van Gelder and Green realized that strikers at the major repair yards were exhausted and that the national union's finances would be in serious trouble unless they terminated the walkout. The choice, as they saw it, was to continue the strike and possibly lose everything, or return to work and at least maintain some organization inside the port's yards. They managed to persuade a majority of workers in the port that the strike should be ended, but in Brooklyn Local 13 a vocal minority was determined to continue the strike. Van Gelder later reported that "certain self-styled leaders of the rank and file, including Organizer Hecht . . . in direct defiance of the National Officers and the Local vote, continued the picketing next morning and sent delegates to Staten Island and Hoboken in an effort to persuade them to stay out on strike. They also approached the National Maritime Union for support in their campaign, but without success."[15]

Under the circumstances, the national office believed that tough action had

[13] IUMSWA, *Proceedings, 3rd National Convention*, pp. 17–18; *New York Times*, July 9, 11, 13, 14, 17, 18, 20, 23, 27, 1936.
[14] IUMSWA, *Proceedings, 3rd National Convention*, p. 18; *Shipyard Worker*, July 21, Aug. 20, 1937.
[15] IUMSWA, *Proceedings, 3rd National Convention*, p. 18.

to be taken against dissenters in order to avoid the complete destruction of union organization in the port. Van Gelder and Green easily extinguished the dissident movement, but their victory did not alter the fundamentally rebellious and independent character of New York port workers. While the dissidents had shown bad judgment, their defiant spirit would be needed if organizing were to succeed in the future.

The AFL remained a highly visible force in the port of New York, particularly through Joseph Ryan's corrupt International Longshoremen's Association (ILA). Ryan and the AFL made some inroads into shipbuilding on the heels of the IUMSWA strike, but their gains were shortlived. The ILA and the AFL Metal Trades Council had actively promoted strikebreaking by their members during the shipyard walkout, and the Boilermakers even brought in scabs from Galveston, Texas. Ryan signed a sweetheart contract with Staten Island once the IUMSWA called off the strike, but those workers who joined the AFL soon returned to the IUMSWA. Despite the temporary defeat of the port strike, the IUMSWA retained a viable, though weakened, organizational base in the New York yards. Through Local 22, which represented the Chelsea (Manhattan) shore gangs, the IUMSWA even began to challenge Ryan's ILA on the docks.[16]

The 1937 strike was not a complete loss, even though Van Gelder's harsh critique gave that impression. The smaller, independent yards settled with the union; twelve agreements were signed by the fall. Workers in the repair yards expanded the ranks of the IUMSWA beyond Federal Shipbuilding. The port of New York had more shipyard workers covered under signed contracts than any other region of the United States. The losses at the major Todd and United yards, which appeared to be so devastating in 1937, were recovered within two years.[17]

By late 1937, the membership base of the IUMSWA had shifted from its early concentration at New York Ship in Camden to a more even distribution between the ports of Philadelphia and New York, as indicated by the number of delegates to the union's national conventions over the decade (Table 4). At

---

[16] IUMSWA, *Proceedings, 3rd National Convention,* p. 18; *Shipyard Worker,* July 16, 23, Aug. 6, 20, 27, 1937.

[17] IUMSWA, *Proceedings, 3rd National Convention,* p. 9; *Proceedings, 5th National Convention,* Sept. 8–11, 1939, "List of Delegates." When Van Gelder spoke with me, he was reluctant to call the strike a "failure," thus disagreeing with Mergen's assessment in "A History of the Industrial Union of Marine and Shipbuilding Workers of America" (Ph.D. diss., University of Pennsylvania, 1968). Mergen did not interview Van Gelder or any other IUMSWA leaders, and his dissertation does not discuss the 1937 New York port strike in any detail. But Mergen did make extensive use of IUMSWA documents, then still in the union's Camden headquarters, and his study is very useful for a general understanding of the union's national administrative policy and for details on a number of local union affairs.

Table 4. Delegates to IUMSWA National Conventions by Region, 1934–1946

Year	N.Y. Harbor	Camden/ Philadelphia*	New England	South	Baltimore	Pacific
1934	0	46	8	0	0	0
1936	0	45	13	0	0	0
1937	30	26	3	2	1	2
1938	19	22	5	0	1	6**
1939	18	26	2***	2	6	5**
1940	22	38	1	2	4	2
1941	56	58	5	5	11	7**
1942	99	100	14	4	27	12**
1943	133	224	29	8	81	28
1944	153	287	49	20	58	20**
1946 (Jan.)	162	259	53	9	58	22
1946 (Sept.)	147	155	22	11	42	11

* Includes yards in Philadelphia, Chester, and Wilmington, all on the Delaware River.

** In 1938, 2 organizers held 6 votes, representing 4 West Coast locals; in 1939, 1 delegate had 5 votes, for 2 locals; in 1941, 3 delegates from San Pedro had 5 votes; in 1942 and 1944, all Pacific region delegates came from San Pedro.

*** Both Fore River (Hicks-absent; and organizer Koch-present).

Other regions include: *Great Lakes*: 1942: 12; 1943: 9; 1944: 12; 1946 (Jan.): 3; *Ohio River*: 1944: 32; 1946 (Jan.): 11; 1946 (Sept.): 7.

GEB members are not included; most came from New York Shipyard during the 1930s. Alternate delegates also are not included.

Source: IUMSWA, *Proceedings of National Conventions, 1934–46.*

the 1937 convention, the New York area had the greatest number of delegates, with seven locals represented; the Delaware River region had slightly fewer delegates and three locals, including Local 1. The delegates from New York Ship still represented the largest number of union members from a single yard. A majority of GEB members came from Local 1, which allowed the founding local to retain its power over the recently established locals in New York and North Jersey. The 1937 strike in New York Harbor reduced that region's delegate strength from 1938 to 1940, but when these delegates allied with delegates from New England and the Pacific region (who frequently took positions independent from Local 1), the core New York Harbor local at Federal Ship represented a threat to Local 1's dominant position in the IUMSWA. By 1941, locals in the New York Harbor region had achieved a rough parity with those in the Camden/Philadelphia region. The locals at Federal Ship and New York Ship now held the balance of power in the national union. By 1943, however, corruption and incompetence almost destroyed the Federal Ship local, which returned the advantage to Local 1. Nevertheless, 1937 represented a turning point for the national IUMSWA, primarily because of the successful drive at

Federal Ship and the union's ability to survive the New York port strike. The shipyard union had genuinely become a national organization.[18]

Shipyard workers at Federal Shipbuilding in North Jersey did not join the New York Harbor strike, but during the months when thousands of others walked picket lines outside area shipyards, workers in the Kearny yard engaged in a series of job actions to enforce their new contract. These limited strikes inside Federal Ship pitted local trade unionists not only against the company but eventually against John Green and national IUMSWA policy. Organizing and consolidating the union at Federal Ship during the second half of 1937 raised the same problems of democracy and centralization that were highlighted so dramatically by the far larger port strike.

The strikes at Federal Ship were not plant-wide actions, but were directed at specific departments. Organization was concentrated in the steel trades, particularly in the plate shop (Department 32) and among the welders and burners (Department 44). Some of the toughest work in the shipyard could be found in these locations, and it was from here that many of the early leaders of Local 16 came. Many younger men were welders and burners who felt they had little to lose by taking a stand for their union rights. This group became one of the main sources for leaders in the shipyard labor movement. Older, more experienced men in these departments, such as shipfitters and riveters, also played prominent leadership roles. These two age groups, combining youthful daring and older leadership capability, were the force that drove the sit-down movement.[19]

Trouble began at the Federal yard almost immediately after the union agreement was signed, when management recognized and began bargaining with the newly formed company union, the Shipbuilding Employees Association (SEA). Although company president Korndorff sought to give the impression that he would deal fairly with both the IUMSWA and the SEA, he had no in-

---

[18] Delegate lists: IUMSWA, Convention *Proceedings*, 1st (1934), 2nd (1936), 3rd (1937), 4th (1938), 5th (1939), 6th (1940), 7th (1941).

[19] Andy Reeder interview, May 21, 1988, Wilmington, Del. The distinction between the union leadership of the early 1930s and that of the late 1930s and the shift from craft to mass production trade union leaders have not been emphasized enough by labor historians. For analyses that stress the craft character of early industrial union leaders, see Ronald L. Filippelli, "UE: The Formative Years, 1933–1937," *Labor History* 17 (1976) 351–71; Ronald Schatz, "Union Pioneers: The Founders of Local Unions at General Electric and Westinghouse, 1933–1937," *Journal of American History* 66 (1979) 586–602; and Roger Keeran, *The Communist Party and the Auto Workers Unions*, (Bloomington: University of Indiana Press, 1980). For a contrasting analysis that considers leadership in sit-down activity in terms of mass production technology and resultant "new" skills, see Daniel Nelson, "Origins of the Sit-Down Era: Worker Militancy and Innovation in the Rubber Industry, 1934–1938," *Labor History* 23 (1982) 198–225; and Daniel Nelson, *American Rubber Workers and Organized Labor, 1900–1941* (Princeton: Princeton University Press, 1988).

tention of acting quickly on IUMSWA grievances, while the SEA made no real demands on management. In response, plate shop workers initiated a half-hour sit-down strike in their area on June 4 to protest the company's refusal to adjust crane operators' wage rates. Like other sit-downs at Federal Ship during these months, this strike was confined to a specific department rather than being plant-wide. But it was, nonetheless, a sympathy strike, a militant direct action taken by shop workers in support of skilled workers who worked both within and outside of their area, indicating high levels of solidarity across job classifications. Over the next few months, three more sit-downs broke out, each aimed at a specific grievance.[20]

When the first work stoppage hit the yard, Federal Ship's industrial relations manager, James H. Love, immediately contacted the national IUMSWA's president, John Green, in Camden. Love stated management's desire "to be cooperative," but he insisted that "one of the first essentials to that end is for both parties to abide absolutely by the routine and measures set up in our arrangement for handling grievances." Green assured Love that he was opposed to such unauthorized job actions and he hoped that "no more instances of this sort eventuate." As the administrator of a growing, but fragile, national trade union organization, Green sought to implement more stabilizing and moderate union policies.[21]

Green made this decision to back management's opposition to direct action on the shop floor within a broader context of shifting trade union values and leadership structure. Concentration of decision-making in the hands of a few key leaders proved crucial for conducting and winning the 1935 New York Ship strike, even though Local 1 members ratified all important decisions. This approach, formerly confined to crisis situations, now became standard operating procedure. A remarkable disparity emerged between Green's public words (such as his speeches in the *Shipyard Worker*) and his behind-the-scenes actions. The IUMSWA's continued advocacy of industrial unionism based on rank-and-file democracy had tremendous appeal to shipyard workers, many of whom revered Green as the founder of industrial unionism in shipbuilding. The union's revised 1936 constitution reflected this sentiment in its new preamble, which read in part: "The Industrial Union of Marine and Shipbuilding Workers of America advocates and practices the program and tactics of militant industrial unionism, based on the principle of One Industry—One Union. . . . It bases itself upon the principle of rank and file control,

---

[20] Korndorff to Oscar Greenberg (SEA counsel), May 25, 1937; James Love to Green, June 7, 1937; Robert P. Brecht ("impartial umpire"), "Case Involving Present Status of [IUMSWA Local 16] Agreement, Decision No. 1," Sept. 10, 1937; all IUMSWA Archives, Series V, Box 50.

[21] Love to Green, June 7, 1937; Green to Love, June 9, 1937; both IUMSWA Archives, Series V, Box 50.

unrestricted trade-union democracy, and at all times an aggressive struggle for an ever higher standard of living." By mid-1937, however, Green feared that the uncertain, often chaotic character of democratic union action was a potential threat to his leadership, to the centrally directed strategy of the national union, and to the organization's growing alliance with the Democratic Party. He opted instead for the certainty of a stable, bureaucratic structure and a top-down line of command from the Camden office. But his *public* words rarely indicated that he operated this way.[22]

When shop-level leaders at Federal defied Green's tactical conservatism, they created a vitality and fighting spirit in Local 16 that contributed to much of its early growth. Capable leaders such as Alex Turoczy and Nat Levin, who initiated job actions when necessary, generally kept the militant tactics of rank-and-filers within realistic bounds. Levin taught the militant welders under him that diplomacy, not just direct action, was often required to win. As welder Andy Reeder recalled, Levin told his men that a good trade unionist had to know how to maneuver and when to compromise, and did not just act out of anger.[23]

The rank-and-file leaders who initiated the tactic of direct action connected it with building shop-level organization, encompassing shop stewards, shop committees, and department-level meetings. While the national union promoted these forms of organization through its publications and policies, actually establishing them in a yard was far more difficult. The shop steward system, which was used by the IUMSWA at New York Ship as early as 1933, originated in the British Isles, including the Clydeside in Scotland, and was particularly strong in munitions, shipbuilding, and coal mining. John Green and his fellow Scotsmen, most of whom were skilled shop tradesmen and shipfitters, had first-hand experience with it during the First World War before they emigrated. The shop steward system also had roots in the American AFL craft unions, including those in the shipyards prior to the 1920s. The organizational outlook of the Scottish shipyard workers, however, was generally syndicalist rather than craft-based. The Scottish version of shop-level organization tended to be closer to industrial unionism because of its radical and egalitarian character, even though craft union divisions existed within the Scottish shipyards. The industrial character of their movement gave the Scottish shop stewards greater power during World War I than their American counterparts were able to attain.[24]

[22] Constitution of IUMSWA, as amended Aug. 22, 1936. This preamble remained in effect until 1966.

[23] Reeder interview, May 21, 1988.

[24] See James Hinton, *The First Shop Steward Movement* (London: George Allen and Unwin, 1973); and G. D. H. Cole, *Trade Unionism and Munitions* (London: Oxford University Press, 1923).

A number of these "Clydebankers" (as the Americans called them) worked at the Federal yard and played influential roles in the union. For example, Frank Mason, a Scottish immigrant shipfitter in the plate shop, left a deep impression on young activists. It was the American-born workers, however, who provided the main initiative for building the Kearny local. They included more conservative, or "traditional," craft-oriented workers, like chipper and caulker Dan Deans, as well as younger, less traditional men, like welder Nat Levin. These workers learned from the example of the Clydesiders, just as many other shipyard workers had learned direct action tactics from the IWW during their hoboing days. These shipyard activists believed there was a spirit of defiance and solidarity in the heritage of the Clydesiders and the IWW that was not found in the staid craft unionism of the AFL shipbuilding Metal Trades organizations.[25]

The American political left also had an important influence on trade union organization at the Federal yard. At New York Ship, the Socialist Party was more influential than other leftist groups, whereas at Federal Ship, the Communist Party (CP) had the greatest influence. The CP at Federal Ship did not necessarily operate directly through party directives. Instead, party members seem to have acted more as left-wing trade unionists who found in the CP a source of workable ideas and a vision of class solidarity. The CP's orientation toward a "left-center" trade union coalition in the late 1930s was especially influential. The CP was not the only left-wing influence, however. Other left-wing groups that had contacts with shipyard union activists included anarchists, Trotskyists, and a variety of independent leftists. This "left" presence was manifested primarily in trade union organizing, rather than in political activity, during the late 1930s.[26]

---

[25] See interviews with Lou Kaplan, Jan. 8, 1983; Arthur Boyson, Oct. 4, 1982, and Sept. 12, 1986; Reeder, Sept. 3, 1986, May 30, 1987, May 21, 1988, and Nov. 17, 1988; Don and Jim Bollen, May 7, 1983, Swampscott, Mass.; Al Petit-Clair, Sept. 15, 1987, Toms River, N.J.; and Terry Foy, April 6 and May 20, 1988. I found traces of this radical trade union tradition in each of the yards covered in this study. Usually, only the most active trade unionists established such links. I found no evidence of any positive AFL influence on industrial unionists present in these shipyards in the 1930s and 1940s.

[26] Interviews with Kaplan, Reeder, Petit-Claire, and Foy. For an analysis of CP trade union strategy utilizing the left-center coalition, see William Z. Foster, *American Trade Unionism: Principles, Organization, Strategy, Tactics* (New York: International Publishers, 1947). While the CP had a well-defined strategy on the united front in the trade union movement, its analysis of bureaucratization and institutionalization did not go beyond a simplistic critique of business unionism. This theoretically and practically weak position led to serious divisions between conventional Leninist (and Stalinist) party leaders and many unconventional trade union party members who were syndicalists. For a broad discussion of this theme, see David Milton, *The Politics of Labor, From the Great Depression to the New Deal* (New York: Monthly Review Press, 1982), esp. pp. 9–24, 139–68.

Those who identified with the Communist Party and were active in ship-building union organizing during the mid- to late 1930s had inherited, and in many ways carried on, the legacy of the syndicalists, which the Socialist Party had by then abandoned. Although these pro-CP left-wingers still believed that direct action was an essential tactic, they also believed that it was imperative to have a stable working relationship with management, which would allow the union to negotiate on grievances. The IWW, with its opposition to contracts and to formal structures, neglected this aspect of organizing. In contrast to those who had been influenced by the Socialist Party, the left-wingers who were close to or belonged to the CP believed that the spirit of the IWW's direct action tactics kept the union alive as a movement, making the union more responsive to workers' immediate needs, even as they helped build the union organizationally.[27]

From the yard-level bosses to the president, Lynn Korndorff, Federal Ship's management made concessions only when forced to do so by workers in the yard. According to Levin, Korndorff set management's style and flaunted his personal prejudices:

> Mr. Korndorff was physically intimidating, at least six foot six inches tall with very rough features and stern expression. He was very shrewd and made it clear, at the start, that no one was going to tell him how to run his company, and that the officers of U.S. Steel in Pittsburgh didn't give a hoot how he runs Federal so long as it makes money for them. . . .
>
> When I was reinstated [in 1937], I met Mr. Korndorff . . . who told me I was the kind of guy he wanted on his side. He offered me a Sub-Foreman job. It was such an obvious bribe and could only have resulted in my being fired again, and without recourse this time. . . . He was absolute boss in that yard, and he intimidated everyone under him. He was protected by his male secretary Oscar Pfister, and the daily grievance handling in all departments was supervised by Jim Love—Personnel Manager. Mr. K. had Nazi (anti-Jewish) post cards and cartoons on his desk and on his office wall until the start of World War II, when they were removed and replaced with American flags. I don't know if Mr. K. ever got used to names like Goldstein, Rothbard [both IUMSWA attorneys], Oxfeld, Levin, and Shapiro.[28]

---

[27] On the CP's shift toward a more flexible trade union policy in the late 1930s, see Bert Cochran, *Labor and Communism: The Conflict That Shaped American Unions* (Princeton: Princeton University Press, 1977); Maurice Isserman, *Which Side Were You On? – The American Communist Party during the Second World War* (Middletown, Conn.: Wesleyan University Press, 1982); and Harvey A. Levenstein, *Communism, Anticommunism, and the CIO* (Westport, Conn.: Greenwood Press, 1981).

[28] Levin letter to Palmer, March 11, 1988.

The stalemate between the union and Korndorff continued after Green, the IUMSWA's national president, and Love, Federal Ship's industrial relations manager, agreed that work stoppages were not a legitimate way to negotiate grievances. On June 14, ten days after the first action in the plate shop, Local 16 members in Department 44, composed of welders and burners, initiated a second sit-down, believing that management had no intention of bargaining seriously regarding adjustment of the burners' rates. Union representatives Deans, Turoczy, and Miskell were in conference with management on the issue at the time, but they immediately went back to the plant in order to get the men back to work. Before they arrived at the shop, however, all the outside tradesmen on the ways and the men on two ships in the wet dock joined the walkout. The wildcat was brief, and by 3 p.m. everyone had returned to work.[29]

Mike Smith, who was busy with the New York port strike at the time, sent a message to Deans and Turoczy through Love directing the strikers to return to work immediately and not to take such action again without authorization from him or the national office. As this message to the strikers came through Love rather than directly from Smith, it is not entirely clear what Smith actually thought of the job action. Later, however, Smith commented in the *Shipyard Worker* that management's attempt to revive the company union and the foremen's failure to abide by the agreement had provoked the action. Did he really mean what he said in this message to Love? Or was this his way of saying that as a national staff organizer he had the obligation to tell the workers to return to work, but their grievances and actions were nonetheless justified? This approach, publicly reminding workers to comply with the contract but taking no effective steps to restrain them, has often been adopted by local officers and organizers who find themselves under a contractual obligation to stop unauthorized strikes. Since Smith was a master of tactics, it is not unlikely that this is what he really meant, considering what followed.[30]

A month later, on July 14, Korndorff charged that "Smith ordered a sit down at 12:40 today in violation of our agreement." When the sit-down ended, Love wrote critically to Green, "I couldn't help but recall the remarks you made during our conference when the agreement was negotiated about disciplining your members. It seems to me that this is essential to the carrying out of the spirit and letter of our agreement." If Korndorff could get Green to "discipline" Smith, the best organizer in the port of New York, Local 16 would cer-

[29] *Shipyard Worker*, June 18, 1937.

[30] *Shipyard Worker*, June 18, 1937; Love to Green, June 15, 1937, IUMSWA Archives, Series V, Box 50.

tainly be tamed, if not broken. Green did not take immediate action to curb Smith, but he was very concerned that his efforts to improve relations with the company had been disrupted.[31]

The July sit-down, the third one in just two months, revealed the frustration Local 16's leaders felt about their meetings with Love to resolve grievances. Management had openly defied the IUMSWA by holding Shipbuilding Employee Association (SEA) meetings on a daily basis at noon in the company store, all under the guise of Credit Union business. Management allowed SEA supporters to organize on company time, but docked the pay of Turoczy's rivet gang when he conducted legitimate union business for the Local 16 grievance committee. Local union president Deans was convinced that Green had to intervene personally to stop these and other violations of the contract.[32]

On August 13, workers in Department 44 initiated their most dramatic sit-down to date. This particular action in the welding department was set off by a typical grievance, which recurred during World War II. The company required welders to be at their workplace, usually out on the ways, at the start of the workday. First, however, they had to pick up their equipment at the welding shed and then walk to their assigned boat or welding bay. This extra walk made men lose from five to twenty minutes a day in wages, because technically they were "off the clock"—not at their assigned workplace—even though they had punched the time clock located in the shed. Workers wanted to stop work five minutes early, or else have the paid workday start when they first picked up their equipment in the shed.[33]

The men initially protested by taking longer to get their equipment from the tool room, but the action soon escalated when the company deducted the lost time from their pay. The welders retaliated with a sit-down. Floyd De Blaker, the shop steward on the day shift and a Local 16 trustee, had followed Smith's lead in the July 14 sit-down, but now he led the action. The company viewed him as the ringleader and fired him. Nat Levin, who worked nights, came in early and encouraged men to join the sit-down. He too was fired, along with Charles Roblesky, but the sit-down continued throughout the day. Green finally got Korndorff to agree to arbitration (with a third party based in the private sector, not a government-affiliated arbitrator), but he concurred with Korndorff that the grievance procedure established by the union agreement,

[31] Korndorff telegram to Green, July 14, 1937; Love to Green, June 15, 1937; both IUMSWA Archives, Series V, Box 50.

[32] Deans to Green, July 7, 1937; Smith on Local 16 letterhead, "The Williams Case . . . ," no date (c. late July 1937); both IUMSWA Archives, Series V, Box 50. *Shipyard Worker*, Aug. 6, 1937.

[33] Brecht arbitration decision #4, IUMSWA Archives, Series V, Box 50.

which prohibited wildcat strikes, must be fully enforced by union leaders in the future.[34]

The arbitration decision issued in October reinstated Levin and Roblesky, but not De Blaker, who was serving as shop steward when the sit-down began and thus was held responsible for the action. The welding department won the five-minute starting time, but not retroactive pay for the disciplinary deductions. Most important for the union, the contract was validated as a legal document. The arbitrator did not accept the company's contention that the contract had been nullified by the sit-downs. The arbitrator ruled that violations of the agreement were to be expected, but that maintaining the agreement was essential because the grievance machinery acted as a "safety valve for ridding the system of threatening pressures." The national union optimistically viewed this decision as an important advance that "inaugurated an era of peaceful solution of disputes between the Industrial Union and Federal Ship."[35]

Commenting on these arbitration decisions, John Green noted the need for a more systematic approach to handling grievances at the Federal yard. He appears to have drawn mainly upon his experience at New York Ship. He suggested that individual meetings with supervisors were preferable to group meetings; that stewards fully investigate grievances before submitting them to the company; and that the industrial relations manager provide written responses to all grievances. He also advocated that stewards be allowed to handle grievances on company time with pay.[36]

Green's approach closely resembled the grievance system that later became standard in most union workplaces. The success of such a system, however, would depend on management's full agreement to process grievances equitably and in a timely manner. Green offered pragmatic and reasonable solutions, but he failed to address the tactical problems of how to break Federal Ship management's anti-union attitudes and practices and how to complete the organization of the local union, which can be identified as the second phase of the organizing process.

Nevertheless, a precedent had been set. Arbitration appeared to be the answer for unsettled grievances, unless management wanted continuous rebellions on the job. If the union accepted this approach, it would have to bring in

[34] Brecht arbitration decision #4; Brecht arbitration decision #5, October 2, 1937; Korndorff to Green, Aug. 17, 1937; all IUMSWA Archives, Series V, Box 50. Neil McMahon interview, June 26, 1987, Kearny, N.J.

[35] Brecht arbitration decisions #4, #5; *Shipyard Worker*, September 17, 1937. See also Brecht arbitration decision #1, Sept. 10, 1937.

[36] Green memorandum on Federal Shipbuilding arbitration cases, no date (c. Oct. 1937), IUMSWA Archives, Series V, Box 50.

more members and strengthen its organization. The local was relatively strong in the plate shop and the welding department, where the sit-downs had originated. But by fall 1937, only a minority of Federal Shipyard workers were union members, despite the groundswell of support during the May 1937 recognition strike.

Green extolled the new system of processing grievances and the benefits of rank-and-file democracy in his September 1937 Labor Day message to union members. While locals required an organizational structure with shop officers, stewards, local officers, by-laws, and so on, "above and beyond all this machinery is the principle of rank and file control. The fullest power is vested in the members. The organization is theirs, theirs to adapt and change as changing times and conditions bring new demands and problems to them." [37]

These words were rhetorical, for national officers Green and Van Gelder were moving the union toward a more centralized system of decision-making and away from "rank and file control." Developments in the New York Harbor strike, in particular, shaped Van Gelder's thinking, but events unfolding at the local level, especially direct action as a means for breaking grievance deadlocks, also contributed to the policy shift.

At the September 1937 IUMSWA national convention, Van Gelder made a major reassessment of the union's approach to leadership, decision-making, and organizing. He observed that "obvious[ly] . . . the New York [port] strike was not very carefully planned or thought out in advance," and concluded: "There is therefore clearly indicated the necessity for more centralized control, so that the interests of the national organization will be protected against the enthusiastic short-sightedness of local groups. It is invariably the case that each Local feels itself the key point and vital cog in the whole Union, and that all other interests must be forgotten when it gets in trouble. To promote and advance our organization nationally, some effective check upon autonomy in this respect is essential." [38] The faction in the Brooklyn local that advocated continuing the strike provided Van Gelder with a rationale for his new position. He suspended this local's autonomy, placing it under the direction of the national office in an effort to save existing union organization and to bring the local in line with national policy.

In succeeding years, the national office used the policy of "lifting" (suspending) autonomy, whether threatened or carried out, for two purposes. First, it was a way of gaining control over insolvent locals suffering from low mem-

[37] *Shipyard Worker*, Sept. 3, 1937.
[38] IUMSWA, *Proceedings, 3rd National Convention*, Sept. 1937, p. 23.

bership, mismanagement of the treasury, or corruption (as happened with Local 16 during World War II). Second, the policy was used to stop local movements that were highly critical of the national office (as was the case with Brooklyn Local 13 in 1937) or too far to the left (as with Baltimore's Maryland Dry Dock Local 31 in 1941). This policy eventually became a tool for shaping the ideological character of union locals.[39]

Kearny Local 16 challenged this drift toward centralization during the next decade, beginning with these unauthorized sit-down strikes. The IUMSWA's 1937 convention, however, outlawed unauthorized strikes in response to Van Gelder's report on the New York port walkout. Leaders from the New York harbor yards—Mike Smith and two Local 22 delegates—opposed the restriction on strikes. Gavin MacPherson, who represented the Chelsea shore gangs, told the convention that "if this goes through, Joe Ryan has a weapon against us." Smith explained his view to the delegates: "There was in my experience the necessity of calling a strike within two hours. If we had waited for a period of a week we would have been in a bad fix because it would have left us in the position of taking a step backward." Van Gelder replied that "if any Local is moving into a position where a strike is necessary the President should be told about it." In a setting like Camden, with its integral connection to the national office, Van Gelder certainly had a point. The dilemma, however, was that the national leadership felt compelled, and legally was required, to honor no-strike clauses in existing contracts. In the case of the Federal Shipyard, located in the port of New York, informing the national office of an impending strike that violated the contract (as sit-down strikes did) would ensure that it was prevented.[40]

At Federal, direct action tactics succeeded because of the presence of staff organizer Mike Smith, who gave the local union movement clear direction. He was militant and socialist, but not a communist, and had excellent credentials as far as the national officers were concerned. His position on the IUMSWA General Executive Board gave him union-wide contacts and respectability. The national office could not just dismiss him as a dissident when he tacitly endorsed the Kearny sit-downs of summer 1937, while publicly opposing them in speaking to the company. As the summer wore on, however, Green sought greater control over both Local 16 and Smith, partly because the lo-

---

[39] Former IUMSWA local officers and stewards whom I interviewed considered the national office's suspension of, or threat to suspend, local autonomy one of the most serious problems they faced. See, for example, interviews with Boyson (Fore River), Oct. 4, 1982, and Sept. 12, 1986; Petit-Clair (Federal); Foy and Kaplan (Federal), April 6, 1988; and Reeder (New York Ship), Sept. 3, 1986, May 30, 1987, and May 21, 1988.

[40] IUMSWA, *Proceedings, 3rd National Convention*, Sept. 1937, p. 42.

cal's officers, stewards, and members began to view Smith as their national leader, but also because Federal Ship was the IUMSWA's second largest local. The combined strength of the growing New York and North Jersey locals could conceivably overwhelm Green's base in Camden Local 1. Consolidating Kearny thus became a question of how power was distributed within the IUMSWA, not simply a matter of adding more members and building local organization.[41]

By September 1937, Green was planning to transfer Mike Smith, even though Smith was immensely popular as Local 16's staff organizer and the yard still was far from organized. In addition to regarding Smith as a potential rival who threatened his special relationship with Federal Shipbuilding's management, Green undoubtedly felt that Smith's talents could be better utilized at a non-union yard where organizing was most needed. In October he had Smith transferred to Sun Ship in Chester, Pennsylvania. Local 16 members elected Dan Deans to act in Smith's place, but Deans complained to Green that the absence of a national organizer gave the company an excuse to avoid processing grievances, for a national organizer was required at the step prior to arbitration.[42]

Late that month Green assigned New York Ship Local 1 president Francis Hunter, a close ally, as Federal's national organizer and Local 16's secretary-treasurer. Hunter was paid a full-time salary from the Kearny local's treasury and displaced William O'Donnell, a rank-and-file shipfitter who had been elected secretary-treasurer in July. This change made it easier for Green to meet privately with Korndorff on grievances not settled at a lower level, while Hunter made every effort to get Green loyalists elected to local office and provided information on internal local politics to the national office.[43]

Hunter entered the local at a good time. With favorable arbitration rulings behind them, local leaders began to give new direction to the union's internal organization. General membership meetings were held monthly, and by February 1938 shop meetings were conducted regularly in fifteen departments. The local formed an education committee with four members: Nat Levin (a future local treasurer), John Dempsey (a future local president), Karl Neugebauer, and James Kavanaugh. As in Camden Local 1, the Kearny Local 16

[41] Lucien Koch interview, June 10, 1987, Alexandria, Va.

[42] Deans to Green, Oct. 15, 1937, IUMSWA Archives, Series V, Box 50. Van Gelder did not deal with Local 16 except when dues or convention delegate issues arose or when the local was involved in an organizing drive, for example, for recognition in 1937 and the NLRB election in 1940.

[43] Minutes of meeting between Korndorff and Green, Smith, probably by the union, Oct. 22, 1937, IUMSWA Archives, Series V, Box 50; *Shipyard Worker*, July 9, Oct. 29, 1937.

education committee became an important means for union men to launch their campaigns for local office. Some used the education committee primarily as a way to teach members how the grievance system and parliamentary procedure functioned; this became Hunter's approach at New York Ship. Others, such as Levin, used the committee to promote a vision of the labor movement by emphasizing broader issues. The local started to sponsor athletic teams organized by departments, as well as social events and dances. Local 16 also expanded its organizational ties with trade unionists outside the Federal Shipyard by bringing Camden and Kearny workers together in joint union and social events and uniting with other IUMSWA locals to establish a "Permanent Port Council of New York Local Officers." Through its support for the CIO's North Jersey organizing drives, Local 16 established stronger relations with other unions, especially the UE and the ACW.[44]

Local 16's apparent success proved deceptive. Membership growth failed to keep pace with advances in the local's organizational structure. Hunter reported that there were only 800 union members out of 3,000 employed at the yard in April; membership rose to 900 in May, when the union contract came up for renewal. Hunter appears to have focused on promoting committees, meetings, and social events but not on developing new leadership (what Van Gelder called "secondary leadership"). Instead, he spent much of his time trying to undercut the indigenous leadership emerging in Local 16. His style may have aggravated this problem. Van Gelder remembered Hunter as a man who liked to give long speeches but did not have the ability to hold the attention of the members. Hunter overlooked the most critical fight, the situation workers faced inside the yard, on the job, where enforcement of the contract was needed. New union structures were essential for a strong local union, but would not succeed unless workers themselves were mobilized to defend their rights.[45]

The anger of Local 16 leaders over the removal of Smith and the unilateral installation of Hunter finally burst into the open in April, during preparations for the second contract. Then, at the May general meeting where the contract proposals were discussed, union members demanded that John Green (who was present in the hall) cease acting as Local 16's national representa-

<hr>

[44] *Shipyard Worker*, Aug. 27, Oct. 29, Nov. 5, 12, 19, 26, Dec. 10, 17, 1937; Van Gelder telegram to Secretary of Local 16, Oct. 21, 1937, IUMSWA Archives, Series V, Box 50; Reeder interview, Sept. 3, 1986; Collins interview, May 22, 1988, Gloucester, N.J.

[45] *Shipyard Worker*, Jan. 14, Feb. 2, March 25, April 8, 1938. Hunter (Local 16 executive secretary) "Official Report" for April 1938; Hunter "Official Report" for May 1938; both IUMSWA Archives, Series V, Box 50. Observations on Hunter's personal style are from Van Gelder interviews, 1987.

tive and stop meeting privately with President Korndorff. They passed a resolution that instructed Green to "straighten out the Agreement that he made with Mr. Korndorff so it will become null and void and that Local 16 choose its own representative to represent them with the Federal Shipbuilding Company." Local 16 went even further, deciding that its own negotiating representatives and committees would be the ones to draw up all agreements with management. "But before they become binding on Local 16 it must be passed by the General Membership at a meeting called for that purpose." The resolution then spelled out other secondary powers of the negotiating committee.[46]

Local leaders did not want Green excluded from negotiations; they simply wanted Local 16's authority to be paramount and private meetings to be ended. Following this difficult session, Green helped negotiate the new contract, which was signed on May 21, 1938. No major gains were made, but the union did win the right to collect dues on company time, to arbitrate individual wage rates, and to have former members in a department fill open jobs.[47]

Local 16 continued in its independent direction by voting at the June 1 executive board meeting to terminate Hunter's "services" in 30 days. Local 16 president Deans wrote to Green that this was done to "curtail expenses of the Local." Apparently aware that this would antagonize Green, he added, "we hope, by this action, that the National Office and Brother Hunter will not feel that we have not appreciated the services he has given us." Hunter himself later revealed the real reason behind the local leaders' action:

> Please try to build up some enthusiasm in this Local, I think some real pep talks by members of the GEB would help. Regarding my stay here as Local Executive Secretary, John you know damn well I am no job seeker, I am not anxious to stay here if these men don't want me. They have not worked with me since I've been here; they do not consult me before taking up grievances; they fight me whenever they can and all of this has made it almost impossible for me to do anything here. If I am not going to get the cooperation of these men I might as well get the hell out.[48]

Hunter blamed the elected leaders of Local 16 for most of his problems. He explained that the records had been in "a very disorderly condition" on his ar-

---

[46] Minutes of Local 16 General Membership Meeting, May 14, 1938, IUMSWA Archives, Series V, Box 50.

[47] *Shipyard Worker*, May 20, June 3, 1938; Agreement between Federal Shipbuilding and IUMSWA Local 16, May 21, 1938, IUMSWA Archives, Series V, Box 50.

[48] Deans to Green, June 2, 1938; Hunter to Green, June 23, 1938 (punctuation as in original), IUMSWA Archives, Series V, Box 50.

rival. He had worked out a plan for keeping the books in shape, but could not enforce it. Since May, Van Gelder had been hounding Hunter for backlogged reports and unpaid per capita dues. In general, Hunter claimed he had improved local officers' attitudes toward the national office, which had been "very antagonistic" at first. Nowhere did he give credit for the building of Local 16 to the leaders who had been elected by the workers themselves. He believed that he had been responsible for the local's stagnation in only one respect: "I have failed in one thing for which I was sent here to do and that is to find a local man who I felt was capable to assume the duties of an executive secretary."[49]

Hunter finally left Local 16 at the end of July, after suffering a breakdown. He wrote to Green, "my wife . . . thinks I have a cold but the fact is I am suffering with my nerves, I was doctoring for this for some time while in Jersey City." He returned to New York Ship where he worked once again with Local 1. Kearny Local 16 was his last assignment beyond Camden.[50]

New local leaders had emerged by the time of Hunter's departure. John Dempsey became the new president; Deans continued in office as vice president. Dempsey established himself as a key figure in Local 16 politics over the next ten years. He came from a Republican background, but had close ties with Jersey City's Mayor Frank Hague, a Democrat, as did a number of Republicans in North Jersey. Alex Turoczy was elected executive secretary in Hunter's place, and Nat Levin was elected treasurer. Both Turoczy and Levin supported direct action as an option. Although Levin was generally identified with the Communist Party, union activists considered his style constructive rather than sectarian and believed that the tactics he advocated made negotiated settlements possible. He was well known for his soft-spoken manner, but as the welders' steward he took firm positions for the rank and file. These four—Dempsey, Deans, Turoczy, and Levin—became the core local leadership of Local 16 from 1938 to early 1940, and generally remained independent despite Green's efforts to control the local. Peter Flynn and George Wright won important committee positions; both were Green loyalists (and Scotsmen) and had ambitions for higher positions.[51]

The first confrontation between Green and the local's new leaders occurred after a two-hour, private meeting between Green and Korndorff in July 1938.

[49] Hunter to Green, June 1, 1938; Hunter to Van Gelder, May 20, 1938; both IUMSWA Archives, Series V, Box 50.

[50] Hunter to Green, August 8, 1938; Green to Hunter, August 15, 1938; Dempsey to Green, August 25; Van Gelder to Hunter, May 24, 1938; all IUMSWA Archives, Series V, Box 50.

[51] *Shipyard Worker*, July 9, 1937; Hunter to Green, June 23, 1938, IUMSWA Archives, Series V, Box 50. Information on Levin and Dempsey is from Foy interview, April 6, 1988.

Industrial Relations Manager Love, who must have known of the rift between the national union and the local, informed several Local 16 officers of the private conference. Dempsey immediately fired off a letter to Green stating: "It is a strange thing that you could be in town on an arranged conference with Mr. Korndorff and Mr. Love, and not even notify Local 16 and any of the officers concerning the matter. We had to get our information that you were coming through *Mr. Love.* Please get in touch with Local 16 immediately as we have matters of vital importance demanding your attention."[52]

Green's response indicated his belief that accommodation with management was now possible and his determination not to yield his authority. "May I point out that our discussions were cordial and Korndorff took the position, in my humble opinion, that if we can convince him things may work out all right." Green assured Dempsey "that there is nothing to be alarmed over at the present time" and suggested that the local transmit "any pertinent matters . . . along with full details so that I may have the opportunity to discuss them with Korndorff."[53]

Local 16 officers and members remained unconvinced that Green could fairly represent their interests in private meetings with the company. At the August 1938 membership meeting, they again voiced their opposition to his acting without a Local 16 representative present. Green's response to Dempsey's criticism revealed that there were limits to the "rank and file democracy" publicly advocated by the IUMSWA. Green bluntly told Dempsey that his approach as Local 16 president "certainly does not tend to harmonize relationships between your Local and the National Office. In fact . . . I am really surprised that you allowed such discussion to come on the floor." He warned Dempsey that if Dempsey had been aware of the contents of the union agreement, "I am sure that no such discussion or no such motion would have been allowed at your general membership meeting. . . . If this condition . . . which caused discontent prior to your going into office, is allowed to continue your efforts as President of Local 16 will be nullified."[54]

This was no idle threat. The national officers had suspended the autonomy and removed elected officers of Brooklyn Local 13 and Baltimore Local 28 in May for making such challenges. Staff organizers Charles Renner (an IUMSWA charter member from Sun Ship Local 2) and John Darling were fired in the process. These actions had been publicized in the *Shipyard Worker* and received the endorsement of the national General Executive Board. A year

[52] Dempsey (as president Local 16) to Green, July 27, 1938, IUMSWA Archives, Series II, Box 50 (emphasis in original).

[53] Green to Dempsey, July 27, 1938, IUMSWA Archives, Series V, Box 50.

[54] Dempsey to Green, Aug. 12, 1938; Green to Dempsey, Aug. 15, 1938; both IUMSWA Archives, Series V, Box 50.

earlier John Diehl, another organizer and IUMSWA charter member from New York Ship, had been fired by the union and then brought up on charges for "making disparaging remarks concerning John Green and this Organization in a sabotaging manner." From this point on Dempsey's correspondence with Green dealt only with grievances from the shop and made no reference to internal union problems.[55]

This experience must have made Green acutely aware of the need for loyal leadership in the Federal Ship local. In George Wright, the sheet metal shop steward and newly elected grievance committeeman, and Peter Flynn, head of Local 16's education committee, he found two reliable allies. Wright was elected to the GEB at the September 1938 national convention, further ensuring support for Green's union machine. Both Flynn and Wright had an affinity with Green, having originally come from the Clyde. Green also may have appreciated Flynn's vocal anticommunism and his criticism of those in Local 16 who used direct action. Dempsey's effort to temper his relations with Green proved to be an intelligent move. Local 16 regained some of its independence when the national office again named Mike Smith its representative. Smith also was appointed regional organizing director for New York port.[56]

Throughout 1938, management continued to test Local 16's ability to enforce the grievance procedure, but workers maintained reliance on direct action to enforce union rights despite Green's open opposition to the tactic. The problem of speed-up in the welding department had been growing for some time, and by the fall of 1938 it could no longer be contained. Management steadily increased welding production by using pace-setters, many brought up from Newport News Shipyard, who tried to outdo all the other welders in an area. Andy Reeder, a welder and union committeeman on the third shift, remembered that "these pace-setters . . . would work from whistle to whistle, never stop, and always get more footage—production—than the average guy would get. And the company would take their footage and set that as what we had to get." Supervisors would keep track of footage and penalize those who failed to match the pace-setters. Once Reeder was called in at midnight by his boss for only having welded 23 feet the previous night, which was below the going rate of these pace-setters. Reeder responded to the charge by saying, "Well I had a little trouble with the machine." The boss replied, "No . . . You were tired. You go home and rest tonight." As a result, Reeder lost an entire night's pay. Reeder remembered that the system was especially hard on work-

[55] *Shipyard Worker*, June 3, 1938; Thomas Gallagher to Green, Aug. 5, 1937.

[56] Foy interview, April 6, 1988; Levin letter to Palmer, March 11, 1988; Boyson interview, June 3, 1988; Neil McMahon interview, June 26, 1987, Kearny, N.J.; Green to Love, Sept. 22, 1938, IUMSWA Archives, Series V, Box 50.

ers who came temporarily from yards in other ports. "Guys used to commute from New York Ship, quite a few New York Ship men were working there. They'd come up five in a car. And at least once or twice a week [the boss would] send one of them guys out [and say] go home, that he didn't have enough work. How could they go home? They had to go out . . . and sit in the car all night. There was no town around or anything like that. . . . It was a way of punishing them."[57]

Reeder was typical of the best rank-and-file organizers inside the shipyards during the 1930s. He had a working-class background, was not an intellectual or a member of a left-wing group, and basically was just trying to make a living. At the same time, he is emblematic of secondary-level leadership emerging in the IUMSWA. He was one of many young welders at the Federal yard recruited as a volunteer organizer by Mike Smith after the first contract was signed. Unlike many of the others, however, he did not come from New York Ship, but had worked at Sun Ship, Fore River, the Philadelphia Navy Yard, and at other East Coast yards. After he got in trouble at Sun Ship in late 1937, Mike Shapiro sent him a telegram from Kearny: "'Come on up, I got a job for you.' And I walked out of Sun Ship. . . . My two brothers [Robert and Wilbert] were welders, both younger than me. . . . So all three of us went up and we got a job . . . at Kearny." The solidarity of the Federal Shipyard workers amazed him, compared to what he had experienced elsewhere. "What a difference to see the solid guys that . . . I run into up there. That's the first solid guys I run into."[58]

Reeder began to sign up new members and handle grievances only a few weeks after getting hired. Nat Levin was his mentor. Although Levin, like Reeder, believed in direct action, he also taught Reeder the necessity of patience in union building. Reeder's early "training" in direct action came from his first-hand experience with IWW organizers. During one of the worst years of the Great Depression, he rode the rails with other men in search of work. Railroad guards once stopped a freight train he was riding and took Reeder and other men in the box cars to a detention camp, where they were told to break rocks with sledge hammers. The Wobbly organizers among them broke the wooden handles with the rocks instead, and others followed, making it impossible to carry out the work. As a result, the men were released. Reeder also worked in many shipyards along the Delaware River, where the IWW had substantial membership during World War I. Philadelphia remained a Wobbly enclave (though organizationally the IWW was ineffective), especially at West-

---

[57] Reeder interview, Sept. 3, 1986. On Green's involvement with this grievance, see Green to Dempsey, Sept. 28, 1938, IUMSWA Archives, Series V, Box 50.

[58] Reeder interview, Sept. 3, 1986.

inghouse and on the docks. This labor environment made Reeder responsive to the IWW outlook, even though he came from a conservative family that was Republican and Presbyterian.[59]

When Reeder and others like him came into the shipyards, they initiated job actions inspired by these earlier experiences. "It was only then," Reeder remembered, "that I fully understood direct action." Their impatience also came from their youth and their drive to change the world. In Reeder's words, "we felt as if we were on the verge of a revolution." These young activists had a deep respect for President Roosevelt and what New Deal politics represented, but they also had a high regard for the left-wing trade unionists they encountered in the shipyards who were fighting for workers' rights. Reeder, in particular, hated red-baiting. He admired John Green, as did many rank-and-file leaders, because Green symbolized the rise of the shipyard union and the empowerment of the workers. Reeder was aware of Green's autocratic tendencies and red-baiting, but he found it hard to blame Green for what seemed to be the fault of second-rate local leaders. Reeder's main concern was for trade union unity based on "brotherhood," solidarity, and "help[ing] one another when times are hard."[60]

Federal Shipyard welders, including Reeder, had waited over six months for the company to answer their grievance on the speed-up and pace-setting. On the shipways they began to take matters into their own hands, led by veteran welder Mike Shapiro. As Reeder recalls, Shapiro and the rest of the union men were "going around threatening these guys. . . . The majority [of the pace setters] went along, you know, scared. But this one guy, he wouldn't listen to us, and that's when Mike crashed him [over the head] with this piece of pipe."[61]

In the *Shipyard Worker*, shop steward Levin called for improved union organization as one way to attack the problem, explaining that union members were "at the crossroads" with this grievance. "Brothers, we may not be able to make the management a friend of labor overnight, but we can neutralize further its antagonism by going along steadily as we have been; by taking up all our grievances and following them through to the finish, and, most important,

[59] Reeder interviews, May 30, 1987, May 21, 1988; Reeder and Kaplan interview, Sept. 3, 1986; Len De Caux, *The Living Spirit of the Wobblies* (New York: International Publishers, 1978), p. 81, Reeder comments on a draft of this chapter (in dissertation form), November 1988. Nat Levin wrote to me regarding Reeder: "Andy . . . was a real hot-head at that time, a 'spark plug' that had to be controlled sometimes, so that it would not explode prematurely"; Levin letter to Palmer, Nov. 18, 1988.

[60] Reeder interviews, Sept. 3, 1986, May 30, 1987, May 21, 1988, and in Shipyard Workers' Reunions, Oct. 25, 1986, June 31, 1987, May 22, 1988; Reeder, "A Story of the Past," personal autobiographical compilation, 1988, given to David Palmer.

[61] Reeder interview, Sept. 3, 1986.

by not allowing ourselves to be provoked by the company into premature action that will be ineffective and unorganized." If job action was required, Levin wanted to make sure that it was effective and under control.[62]

In mid-October 1938, a special meeting for Department 44 welders and burners called by Mike Smith gave membership backing for the union's negotiating position on the footage issue. Smith and Levin met with Industrial Relations Manager Love during the following week, but the company refused to bargain on the grounds that welding production was not a fit subject for arbitration. In response, the welders decided to work at a "fair production level," that is, the rate of production desired by the union, rather than the higher rate pushed by the company. In plain words, the action was a slowdown. The company then fired welder John Marlow and laid off sixty others who had engaged in the action. John Green joined the talks with management and advocated arbitration of all issues. When the company again refused, the welders unanimously backed a work stoppage. Over 400 welders struck the following Monday, along with 200 shipfitters, and refused to resume work for the rest of the week.[63]

Reeder and his union brothers on the third shift took the fight a step further, using sabotage. Reeder recalled that the company had installed "four huge portable welding machines that had some kind of a ticker tape arrangement on it." These machines kept track of the length of time a welder's arc was broken (not lit), such as when a welding rod had to be changed. "The company could take that tape and read it and tell how long you was off the job at any one time. Well, we couldn't have that. So, a half a dozen of us got together and we decided we was going to destroy that machine . . . teach 'em a lesson." The welders agreed to meet at 4 a.m., suppertime on the third shift, under the ship, where these machines were located.

Ten or fifteen guys was to meet there. But the result was twenty-five, thirty-five guys come. Well we decided we needed a diversion. So I told the fellows go down to the end of the yard and start a fire on a tanker down there that was under construction. . . . Maybe fifteen or twenty guys started down there, but on the way . . . it wound up with fifty guys. . . . Everyone was carrying a five gallon can of paint, and turpentine, gasoline, rags. They got down on the boat, and they poured all this flammable fluid down the tanker's tank. They soaked rags and put 'em down there, and they lit it. Well guys left that boat like rats leaving a sinking ship.

[62] *Shipyard Worker*, Sept. 23, Oct. 7, 1938.
[63] Ibid., Oct. 21, Nov. 4, 11, 1938.

When Reeder and his workmates reached the welding machines they heard a "terrible explosion."

> Then we heard a fire engine and everything. We had these four by fours to throw the machine overboard. But instead of one we throw'd all four overboard. And then we took off. Well it was hell to pay about that. But they didn't do a thing. And they had to cut around thirty-five feet back off the bow of the boat, had it cut and reset. It had lifted the forepeak keel about eight inches off the keel blocks, from the explosion. So when that settled down—the strike brought this on—there [was] no more counting. . . . Things worked out good then.

Within days the company agreed to arbitrate the entire matter, bringing the strike to an end.[64]

The *Shipyard Worker* revealed two different perspectives on this strike. The view of many Federal Ship workers, led by Levin, Reeder, and Shapiro, was summed up in a letter from "The Observer, Kearny Local 16." It praised the strikers' solidarity and their strategy of a limited rather than general walkout, and commended the democratic way decisions were made through mass meetings, such as the one a few days before the final settlement. "Every proposal which was adopted was purely a spontaneous observation from rank and file members of the Union." Only "a minimum of direct action" had been required, but the writer urged workers not to be lulled by this victory and to continue the fight. In contrast, the lead article in the same issue reflected a more conservative perspective on the strike victory, in line with Green's views. It noted that "it was only by the slenderest margin that the more judicious and calm members were able to restrain the fire-brands from hasty and untimely action."[65]

Union activity at Federal Ship during 1937 and 1938 illustrates the larger strategic choice that the IUMSWA faced: whether to encourage continued rank-and-file activity and allow considerable local autonomy as a basis for union organizing and consolidation; or instead to move toward greater centralization of decision-making, emphasizing uniform contracts with clear legal negotiating and enforcement conditions. Both approaches could be utilized tactically depending on particular conditions. Only one approach, however, could serve as the main strategy, that is, the long-term organizing outlook and practice.

Arguments could be made for either strategic position. Trade unionists

---

[64] Reeder interview, Sept. 3, 1986; *Shipyard Worker*, Nov. 18, 1938.
[65] *Shipyard Worker*, Nov. 18, 1938.

needed local democracy and freedom of action to organize effectively and to protect workers' rights on the job. Many of these union activists believed that organizing demanded direct challenges to management abuses, at times making upheaval preferable to stability in labor relations. At the same time, however, the national office clearly needed to coordinate local initiatives more directly, to promote uniform bargaining policies and to maximize organizing resources, all concerns that often were not adequately appreciated by local activists.

By the following year these differences over tactics began to divide Local 16 leaders themselves. Sharp differences on tactics led, in turn, to two possible strategies for consolidating the Kearny yard: to rely primarily on legal means, including negotiations and a certification election; or to combine this approach with continued rank-and-file mobilization and selective use of direct action.

From late 1938 on, IUMSWA Local 16 steadily increased its standing among Federal Ship workers and its power to represent their interests to yard management. Direct action did not cease, but it had clearly been circumscribed by the union's national officers, and a more workable grievance system made the legal route through the contract more viable. Although Federal Shipbuilding's management nominally recognized Local 16 as early as May 1937, when the first contract was signed, the union decided to get official NLRB certification through a representation election, held in March 1940.

The IUMSWA waged a highly effective campaign for this election, which was overseen by national secretary-treasurer Van Gelder, still the head of organizing initiatives. The union relied mainly on internal yard leadership contacts and face-to-face persuasion in every department, rather than using extensive leaflet distributions or housecalls. The Federal yard, after all, was in the middle of a vast industrial complex, and workers, by 1940, came from every part of the New York metropolitan area. Aside from the small Scottish immigrant neighborhood in Kearny, which was separated from the yard by highways and factories, the Federal Shipyard had no "workers' community" in the traditional sense. The outcome of the election was never in doubt. The IUMSWA won by a landslide, receiving 4,683 out of 5,712 votes cast. The SEA, Federal's revamped company union and the IUMSWA's only competitor, received only 693 votes, while 263 workers voted for no affiliation. Legally, at least, there could be no question that the IUMSWA spoke for Federal Shipyard workers.[66]

---

[66] Van Gelder to Dempsey, Jan. 22, 1940, IUMSWA Archives, Series V, Box 51; *Shipyard Worker*, Jan. 26, Feb. 9, March 8, 1940.

More doubtful, however, was the *depth* of commitment that the union achieved among Federal Ship workers. Union membership was not yet a condition of employment, and many who voted for the IUMSWA in the NLRB poll did not subsequently take up membership. The IUMSWA had organized Federal Ship on one level by winning contracts and NLRB certification, but on another level much had yet to be done. Federal Ship was anything but consolidated as a union yard, despite the militancy of local activists.

Reeder's observation about "what a difference" it made "to see the solid guys there" was an accurate assessment of the intense militancy at Federal Ship *relative* to other shipyards, especially those in New England. Nowhere did the IUMSWA try so hard to organize over such a length of time and meet such resistance, both from management and from workers, as at Bethlehem's Fore River Shipyard in Quincy, Massachusetts. This yard had been the target of one of the young industrial union's first campaigns in the early 1930s, but it would become, by the end of World War II, the target of the IUMSWA's last major organizing campaign.

PART III

THE FINAL CAMPAIGN:
FORE RIVER, 1923–1945

CHAPTER 6

Company Union in Control:
Fore River, 1923–1939

Bethlehem Shipbuilding proved a far more formidable opponent for the IUMSWA during the 1930s than either Federal Shipbuilding or New York Shipbuilding. The most important yard in the Bethlehem chain was its Fore River Shipyard in Quincy, Massachusetts, and it proved to be the most difficult to organize.

During World War I, Fore River workers had shown their militancy through strike actions and craft union organization. The company tried to tame this movement through paternalist welfare programs, a relatively modern personnel system, and a management style that emphasized personal contact between supervisors and workers. Fore River's AFL craft unions disintegrated in the postwar period, not as a result of these fairly liberal management schemes, but because the unions engaged in strikes individually, on a craft basis, an ineffective tactic that allowed Bethlehem to defeat them relatively easily.[1]

By the mid-1920s, the few workers who retained their AFL union membership could not sustain viable local organization or mount effective protests. Fore River management retained its personnel and welfare policies while isolating the remaining handful of craft unionists without violence or massive firings. To solidify its control over Fore River workers, management introduced a company union, the Employee Representation Plan (ERP).[2] Abuses

---

[1] For the history of the AFL unions and management policies at Fore River from 1898 to the 1920s, see David Palmer, "Organizing the Shipyards: Unionization at Fore River, New York Ship, and Federal Ship, 1898–1945" (Ph.D. diss., Brandeis University, 1990), pp. 39–220; reports on Fore River in *Boilermakers' Journal* (1899–1922) and *Machinists' Monthly Journal* (1898–1924); and *Fore River Log* (1916–1919).

[2] Bethlehem Fore River Shipyard company newspaper clippings book, Quincy Historical Society, Mass.; "Intermediate Report" by Henry W. Schmidt (NLRB Trial Examiner), 1937,

at Fore River rarely accumulated to the point where they could be exploited by union organizers. The company tended to address some complaints, but let others stand, including favoritism, inadequate rate upgrading within a classification, and "chiseling" (failure to pay full wages on piece work). Fore River had one of the highest base pay rates on the East Coast, which made it more difficult to organize around wage issues than it was elsewhere. Furthermore, the existence of a well-organized company union convinced many workers that they had a voice, however limited.

By the late 1920s, workers at Fore River had become relatively passive compared to those in other shipyards. They also had a special dislike for any person or organization that was accused of being "communist." People in the town of Quincy, whether middle class or working class, were relatively conservative, reflecting the less militant social and labor environment of the Boston region compared to the Camden-Philadelphia region and the port of New York.[3]

Quincy's local government was dominated by conservative Republicans, unlike Camden, where liberal Republicans, New Deal Democrats, and moderate socialists coexisted. Nor was Quincy a cosmopolitan urban environment like the port of New York, where widely differing ethnic, racial, and political groups fought for turf and built their own enclaves but came together in the shipyard. Quincy resembled a large village on the edge of a metropolitan area. It was not a company town in the strict sense, but Bethlehem influenced the political and cultural atmosphere far more than New York Ship did in Camden.

During the 1930s, about 75 percent of Quincy's 71,000 residents were native-born whites, and the other 25 percent were European-born immigrants; only seventeen black people were counted among its residents. The commu-

---

for Bethlehem Shipbuilding v. IUMSWA Local 5 (case no. I-C-25) and Bethlehem Shipbuilding v. IUMSWA (case no. I-C-536), NA, RG 25, Box 1669, (file) "Bethlehem Shipbuilding, case no. R-30, Quincy, Mass" (hereafter cited as Schmidt, "Intermediate Report"). Bethlehem's industrial relations policy at Fore River stands in marked contrast to that of its steel division, infamous in the 1930s (along with other "Little Steel" corporations) for its use of special police and anti-union violence to stop the Steel Workers Organizing Committee. See, for example, Jerold S. Auerbach, *Labor and Liberty: The La Follette Committee and the New Deal* (Indianapolis: Bobbs-Merrill, 1966), pp. 89, 101, 135.

[3] An indication of Boston's relatively conservative labor environment can be seen in union growth figures for the 1930s. Between 1932 and 1940, Boston's trade union membership increased by 95 percent, while that for the United States as a whole (according to the U.S. Bureau of Labor Statistics) was 213.7 percent; Charles H. Trout, *Boston: The Great Depression and the New Deal* (New York: Oxford University Press, 1977), p. 217. Before the First World War, however, the Boston region had been a volatile labor environment, especially in outlying industrial cities such as Lawrence, Lowell, Lynn, and Fall River, where textile mills and shoe factories were concentrated. By the 1930s, many of these mills and factories had moved to the South.

nity's racial homogeneity and its residential exclusion of African Americans made Quincy a more extreme version of neighboring Boston: during the Great Depression, only three percent of Boston's approximately 770,000 residents were black, while almost 30 percent were European-born immigrants (mainly Irish, Italians, and Russian Jews). The town, which was formerly part of Braintree, had a long and distinguished history, for it had been settled early in the colonial period; as the birthplace of presidents John Adams and John Quincy Adams, it could claim to be the bastion of "Yankee" tradition. By the twentieth century, this image was little more than a myth. Quincy's immigrants, however, were heavily Northern European and tended to accept the culturally conservative mentality common throughout much of small-town industrial and rural New England. This "traditional" outlook valued hard work, individualism, and plain living while rejecting "outsiders," whether they were Southerners, speakers of "foreign" languages, or non-whites. Although many workers at Fore River came from Boston, people from Quincy and similar towns on the South Shore predominated in the shipyard's labor force before World War II.[4]

These social conditions, combined with formidable managerial policies, made organizing in Quincy an extremely difficult task in the interwar years. The durability of the company union, however, was by far the greatest obstacle.

Bethlehem management established the Fore River Employee Representation Plan in 1923. It tried to create the impression that workers had initiated the ERP on their own, with management's encouragement. Within the business community, however, there was no such illusion. In assessing Bethlehem's original plan at its Sparrows Point steel and shipbuilding complex, *Iron Age* sympathetically noted: "The seeds of the plan may be silently sown by management. . . . The whole idea is that it must be created sufficiently within the ranks of the employees so that they will regard it as their own and will be loyal to it accordingly."[5]

Management control of the ERP began at its inception. In late February 1923, the company's industrial relations manager, Harry Parker, called

---

[4] U.S. Dept. of Commerce, Bureau of the Census, *Sixteenth Census of the United States: 1940, Population*, vol. 2, part 3, *Massachusetts* (Washington, D.C.: GPO, 1943); *Seventeenth Census of the United States: 1950, Population*, vol. 2, part 21, *Massachusetts* (GPO, 1952). My cultural observations are based on interviews conducted in Quincy and the Boston area.

[5] *Iron Age*, April 29, 1920. For a contrasting and generally favorable view of company unionism in the 1920s, see Daniel Nelson, "The Company Union Movement, 1900–1937: A Reexamination," *Business History Review* 56 (August 1982) 335–57. For a critical view of ERPs, see David Brody, "The Rise and Decline of Welfare Capitalism," in Brody, *Workers in Industrial America: Essays on the Twentieth Century Struggle* (Oxford: Oxford University Press, 1980), pp. 48–81.

twenty-five workers to the company board room, with Fore River President Samuel Wakeman and General Manager Harry Gould present. None of these workers knew why they had been summoned. Parker informed them that Joseph Larkin, head of industrial relations for all Bethlehem plants, had "arranged a plan of what they would call the Employees' Representation Plan" and told the men to go back to their departments and "explain it to the other employees in the yard." Parker concluded by stating that another meeting would be held soon and that notices announcing that the Plan was operational would be posted in the yard.[6]

No general meeting for ratification by Fore River workers was ever held. Instead, the posted notices listed the twenty-five workers who had participated in the ERP's founding. When the same group of workers was again called to the board room about ten days later, Parker told them that nominations for positions in the ERP would be conducted in the yard and that anyone could run. An election committee of five then was appointed, which oversaw nominations and elections. The original group of twenty-five came from a variety of departments and crafts, as did the twenty-one representatives who subsequently served on the ERP. The AFL believe that it should try to get representation on the ERP. Two AFL candidates were subsequently elected to the open seats, while those elected to the other positions were from the original, founding group. The ERP had a "General Body" consisting of all twenty-one elected employees and three "Joint Committees" to deal with specific issues. The Joint Committees, however, each had equal numbers of worker and management representatives.[7]

Consistent with Bethlehem's original Sparrows Point plan of 1918, management retained the power to veto any decision, because tie votes in the Joint Committees could be broken by management or else declared invalid. Only the Joint Committees could pass motions of any substance. The company could be present at any meeting through "Management's Special Representative," who was always the industrial relations manager. Even though the Special Representative could not vote, the presence of such a powerful company official usually had a strong persuasive effect on the employees present.[8]

Management also used its authority in various informal ways. Industrial Re-

[6] Schmidt, "Intermediate Report"; Bethlehem v. IUMSWA, 3 LRR Man. 569–576 (NLRB 1939).

[7] Schmidt, "Intermediate Report"; "Plan of Employee's Representation, Fore River Plant, 1934–1935," card listing committees and representatives, NA, RG 25, Box 2375, (file) "Bethlehem Shipbuilding, C-906, #1." The three Joint Committees were: wages, bonus, and piecework; safety, pensions, and relief; and rules, ways and means, apprenticeship, suggestion systems, board of appeals, and miscellaneous matters.

[8] Schmidt, "Intermediate Report."

lations Manager Parker's office handled all correspondence between the committees. Parker, General Manager Gould, and President Wakeman thus had access to all ERP activity, including that of the all-worker General Body. When the organization was first established, Wakeman and Gould issued reprimands to representatives who were either late or absent from meetings. The two managers also prevented the General Body from taking action on its own on a number of occasions. In July 1927, for example, the General Body passed a resolution that all Bethlehem ERPs hold joint conferences to correct negative impressions of the Plans. Management simply ignored the resolution, and no company-wide conferences were ever held.[9]

Management offered men strong incentives to follow the direction it gave the ERP. Representatives received full pay (base rate plus one-third extra as piece rate wages) for time spent on company union business. Joint Committee management representatives usually were foremen, and contact with them provided workers with excellent opportunities for advancement and special treatment, including job upgrades, transfers, and the hiring of relatives.[10]

Rank-and-file opposition to pro-company ERP representatives was minimal between 1923 and 1933, when there was no large-scale independent trade union activity at Fore River. Employees usually owed their jobs to foremen who got them hired through networks of family or friends. ERP representatives acted as go-betweens in this process. Some foremen expected these new workers to give them gifts or to perform personal services, such as cutting their lawn. Italian workers, the second-largest group of immigrant employees (outnumbered only by those from the British Isles), feared that their lack of ability to speak English might hinder their job security and were known for providing their foremen with cheeses and other items. Andy Reeder, who (like many shipyard workers) held jobs for short periods of time in a number of East Coast yards, claimed that no other yard in which he worked had such docile employees.[11]

Despite these difficult organizing conditions, AFL trade unionists continued fighting on an individual basis for the rights of Fore River workers. In 1923 the AFL elected two of its members, Jake Van Vloten and Jimmy Furse, as ERP delegates. Van Vloten maintained his pro-labor and socialist convictions even as he served on the ERP from 1923 to 1928. Both Van Vloten and

[9] Ibid.

[10] Ibid.

[11] Schmidt, "Intermediate Report"; Milton Vogel, "The Fore River Strikers, A Study in Allegiance Dynamics" (MA thesis, Massachusetts Institute of Technology, 1948), pp. 85–86, 92–96; Don and Jim Bollen joint interview, May 7, 1983, Swampscott, Mass.; Vincent Hennebary interview, Nov. 22, 1982, Norwell, Mass.; Alex, Tom, and Agnes Mitchelson interview, May 8, 1987, Quincy, Mass.; Andy Reeder interview, Sept. 3, 1986.

Furse actively spoke for workers in their departments, while other representatives generally carried grievances no further than the immediate foreman, where problems invariably got lost.[12]

The Fore River ERP did provide workers with some minimal benefits. No other American shipyard had a company union so well connected to programs associated with welfare capitalism; Fore River had, in fact, pioneered such reforms in the industry during the 1910s. In December 1928 a Community Chest Fund was established, which provided money for shipyard families in times of personal crisis. It also served as the ERP's primary source of operating funds, while outwardly appearing independent. No workers paid dues or an initiation fee to the ERP, although dances, socials, and general solicitations raised small sums from workers. Bethlehem established a company-wide workers' pension plan in 1923, publicly claiming it was a creation of the ERPs. In 1932 Bethlehem initiated a company-wide relief plan; by the third year of the Depression, many of its workers, including those at Fore River, were on shorter hours or in need of family assistance. The corporation channeled this relief through its shipyard and steel mill ERPs.[13]

The Depression put great strain on the Fore River ERP. Heavy layoffs came to Fore River, as they did everywhere in the shipbuilding industry. Some 4,400 men worked at the yard in March 1932; a year later the number had dropped to 830 (Table 5). Bethlehem tried to lessen the inevitable discontent through relief, work-sharing, and related measures. The deterioration of wages, hours, and job security aroused less anger among workers in Quincy than it did in Camden or the port of New York. In the 1932 Fore River ERP election, the percentage of workers voting was lower than in any other year between World Wars I and II, indicating a significant level of discontent with the status quo. At the May 13 meeting of the General Body, which took place shortly after the election, General Manager Gould announced that the company planned to cut wages by 15 percent. Not a single ERP representative raised his voice in protest, nor was there any discussion on the matter.[14]

Fore River workers got a 10 percent wage increase in 1934, following the IUMSWA's successful Camden strike. Bethlehem made a point of keeping Fore River wages on a par with those at New York Ship to prevent pay from

[12] Arthur Boyson interview, Dec. 22, 1982; Daniel Nelson, "The Company Union Movement," pp. 345–46.

[13] Schmidt, "Intermediate Report"; *Bethlehem Review*, Sept. 25, 1933. For the development of Fore River's welfare capitalism, see Palmer, "Organizing the Shipyards," pp. 81–134.

[14] Schmidt, "Intermediate Report"; *Bethlehem Review*, Sept. 25, 1933; "Statement of Bethlehem Steel Co. . . . ," May 29, 1942, Bethlehem Shipbuilding v. IUMSWA, NWLB Case No. 38, p. 9.

Table 5. Employment and ERP Voting at Fore River Shipyard, 1923–1938

Year	Total Employed	ERP Votes Cast	% of Workers Voting for ERP
1923	2,254	2,086	92.5
1924	2,080	2,049	98.5
1925	2,795	2,597	92.9
1927	3,177	2,849	89.7
1928	1,649	1,471	89.2
1929	1,879	1,577	83.9
1930	2,122	1,793	84.5
1931	3,020	2,660	88.1
1932	4,408	2,987	67.8
1933	830	737	88.8
1934	2,138	1,655	77.4
1935	3,784	3,640	96.2
1936	4,769	4,579	96.0
1937	3,850	3,776	98.1
1938	3,959	3,254	82.2

There were no elections in 1926 because the ERP changed the election date from October to March, leaving a year and a half between those in 1925 and 1927. Supervisory personnel did not vote, because their representatives were appointed to joint committees.

Source: "Statement of Bethlehem Steel Co. with regard to the Union Shop and Check-off Issue, before the NWLB Mediation Panel," May 29, 1942, Bethlehem Shipbuilding v. IUMSWA, NWLB Case No. 38, p. 9.

becoming a subject that union organizers could exploit. Wages nevertheless became an issue at Fore River because upgrades to second and first-class rates often depended on how well a worker was liked by his foreman, rather than on an objective evaluation of his proficiency in the trade.[15]

General Body representatives unsuccessfully proposed a general wage increase at three meetings in 1935 and at another in 1936. When the proposal finally reached the Joint Committee that dealt with appeals, a tie resulted: all the worker representatives supported the raise and all the management representatives, who were foremen, opposed it. The industrial relations manager then ruled against the motion, and it was defeated. Although William Collins, the yard's new general manager, granted a 5 percent increase many months later, the ERP failed to protest the Joint Committee's deadlock and management's veto through alternative means, such as strike actions or slowdowns.[16]

The ERP's capitulation to the company went beyond its failure to represent

[15] Schmidt, "Intermediate Report"; *Quincy Patriot Ledger*, June 8, 12, 1934.
[16] Schmidt, "Intermediate Report."

Fore River workers. In 1933 it began to lobby in Washington on behalf of Bethlehem policy positions. That summer, ERP Chairman William McDermott and Vice-Chairman Charles MacKenzie spoke at the NRA Shipbuilding Code hearings against the thirty-two-hour week and in support of the forty-hour week, which industry executives were promoting. They financed their trip with $500 from the ERP's Community Chest Fund, which Industrial Relations Manager Parker personally approved. While this delegation was out of town, Arthur Boyson, a newly elected ERP representative who belonged to the machinists' union (IAM), organized Fore River workers to vote in support of the lower hours, even though the General Body later endorsed the pro-company actions of McDermott and MacKenzie. In 1934, McDermott and five other ERP representatives backed management by testifying against the prospective National Labor Relations Act before a Congressional Committee, even though many Fore River workers supported it. As before, Industrial Relations Manager Parker coordinated the campaign.[17]

After the successful resolution of the 1934 New York Ship strike, Fore River became a critical target for the IUMSWA. Discontent among some workers surfaced at the yard, in part because wages still had not been restored to pre-1932 levels. A few Fore River workers and their wives wrote in protest to President Roosevelt that they still received less than workers employed at the Charlestown Navy Yard in Boston. Expectations for improvements rose as FDR's new naval shipbuilding program dramatically increased shipyard employment in 1933. However, jobs were no more secure than before; men were freely hired and fired, employed only to work on individual vessels for the duration of the contract, in much the same way that construction workers were hired and fired at building sites. One worker's wife wrote to President Roosevelt about these difficult conditions: "We had to ask aid for the first time from the welfare; then he was put on the CWA and then called back to Fore River, but is it fair that he risk his life on high cranes etc. for a sum not enough to take care of one family in the very meanest cheapest way?"[18]

Phil Van Gelder, acting as a national IUMSWA organizer, made his first trip

---

[17] Schmidt, "Intermediate Report"; Boyson interview, Dec. 22, 1982. McDermott to Whiteside (NRA), July 21, 1933; NRA Proceedings on Shipbuilding Code, July 21, 1933, pp. 1000–2; both NA, RG 9, Box 5249. McDermott testimony against NLRA, as quoted in "Employee Representation in the Iron and Steel Industry—As Set Forth by Men and Management before the Senate Committee on Education and Labor," American Iron and Steel Institute, New York, c. 1934, in Hagley Museum and Library.

[18] "Case of IUMSWA on Behalf of Jack McGill," Van Gelder, c. June 19, 1934. "Mr. and Mrs. 'America'" to President Roosevelt, Feb. 16, 1934; "A worried tax-payers wife" to Hugh Johnson, March 10, 1934; both NA, RG 9, Box 5253.

to Quincy in April 1934 to investigate the situation at the Fore River yard. He stayed at the home of Jack McGill, a fellow Socialist Party member who had recently been hired as a driller. McGill had worked in the yard for about six months during the early 1920s, and he was no stranger to the Boston area or its shipyards. He had originally immigrated from Scotland and had experience in the Clydeside shipyards, where he was educated in militant trade unionism and syndicalism and had belonged to the same union as John Green.[19]

The Socialist Party network of union activists was instrumental in these and other early contacts between the IUMSWA and workers at Fore River. The SP leadership in the Boston area independently made direct contact with IUMSWA national secretary Francis Hunter in Camden at about the same time that Van Gelder journeyed up the coast. The SP's New England district secretary, Alfred Baker, wrote to Hunter on May 16, a month after Van Gelder's initial visit, that the party was planning an organizing drive at Fore River. Baker's plan was "to form one industrial union for the plant" and to affiliate with the IUMSWA, with the final decision, of course, in the hands of the workers themselves. Baker had read about the successful New York Ship strike in the *Camden Courier Post* and wanted to distribute copies of the article to Fore River workers. Within a week, Hunter sought support for the Fore River organizing from the skeletal Central Council of IUMSWA, the union's earliest national leadership body, and listed McGill among the union's contacts. Hunter also suggested that the union contact SP members in other East Coast shipyards.[20]

When Alfred Lewis and other SP activists called the first organizing meeting for the IUMSWA on Saturday morning, May 26, at Quincy's Labor Lyceum (the SP's local meeting hall), about 125 workers showed up. AFL Metal Trades Council representatives who were present argued against the industrial union strategy and claimed some 200 IAM members in the machine shop. Nothing was decided. Lewis admitted in correspondence to Hunter that "there is no strong organization sentiment as far as I can judge." He also indicated that Van Gelder's presence, along with specific information on the IUMSWA, would make a difference.[21]

---

[19] "Case of IUMSWA on Behalf of Jack McGill, Hugh Wallace, and Thomas Kelly [sic] vs. Bethlehem Shipbuilding Corp., Fore River Plant," by Van Gelder, c. June 19, 1934, NA, RG 25, "Fore River Shipyard, Docket #280, NLRB." Vogel, "The Fore River Strikers," pp. 75–97; Vogel used the pseudonym "Jack McCann" for McGill.

[20] Francis Hunter to Charles Renner, May 5, 1934; Alfred Baker to Hunter, May 16, 1934; Hunter to Renner, May 21, 1934; all IUMSWA Archives, Series I, Subseries 3, Box 1, Special Collections, University of Maryland at College Park Libraries.

[21] A. Lewis to Renner, May 29, 1934; "Fore River Plant Employees Mass Meeting" (organizing leaflet) scheduled for May 26, 1934; both IUMSWA Archives, Series I, Subseries 3, Box 1.

When Van Gelder led the second organizing meeting on Saturday, June 2, far fewer workers attended. He later claimed that thirty-six were present, but other sources indicate there may have only been eight. Van Gelder informed his Camden colleagues, however, that there was great potential for organizing at Fore River. His view of how to attack Bethlehem in Quincy emphasized strength of will, increased organization, and long-term commitment, which in many ways represented his vision for the national expansion of the union:

> The yard will not be organized overnight, but from the enthusiasm shown this morning I am confident that it is just a question of time before we get them. The AFL meeting last night was a flop—they didn't sign up a single man & they already act as if they were licked. I want to impress upon you the necessity for continuing this work here. . . . The men . . . are depending upon us. . . . The Central Council must realize that any backsliding on its part will seriously hamper the work we have started. We need more money, more organizers for other yards, & an efficient central office in order to capitalize on our reputation.

Charlie Purkis, who had been appointed temporary organizer, accompanied Van Gelder to the meeting. Van Gelder pushed hard to have Purkis put on permanently as the union's first full-time staff (non-office holding) organizer. Two of the Fore River workers who were present at the meeting, veteran trade unionist Jake Van Vloten and new hire Jack McGill, were socialists like Van Gelder. McGill, Hugh Wallace, and Thomas Kelley were chosen to run the organizing committee, even though they had worked less than a year at the yard.[22]

On the following Monday morning, McGill and the others on the organizing committee immediately tried to sign up members inside the yard. By midweek the boiler shop foreman notified McGill and two other workers in the department that they were being laid off indefinitely. The foreman seemed reluctant to take this action, because he liked the men and evidently felt that "the cream of his workers were being let go." Upper-level management, however, had decided to redesign the condensers on which they were working, thereby "eliminating" their jobs. The boiler shop also happened to be ERP Chairman McDermott's department and was a stronghold for the company union. Normally, when work in one area became slack, employees were temporarily transferred to another area, but in this case the company laid off the

---

[22] "Case of IUMSWA on Behalf of Jack McGill"; Vogel, "The Fore River Strikers," p. 97; Bethlehem Shipbuilding v. IUMSWA Local 5, NLRB case no. 135, Feb. 13, 1935, NA, RG 9, Box 5242. Van Gelder to John Green et al., June 2, 1934, IUMSWA Archives, Series I, Subseries 3, Box 1.

three leaders of the IUMSWA organizing committee, along with two other union members.[23]

These men were not in a position to challenge this action because their short employment service gave the company a strong legal position. Fore River's management did not lay off other union members with longer service, such as Van Vloten, nor did it have a standard layoff procedure that the discharged men could cite in their own defense. Usually older men and those with families were retained, while unmarried younger workers were discharged even though they might have had more time with the company. Transfers and recalls also were arbitrary. Technically, the company had not gone outside its usual layoff and transfer policy when it discharged the five union members.[24]

The IUMSWA now had a concrete issue around which to rally. More than 150 workers joined over the next two weeks, including many who did so as a protest against the firings. ERP representatives kept a close eye on this activity and reported regularly to management. To keep more organizers from entering the yard, the employment office instituted a new policy not to hire anyone who had not worked at Fore River previously.[25]

The IAM, the AFL's most active union at Fore River, also tried to pick up new members. Although the IAM was no real competition for the IUMSWA and had only limited success in recruiting workers, its presence inhibited the industrial union's growth because it prevented a united effort by all trade union activists in the yard. Arthur Boyson, the yard's leading IAM member and the Quincy Central Labor Union's vice-president, remained loyal to the AFL. The International Brotherhood of Electrical Workers (IBEW), the Boilermakers, the Patternmakers, and a number of other AFL craft unions also brought in a scattering of new members.[26]

During June and early July, the IUMSWA and the ERP waged a war of words through leaflets distributed at the gate, as well as statements and interviews published in the *Quincy Patriot Ledger*. Although the *Patriot Ledger* printed both sides of the story, it was not pro-labor, like the *Camden Courier Post*. McDermott, acting on behalf of the ERP, issued a lengthy statement

[23] "Case of IUMSWA on Behalf of Jack McGill"; Vogel, "The Fore River Strikers," p. 97; Bethlehem Shipbuilding v. IUMSWA Local 5, NLRB, Feb. 13, 1935. Hugh Wallace to New England Regional Labor Board, July 5, 1934; Thomas Kelley to New England Regional Labor Board, July 5, 1934; both NA, RG 25, "Fore River Shipyard, Docket #280, NLRB."

[24] Bethlehem Shipbuilding v. IUMSWA Local 5, NLRB, Feb. 13, 1935; Frederick Stevens to New England Regional Labor Board, July 24, 1934, NA, RG 25, "Fore River Shipyard, Docket #280, NLRB."

[25] Vogel, "The Fore River Strikers," p. 98; "Case of IUMSWA on Behalf of Jack McGill"; Van Gelder to Bartlett, July 10, 1934, RG 25, "Fore River Shipyard, Docket #280, NLRB."

[26] Vogel, "The Fore River Strikers," p. 98; Boyson interview, Sept. 12, 1986.

claiming among other things that workers at Fore River received better pay
than those at New York Ship; that all ERP representatives were "working men"
in contrast to Van Gelder's "present outside agitation"; and that the ERP provided Fore River workers with many benefits, such as a pension, a relief plan,
a community chest fund, and even free parking.[27]

IUMSWA organizer Charlie Purkis responded by explaining that the Fore
River workers' 10 percent raise resulted not from ERP efforts but from the
strike by union workers in Camden, who won a 14 percent wage increase;
Bethlehem felt obliged to follow suit and raised wages in Fore River as a way
to prevent unionization. IUMSWA Local 1 was in good shape, and the union
was not organizing in Quincy to build up a dues "war chest" for Camden, as
McDermott had alleged. Finally, Purkis declared that pension and relief plans
like the ERP's were merely "devices of capitalism" to keep workers from joining genuine unions, such as the Amalgamated Clothing Workers, which had
their own worker-run plans.[28]

Purkis and Van Gelder continued to organize at Quincy, while starting new
campaigns at the Bath Iron Works Shipyard in Maine, in East Boston where
Bethlehem had two repair yards, and at Electric Boat in New London, Connecticut. By July, the IUMSWA was operating at Fore River as Local 5, with
some 350 members, even though the local had not yet been chartered.
IUMSWA organizing meetings for Fore River were also held throughout the
metropolitan area. McGill now worked as a full-time organizer for the local,
accompanying Van Gelder and Purkis on home visits where they asked workers to sign cards for a union election. By late July, however, IUMSWA membership at Fore River had reached a plateau, and Van Gelder concluded that
strike action to build the union "was impossible."[29]

Initially Van Gelder had faith that the Roosevelt administration's early New
Deal policies, including Section 7(a) of the NRA and the establishment of the
National Labor Board, would provide government protection for union organizing, but in Quincy he soon learned the serious limitations of relying too
heavily on legal procedures to promote trade unionism. When the five union
men were fired, Van Gelder immediately filed a complaint with Arthur Wharton, the IAM national president who sat on the NRA Shipbuilding Authority's

[27] *Quincy Patriot Ledger*, June 8, 12, 1934.
[28] Ibid.
[29] Van Gelder interview, Oct. 25, 1982; Van Gelder letter to David Palmer, Nov. 27, 1982;
Vogel, "The Fore River Strikers," p. 98. IUMSWA's 1934 leaflets for meetings at Quincy
(June 16, July 4, 17), Weymouth (June 14), Dorchester (June 19), and East Boston (June 27);
all NA, RG 25, "Fore River Shipyard, Docket #280, NLRB." Van Gelder to H. Newton Whittelsey, Aug. 17, 1934; Whittelsey to Van Gelder, Aug. 21, 1934; both NA, RG 9, Box 5250.
IUMSWA, *Proceedings, 2nd National Convention*, Aug. 1936, Van Gelder report.

newly formed Industrial Relations Committee (IRC). Van Gelder also wanted the New England Regional Labor Board to take up the case, so that he could stay in Quincy to organize. The IRC's Wharton appeared to be sympathetic to Van Gelder's inquiry at this point, but the business representatives on the Shipbuilding Authority, who included former Fore River executive H. G. Smith, were not. A round of bureaucratic wrangling ensued over which government agency should have jurisdiction in the case, and finally the Labor Board gained control.[30]

Finally, on July 17, the Regional Board began hearings in Boston, but the company refused to attend. Instead, Employment Manager Stevens sent two memoranda detailing the service records of the discharged men and others still working at the yard. The Board did not make an investigation on its own and agreed with the company's claim that it had not discharged the men for union activity. The investigative process prior to the hearing was a travesty, compared to later procedures adopted by the NLRB after the passage of the National Labor Relations Act in 1935. The Regional Board ambivalently concluded that the complainants, now reduced to three, had not been subjected to discrimination, but found fault with the company "on account of the intentional failure . . . to send representatives to answer the questions of this Board."[31]

The NLRB (the board in Washington, D.C., that preceded the Wagner Act) responded by demanding that the Regional Board take a clearer stand in finding fault with the company's failure to appear. When the Regional Board was unable to resolve the issue, officials from the National Board assumed responsibility over the hearings in Boston. This time, ERP head McDermott and other company union representatives expressed interest in attempting to counter Local 5's efforts to get a union election at the yard. Controversy in the case

---

[30] Van Gelder to Wharton, June 8, 1934; Van Gelder to Robert Wagner (Chairman NLB), June 13, 1934; H. G. Smith to Doyle, June 14, 1934; Wharton to Van Gelder, June 14, 1934; B. M. Stern (NLB) to Van Gelder, June 19, 1934; Van Gelder to Wharton, June 19, 1934; Doyle to Van Gelder, June 22, 1934; Benedict Wolf (NLB) to IRC, June 28, 1934; all NA, RG 9, Box 5242. Van Gelder to Doyle, June 19, 1934; Doyle to Chairman NLB (Wagner), June 22, 1934; Van Gelder to Bartlett, July 10, 1934; Bartlett to Bethlehem Shipbuilding, July 13, 1934; all NA, RG 25, "Fore River Shipyard, Docket #280, NLRB." "Conference on Shipbuilding," NRA Shipbuilding Code Authority, June 22, 1934, NA, RG 9, Box 5255.

[31] "Notes of Hearing on Fore River Shipyard," NLRB Docket No. 240; Stevens memos, July 24, 1934; Bartlett to Bethlehem Shipbuilding, July 18, Aug. 3, 1934; Van Gelder to Bartlett, July 24, 1934; Bethlehem Shipbuilding v. IUMSWA, Docket No. 240, Decision, issued by Edmund Blake (New England Regional Labor Board), Aug. 30, 1934; all NA, RG 25, "Fore River Shipyard, Docket #280, NLRB." It is not exactly clear why the discrimination cases dropped to three, but it can be assumed that the others had either lost contact with the union or preferred not to be part of the Board case.

escalated when the IUMSWA Local 5 secretary, James Hardie, notified the Regional Board on Thursday, September 6, that the union had "a substantial number" of signed cards requesting an election. Over the next two days, union activists passed out as many cards as they could, but the ERP General Body quickly mobilized its own supporters to pass out anti-election cards, effectively blocking the election push. As workers saw it, the IUMSWA had lost the "battle of the postcards" at Fore River.[32]

By Tuesday, Local 5 president Jeremiah Mitchell and secretary James Hardie knew they had been beaten, but tried to make the best of the situation. When they submitted their cards petitioning for an election to the Regional Board, they protested: "We feel that this number . . . should be considered sufficient in view of the wholesale intimidation that has run riot in the Fore River yard since early last June." The Board received only 308 workers' cards from the IUMSWA, out of some 3,000 employees, compared to 1,524 cards from the ERP opposing an election. It saw no reason to investigate Mitchell and Hardie's accusations against the company, believing that the card count spoke for itself.[33]

To strengthen the campaign, the IUMSWA decided to hold its first national convention at Quincy Point, near the shipyard, in late September. Those elected as national officers included Local 5's Mitchell, who became vice-president, and Sinclair, who joined the General Executive Board. Union leaders hoped that this attention to Quincy would somehow translate into a larger union movement at Fore River, but Local 5 continued to attract only a small membership.[34]

A second round of NLRB hearings on behalf of the discharged workers lasted from October to December 1934. Van Gelder did his best in this lopsided contest with the giant steel and shipbuilding corporation. The case was conducted in Boston before hearing examiner Calvert Magruder, then a law professor at Harvard. Bethlehem was represented by the Wall Street firm of Cravath, de Gersdorff, Swaine and Wood, with partner Hoyt Moore, who had organized the original Bethlehem Steel Corporation, presenting the com-

---

[32] Wolf to Bartlett, Sept. 15, 1934; Harry Knight to Bartlett, Sept. 20, 1934; Wolf to Regional Labor Board, Sept. 25, 1934; McDermott to Calvert Magruder (NLRB, Boston), Sept. 26, 1934; Magruder notes on conference with ERP representatives, Sept. 29, 1934; James Hardie (two Local 5 letters) to Regional Labor Board, both Sept. 6, 1934; Jeremiah Mitchell and Hardie to Regional Labor Board, Sept. 13, 1934; all NA, RG 25, "Fore River Shipyard, Docket #280, NLRB."

[33] Mitchell and Hardie to Regional Labor Board, Sept. 13, 1934; Report by Blake (New England Regional Board), Oct. 17, 1934, NA, RG 25, "Fore River Shipyard, Docket #280, NLRB."

[34] IUMSWA, *Proceedings, 1st National Convention*, Sept. 28–30, 1934.

pany's case. The IUMSWA could not afford a lawyer, so Van Gelder conducted the case, in his words, "after a fashion." Bethlehem submitted a printed brief, while Van Gelder typed the IUMSWA's. On February 13, 1935, the NLRB announced its decision: there had been no discrimination against the three discharged workers. The Board did not consider the fact that these men belonged to the organizing committee leading the drive, nor did it address the accusation that foremen had coerced workers to sign anti-election cards. By present-day standards, the Board's investigative process, which relied on Regional Board investigators who had never left their offices, was heavily biased against the IUMSWA. When Van Gelder learned of the outcome, he recalled, "I was furious. . . . I thought this was really going to do something for us. I was young and innocent. . . . I never forgave [NLRB Chairman Francis] Biddle for finding for the Company. Among his reasons was that there were other IUMSWA members in the yard and they weren't fired! . . . Well, that was a set-back for us, because we couldn't protect people. I have always felt that this loss was the key to our failure to organize the yard in those early years." [35]

Immediately after the NLRB's Fore River decision, Van Gelder stopped expecting positive action from new government agencies, although he continued to work with the Labor Department and pro-labor elected officials. The breakthrough, he now believed, depended on action by workers themselves. As he explained to Paul Porter, the Socialist Party's national labor secretary: "We are having a tough time keeping our new Locals together. They haven't been able to get recognition or any conditions and the Labor Boards and Industrial Relations Committee have given us a terrible jerking around. Everyone is completely fed up with them. They are really worse than nothing. That's why we are trying to work up sentiment for direct action. Am looking for a strike wave this spring, which would help us a lot." [36]

Van Gelder proposed an alternative tactic at Fore River. Local 5 would run candidates for the March 1935 ERP election in an effort to expose the company union from the inside, as Purkis and Mullin had done at New York Ship in 1933. Instead of immediately taking over the company union, the IUMSWA's representatives on the ERP would first push a program calling for better wages and working conditions. Van Gelder outlined the idea to John W. Brown, then organizing at the Bath Iron Works shipyard in Maine. "They . . . will fight for wages and shop conditions, and call meetings of their depart-

---

[35] Bethlehem Shipbuilding (Quincy) v. IUMSWA Local 5, NRLB Decision, Feb. 13, 1935; NLRB press release, Feb. 14, 1935; both NA, RG 25, "Fore River Shipyard, Docket #280 NLRB." Van Gelder letter to Palmer, Nov. 27, 1982; Van Gelder interview, Oct. 25, 1982. Biddle later became Attorney-General in the Roosevelt administration.

[36] Van Gelder to Paul Porter, Feb. 12, 1935, Van Gelder personal papers.

ments to back them up. Then when they can't get anywhere in the company union set up they will resign in a body and organize the men on the basis that the Company union is a fake and a delusion. Mitchell, Sinclair, and Hardie will pick only dependable men for candidates, who will pledge themselves to obey the orders of the Union."[37]

Local 5 adopted Van Gelder's plan for entering the ERP, but anticipated that the union could "break . . . it up from within" from the start. When the local fielded eleven candidates in a race in which sixty-three men competed for eighteen open positions, the IUMSWA men won only six seats; Local 5 members were a minority on the General Body and were unable to gain top committee posts. Nevertheless, the local now had five of its key leaders— Mitchell, Sinclair, Hardie, Westland, and John Hicks (a former AFL pipe-fitter)—positioned where they could make open demands on the company. As IUMSWA representatives, they also put forward parallel demands through Local 5 for union recognition, seniority rights, and better pay, which led to what may have been the first company meeting with the local's committee.[38]

Although the IUMSWA representatives worked in the ERP, "they did not publicize the closed-door activities of the company union, they did not call meetings of their shops to denounce the Plan and its workings, they did not make any real fight in the General Body meetings against management," according to Van Gelder. The national union decided in May to apply its own pressure on Fore River management. Camden was again out on strike, and Green and Van Gelder called on IUMSWA locals to join in a general ship-building strike. Van Gelder put forward the idea in a special visit to Quincy. Then on May 18 and 19 a special GEB meeting was held in Camden to discuss implementing the general strike plan.[39]

A year later, Van Gelder claimed that Fore River workers were "boiling" and that "the yard could have been pulled." Perhaps he mistakenly believed that the militancy and solidarity of New York Ship workers, then in their second strike, could easily be transferred to Quincy. More likely, however, Van Gelder was excusing his own misjudgment of Fore River's workers by blaming the local union leadership for being conservative and passive. Local 5's executive board at first agreed to the strike call "upon advice of the [national] GEB," according to Van Gelder, but then it backed off. When the membership meeting for the strike vote was finally held, with Van Gelder and Green both present, Jake

[37] Van Gelder to John W. Brown, Feb. 20, 1935, IUMSWA papers (prior to University of Maryland accession) quoted in Mergen, "History of the Industrial Union of Marine and Ship-building Workers of America," p. 49.

[38] Vogel, "The Fore River Strikers," pp. 100–1.

[39] IUMSWA, *Proceedings, 2nd National Convention*, Aug. 1936, Van Gelder report; John Green to GEB members, May 13, 1935, Van Gelder personal papers.

Van Vloten and Andrew Banks, an emerging leader, restated their allegiance to the IUMSWA but made it clear that they feared the local could not survive a strike. Every other local leader agreed with their position. When Green tried to argue for a strike at the yard, Local 5's president Mitchell refused to let him speak and blocked a vote on the issue. McGill supported the national office, but he was not working in the yard and seems to have had no other allies at the meeting. Some of Local 5's leadership, as Van Gelder recalled, "blamed the strike agitation on Camden, called it a sympathetic strike, and asserted that they were being forced to pull Camden's chestnuts out of the fire, and would then be left out on the street." Van Gelder believed that this local misleadership, as he perceived it, "effectively killed the fighting spirit in the yard." In his eyes, Local 5's leaders had "lost their guts completely." [40]

But had they? Even Van Vloten, a socialist like Van Gelder and a veteran of many union struggles in the yard over the years, could not agree with the national office on the proposed strike. The real issue was whether or not Fore River's workers were ready to strike. There is no record of any direct action by workers between the time the IUMSWA began organizing in the spring of 1934 and May 1935, when this meeting took place. How, then, could they be expected to carry out an effective strike that *no* local leaders considered realistic? No shipyard strikes materialized on the East Coast when the national call was made, aside from the one already underway in Camden. The Camden walkout succeeded because it was based on worker sentiment inside the yard, had a united local leadership, and did not have to contend with a company union. These conditions did not exist at Fore River.

The leaders of Local 5, whatever their limitations, were realistic when they refused to follow Van Gelder and Green's plan. The national office, however well intentioned and dedicated to furthering militant unionism, seems to have split an already weak Quincy leadership. Van Gelder later concluded that these leaders were responsible for the "terrific letdown [which] broke the morale of the Local, and it died right there [at the May meeting]," but national leadership was hardly blameless under the circumstances. [41]

Local 5 provided no financial assistance to the New York Ship strike over the summer, nor did the local's representatives on the ERP take any further actions on behalf of the IUMSWA. In September, Van Gelder moved against Local 5 leaders Mitchell, Sinclair, and Hardie. He persuaded the national GEB to drop Mitchell and got the national board to endorse an order for IUMSWA members to resign from the Fore River ERP. Mitchell and the IUMSWA's

---

[40] IUMSWA, *Proceedings, 2nd National Convention*, Aug. 1936, Van Gelder report; Green to GEB members, May 13, 1935; Vogel, "The Fore River Strikers," pp. 101–2.

[41] IUMSWA, *Proceedings, 2nd National Convention*, Aug. 1936, Van Gelder report.

other ERP representatives, Hardie, Sinclair, and Westland, refused to abide by the GEB's order and instead met with Industrial Relations Manager Stevens on their own. They turned on the IUMSWA, attacking it as corrupt and communist-influenced. In later years Mitchell became a foreman, Sinclair an assistant foreman, Westland a quarterman (lead hand with supervisory status), and Hardie a company union official. The IUMSWA's two other ERP representatives, McLean and Hicks, resigned from the company union.[42]

IAM activist Arthur Boyson, who had served on the ERP in the early 1930s, refused to run again in 1935 when the IUMSWA fielded its candidates. Although he remained loyal to the IAM at this point, he began to take a position independent of both the AFL and IUMSWA activists at the yard by strongly opposing any involvement with the ERP, having lost patience with its corruption. Boyson recalled that Sinclair talked to him about the infiltration plan. "I was dropping out as a representative at that time. . . . They put a lot of pressure on me . . . to stay in, because I was a curiosity. I was an AFL lobster in the Representation Plan." But Boyson "got the hell out of there," even though the IUMSWA "wanted me to stay in . . . as sort of a spy." Boyson warned Sinclair that if the union members stayed in the ERP, they would end up like all the other representatives.

> I told [him] "you can come in out of the yard if you want to . . . and nobody wants you to do any work. They pay you time and a third for doing nothing, and nobody questions you. . . . They can go up to the board room, and they sit there and talk . . . about nothing, and fall asleep and everything else. Or [they] go over [to] the apprentice school . . . and sit there. First thing you know it will rub off on some of you guys . . . and you'll find out you're in a mess." So that's just what happened. And that's why they went sour. In order to cover themselves up they got sour on the union and called it a communist outfit and a red outfit and every other damn thing. . . . That was Jerry Mitchell. . . . The only one who didn't was Johnny Hicks. He was a representative, and he got the hell out of it. . . . Johnny never wavered an inch.

In later years, Boyson and Hicks became Local 5's core leaders from the older group of workers who had been affiliated with the AFL.[43]

From the fall of 1935 to early 1937, there was little or no IUMSWA organization at Fore River. Organizer John W. Brown came down from Bath, Maine,

---

[42] Ibid.; Vogel, "The Fore River Strikers," pp. 101–2.
[43] Boyson interview, Sept. 12, 1986.

in November 1935 to try to revive the local, but in February 1936 John Green suspended Local 5's autonomy, putting Brown in charge. Andrew Banks was appointed temporary secretary-treasurer and John Hicks was named president. Brown stayed for a year, but had to resort almost exclusively to legal maneuvers.[44]

In March 1936, Brown and a group of Fore River workers filed a new charge with the Boston NLRB, claiming that Bethlehem dominated the ERP, which made it impossible to organize or hold a fair election. Interviewing ERP representatives and company officials, Boston NLRB director Howard Myers soon uncovered substantial new evidence of company domination, an unfair labor practice under the new NLRA. In early April, the Washington NLRB authorized him to issue a new complaint against Fore River. Myers proved to be the single most important government official in the prosecution of Bethlehem Fore River over unfair labor practices during the 1930s and 1940s. He eventually led the Board's fight for jurisdiction in the landmark Supreme Court case of *Myers v. Bethlehem Shipbuilding Corp.*[45]

The Board scheduled hearings for April 27, but on that day Bethlehem filed successfully for an injunction that blocked the NLRB from proceeding. Delays continued until July, when a District Court judge issued an injunction prohibiting the NLRB from investigating or holding hearings in response to the Fore River workers' complaint. In essence, the court ruled that the Board had no jurisdiction in labor relations at Fore River. A long process of appeals by the Board ensued over the next two years, leaving the IUMSWA organizers with no immediate legal protection at the shipyard. The union hoped that the legal battle would be resolved in a matter of months, but it seriously underestimated the staying power of the Bethlehem Corporation and its lawyers. By February 1937, all IUMSWA locals organizing at Bethlehem yards around the country had complaints before the NLRB, which the company was blocking by contesting the Board's jurisdiction in the courts.[46]

At the same time, workers nationwide were initiating strike actions, espe-

[44] IUMSWA, *Proceedings, 2nd National Convention*, Aug. 1936, Van Gelder report; Minutes of Local 5 monthly meeting regarding suspension of autonomy, signed by John Hicks and Andrew Banks, Feb. 4, 1936, IUMSWA Archives, Series V, Box 19.

[45] Wallace Cohen to "The Board," chronology of Bethlehem Shipbuilding v. IUMSWA Local 5, Oct. 21, 1938; Myers memo "Re: Bethlehem Shipbuilding Corp., I-C-25," March 3, 1936; NLRB 1st Region, "Weekly Report on Pending Cases," March 28, 1936; Myers to Wolf, April 3, 1936; Wolf to Myers, April 6, 1936; NLRB 1st Region, "Weekly Report on Pending Cases," April 11, 1936; all NA, RG 25, Box 2357.

[46] IUMSWA, *Proceedings, 2nd National Convention*, Aug. 1936, Van Gelder report; Vogel, "The Fore River Strikers," p. 103; *Shipyard Worker*, Nov. 5, 13, 27, Dec. 4, 1936, Jan. 15, Feb. 5, 1937.

cially sit-downs. Even the shipyards of staid New England were affected by the changed atmosphere. In late February 1937, 60 workers at Electric Boat, in New London, Connecticut, conducted a sit-down strike to protest the firing of union activists. At Fore River, 200 workers in the pipe shop, where John Hicks was organizing, held a twenty-two-minute sit-down after the company fired a worker for smoking on the job. The foreman responsible quickly reversed his decision when it appeared that the protest might spread. Fore River general manager William Collins vowed that he would discipline yard foremen rather than workers if there were any more protests.[47]

Two months later, on April 26, a major new campaign got underway at Fore River with the arrival of Lucien Koch. Koch had just been hired by the IUMSWA to replace organizer John Diehl, who had come up from New York Ship in August 1936 when John W. Brown returned to Bath, Maine. Although Koch had never worked in a shipyard or been a full-time union organizer, he brought experience from his years in Arkansas as director of Commonwealth College. This alternative school educated workers and social activists, and paid special attention to the needs of sharecroppers and others who lived in the rural South. Koch himself had been beaten and jailed while helping the Southern Tenant Farmers' Union organize black and white sharecroppers. Commonwealth College had a practical curriculum for organizing, but it also had a radical political and cultural bent, which made Koch controversial. As head of the school, he had toured the country to raise funds and gather support. He had also used this forum to promote solidarity in workers' struggles; for example, he had addressed New York Ship strikers in 1934, supporting their walkout. Koch brought a useful research background to the Fore River campaign. He had studied labor economics with John R. Commons and Selig Perlman at the University of Wisconsin, where he received a Masters Degree in 1931. In 1935 he left Commonwealth College in Arkansas to work for the National Recovery Administration, and he later joined the Labor Department under Secretary Frances Perkins as a consumer interest researcher.[48]

Koch aimed to set the Fore River campaign on a new footing. He and the national officers viewed the restructured organizing drive and the new level of worker activism, such as the pipefitters' sitdown, as a major departure from the

---

[47] *Shipyard Worker*, Feb. 26, March 5, April 16, 1937. State police ejected the Electric Boat workers and placed them under arrest. Pickets outside the plant kept the strike going, even though the company union led some 300 strikebreakers through the lines.

[48] *Shipyard Worker*, April 2, 9, May 7, 1937; Lucien Koch interview, Jan. 7, 1983, Alexandria, Va.; Koch resume, Koch personal papers. For background on Koch's support for tenant farmer organizing while at Commonwealth College, see H. L. Mitchell, *Mean Things Happening in This Land: The Life and Times of H. L. Mitchell, Co-founder of the Southern Tenant Farmers Union* (Montclair, N.J.: Allanheld, Osmun, 1979), pp. 50–51, 62–67.

1934 organizing campaign. Momentum for a new movement in the yard appeared to be growing, as workers in other departments began to raise grievances with management. Many were reportedly turning to IUMSWA activists for support because ERP representatives appeared complacent and ineffective. Koch and the national officers also sought to expand the scope of the IUMSWA's operations by renewing drives at Bethlehem's East Boston repair yards and the Charlestown Navy Yard.[49]

Over 500 workers attended the first Quincy meeting for the new campaign on May 1. Koch and Green explained the Supreme Court's *Jones & Laughlin Steel* decision upholding the constitutionality of the NLRA, which gave legal protections to union organizing. Koch's observations seemed to be borne out in Quincy. About 90 percent of the welders had joined the union during a recent surge of inside organizing. Former AFL loyalists, such as machinist Arthur Boyson, were beginning to sign workers into the new union. They retained their AFL craft union membership while joining the IUMSWA, thereby disregarding the prohibition against "dual unionism" held so dear in labor circles. Koch could confidently report that there was "much interest among the men. . . . Here in Quincy there is some meeting almost every night."[50]

Anticommunism within the local leadership and the workforce, promoted by Fore River management and the ERP, surfaced as soon as Koch arrived. The company and the ERP immediately attacked him as a communist. ERP representatives discreetly circulated an article from *Liberty*, a right-wing, anti-CIO magazine, which claimed that Koch had promoted communism, nudism, atheism, and other unorthodox activities while at Commonwealth College. In culturally conservative Quincy, these accusations had a receptive audience. Unfortunately, Koch's conspicuous long hair and his lack of shipyard work experience stereotyped him in the minds of many workers. Although he was American-born, he was not a native New Englander. All these personal factors, which defined Koch's public image, led many workers to believe that he was an outsider who did not belong in Quincy. To complicate Koch's problems, Local 5 president Andrew Banks, who had a strong base in the welding department, saw Koch as a threat to his position and his free access to Local 5's dues money. Banks and his allies, Michael Woodford and Charles Smith, demanded that national president John Green remove Koch, citing *Lib-*

---

[49] *Shipyard Worker*, April 16, Aug. 6, 1937. IUMSWA leaflet, "Men of Fore River—A New Drive is in Progress," May 7, 1937; Van Gelder to Jack McGill, May 3, 1937; Green to Koch, May 4, 1937; IUMSWA leaflet, "Ship Repair Workers of Boston," May 5, 1937; Koch to Van Gelder, May 7, 1937; all IUMSWA Archives, Series V, Box 19.

[50] *Shipyard Worker*, May 7, 1937. IUMSWA leaflet, "To All Shipyard Workers—Mass Meeting—Saturday, May 1," c. April 1937; Koch to Van Gelder, May 9, 1937; Koch to Van Gelder, May 6, 1937; all IUMSWA Archives, Series V, Box 19.

erty's allegation that he was a "communist." They warned Green, "if you do not arrive within 24 hours the situation in Quincy is a disaster." The words of these Local 5 leaders made their way into the *Quincy Patriot Ledger*, providing further bad publicity for the union. Although he was left-wing, Koch was not a Communist. Green and Van Gelder backed Koch without reservation, and Koch soon had complete oversight of Local 5's finances and gained the trust of most members.[51]

Arthur Boyson became the key link to rebuilding the IUMSWA at Fore River, following the eclipse of Banks's power in Local 5. Boyson advised Koch on how to adapt to Quincy's conservative New England culture, suggesting that he join a church that shipyard workers attended and downplay his left-wing politics. He and Koch quickly established good relations, attesting to Koch's organizing abilities, his effective style with workers, and his genuine interest in people. Koch also won the confidence of other veteran activists, such as John Hicks and Charlie Palmer, who like Boyson had AFL backgrounds. These three became the backbone of the new leadership. By June 1937, Local 5 had a functioning organizing committee with representatives in seventeen departments, and by the fall over 1,000 Fore River workers had become union members. The rapid progress of simultaneous drives at the Navy Yard and in East Boston, where locals were chartered that month, further galvanized the Fore River organizers.[52]

A major legal breakthrough occurred on January 31, 1938, when the Supreme Court handed down its decisions in *Myers v. Bethlehem Shipbuilding* and *Newport News Shipbuilding v. Schauffler*. It ruled that lower courts had acted improperly when they issued injunctions preventing the NLRB from investigating unfair labor practices at these two shipyards. Justice Louis Brandeis, who wrote the majority opinions, established that the NLRA's provision

---

[51] *Shipyard Worker*, May 28, 1937; *Quincy Patriot Ledger*, May 5, 1938. Nolen Bullock, "Rah, Rah, Russia!", *Liberty*, Dec. 19, 1936, reprinted in Vogel, "Fore River Strikers," between pages 104 and 105; James Rowan, "Mr. Koch Comes to Town," *Iron Age*, April 21, 1938, pp. 26–27; Boyson interviews, Oct. 4, 1982, Sept. 12, 1986. Koch to Van Gelder, May 6, 9, June 7, 1937; Banks to Green, May 10, 1937; Van Gelder to Koch, May 11, 25, early June, 1937; Woodford to Green, May 12, 15, 1937; Koch to Green and Van Gelder, May 24, 1937; Charles Smith, Banks, Woodford to Green, May 3, 1937; Local 5 Executive Board to Koch, May 15, 1937; Green to Banks, May 14, 1937; Green to Woodford, May 15, 1937; all IUMSWA Archives, Series V, Box 19. Koch associated with leftists of every persuasion but was not in the Communist Party. He told me how, when he was red-baited during the McCarthy era, the anticommunist CIO leader James Carey spoke publicly in his defense.

[52] Boyson interviews, Oct. 4, 1982, Sept. 12, 1986; Koch interviews, Jan. 7, 1983, June 10, 1987. Koch to Van Gelder, May 25, Oct. 26, 1937; both IUMSWA Archives, Series V, Box 19. *Shipyard Worker*, June 18, 1937; IUMSWA, *Proceedings, 3rd National Convention*, Sept. 1937.

granting the NLRB full jurisdiction to investigate and decide labor relations cases was indeed constitutional. The NLRB could now conduct its long-delayed Fore River hearing on unfair labor practices and the company union, but the IUMSWA still had to contend with the unresolved problem of enforcement of the Board's findings.[53]

The Supreme Court rulings stimulated the Fore River organizing drive, and the scheduling of NLRB hearings for the spring of 1938 gave the impression that the IUMSWA was headed toward victory. After four long years, it finally appeared that the ERP was on its last legs and Bethlehem would have to accept an election. On February 12, a meeting for the nomination of local union officers was "jammed," and workers spilled out into the streets. Two weeks later the national office restored Local 5's autonomy and reissued its charter at a special meeting that filled the Quincy Arena with over 2,000 workers.[54]

Under the new local leadership of Boyson (president), Hicks (vice president), and Palmer (financial secretary), Koch proclaimed that the union now had a safe majority of the yard's 3,500 employees. Internal organization appeared to keep pace with this increase. Shop officers represented six of the yard's departments: the pipe shop, blacksmiths, outside machinists, chippers and caulkers (which included the central tool room), welders, and electricians. In line with this growing strength, Local 5 officers called on all Fore River workers to boycott the ERP's March elections.[55]

Events in March showed how skillful Bethlehem was in the art of public relations. Without once resorting to physical force or blatant coercion, the company completely reversed the union's gains. On the morning of March 10, a large police contingent stood guard over a group of young boys in front of the yard, who passed out a four-page reprint of the *Liberty* magazine article, "Rah, Rah, Russia," attacking Koch as a communist.[56]

The impact on yard workers was devastating. As Boyson recalled, "the men ran like flies" from the union. The boycott of the ERP election completely collapsed: 82 percent of all Fore River workers voted in it. Although the NLRB hearings revealed complicity between the ERP and Bethlehem, Local 5's membership dropped precipitously. The company kept up its attack on Koch in April through a second handout. Published in the industry magazine *Iron*

---

[53] Myers v. Bethlehem Shipbuilding, 1A LRR Man. 575–580 (U.S. Supreme Court 1938); Newport News Shipbuilding v. Schauffler, 1A LRR Man. 580–582 (U.S. Supreme Court 1938); Irving Bernstein, *The Turbulent Years: A History of the American Worker, 1933–1941* (Boston: Houghton Mifflin, 1960), pp. 646–48.

[54] Schmidt, "Intermediate Report"; *Shipyard Worker*, Feb. 25, March 11, 1938.

[55] Schmidt, "Intermediate Report"; *Shipyard Worker*, Feb. 25, March 11, 1938.

[56] Vogel, "The Fore River Strikers," p. 104, and reprint of article's first page; Rowan, "Mr. Koch Comes to Town."

Age, this article retold the "Rah, Rah, Russia" story, but put it in the context of the steel industry's employee representation plans. Koch and Local 5 had compared the ERP election to those conducted under the dictatorships of Hitler and Stalin. *Iron Age* replied in a similar vein, but also took aim at the larger CIO movement. "That Mr. Koch's efforts to cram the socialistic and communistic philosophies of Commonwealth College down the throats of the Yankee shipbuilders along with their beans, brown bread and fried clams have just met a stunning defeat does not reflect particularly on Mr. Koch. . . . Quincy of Massachusetts is not Mena of Arkansas nor is it one of the somewhat more fertile fields for unionism which Mr. Lewis and the CIO have cultivated industriously with varied degrees of success for about two years now." Koch and Local 5 clung to the hope of a victory at the Boston NLRB hearings, but the damage had been done.[57]

Koch had great difficulty countering this anticommunist slander from Bethlehem, even though equally insidious forms of propaganda had failed earlier at New York Ship and Federal Ship. Fore River workers had less tolerance of the left than workers at these other two yards did. Union leaders at these other worksites, such as Green and McAlack in Camden and Shapiro and Levin in Kearny, had openly acknowledged their left-wing views and had a strong following, both on a trade union and a personal level. In Quincy, Koch worked with a number of inside leaders whose philosophy did not go beyond liberal trade unionism and who generally mistrusted the left, even if they were not strictly anticommunist. (Boyson was a striking exception.) Local leaders of this type had difficulty with anticommunist assaults by those opposed to the IUMSWA.

The level of conformity and fear induced by Bethlehem Fore River's company union environment created a "herd mentality" among many of the workers. Management's attack was led by worker leadership in the company union, not simply by foremen. Meg McGill, the wife of IUMSWA organizer Jack McGill, recognized the level of fear among the men: "Lots of them . . . were such slaves to the bosses that they would spy and report on their fellow workers. . . . The majority of them liked Roosevelt and had just gotten a little security in their lives—many just got back their houses from the banks through the government's help. They didn't want any trouble."[58]

Finally, Koch's conventional tactics at this point contributed to his inability to launch an effective counter-attack. At New York Ship from 1933 to 1935

---

[57] Vogel, "The Fore River Strikers," p. 104, reprint; Boyson interview, Oct. 4, 1982; Rowan, "Mr. Koch Comes to Town"; "Statement of Bethlehem Steel Co. . . . ," May 29, 1942, Bethlehem Shipbuilding v. IUMSWA, NWLB, Case No. 38, p. 9.

[58] Meg McGill interview, quoted in Vogel, "The Fore River Strikers," pp. 95–97.

and at Federal Ship from 1937 to 1939, local leadership and staff organizers used an array of "surprise" tactics against management. These included rapid takeover of the company union, unexpected forms of direct action inside the yard, and mass pickets involving thousands at the gates. Koch, however, relied on more passive and open tactics, focusing on the NLRB hearings and the boycott of the ERP election. Even if he had tried more ambitious tactics, Koch had neither the bold leaders inside the yard nor the critical mass of militant workers that would have been required to carry out direct action. The momentum remained with the company union and its sponsor, Bethlehem management; the industrial union was unable to match their creative tactics and effective mobilization.

As Local 5 passed through this new crisis, secretary-treasurer Charlie Palmer kept careful track of the local's finances and membership files. His monthly reports to the Camden office revealed a sharp, demoralizing decline in membership from 1,800 in May to 800 in June, 400 in July, and 350 in August. The NLRB's "Intermediate Report," based on the hearings, found full justification for the union's charges against the Bethlehem Corporation and the Fore River and East Boston ERPs. This particular legal victory obviously did not translate into increased membership.[59]

The union continued to issue optimistic leaflets promising that "The Election Lies Ahead!," but the campaign's momentum disintegrated as Bethlehem continued its legal fight against the union. Despite strong evidence from the Boston NLRB hearings of Bethlehem-ERP complicity, the company union showed no signs of weakening its hold over Fore River workers. In December IUMSWA Local 4 narrowly lost an NLRB election in Bath, Maine, adding to the frustration of Fore River's union members. Some hope appeared in February 1939, when the NLRB officially ruled that Bethlehem controlled the ERPs at Fore River and East Boston and ordered an election. In the ensuing months, however, Bethlehem challenged this decision in the courts, delaying an election.[60]

In response to the company's stalling tactics, Koch adopted a new slogan, "Digging In," but as 1939 progressed, his sense of frustration and powerless-

---

[59] Official Report Sheets, Charles Palmer to IUMSWA GEB: June 4, July 9, Aug. 20, Sept. 17, 1938; Koch to Van Gelder, Aug. 29, 1938; all IUMSWA Archives, Series V, Box 20. Schmidt, "Intermediate Report."

[60] Local 5 leaflet, "What Is Ahead?," for Sept. 17, 1939 meeting; Koch to Van Gelder, Aug. 29, Sept. 20, 27, 1938; Van Gelder to Koch, Sept. 21, 28, 1938; all IUMSWA Archives, Series V, Box 20. *Shipyard Worker*, Oct. 21, Nov. 4, Dec. 30, 1938, Feb. 24, 1939. Bethlehem Shipbuilding v. IUMSWA, 3 LRR Man. 569–576 (NLRB 1939). Bethlehem Shipbuilding against NLRB, "Petition for Review of Order of NLRB," March 2, 1939, NA, RG 25, Box 2357, "Bethlehem Shipbuilding, C-906, #1."

ness grew. In August he reached the breaking point, and in a letter to Van Gelder he bluntly criticized the union's reliance on a legal strategy for organizing. Koch had gone by the Circuit Court, as he did every few days, to check on the status of the Bethlehem case.

> A day or two ago Bethlehem lawyers notified the court that the stipulation had been completed. But now it seems there is not sufficient time left for printing and preparation of briefs.
>
> This new delay, if it is allowed to occur, may be the last straw. I have assured the men that the case would be ready by October. . . . The Board had from Feb. 10 to get a certified copy of the record to the court, yet it failed to do so until a few weeks ago. Something drastic needs to be done to push this thing through. It's time the Board took its fingers out of its asshole where Bethlehem is concerned at least. Otherwise our two years up here will go to hell sure. . . . This [Circuit] court will pay no more attention to a Supreme Court ruling than it will to me. . . . What are you going to do about it?[61]

In his sympathetic reply, Van Gelder reported that "Green, before the House Labor Committee, dwelt on the Bethlehem Fore River case at considerable length and blasted the Board for its delinquency in this and other cases." Koch was not satisfied with Van Gelder's answer, and responded: "The frustration that accompanies dealings with the Board is fierce." But he did not undertake any "drastic" actions; instead, he continued to adhere to the policy position taken by the national office.[62]

Local 5 activists tried to overcome the pessimism created by these difficult conditions and aimless strategy. Palmer and Boyson revitalized the local's Friday night "smokers" by combining entertainment (such as vaudeville and boxing) with CIO speeches. The local won a number of small gains for workers, including a raise for bonus workers, through a grievance committee run by Boyson, Hicks, and Whiteside. Union victories in other shipyards also improved the IUMSWA's reputation in Quincy. By late 1939, the IUMSWA had won a number of local contracts with Bethlehem in the ports of New York and Los Angeles, and in December the Supreme Court handed down its decision outlawing the company union at Newport News Shipyard.[63]

---

[61] *Shipyard Worker*, July 14, 1939; Koch to Van Gelder, Aug. 8, 1939, IUMSWA Archives, Series V, Box 20.

[62] Van Gelder to Koch, Aug. 10, 1939; Koch to Van Gelder, Aug. 14, 1939; both IUMSWA Archives, Series V, Box 20.

[63] Koch to Van Gelder, Sept. 18, 24, Oct. 2, Dec. 2, 10, 18, 1939; Van Gelder to Koch, Oct. 24, Dec. 9, 1939; Local 5 leaflets, Aug. 5, Oct. 23, c. Nov. 1939, c. mid-Dec. 1939; Charles Palmer to Van Gelder, Nov. 27, 1939; all IUMSWA Archives, Series V, Box 20. *Shipyard Worker*, Oct. 20, Nov. 3, Dec. 1, Dec. 19, 1939.

Local 5's leaders still believed that persistence and hard work would bring the rewards of unionization and that it was simply a matter of time until a majority of Fore River workers came over to their side. The difficult years from 1934 to 1939 had taught them many lessons, and the bitter memory of the betrayal by former Local 5 officers Mitchell and Hardy gave them a sense of who could really be trusted. These leaders did not anticipate the enormous difficulties of organizing under wartime conditions. Nor did they suspect that one of the greatest obstacles to organizing over the next few years would come from within the IUMSWA itself, as local initiative at Fore River lost ground to national union priorities, and as legal maneuvering by Bethlehem and the IUMSWA's top officers temporarily pushed aside the possibility of building a revitalized movement in Quincy.

CHAPTER 7

Fighting for a Lost Cause:
The Fore River Drive of 1941

On the eve of World War II, Fore River was the jewel in the Bethlehem Ship-building system, evident in the scale of its production, the size of the ships it built, and the profits it earned. Bethlehem had a major stake in maintaining management control at the Quincy shipyard, which it achieved by preventing genuine union organization there. Even with the IUMSWA's decade-long organizing campaign and continuous legal battles, Bethlehem kept its company union as the cornerstone of Fore River's anti-union industrial relations system. In 1941, as in the 1930s, the ideological underpinning of this system was to attack the IUMSWA as left-wing, un-American, and alien to Quincy.

Fore River specialized in capital naval ships (the largest class of warship) when World War II approached, as it had done during World War I. Employment increased with the wartime expansion of production. In March 1938, Fore River employed 4,000 workers; in September 1940, only two-and-a-half years later, almost 9,000 men worked in the yard. The revenues and income of the Bethlehem Steel Corporation, which included the Shipbuilding Division, rose dramatically during this period (Table 6). Bethlehem increased its investment in shipbuilding, first with the 1938 purchase of United Shipyards in the port of New York (the Hoboken, Brooklyn, and Staten Island yards), and then with the construction of two new, World War II shipyards (Fairfield in Baltimore, and Hingham in Massachusetts). The corporation also expanded facilities in its existing Atlantic and Pacific Coast yards, including major new additions at Fore River and the Sparrows Point steel-shipbuilding complex in Baltimore. Bethlehem Steel's investments in shipbuilding proved extremely valuable. The proportion of the American steel industry's output that was used

**Table 6. Bethlehem Steel Total Revenue and Net
Income, 1935–39, 1941–45 (in millions of dollars)**

Year	Total Revenue	Net Income
1935	$ 198.7	$ 4.3
1936	294.1	13.9
1937	424.5	31.8
1938	271.9	5.3
1939	414.9	24.6
1941	962.2	34.5
1942	1,497.7	25.4
1943	1,906.2	32.1
1944	1,750.4	36.2
1945	1,329.5	34.9

Sources: Bethlehem Steel Corporation, *Annual Reports,* 1941–1945, 1953.

in shipbuilding rose from 2.1 percent in 1940 to 19.2 percent in 1943; Bethlehem was the leading producer of steel for shipbuilding.[1]

The IUMSWA also grew as production accelerated before the war. For most of the 1930s, the IUMSWA's national membership had never exceeded 10,000 (when seasonally adjusted). By 1939 some 11,000 workers belonged to the union, and the number was increasing rapidly. Membership doubled within a year and then grew at an even faster rate as war workers flooded into the shipyards (Table 7). This growth meant new union revenues and the opportunity to hire more organizing staff.[2]

At the biggest yards, including Fore River, the rate of hiring grew faster than the union's ability to organize. Between 1939 and the spring of 1941, employment at Fore River increased from 7,000 to 11,000. Five months later, an additional 6,000 workers had been hired, bringing the total yard employment to about 17,000 (Table 8). Only the local at New York Ship, with its highly

[1] Bethlehem Steel Corporation, *Annual Reports,* 1941–45, 1953; Frederic C. Lane et al., *Ships for Victory: A History of Shipbuilding under the U.S. Maritime Commission in World War II* (Baltimore: Johns Hopkins University Press, 1951), p. 293; William T. Hogan, *Economic History of the Iron and Steel Industry in the United States,* vol. 3 (Lexington, Mass.: Lexington Books, 1971), pp. 1216–25, 1361–77. For employment data, see sources for Table 8.

[2] Bernard Mergen, "A History of the Industrial Union of Marine and Shipbuilding Workers of America, 1933–1951" (Ph.D. diss., University of Pennsylvania, 1968), pp. 87, 194.

Table 7. National Membership of the IUMSWA, 1934–1950 (to nearest hundred)

Year	Members
1934	3,400
1935	2,300
1936	4,000
1937	13,600
1938	9,000
1939	11,800
1940	22,600
1941	57,300
1942	51,600
1943	155,100
1944	218,100
1945 (June)	199,500
1945 (Dec.)	85,400
1946	78,600
1947	69,200
1948	48,400*
1950	25,000*

*Shipyard division only. After 1947 the IUMSWA organized in other industries, especially railroads. All figures are for working members in the summer of each year, except 1935 and 1942 when figures are for winter.
Source: Mergen, "A History of the Industrial Union of Marine and Shipbuilding Workers of America, 1933–1951," pp. 87, 194.

active and dedicated network of stewards, committeemen, and members, was able to absorb this enormous influx.

Local initiative for a new Fore River organizing campaign came in early 1940 from Local 5 secretary-treasurer Charlie Palmer, who chaired a new organizing committee. He had emerged as the Local 5 officer most loyal to the national office and had proven he was an able administrator, in contrast to previous Local 5 financial officers. Palmer wanted the organizing committee to focus on signing up new members and bringing back financially delinquent ones. Beyond these immediate tasks, his plans were vague. He was optimistic about the prospects, in part because of the recent Supreme Court decision outlawing the Newport News company union.[3]

---

[3] Arthur Boyson interview, Feb. 11, 1987; Charles Palmer to Phil Van Gelder, Dec. 20, 1939, IUMSWA Archives, Series V, Box 20, Special Collections, University of Maryland at College Park Libraries.

**Table 8. Employment at Fore River Shipyard,
1936–1946 (to nearest thousand)**

Year	Employees
1936	5,000
1937	4,000
1938	4,000
1939	7,000
1940	9,000
1941 (April)	11,000
1941 (May)	12,000
1941 (Sept.)	17,000
1942	25,000
1943 (Jan.)	31,000
1943 (July)	30,000
1943 (Oct.)	29,000
1944 (Oct.)	22,500
1944 (Dec.)	18,000
1945	15,000
1946 (Jan.)	11,000
1946 (May)	6,000
1947	2,400

Sources: "Statement of Bethlehem Steel Co. to the NWLB with regard to the Union Shop and Check-Off Issue," Bethlehem Shipbuilding v. IUMSWA, Case No. 38, Feb. 1942, p. 9. Arthur Boyson to U.S. Coordinator for Housing, Sept. 1940, Box 20; Charles Palmer, Local 5 April and May Reports, Box 20; Gavin MacPherson to Boston-area CIO locals, Sept. 1941, Box 21; Bill Hartwick report on Fore River, Dec. 16, 1944, Box 21; all IUMSWA Archives, Series V, Special Collections, University of Maryland at College Park Libraries. NLRB, Charge by George Katz against Bethlehem Fore River, Aug. 12, 1942, NA, RG 25, Box 2357; U.S. Dept. of Labor, Conciliation Service, Fore River Reports, July 25, 1943, Oct. 13, 1943, Oct. 10, 1944, NA, RG 25; *Shipyard Worker*, July 30, 1945; *New England Shipbuilder*, May 10, 1946; Milton Vogel, "The Fore River Strikers: A Study in Allegiance Dynamics" (M.A. thesis, Massachusetts Institute of Technology, 1948), p. 46.

Lucien Koch, the organizer at Fore River for almost three years, was more skeptical. He put greater stress on reinstating previous members, and set an initial goal of 300 to 400. He also sought more organizers and CIO assistance. The CIO responded by assigning Powers Hapgood, a nationally known UMW organizer and former Socialist Party leader, to the IUMSWA. Hapgood did well as a speaker at meetings and provided some brief training for new organizers who came to Quincy in early 1941. But Koch recalled that Hapgood "didn't do . . . any real digging," even though he was a "wonderful guy." A drinking problem also interfered with his work. His past activity in the Socialist Party stirred the usual fear of radicals, which resurfaced in Local 5. Koch noted that "some of the fellows were nervous about having him speak [at the smoker]. They feared re-opening the red issue." The company union, however, did not exploit his appearance in Quincy.[4]

Hapgood's presence symbolized another problem for the Fore River organizers: CIO assistance invariably meant assigning UMW organizers who had no shipbuilding background. Although Local 5 benefited from the CIO's financial help, the IUMSWA ultimately was better off when it conducted its own organizing efforts. The IUMSWA, however, did not have the resources of the Steel Workers' Organizing Committee (SWOC), which could call on dozens of paid staff to descend on a single plant. For the most part, Koch had to work independently, covering not only the port of Boston but the entire New England coast from Maine to eastern Connecticut, assisted by one organizer at best.[5]

By late spring, Koch concentrated on the election drive at the Bath shipyard in Maine, where the IUMSWA had narrowly lost a "union" versus "no union" poll in 1938. In 1941, the IUMSWA ran against the company union and lost badly. The situation was no better at Electric Boat in New London, where Koch felt it was "like starting over again." In the New England region, unlike other places, company unionism seemed to be on the ascendancy in the big shipyards.[6]

Continued lack of progress in New England compelled Van Gelder to redirect the organizing effort by initiating "a concerted drive on Bethlehem." He focused his attention on the Sparrows Point yard in the port of Baltimore, where workers were on the verge of calling a strike for recognition. Van Gelder hoped that news of this type of activity would spread to Fore River and create "some enthusiasm" there. This change indicated that the IUMSWA was shifting its focus to areas where its Bethlehem organizing was strongest: the ports of Baltimore and New York. In New England, the IUMSWA's only base was in the East Boston repair yards. In November 1940, Van Gelder assigned Koch to direct the East Coast campaign against Bethlehem and designated

---

[4] Lucien Koch to Van Gelder, Dec. 23, 1939, Jan. 8 and 29, Feb. 12 and 19, 1940; all IUMSWA Archives, Series V, Box 20. Koch interview, June 10, 1987.

[5] Koch interview, June 10, 1987.

[6] Koch to Van Gelder, March 11 and 16, April 8, May 2, June 3, 9, 17, 1940; Charles Palmer to Local 5 members, March 25, 1940; all IUMSWA Archives, Series V, Box 20. Mergen, "History of the Industrial Union of Marine and Shipbuilding Workers of America," p. 111. In 1941, Bath Iron's company union received 2,197 votes, the IUMSWA received 1,094 votes, and 291 workers voted for "no union."

Quincy as its headquarters. In reality, organizing in the Bethlehem shipyards continued to be conducted autonomously in each port. Koch recalled that his role as Bethlehem campaign director was "a title only," and that making Quincy its center had no impact on organizing the corporation's national shipbuilding chain.[7]

There was other evidence that the IUMSWA national office no longer gave Fore River top priority as an organizing target. Activists in Quincy made numerous efforts to broaden the Fore River organizing to the national level, including an initiative led by Local 5 president Arthur Boyson to get federally sponsored area housing built for shipyard workers. Boyson was seeking a solution to a major problem created by the rapid growth of shipyard employment. By 1940, the massive influx of new workers into the Quincy area had exhausted the town's available housing. The national IUMSWA was focusing its Washington lobbying efforts elsewhere and concentrating its organizing resources on shipyards in the mid-Atlantic ports of New York, Philadelphia, and Baltimore. As a result, Quincy did not gain major government-financed projects like those undertaken in Camden and Kearny-Newark.[8]

In October 1940 the Circuit Court of Appeals in Boston upheld the original NLRB ruling that Bethlehem had interfered with and dominated the Employee Representation Plan, and it ordered Bethlehem to disband the ERP. The next day, Local 5 representatives met with company managers and requested that IUMSWA officers and stewards be given privileges equal to those in the company union, but management claimed that IUMSWA representatives already had equal rights. Later NLRB findings revealed, however, that total weekly hours spent by company union representatives on grievances ranged from 500 to over 1,000, compared to a range of 7 to 86 hours for Local 5 stewards. Management also paid company union representatives time-and-a-third (base pay plus estimated bonus and piece rate) for hours they spent off the job on union business, while it compensated IUMSWA representatives at only the base rate.[9]

[7] Van Gelder to Koch, July 9, 1940; Van Gelder to all Bethlehem IUMSWA organizers, Nov. 2, 4, 1940; Koch to Van Gelder, Nov. 4, 1940; all IUMSWA Archives, Series V, Box 20. Koch interview, June 10, 1987.

[8] Koch interview, June 10, 1987; Boyson to U.S. Coordinator for Housing, Sept. 1940, IUMSWA Archives, Series V, Box 20. The Quincy housing crisis was so severe by 1940 that Powers Hapgood had to commute from a hotel in Boston while working with Koch at Local 5.

[9] Bethlehem Shipbuilding v. NLRB, General Body of Employees' Representatives v. NLRB, U.S. Circuit Court of Appeals, Oct. 8, 1940, 7 LRR Man., 330–341; Harold Roberts (NLRB) to Gerhard Van Arkel (chief, NLRB Compliance Unit), May 23, 1941, NA, RG 25, Box 2894. The judge who wrote the decision in the Circuit Court case was Calvert Magruder, the former NLRB investigator who had ruled against the IUMSWA in its original 1934–35 Fore River case.

Meanwhile, ERP leaders disbanded their organization, even though this was technically impossible under Bethlehem's rules, and reconstituted themselves as the Independent Union of Fore River Workers. Management professed total non-involvement but permitted dozens of Independent Union delegates to sign up new members during regular working hours. The Independent Union told workers that it was "unaffiliated" and "primarily for employees of the Fore River yard." It also promised that it would hold mass meetings (a promise it never kept) and that dues would not be higher than 25 cents.[10]

When the Independent Union held an election for officers inside the yard in January 1941, polls stayed open until 11 pm for seven days straight. The IUMSWA angrily protested management's tolerance of such open violations of labor law. Charlie Palmer commented that the new company union would have no trouble getting a majority "if the pencils and ballots hold out," but an NLRB investigator on the scene noted myopically that supervisors did not "interfere" with the balloting. A month later Bethlehem's management recognized the Independent Union as sole bargaining agent for the yard.[11]

In the face of Bethlehem's flagrant unfair labor practices, the IUMSWA's national officers continued their strategy of relying on the courts. Koch faithfully carried out the policy, filing a new complaint with the NLRB in late 1940. The union wanted the NLRB to find Bethlehem in contempt of the Circuit Court decision, as the Independent Union was nothing more than a successor to the ERP. When the campaign to revitalize organizing at Fore River accelerated in early 1941, Koch reiterated the legal strategy to IUMSWA organizers at other Bethlehem yards: "Once we are clear of the company union and its successor, we have only a straight organizational job left to do and it has got to be done." It was the courts and the NLRB who were to "clear" the way, not volunteer organizers in the yard. Members and staff were to focus on signing up new members and developing new departmental leadership, rather than attacking the new company union.[12]

IUMSWA national president John Green reinforced this position when he proposed to Bethlehem president Eugene Grace in December 1940 that the na-

---

[10] Roberts to Van Arkel, May 23 and 26, 1941, NA, RG 25, Box 1894. Charles Palmer to Van Gelder, Oct. 16, 1939; Independent Union leaflet, "Important Notice!", Oct. 17, 1941; Koch to Van Gelder, Oct. 28, 1939; all IUMSWA Archives, Series V, Box 20. *Quincy Patriot Ledger*, Oct. 18, 1939.

[11] Roberts to Van Arkel, May 23 and 26, 1941; Malcolm Halliday memo on Bethlehem case, Feb. 13, 1941; Myers to NLRB, Jan. 13, 1941; all NA, RG 25, Box 1894. *Quincy Patriot Ledger*, Feb. 5, 1941; Charles Palmer to Van Gelder, Jan. 10, 1941, IUMSWA Archives, Series V, Box 20.

[12] Koch to Myers, Nov. 29, 1940, NA, RG 25, Box 2894. Koch to Bethlehem IUMSWA organizers, Dec. 3, 1940, and Jan. 2, 1941, IUMSWA Archives, Series V, Box 20.

tional union and the corporation bargain for contracts in plants where the IUMSWA had a recognized majority. Green explained to Grace that he believed the federal government's recent formation of the Shipbuilding Stabilization Committee indicated that the time had come for this new step.[13]

The IUMSWA, particularly John Green, had pioneered plans in 1937 and 1938 for federal intervention to stabilize the shipbuilding industry nationally. The union focused on securing employment, but also advocated a single minimum wage rate, the simplification of job classifications, and the reduction of wage differentials. It also endorsed a tripartite bargaining approach. Although this proposal was rejected by the Roosevelt administration, the IUMSWA's plan anticipated developments that took place in industrial relations during World War II.[14]

President Roosevelt had established the National Defense Advisory Commission (NDAC) in May 1940 to coordinate America's growing military production, which was supplying its European Allies as well as preparing the United States for the possibility of entering the war. By September, Roosevelt saw the need for the formation of a labor-management committee to stabilize wages as part of this process. In response, the Director of the Labor Division of the tripartite NDAC, Sydney Hillman, announced the creation of the Shipbuilding Stabilization Committee in late November 1940.[15]

The Shipbuilding Stabilization Committee's first action was to publicize a new "no-strike pledge" that was backed by the IUMSWA and the AFL Metal Trades, which both sat on the new government body. The labor and employer representatives agreed, at least in principle, "that there should be no interruption of production on the part of shipyard employers and shipyard employees before all facilities . . . of the National Defense Advisory Commission for adjusting differences have been exhausted." This "pledge," subsequently endorsed by a majority of CIO unions, became the most controversial aspect of American labor relations during World War II.[16]

---

[13] Green to Eugene Grace, Dec. 10, 1940, IUMSWA Archives, Series V, Box 20.

[14] Horace B. Drury, "History of Shipbuilding Stabilization: Part II, Stabilization in the Framework of National Defense," pp. 23–31, NA, RG 254, Shipbuilding Stabilization Committee "Finding Aids" Box. Drury generally disclaims the IUMSWA-Committee connection, but the actual outcome of its policies would seem to vindicate Green's claim. For later developments, see also National War Labor Board, *Termination Report*: vol. 1, *Industrial Disputes and Wage Stabilization in Wartime* (Washington, D.C.: GPO, 1947), pp. 831–99 ("The Shipbuilding Commission"). The Committee (later changed to Commission) obviously drew from the example of the World War I–era Shipbuilding Labor Adjustment Board.

[15] Nelson Lichtenstein, *Labor's War at Home: The CIO in World War II* (Cambridge: Cambridge University Press, 1982), pp. 32–43; Lane, *Ships for Victory*, pp. 268–73.

[16] Shipbuilding Stabilization Committee Meeting Minutes, Dec. 5, 1940, quoted in Lane, *Ships for Victory*, p. 274.

The Committee made substantial progress by the spring of 1941, holding four zone conferences (Pacific, Atlantic, Gulf, and Great Lakes) that negotiated "zone standards" for wages. It avoided any discussion of union recognition, which would have prevented any positive outcome. The IUMSWA, clearly the principal shipbuilding union on the Eastern seaboard, was the sole union representative in the Atlantic Zone Conference. The AFL, dominant in the Pacific and Great Lakes zones, refused to participate, since in practical terms it had little power in the Atlantic region. Company unions, like those at Fore River, Bath, and Newport News, were refused seats, although informal concurrence with them was obtained by the Committee's government representatives after the zone conference. Government representatives came from the Maritime Commission and the Navy, while employers were represented by industry spokesmen, such as H. Gerrish Smith from the National Council of American Shipbuilders. Executives from Bethlehem, Sun Ship, and Newport News refused to participate because they did not want to be seen as negotiating with the IUMSWA.[17]

Green and Van Gelder viewed the Shipbuilding Stabilization Committee's negotiated "zone standards" as a pattern to be emulated in specific, company-based agreements. They pursued a strategy of seeking national pattern agreements with companies like Bethlehem as a way to advance the IUMSWA's membership and standing. This approach demanded, even more than before, the subordination of local concerns to national union interests. Serious problems in bargaining at Federal Ship, especially during the summer strike of 1941 over the union shop, contributed to this shift in focus, as did the SWOC's national campaign to organize Bethlehem's steel mills.[18]

Green and Van Gelder's reformulation of the union's strategy, from a local and regional focus to a national one centered on bargaining, had the potential to undermine organizing. While bargaining, especially in terms of wages, clearly benefited from a national, highly centralized approach, organizing required a balance between national and local interests, as well as substantial contributions and direction from local leaders. Furthermore, the volatile conditions and militant attitudes in Bethlehem's steel mills, where workers spontaneously struck under local leadership in some places, were far different from the dominance of management at Fore River, Sun Ship, Electric Boat, Bath,

---

[17] Lane, *Ships for Victory*, pp. 273–87.

[18] For a discussion of the centrality of the Shipbuilding Stabilization Committee for the national IUMSWA officers during World War II, see Mergen, "History of the Industrial Union of Marine and Shipbuilding Workers of America," pp. 102–63. For the situation at Federal Shipbuilding from 1941 to 1944, see Palmer, "Organizing the Shipyards," pp. 676–787.

and Newport News, where major assaults on company unions were vitally needed.[19]

In this new environment, the initiative for a viable organizing strategy at Fore River came from local union activists and organizers, not from the IUMSWA national office. Charlie Palmer had tried to activate the local in 1940, but used a conventional organizing approach restricted mainly to general meetings and regular union publicity. He had been elected national vice president at the September 1940 IUMSWA convention, but even with this advantage he had virtually no power to influence policy at the national level. Nevertheless, he tried to persuade Van Gelder that the old organizing strategy had failed and a new, far more aggressive approach, combining pressure in Washington with activism in the yard, had to be adopted. Palmer told Van Gelder that he believed "the regional board in Boston is more impotent than Local #5 in getting any concessions from Fore River." He had little faith that the NLRB in Washington would be any better, but "with more men working harder than any time in the last three years," pressure on the national board might make a difference.[20]

Green was more interested in winning contracts from Bethlehem than in launching a major lobbying campaign in Washington aimed at attacking the Fore River company union and management complicity. Van Gelder, too, had his sights on drives in the ports of New York, Baltimore, and other locations where there was more activity. Nevertheless, Koch began to gradually move away from reliance on the Labor Board, in part because he could now work with a new, younger group of activists in the yard who wanted to initiate more militant actions. Koch commented to Van Gelder in early 1941: "We are considering the advisability of stoppages in some departments to make the resentment of the men known, but whether the feeling is strong enough for this procedure remains in doubt."[21]

Green did allow Koch to hire two new organizers, Paul Mulkern and Louis Torre, by early 1941. Both of them were well suited to Boston-area shipyard organizing. Mulkern came from a working-class family in heavily Irish South Boston, a major asset at Fore River where Irish Americans formed a large majority of the workforce. He had acquired a progressive Catholic background while a student at Boston College High School and Boston College, where the

---

[19] For the SWOC Bethlehem campaign of 1941, see Irving Bernstein, *The Turbulent Years: A History of the American Worker, 1933–1941* (Boston: Houghton Mifflin, 1969), pp. 727–34; and Art Preis, *Labor's Giant Step: Twenty Years of the CIO* (New York: Pathfinder Press, 1972), pp. 107–12.

[20] Charles Palmer to Van Gelder, Jan. 10, 1941, IUMSWA Archives, Series V, Box 20.

[21] Koch to Van Gelder, Feb. 6, 1941, IUMSWA Archives, Series V, Box 20.

Jesuit tradition was strong. He also had a masters degree from the Boston School of Social Work, where he had studied under New England NLRB Regional Director Howard Myers. When Mulkern graduated, Myers suggested that he apply for an organizing job with the IUMSWA at Fore River. Mulkern proved to be a fine speaker at meetings, got along well with the workers, and had a tolerance for differing opinions comparable to Koch's.[22]

Louis Torre, an Italian American, also represented a constituency that was critical for Boston-area shipyard organizing. He spoke Italian fluently, a valuable skill in the effort to revitalize the union at Bethlehem's yard in predominantly Italian East Boston. He also assisted with organizing Fore River, where there were many Italian workers. Torre had experience as an organizer with the UE and the Transport Workers, and had been recommended by James Carey and Mike Quill, the leaders of the two unions. Torre was probably a member of the Communist Party, although he did not make his membership public, and he strongly believed that workers should use militant action as an organizing and bargaining tool.[23]

Mulkern could see the hold of the company union over Fore River workers as soon as he began organizing there. He reported to Green: "The chief difficulty that we have to contend with here is the phony Beth. Union. As you know, all hiring is done thru these representatives and out of a misguided sense of gratitude the workers feel that they must toe the line. The vast majority of men hired are between 18 and 23 and they look on the Fore River Yard as the promised land." He also noticed "two separate factions" emerging within Local 5. One faction preferred "straight organizing work," that is, signing up workers into the union, holding meetings, and distributing union publicity. The other faction advocated more direct action on the job as a way to mobilize support for the union and activate potential rank-and-file leaders. Mulkern did not outline for Green the depth of this division, stressing instead that "the members are more active and we can only hope that they will relay this attitude to the general rank and file." The moderate faction was led by "oldtimers" Palmer, Boyson, and Hicks, while the more militant group was comprised of younger workers who were new to the yard and identified openly with radical left-wing politics. Some members of the new group, such as Cliff

---

[22] Koch to Van Gelder, Dec. 23, 1940; Green to Koch, Dec. 30, 1940; Paul Mulkern to Green, April 24, 1941; all IUMSWA Archives, Series V, Box 20. Paul Mulkern interview, Sept. 3, 1987, Quincy, Mass. Myers did not intercede on behalf of Mulkern when he sought an IUMSWA position because of Myers' connection with the pending IUMSWA v. Fore River NLRB case.

[23] Koch to Van Gelder, Dec. 23, 1940; Green to Koch, Dec. 30, 1940; Paul Mulkern to Green, April 24, 1941; Mulkern interview; Mike Quill to Koch, Dec. 27, 1940; James Carey to Koch, Dec. 30, 1940; Louis Torre to Green, April 23, 1941; all IUMSWA Archives, Series V, Box 20.

Crozier, were Communist Party activists. While Mulkern admired the spirit of these younger men, he became concerned that they were organizing a "rump group," which held private home meetings on union matters and was led by the Communist Party. He did not express his doubts about the actions of this group to the national office, but instead did his best to work with both sides.[24]

Torre, on the other hand, was a harsh critic of what he considered conservatism among local leaders and in contract negotiations, as well as of over-reliance on legal tactics. His April report to Green, while highlighting the same problems as Mulkern, was much blunter, as well as more sympathetic to the left wing of the local union. "The Company Union is the main obstacle to our work in Fore River," Torre wrote.

> It seems to me that our failure to make more progress . . . is due to the fact that the men in the Yards are waiting for the Labor Board and the Courts to give them a union, instead of taking matters in their own hands and forcing the Company to obey the law. There has been too much reliance on the Labor Board and Courts and not enough reliance on the union itself. Until this wrong idea is broken down, first among our own members and the unorganized men in the Yard, we will not make . . . gains.[25]

Although Torre worked part of the time at Fore River, his main assignment was in East Boston. Bethlehem recognized the IUMSWA at its East Boston repair yards, but had never agreed to a written contract there. In January, national-level talks began between Bethlehem and the IUMSWA, after the corporation dropped its Supreme Court appeal of the Fore River Circuit Court case. Negotiations at the local level progressed most rapidly at Bethlehem's shipyard in Hoboken, New Jersey, where Green and Van Gelder hoped to settle as quickly as possible. On May 3, 1941, the IUMSWA won a written agreement there; this victory put it ahead of the SWOC, which was pushing for contracts in Bethlehem's many unorganized steel plants. The Hoboken Bethlehem contract, the national IUMSWA officers told Torre, should serve as the model for East Boston. But Torre refused to make compromises in the East Boston negotiations, even though Green and Van Gelder told him to settle at any cost

---

[24] Mulkern to Green, April 24, 1941; Mulkern interview. Hicks was probably a member of the Communist Party by this time, despite his moderate union tactics and status as an "old-timer." (Conversations with Don Bollen.) He seems to have drawn a line, however, between his union work and his political views. This conclusion would confirm Jim Bollen's contention that the division in Local 5 (in contrast to that in Local 16) had more to do with generational differences than with political ideology.

[25] Torre to Green, April 23, 1941.

so that the union could at least claim to have a contract at the repair yards. Despite their political differences, both Torre and Palmer began to suspect that the union's national office was usurping local initiative in order to obtain a larger, national agreement with Bethlehem. All sides at the local level still believed, however, that the national office was committed to pursuing the legal fight against the Bethlehem company unions at Fore River and East Boston.[26]

Local 5 leaders had not made the national talks between Bethlehem and the IUMSWA the center of their work, but on June 10, every IUMSWA activist at Fore River was suddenly drawn into the national negotiations when John Green and Bethlehem vice president Joseph Larkin signed a "Memorandum of Understandings" in New York. This agreement committed Bethlehem to union elections at its Atlantic Coast shipyards, including Fore River. Nationally, the IUMSWA declared the Memorandum "one of the greatest victories of organized labor in recent years" because it "provid[ed] for negotiation of a master agreement for all Bethlehem shipyards on the Atlantic Coast in which the Industrial Union is certified as the bargaining agency, or becomes certified in the future." The Memorandum also stipulated that the IUMSWA drop its NLRB contempt charge against Bethlehem and the Fore River Independent Union. The Memorandum became effective in the very week that the NLRB was to conduct the contempt hearing in Boston. Local 5 had made the hearings the centerpiece of its organizing work, believing that the government would finally disband the company union. This organizing strategy now had to be scuttled completely; the Memorandum established a hands-off policy toward the Independent Union except as a rival organization.[27]

News of the agreement shocked everyone in Quincy who was connected with the IUMSWA. Koch was caught by surprise, revealing the extent to which he was only a figure-head as "director" of Bethlehem organizing and the very limited role he had played in the national Bethlehem talks. Torre considered the union's abdication of the NLRB case a complete betrayal of the workers, as did the young, left-wing activists in the yard. Palmer, Boyson, Hicks, and the rest of the old-line leadership were equally outraged, because they had

---

[26] Torre to Green, April 23, 1941; Koch to Bethlehem IUMSWA organizers, Feb. 13, 1941; Van Gelder to Koch, Jan. 30, 1941, and Feb. 6, 1941; Koch to Bethlehem IUMSWA organizers, April 15, 1941; Green to Koch, May 2, 1941; Torre letter of resignation, June 25, 1941; all IUMSWA Archives, Series V, Box 20. *Shipyard Worker*, May 9, 1941.

[27] *Shipyard Worker*, June 13, 1941; Bethlehem Shipbuilding v. NLRB, General Body of Employees' Representatives v. NLRB, NLRB motion filed May 27, 1941, NA, RG 25, Box 2894; Bethlehem Shipbuilding v. NLRB, General Body of Employees' Representatives v. NLRB, U.S. Circuit Court of Appeals, June 3, 1941, 8 LRR Man., 500–502; *Fore River Facts*, April 17, May 23, 1941.

put years of work into the case. Even the IUMSWA's Boston attorney, Sam Angoff, was caught off guard, although he had sat in on some of the talks.[28]

The furor led to one of the best-attended general membership meetings in months, which was held on June 11. Harold "Nick" Stephenson, a young steward for the welders, spoke against ratifying the Memorandum and called for returning the local's charter to Camden. Implicit in his stand was the idea that Local 5 should disaffiliate from the IUMSWA and join another industrial union. Veteran union members such as Boyson did not go this far. Attorney Angoff spoke in support of the Memorandum, even though he personally opposed it. Koch and Mulkern did the same, believing that their responsibilities as staff organizers required that they carry out the policy of the national office. This reluctant support from the union's staff swayed the majority of those present. The local's executive board accepted the Memorandum under protest, warning that they did not intend to approve any such action in the future. Koch relayed the sentiment of Local 5 members to Van Gelder: "The men resented particularly the fact that they were not consulted prior to the agreement being negotiated."[29]

The matter seemed to be closed, but a week later the Local 5 executive board went to the NLRB and reopened the contempt charge. Green and Van Gelder concluded that Koch either could not handle the situation or was contributing to the crisis, and the next day they sent Gavin MacPherson, business agent for the Chelsea (Manhattan) shore gang local and a newly elected national IUMSWA GEB member, to take charge of Local 5. MacPherson became Green's eyes and ears in the Boston area, reporting all activity he deemed disloyal or subversive.[30]

The challenge of Fore River exposed MacPherson's many weaknesses. Although he had represented dock workers in the port of New York, he was unprepared for the more conservative and skilled Fore River workers. Quincy's

---

[28] Koch interview, June 10, 1987; Vogel, "The Fore River Strikers," pp. 109–11; Boyson interviews, Oct. 4, 1982, and Aug. 8, 1989. Torre resignation letter, June 25, 1941; Samuel Angoff to M. H. Goldstein (two letters), July 24, 1941; both IUMSWA Archives, Series V, Box 20..

[29] Koch to Van Gelder, June 12, 1941; Sabens to Van Gelder, June 11, 1941; Angoff to Goldstein, July 24, 1941; all IUMSWA Archives, Series V, Box 20. Mulkern interview; Koch interview, June 10, 1987; Boyson interview, Oct. 4, 1982; *Fore River Facts*, July 25, 1941.

[30] Norman Edmonds (NLRB Boston) to Robert Watts (NLRB Washington), June 18, 1941, NA, RG 25, Box 1669. Gavin MacPherson to Green, June 25, 1941; Green to MacPherson, July 2, 1941; both IUMSWA Archives, Series V, Box 20. IUMSWA, *Proceedings, 6th National Convention*, Sept. 13–15, 1940. Koch interview, June 10, 1987.

shipyard workers had a stable, craft-based work culture that contrasted sharply with that of the rough shore gang laborers, who were accustomed to heavy manual work and casual employment. Although MacPherson spoke with a Scottish accent and claimed he had worked on the Clyde, such credentials meant far less in Quincy than in the port of New York. Many of the Scots at Fore River had grown to like the company union, in contrast to those at Federal Ship in the New York port region, who had looked to IUMSWA organizer and former Clydesider Mike Smith for leadership. Almost all of Local 5's leaders were native-born Americans, even though some, such as Boyson (of Swedish ancestry), were second-generation and retained some ethnic consciousness. Boyson believed that MacPherson was self-promoting, crude, and unsuited to the type of workers who lived in and around Quincy. MacPherson's major obstacle was that Local 5 activists initially saw him as a tool of the national office, and his abrasive personal style only added to the resentment they felt.[31]

Green and Van Gelder staunchly defended the Memorandum as it applied to Fore River, and they did what they could to bring the local into line. When Van Gelder heard of the executive board's new appeal to the NLRB, he wired Charlie Palmer that since all levels of the union had approved the Memorandum it was "impossible and unwise to attempt to change this program now in any respect." A month later, when the local persisted in pursuing the contempt case with the help of Attorney Angoff, Van Gelder warned MacPherson, "the Union would just be made to look ridiculous if the Locals and National Officers keep running to the Board and asking for different things." At the end of July, Van Gelder restated his position that the national office, not locals, set policy: "No small, irresponsible group is going to be allowed to upset a program which vitally affects eight Locals of this union."[32]

The procedure for acceptance of the Memorandum had hardly been democratic. The issue was so poorly handled by the national IUMSWA that the National Labor Relations Board decided to wash its hands of the whole affair. New England Regional Director Myers, who was angry with the IUMSWA's change of heart after he had spent seven years on the case, sought to remove the Board from further complications at the yard after June by expediting election procedures while removing NLRB investigators.[33]

---

[31] Don Bollen interview, July 29, 1989; Boyson interview, Aug. 8, 1989; Van Gelder interview, Aug. 11, 1989; Alex, Tom, and Agnes Mitchelson, joint interview (on Scottish workers at Fore River), May 8, 1987, Quincy, Mass.

[32] Van Gelder to Charles Palmer, June 19, 1941; Van Gelder to MacPherson, July 15, 1941, and July 24, 1941; all IUMSWA Archives, Series V, Box 20.

[33] Koch interview, June 10, 1987; Myers to Patterson, Oct. 7, 1941, NA, RG 25, Box 1669.

With MacPherson advocating the national office's position in Quincy, Van Gelder came to town in mid-June to help present his and Green's side of the story. At this membership meeting, Boyson recalled, staff organizer Louis Torre "lit into" Van Gelder, who could only listen to Torre "with his head down." Torre certainly reflected the feelings of many in Local 5. Within days Torre resigned in anger, calling the IUMSWA "anti-labor and anti-CIO" in a letter published in the *Quincy Patriot Ledger* and circulated throughout the labor movement, including to John L. Lewis. Torre's conclusion that the Memorandum set back the Fore River organizing campaign irreversibly may have been correct, but his public attack on the national officers alienated both Koch and Mulkern and made MacPherson more acceptable to the leaders of Local 5, who still mistrusted the national officers. Finally, Torre's identification with the Communist Party, even if he did not openly admit membership, inadvertently opened the floodgates of anticommunism, an ideology always just below the surface at Fore River.[34]

MacPherson now had the excuse to launch a crusade against "communist" influence in Local 5. He began secretly gathering information for Van Gelder and Green, who both had become highly suspicious of Communist Party activity in the union movement. Their turn to the right reflected a general trend within the union. In January 1941, the IUMSWA's GEB had unanimously endorsed a motion to bar "Communists, Nazis, or Fascists" from holding positions in the union. In April, the national officers suspended the autonomy of Local 31 at Maryland Dry Dock in Baltimore and expelled several of its elected leaders on the grounds that they were Communists and had advocated reaffiliation with the left-led National Maritime Union (NMU). A week before MacPherson arrived in Quincy, the *Shipyard Worker* attacked Communists involved in the North American Aviation strike on the West Coast. MacPherson was only carrying out a policy condoned by the national union. He had firsthand experience with the CP in New York City; indeed, he had previously supported CP positions within the labor movement. Now MacPherson believed that there was a conspiracy within Local 5 and that Koch was simply oblivious to it. "The Officers here resent anyone who may come from the National Office and want Lucien Koch to be here with them," MacPherson wrote to Green. "IT IS MY OPINION THAT THEY WANT KOCH BECAUSE HE IS KIND OF WEAK AND THEY CAN HANDLE HIM EASILY, NOT FOR ANY OTHER REASON. The tactics here and the whispering meetings are all

[34] Boyson interview, Aug. 8, 1989; Vogel, "The Fore River Strikers," pp. 110–11; Torre resignation letter, June 25, 1941; MacPherson to Green, June 26, 1941; *Shipyard Worker*, June 27, 1941; Koch interview, June 10, 1987; Mulkern interview.

in Communistic style and although they may not all be in the party, they are certainly more with the party than they are with the National Office."[35]

Although the Communist Party was active in Quincy, it was hardly the threat that MacPherson imagined, especially given the party's relative weakness in the Boston area compared to other American cities. The CP attained its largest membership at Fore River during World War II, when probably no more than eighteen shipyard workers were active members. Many of these, such as Cliff Crozier, were respected trade unionists. Some, including Don Bollen, refused to go along with the party's strict line supporting the no-strike pledge. Local 5 certainly was not in danger of becoming a "communist front."[36]

Most of those connected with the political left in Quincy had originally been members of the Socialist Party. With the decline of the Socialist Party nationally in the 1930s, sharp divisions emerged in the local Quincy organization, which led to its collapse. The party had run a cooperative store with a Workman's Circle meeting hall attached. Some in the organization thought that badly needed money could be raised by renting the hall to a local group that supported the anti-Semitic right-wing priest, Father Charles Coughlin. A number of members strongly opposed this idea as politically reactionary. After the majority voted to rent the hall to the Coughlinites, the cooperative fell apart and most people simply drifted away from the party. The handful who had opposed the fund raising idea formed the local nucleus of the Communist Party.[37]

Some former socialists, such as Don Bollen, worked in the Fore River yard. Don's brother Jim, who did not have a shipyard job, was involved with labor organizing in the area and wrote a regular series of letters to the editor published in the *Quincy Patriot Ledger*. Other former SP members who joined the CP included Abe Cohen, a local dentist whose family had immigrated to America after participating in the 1905 Russian Revolution. He conducted left-wing study groups for workers and promoted sales of the *Daily Worker* at

[35] Van Gelder interview, Aug. 11, 1989; Mergen, "History of the Industrial Union of Marine and Shipbuilding Workers of America", pp. 172–74; *Shipyard Worker*, June 13, 27, 1941; MacPherson to Green, June 25, 1941, IUMSWA Archives, Series V, Box 20 (emphasis in original). Van Gelder told me that MacPherson had been close to the CP in Chelsea during the late 1930s and that his apparent turnaround was probably due to personal opportunism rather than any political convictions.

[36] James R. Green and Hugh C. Donahue, *Boston's Workers, A Labor History* (Boston: Boston Public Library, 1979), p. 109; Vogel, "The Fore River Strikers," p. 115; Len De Caux, *Labor Radical: From the Wobblies to the CIO, A Personal History* (Boston: Beacon Press, 1970), pp. 487–88 (for related background on Cliff Crozier); Jim and Don Bollen joint interview, May 7, 1983.

[37] Jim and Don Bollen interview, May 7, 1983.

the shipyard. The party's political education efforts had little effect on most Fore River workers, but a few activists who did become involved learned intellectual and leadership skills that equipped them for organizing. By 1940, a political nucleus had developed at Fore River. This group had a strong interest in organizing at the yard and appeared more interested in promoting militant unionism than in recruiting party members.[38]

MacPherson quickly sought to establish his own operation, writing that Koch "must be relieved of all responsibility here" and recommending that Mulkern be transferred out of the district "to break up his present connections and for more seasoning." As director at Fore River, Koch had labored to unite as many workers and groups as possible through a modest organizing style. MacPherson tried to play one group off against another and to create the impression, when communicating with Green and Van Gelder, that he was making big changes in the Fore River campaign.[39]

Anger over the Memorandum helped bridge the gap between the younger and older groups in the local, pitting both against the national union. MacPherson quickly discovered that "communists" were hardly to blame for the mess in Quincy. When the national IUMSWA's *Shipyard Worker* ran an article entitled "Torre, Exposed as Red Stooge, Quits His Post," local leaders refused to distribute the newspaper. MacPherson urgently wired Van Gelder: "Article in Shipyard Worker on Torre very bad. Please let me know in advance what will appear in our paper."[40]

The Independent Union used the division within the IUMSWA to its own advantage. Shortly after the Memorandum was signed, the Independent's *Fore River Weekly* devoted much of its June 26 issue to the "sellout," highlighting an enormous banner headline that read, "CIO QUITS." The company and the Independent Union had defeated the CIO, the paper claimed. "Were the faces of the CIO Shop Stewards red when they went up to negotiate with [Industrial Relations Manager] Fenninger and he turned them down. Wow! They were going to have the same rights as the Independent so they thought. They didn't read the agreement very carefully. He bounced them out on their ears. THERE WILL ALWAYS BE AN INDEPENDENT UNION."[41]

The Independent Union did more than slander its CIO opponents, however. It maintained representatives in every department and claimed to handle workers' grievances, using these to promote its viewpoint. Although the Indepen-

---

[38] Jim Bollen interview, May 7, 1983, and subsequent informal conversations with him about Fore River organizing; Abe Cohen interview, Feb. 19, 1987, Quincy, Mass.

[39] Boyson interview, Sept. 12, 1986; MacPherson to Green, June 26, 1941.

[40] *Shipyard Worker*, June 27, 1941; MacPherson to Van Gelder, June 30, 1941, IUMSWA Archives, Series V, Box 20.

[41] *Fore River Weekly*, June 26, 1941 (emphasis in original).

dent Union had a full set of elected officers, its main spokesman was its attorney, Robert Zottoli. A week after the "Memorandum of Understandings" bombshell, Zottoli announced that the Independent Union would not run in an NLRB election, thereby turning the contest into one that pitted the status quo (a "no" vote) against an uncertain and seemingly unstable "outside" union. He told the press, with management consent, that "the Independent won a tremendous victory in bringing about the establishment of the new wage scale" averaging an increase of 13.1 per cent. "Fore River is the highest paid yard in the East Coast. . . . I can't help but feel mighty proud of the Independent Union." This wage gain actually came in the wake of the Atlantic Zone Shipbuilding Stabilization Conference, where the IUMSWA represented labor but not one company union was present. The claim that Fore River had the highest pay also was misleading, because the yard's rates varied considerably from job to job and by type of contract per job where bonuses applied. At this stage, however, the damage had been done; most Fore River workers believed what they were told by the Independent Union, Bethlehem management, and the conservative *Quincy Patriot Ledger*.[42]

Boyson and other local leaders considered the Memorandum incident the campaign's turning point, after which victory was out of the question. New membership had increased slowly but steadily during the spring. In February, 700 out of about 10,000 workers belonged to Local 5; in April, 1,200 out of 11,000; and in May, 1,400 out of 12,000. After June 10, membership gains virtually came to a halt. Unlike Local 5 secretary-treasurer Charlie Palmer, MacPherson did not tally the actual membership or even the total number of workers in the yard. But two months after MacPherson arrived in Quincy, it was obvious to him that the drive was in serious trouble. Ironically, his diagnosis of the problem was, by this time, similar to that of local leaders Boyson, Palmer, Stephenson, and others. "The election must be again postponed, because it would be impossible to hold an election and expect to win when the management at Fore River Yard are still recognizing the Independent Union. . . . How can the NLRB hold a fair and honest election . . . when at the very same time an Independent Union has Hundreds of Walking Delegates inside the Yard coercing the men in every possible way." MacPherson wrote this report for Van Gelder when employment at Fore River was almost 17,000 but Local 5's membership probably did not exceed 2,000.[43]

With the campaign in shambles, MacPherson's only hope was with the

---

[42] *Quincy Patriot Ledger*, June 19, July 3, 1941; *Shipyard Worker*, June 27, 1941.

[43] Boyson interview, Oct. 4, 1982. Koch to Bethlehem IUMSWA organizers, Feb. 13, 1941; Charles Palmer's Local 5 April and May Reports; MacPherson to Van Gelder, Aug. 21, 1941; all IUMSWA Archives, Series V, Box 20.

young militants whom he had originally tried to dislodge. In July, he told Green to disregard any attempts by the local to reopen the NLRB contempt case. "I am building up new blood here that will eventually overthrow this bunch of nuts that have been sitting on their heinies [sic] for years awaiting the courts and President Roosevelt doing their organizing."[44]

MacPherson seems to have had grudging respect for less flamboyant leftists, especially those who excelled in signing up members and fearlessly carried out direct action on the job. One of these was the IUMSWA's steward in the steel mill, Marty Williams. He had helped sixty crane operators and riggers petition the company for bonus adjustments back in April, when they got no help from their Independent Union delegates. Workers then elected a committee with Williams as head representative. Williams arranged a conference with management, handing in the workers' petition, but when he tried to start a wildcat strike the next day, everyone else continued to work. The company fired him for "loafing," even though he had six years' service. Forty IUMSWA stewards from all departments later gathered at Industrial Relations Manager Houghton's office to protest the firing, but management refused to give an answer, forcing the union to file yet another NLRB charge. In the fall, MacPherson managed to get Williams rehired on the organizing staff, reassuring Van Gelder that Williams was an asset to the campaign, despite his radical reputation: "I have assigned Marty Williams to house to house canvassing. It is very difficult to get organizers as you know and I believe that Williams will be effective and safe in this end of the campaign."[45]

Workers conducted several job actions over the summer. In July, all the drillers and reamers on hull 1490 (for the tanker *Superflame*) walked off the job after they were denied a full bonus on completed work. These workers had tried unsuccessfully to get help from their Independent Union delegate and took matters into their own hands.[46]

Another job action was led by Don Bollen, a young left-wing activist. Showing no fear in his organizing activity, he started wearing CIO buttons almost as soon as he was hired, despite John Hicks's advice to be more cautious. Bollen soon surpassed Hicks in the number of IUMSWA recruits he signed up. He also got elected as second-shift steward in the Q Department (outside machinists). On September 22, when a foreman arbitrarily fired Lloyd Raymond, another steward in Bollen's area, Bollen and fellow IUMSWA steward Waite decided to take immediate action to win back Raymond's job. Bollen recalled:

---

[44] MacPherson to Van Gelder, July 16, 1941, IUMSWA Archives, Series V, Box 20.

[45] Vogel, "The Fore River Strikers," p. 108; *Fore River Facts*, April 17, 1941; Don Bollen interview, Sept. 23, 1982; MacPherson to Van Gelder, Sept. 16, 1941, IUMSWA Archives, Series V, Box 21.

[46] *Fore River Facts*, July 25, 1941; Fore River ship list.

I told [Raymond], "Don't get your tool box or punch out. Round up everybody, tell them you're fired, and meet at the top of the gang plank, to teach them how to organize." We passed word from area to area [on the battleship *USS Massachusetts*] and 100 percent of the Q Department showed up, including non-signers. We led them to the bottom of the gang plank, talked about the Raymond case, and read other [unsettled] grievances. We formed a committee on the spot. Then I said, "What do you think of stopping work until Raymond's rehired, but also the grievances settled?" So the personnel manager came down like a bat out of hell. The company agreed to all of our points.

But the key to it was [that] this was the last shift to complete work [on the ship]. The next day, dignitaries, including the U.S. vice president [Henry Wallace], were to be there. A leaflet came out the next day. It became one of the key things in the 1941 campaign to teach workers what they can do through organization. I had been preaching: don't organize by leaflets and money, but by action on the floor, taking militant steps to win grievances.

The stoppage lasted only eight minutes, but it restored some confidence in the union throughout the yard. The action violated the IUMSWA's adherence to the no-strike pledge, but received the quiet praise of the union's staff organizers. Bollen, although a Communist, had no qualms about disregarding the CP's support for the pledge either. These few challenges, however, could not revitalize the campaign by themselves. It became clear by the fall that there was no groundswell of support for the IUMSWA.[47]

In October, Green moved even further from militant organizing tactics, directing Fore River organizers to conduct a "hands off" policy toward the company union, except secondarily to "answer specific charges or attacks." "It is my firm opinion that we should drop altogether our campaign of slandering abuse against the Independent Union, and propagandize on a high and constructive level. In other words, the campaign should not be a negative one, consisting of abuse or opposition to a certain group, but should be a constructive appeal to the men." Green's approach further demobilized the IUMSWA's challenge to the Independent Union.[48]

MacPherson intended to get the "Victory Drive" under way in early September, but the final stretch of the campaign did not begin until October, when CIO Organization Director Allan Haywood offered the IUMSWA organizing

[47] Don Bollen interview, Sept. 23, 1982; Fore River ship list; *Fore River Facts*, June 6, 1941 (for background on Raymond); Ken Kramer report, Sept. 27, 1941, IUMSWA Archives, Series V, Box 21.
[48] Green to MacPherson, Oct. 6, 1941, IUMSWA Archives, Series V, Box 21.

and financial assistance for Fore River. The IUMSWA national officers put George Craig, a UMW colleague of Haywood and John L. Lewis, in charge, brought back Mulkern from New York, and enlisted recently fired Fore River worker Vincent Porpola, which gave the campaign some local roots. Most of the IUMSWA staff and the non-shipbuilding CIO organizers came from outside New England.[49]

Bringing in the CIO led to the exclusion of Local 5's leaders from any real decision-making. As Boyson recalled, "I met with Green and [CIO Organization Director Allan] Haywood, and Haywood said, 'We're running the campaign, we will pay for it.' . . . We were just figureheads. They handled all the publicity, but they didn't seem to realize we knew the guys. I knew it was a lost cause, we weren't going to win. I felt it in my bones. I could go by the talk and the fellows around."[50]

Fifteen staff organizers worked for a month in an effort to build support for the union. National IUMSWA attorney Goldstein managed to get the election postponed until November 19, but this play for time failed to revive the campaign. Relying on the CIO proved disastrous. The new director, George Craig, set up his own private office in the local and spent most of his time barking orders to staffers and workers. At one point, the staff suggested that he change his style after he gave a miserable radio talk. Craig replied that he would run things the way he wanted, even though Boyson and Hicks had given a far more effective radio presentation just days before. All Local 5 dues money for October and November went to the campaign, and the national IUMSWA and CIO donated several thousand dollars, but Craig failed to maintain adequate records of expenditures. The campaign was a case study in disorganization and waste, even though dedicated organizers such as Mulkern and workers such as Boyson and Bollen tried their best to carry on the fight.[51]

Finally by late October, even John Green himself realized how badly the campaign was going and desperately wrote to Haywood:

[49] MacPherson to Van Gelder, Sept. 2, 1941, Oct. 3 and 10, 1941; MacPherson to Green, Sept. 12, 1941; Van Gelder to MacPherson, Sept. 12, 1941; all IUMSWA Archives, Series V, Box 21.

[50] Boyson interview, April 26, 1983.

[51] Watts (NLRB) file memo on Bethlehem Shipbuilding case, June 19, 1941; Supplemental Decision and Amendment to Direction of Election, Bethlehem and IUMSWA Local 5, NLRB, Aug. 18 and Oct. 20, 1941; Goldstein to NLRB, Oct. 9, 1941; all NA, RG 25, Box 1669. Green to MacPherson, Oct. 6, 1941; S. A. Macri, Sr., to Allan Haywood, Nov. 22, 1941; Joseph Hellinger to Green, Nov. 1941; Vincent Porpola (unsigned), Nov. 1941; Mulkern to Van Gelder, Nov. 27, 1941; MacPherson to IUMSWA national officers, Nov. 29, 1941; Van Gelder to Mulkern, Dec. 2, 1941; MacPherson report on Local 5, Dec. 27, 1941; Walter Walker to Van Gelder, Jan. 17, 1942; MacPherson to Van Gelder, Jan. 21, 1942; Report on Fore River campaign (no author listed), Jan. 30, 1941; all IUMSWA Archives, Series V, Box 21.

I have had some very disturbing reports from Quincy, and am convinced that immediate action is necessary to insure the success of the campaign there. . . . Craig has had only two staff meetings since he went up there, and . . . has failed completely to win the full confidence and cooperation of the organizing staff. He issues orders, then cancels them, and then orders them again. . . .

The C.I.O. organizers . . . meet together, but not with the I.U.M.S.W.A. organizers. . . . As a result of this ineptness and general incompetence, the morale of the organizing staff is bad, and this is beginning to be reflected in the morale of the organizing committee in the yard.

CIO Assistant Director of Organization Michael Widman promised to look into the situation, but Craig's supervisors failed to intervene effectively.[52]

Even under Craig's incompetent direction, MacPherson persevered in following Green's orders and did his best to conduct a bland, respectable "Victory Drive." The mundane phrase, "Yes Means Collective Bargaining," was the campaign's slogan. MacPherson told the national office that there were departmental meetings every night and "plenty of activity." In the summer, Van Gelder temporarily shifted publication of *Fore River Facts* to Camden to assert the national office's control of policy, but by late fall the newspaper had reverted to local publication under the editorial direction of Craig, MacPherson, and the organizing staff. Local 5 leadership was excluded from involvement. The newspaper took the place of leaflets and included virtually no departmental information, highlighting instead various speeches by Haywood and Craig. Loaded with copy, it promised better bonuses and job security while offering no criticism of the Independent Union. Rather than making issues comprehensible and personal for the average worker, the paper offered abstract rhetoric wrapped in patriotism. "To Defense workers and their families! . . . What has been done by the shipyard workers in other yards for the defense of their families can be done by the men in the Fore River. 110,000 Shipyard Workers have joined together to defend their job, their homes, and their country!"[53]

The Independent Union, with the backing of yard supervisors, waged a relentless anti-union campaign against the IUMSWA-CIO forces. Supervisors tolerated Independent delegates campaigning and passing out "Vote No" buttons on company time. They also permitted "Vote No" signs on company

---

[52] Green to Haywood, Oct. 27, 1941; Michael Widman to Green, Oct. 29, 1941; both IUMSWA Archives, Series I, Subseries 2, Box 2.

[53] MacPherson to Van Gelder and Green, Oct. 10, 1941; Ken Kramer to Green, Oct. 11, 1941; both IUMSWA Archives, Series V, Box 21. Van Gelder to MacPherson, July 15 and 24, 1941, IUMSWA Archives, Series V, Box 20. *Fore River Facts*, Oct. 16, 1941; IUMSWA leaflet, c. Nov. 1941, Littauer Labor Collection, Harvard University.

property and machines until they were reprimanded by Labor Board observers. One Independent Union delegate was even allowed to use a foreman's office for campaigning, where he systematically interviewed workers from a number of departments. In the community, several Independent Union delegates beat up a Local 5 activist who was passing out leaflets. When Marty Williams filed a complaint with the Quincy police, they did nothing. Craig and MacPherson did not publicize these unfair labor practices, but followed the "high road" as Green and Haywood had advised.[54]

Money and extra IUMSWA and CIO staffers were no substitute for a united campaign based on widespread local support. By the end of the drive, the organizers and Local 5 activists had enlisted less than 3,000 signed members, of whom only 2,700 were members in good standing. In six months the Fore River union grew by only 1,300 members, while employment at the yard had increased by some 5,000.[55]

The IUMSWA lost badly in the November 19 election. Of 12,608 votes cast, only 3,564 went to the union, while 8,991 workers voted "no union." (Table 9). This was the largest NLRB poll held in New England up to that time, and constituted a major setback for the CIO both regionally and nationally.

Some of the organizers believed that the influx of younger workers hurt them, but these workers proved to be among the most favorable to the union. Workers concentrated in the "steel trades" (welders, burners, rivet gangs, drillers and reamers, and chippers and caulkers) were most likely to vote for the union. The training department, which was full of younger workers, also had more union supporters than the rest of the yard.. Even in these departments, however, the pro-union vote did not quite reach 50 percent.[56]

Workers in the most highly skilled trades, especially shipfitters, the boiler shop, inside machinists, electricians, painters, pipefitters, and shipwrights, were least likely to support the union. It is difficult to determine whether the "old-timers," most of whom had jobs in these skilled trades, voted for or against the union, because so many new workers entered the yard in 1941. Nevertheless, the sentiment in the shops, compared to the ways, was overwhelmingly against the IUMSWA. Fore River's shops were much larger than those at Federal and New York Ship, giving this group of skilled men virtually equal numerical strength to that of workers on the ways. (A number of trades,

---

[54] Affidavits filed with NLRB, by stewards Giogrande, Raymond, and others, Oct. 11, 1941; Martin Williams to Green, Dec. 11, 1941; all IUMSWA Archives, Series V, Box 21. *Fore River Facts*, Oct. and Nov. 1941.

[55] MacPherson election report, Nov. 19, 1941, IUMSWA Archives, Series V, Box 20.

[56] *Boston Herald*, Nov. 20, 1941. For sources of election data, see Table 9.

Table 9. Results of Fore River NLRB Election, November 19, 1941

Voting area	Votes Yes	Votes No	% Yes	% No
No. 1: (Plate Yard, Mold Loft, Fabrication, Galvanizing, Stores/Materials)	438	1,167	37.5	62.5
No. 2: (Blacksmith, Foundry, Pattern, Machine Shop, Boiler Shop)	350	1,029	34.0	66.0
No. 3: (Electrical, Paint Shop)	381	1,075	35.4	64.6
No. 4: (Shipfitting, Erecting)	377	1,166	32.3	67.7
No. 5: (Pipe/Copper, Shipwright)	273	766	35.6	64.4
No. 6: (Outside Machinists, Yard)	260	681	38.2	61.8
No. 7: (Riveting, Drilling & Reaming, Chipping & Caulking, Turret Shop)	368	800	46.0	54.0
No. 8: (Electric Welding, Acetylene Welding & Burning)	643	1,299	49.5	51.5
No. 9: (Training, Sheet Metal, Central Tool Room, Transportation)	474	1,008	47.0	53.0
Total	3,564	8,991	39.6	60.4
Total votes cast:	12,555			

Table does not include challenged, blank, or void ballots.

Sources: Certification of Counting and Tabulation of Ballots, Bethlehem Fore River Shipyard, NLRB, 1st Region, Nov. 19, 1941; NLRB Notice of Election (Fore River), Oct. 1941; both NA, RG 25, Box 1669. *Fore River Facts*, steward list, July 25, 1941; Boyson interview (for job classification and department crosslisting for 1941 campaign), Feb. 11, 1987.

such as shipfitters and electricians, worked both on the ways and in the shops.) The relative strength of skilled shop workers may have contributed to Fore River's conservatism compared to other yards.[57]

Some argued that the major problem for organizing came from the recent, overall wartime employment increases, rather than just from younger workers. Fore River did experience enormous growth in the workforce during this period and the following two years: between 1940 and 1943, about 1,000 new workers a month entered the yard. Beyond Fore River, however, this explanation did not hold. Other Bethlehem shipyards with equal if not more rapid hir-

[57] For sources of election data, see Table 9.

Table 10. IUMSWA Elections at Bethlehem Shipyards, 1938–1941

Date	Shipyard	Local Vote	IUMSWA	other/no union
12-22-38*	Brooklyn 56th St.	13	940	AFL 117
12-22-38*	Hoboken	15	736	AFL 93
12-22-38*	Brooklyn 27th St.	13	680	AFL 67
06-12-41	Baltimore Drydock	24	1,878	Ind. 1,597
08-29-41**	Staten Island	12	2,193	no 625
09-16-41	San Pedro, Ca.	9	1,367	no 67
09-30-41	Sparrows Point	33	2,567	Ind. 1,386, no 307
10-17-41	Fairfield, Baltimore	43	3,570	no 533
11-19-41	Fore River	5	3,564	no 8,991

* Independent public accountants' report verifying union majorities; results certified by NLRB, Aug. 2, 1939.

** At Staten Island the IUMSWA had defeated the AFL Metal Trades in an election conducted by an independent impartial board in June 1936, and the owner, United Drydock, made a written agreement with the IUMSWA. The 1941 election was run by the NLRB after Bethlehem had taken over ownership. Although Bethlehem's East Boston repair yards never held an NLRB election, the company recognized Local 25 there and signed a contract with it in May 1941.

Sources: Mergen, "History of the Industrial Union of Marine and Shipbuilding Workers of America," p. 111; Lane, Ships for Victory, p. 293; "Statement of Bethlehem Steel Co. to NWLB with regard to the Union Shop and Check-Off Issue," Bethlehem Shipbuilding v. IUMSWA, Case No. 38, May 29, 1942, pp. 70–72, 78; Shipyard Worker, Sept. 19, 1941.

ing rates still voted in favor of the union in 1941. Bethlehem was the CIO's main national organizing target that year, and the IUMSWA organized all of the company's yards in the ports of New York, Baltimore, and Los Angeles (Table 10). Some had company unions (Sparrows Point, for example), while others did not.

In 1941, a tremendous surge of union organizing, led nationally by the UAW, the SWOC, and the IUMSWA, swept through the massive automobile manufacturing complex at Ford's River Rouge and the steel mills and ship-yards of Bethlehem. In the port of Baltimore, for example, the SWOC's election victory at the Sparrows Point steel mill was followed a week later by an IUMSWA victory at the adjacent Sparrows Point shipyard. This momentum bypassed the workers at Fore River. The odds against winning at Fore River were high, but defeat was not inevitable in 1941.

Fore River trade unionists suffered heavily not only from the Memorandum's impact on the yard's workers but also from the loss of competent staff leadership resulting from the replacement of organizer Lucien Koch with Gavin MacPherson. Anticommunism and suspicion from the national office led to this upheaval and exacerbated already strained relations between the local and the national office. Furthermore, when MacPherson told Van Gelder in September 1941 that "the need for organizers here is very great," he confused staff numbers with staff ability. The campaign's fifteen staff organizers, most of whom came from the national office and the CIO, were ineffective in mobilizing Fore River workers. In 1945, when another election drive got under way at the shipyard, the IUMSWA had no outside CIO organizers and only four regular staff organizers, even though the numbers of workers in the yard in late 1941 and early 1945 were roughly the same.[58]

Some of the union leaders inside the yard, as well as a few of the organizers, tried to keep the spirit of the campaign alive after the defeat. Among these was Marty Williams, who was dropped from the IUMSWA payroll immediately after the election and then became a UE organizer. Williams astutely pointed out that if the union wanted to win at Fore River, more work had to be done in the community, where MacPherson had no real experience.[59]

MacPherson, who asked for an immediate transfer, blamed the loss on the UMW's November coal strike, which made many Fore River workers fearful of unionism. Independent Union campaigners had stood at the shipyard gates and held up Boston newspaper headlines about the UMW strike, but the election had been lost long before November. When MacPherson and Craig departed from Quincy, they left Local 5 in a financial hole. Paul Mulkern stayed on to try to unravel the mess, but despite his efforts the debt was never resolved.[60]

Local 5 continued to meet over the following year under Arthur Boyson's leadership, but divisions between the two factions within the local grew worse as union membership dwindled. In the fall of 1942, Don Bollen was elected as Local 5's sole delegate to the IUMSWA national convention. As union veterans, Palmer and Boyson resented Bollen representing them. Bollen and the younger group challenged the "old-timers" in this minor election because they believed that the established leaders' low-key style was holding back the local.[61]

Despite their differences, both groups in Local 5 believed that the national officers' policies were the main cause of the failures at Fore River. As a protest over the debt that the national would not pay, Boyson and the Local 5 leadership refused to pay the national union's per capita allocation drawn from local dues collections. Van Gelder summarily resolved the issue when he withdrew Local 5's autonomy in October 1942. Bollen soon left the shipyard and, like

[58] MacPherson to Van Gelder, Sept. 6, 1941, IUMSWA Archives, Series V, Box 21.

[59] Williams to Green, Dec. 11, 1941; Hellinger to Van Gelder, Jan. 23, 1942; Russell to Green, March 9, 1942; all IUMSWA Archives, Series V, Box 21.

[60] MacPherson report on Fore River, Dec. 27, 1941; Green to MacPherson, Nov. 25, 1941; MacPherson election report, Nov. 19, 1941; all IUMSWA Archives, Series V, Box 21.

[61] Boyson interview, Oct. 4, 1982; Don Bollen interview, Sept. 23, 1982; IUMSWA, *Proceedings, 8th National Convention*, Delegate List, Sept. 1942.

Williams, became a UE organizer, realizing that he had a better chance of contributing to trade unionism elsewhere. Boyson and the older group decided to withdraw completely from local activity. A handful of inside activists, mostly on the left, continued to try to organize, but they received little help from the national office's appointed director, Richard Kelleher. The IUMSWA had lost not only the election but Local 5 as well.[62]

By 1942 there was little that any skilled organizer could do at Fore River. The IUMSWA had been discredited, and the Independent Union appeared stronger than ever. It is probably fair to say that in 1941 workers did not vote "for" either the company union or Bethlehem management. They voted "against" the IUMSWA. John Green believed that his "historic" first—getting Bethlehem to the bargaining table before the SWOC in the spring of 1941— justified the termination of legal action against the Fore River company union, but the pact led to the collapse of the IUMSWA in Quincy. Green himself could not devise a strategy to win at Fore River, or even one that would revive the movement there. Such a strategy would come, instead, from those who maintained a rank-and-file orientation toward organizing and who would not compromise local initiative or fear its political consequences.

[62] Green and Van Gelder to Local 5, Oct. 17, 1942; Van Gelder to Richard Kelleher, Oct. 17, 1942; both IUMSWA Archives, Series V, Box 21. Don Bollen interview, Sept. 23, 1982; Boyson interview, Oct. 4, 1982.

CHAPTER 8

From Defeat to Victory: Returning to a Rank-and-File Organizing Strategy at Fore River, 1942–1945

During World War II, the CIO and its affiliated unions established themselves as the new cornerstone for organized labor in America. The CIO's expansion was remarkable: it had 1,838,000 total members in 1939; 2,659,000 in 1941; and 3,937,000 by 1944. The IUMSWA shared in this spectacular growth, moving from tenth rank in the CIO in 1939, with 35,000 members, to sixth in 1944, with over 209,000. Its growth rate was greater than that of the CIO as a whole. In recognition of the IUMSWA's new power, national president John Green was elevated to an important CIO vice-presidency. He became a close confidante of CIO secretary-treasurer James Carey, who shared his Socialist Party and anticommunist background. By 1944, however, the CIO's momentum and prestige had not translated into organizing success at Fore River.[1]

From 1942 to 1944, the IUMSWA's national officers failed to alter the policies toward Fore River that they had set down in the 1941 campaign. Momentum for change came instead from young, innovative staff organizers and a revived rank-and-file initiative. Turmoil at Federal Shipbuilding in Kearny, where progressives scored an important victory in 1944, provided a training ground for staff organizers who later came to Fore River. Lou Kaplan, the leader of the 1945 IUMSWA drive in Quincy, was the most prominent of these new organizers; like many of them, he had a left-wing orientation.[2]

---

[1] Nelson Lichtenstein, *Labor's War at Home: The CIO in World War II* (Cambridge: Cambridge University Press, 1982), pp. 80–81; Bernard Mergen, "A History of the Industrial Union of Marine and Shipbuilding Workers of America, 1933–1951" (Ph.D. diss., University of Pennsylvania, 1968), pp. 87, 194.

[2] For the struggle to consolidate IUMSWA Local 16 at Federal Shipbuilding in Kearny from 1941 to 1944, see David Palmer, "Organizing the Shipyards: Unionization at Fore River,

The leaders of the Independent Union believed they had won a secure victory at Fore River that would last for the duration of the war. The Atlantic Coast Shipbuilding Stabilization wage standards applied to both union and non-union yards by mid-1941, although the IUMSWA was the only union that held a voting position on the Atlantic Zone Committee. The Independent Union, which falsely claimed full credit for the pay raises that accompanied Shipbuilding Stabilization, continued to benefit from this arrangement over the next two years.[3]

One hope for expanded union organization in the Quincy area was the new Hingham yard, constructed in 1941 by Bethlehem about two miles east of the Fore River yard. Hingham specialized in landing ship tanks (LSTs) and destroyer escorts, and was typical of many new shipyards built specifically for World War II emergency production. By 1944 the yard employed about 23,000 workers on three shifts, probably a fourth of whom were women. A relatively small number of African Americans and Cape Verdeans also worked at Hingham. In contrast, few women and virtually no African Americans worked at the Fore River yard.[4]

The national IUMSWA did little during World War II to focus its organizing campaigns or other activities on the needs and concerns of women, despite the fact that over 100,000 women worked in private shipyards by 1943. This neglect stood in marked contrast to the other big wartime unions of the CIO, such as the UAW and the UE. The IUMSWA's lack of response may have stemmed in part from the fact that for nearly two decades before the war the industry had been totally male. In December 1943, women still made up less than 10 percent of the workforce at the biggest East Coast shipyards, which built mainly capital naval ships. At Federal Shipbuilding's Kearny yard, women comprised less than 1 percent of the labor force. Women were overwhelmingly relegated to auxiliary wartime yards. This characteristic distinc-

New York Ship, and Federal Ship, 1898–1945" (Ph.D. diss., Brandeis University, 1990), pp. 676–787.

³ *Shipyard Worker*, June 27, 1941; *Fore River Weekly*, June 12, 26, 1941.

⁴ Background on the Hingham yard, including employment numbers and the IUMSWA drive, is drawn from Fran Bollen interview, July 29, 1989; Don Bollen interview, July 29, 1989; *Quincy Patriot Ledger*, Jan. 26, 1945, p. 7; Bethlehem Shipbuilding, Hingham and AFL, April 16, 1943, LLR Man. 12, pp. 97–98; *The Shipyard Worker, Fore River Edition*, Feb. 3, 1944; James Bilotta, Ernest Trueman, Lawrence Parrish et al., to Thomas Gallagher, Feb. 20, 1944, IUMSWA Archives, Series V, Box 21, Special Collections, University of Maryland at College Park Libraries. For the number of women employed in World War II shipyards, see Deborah A. Hirschfield, "Rosie Also Welded: Women and Technology in Shipbuilding during World War II" (Ph.D. diss., University of California, Irvine, 1987), esp. pp. 95–205, 256. Fran Bollen believed that about one-third of Hingham workers were women, but Hirschfield's data shows that women comprised no more than 25% of the workforce at any U.S. shipyard during World War II.

tion between the permanent and emergency shipyards shaped organizing dynamics at Fore River and Hingham as well.[5]

The IUMSWA launched a campaign at Hingham in 1943. After a year's preparation, it sought an NLRB election. In contrast to earlier IUMSWA organizing initiatives, Communists and other left-wing activists in the Hingham yard openly fought for an end to discrimination against women and blacks, rather than just for union rights. The movement to involve women and minorities came almost entirely from these inside radicals, rather than from the IUMSWA staff organizers and national office. This effort to unite different groups behind the IUMSWA did not translate into a union victory, however, and a majority of Hingham workers voted for "no union." The margin of defeat was not as great as it had been at Fore River in 1941, but the loss was seen as another humiliation handed to the Boston-area IUMSWA by Bethlehem.[6]

Despite the Hingham defeat, activists at the Fore River yard were strongly committed to a new drive. Prominent among them was Larry Parrish, an electrician at the yard since 1932. He became active late in the ill-fated 1941 campaign through the encouragement of Joe Hellinger, a left-wing staff organizer from Federal Ship. After that defeat, Parrish emerged as a key leader among the younger group on the left. He became good friends with Local 5 president Arthur Boyson, despite Boyson's dislike for those leftists whom he believed did not appreciate the contributions of older Fore River trade unionists. Parrish and his associates, such as Ernie Trueman, Cliff Crozier, and Carl Carlson, remained active in 1943, even though the national officers refused to

[5] U.S. Dept. of Labor, Bureau of Labor Statistics, "Wartime Employment, Production, and Conditions of Work in Shipyards," Bulletin No. 824 (Washington, D.C.: GPO, 1945), pp. 6–7; Hirschfield, "Rosie Also Welded," p. 256. See also Amy Kesselman, *Fleeting Opportunities: Women Shipyard Workers in Portland and Vancouver during World War II and Reconversion* (Albany: State University of New York Press, 1990). Federal Shipbuilding built a huge wartime auxiliary yard at Port Newark, where 8.4 percent of the workers were women in 1943. New York Shipbuilding, which did not have an auxiliary yard, employed the same percentage of women; Hirschfield, p. 256. For contrasting wartime policies of the UAW and UE toward women, see Ruth Milkman, *Gender at Work: The Dynamics of Job Segregation by Sex during World War II* (Urbana: University of Illinois Press, 1987). For the UAW in particular, see Nancy F. Gabin, *Feminism in the Labor Movement: Women and the United Auto Workers, 1935–1975* (Ithaca: Cornell University Press, 1990).

[6] Fran Bollen interview, July 29, 1989; Don Bollen interview, July 29, 1989; *Quincy Patriot Ledger*, Jan. 26, 1945, p. 7; Bethlehem Shipbuilding, Hingham and AFL, April 16, 1943, LLR Man. 12, pp. 97–98; *The Shipyard Worker, Fore River Edition*, Feb. 3, 1944; Bilotta et al. to Gallagher, Feb. 20, 1944. A breakdown of votes by race and sex does not exist for the Hingham election (or for any NLRB election), so it is impossible to determine empirically the extent to which race or sex determined the poll's outcome. At Hingham, IUMSWA rank-and-file organizers (though not national staff members) explicitly supported the rights of women and black workers in the yard, in contrast to the IUMSWA's equivocation in the Mobile, Alabama, campaign during the same period.

commit more than one organizer full-time to Fore River. They faced additional obstacles in the lead Fore River staff organizer, Richard Kelleher, who openly expressed contempt for the left, and IUMSWA New England Regional Director Hugh Brown, who blamed the left for the Hingham loss. Brown in particular had a reputation as a hard-line anticommunist and was determined that a new Fore River campaign should not be led by workers like Parrish.[7]

Parrish, Trueman, Carlson, Fred Coolen, and other workers who had organized during the 1941 drive decided to form their own "Volunteer Organizers" group, based on their Hingham support committee, as a way to promote a new Fore River campaign. They called on Tom Gallagher, the national union's new organizational director, to remove Brown, Kelleher, and another organizer assigned to Fore River and Hingham. Brown responded by "dissolving" the existing committee so that he could form his own, drawn from the older, more conservative group that included Palmer, Boyson, and others.[8]

John Green sustained Brown's decision and went further, expelling some twenty members of the Volunteer Organizers from the IUMSWA. As a pretext for this action, Green claimed that they had been selling the *Daily Worker* at Fore River. Many workers, including a number of the "old-timers," read the paper even if they disagreed with the party's politics. Brown and Green took this action as much to exert their power over the union as to suppress left-wing ideology. Already there had been talk in other locals, including New York Ship's Local 1, of running someone against Green. This insurgent movement grew as the progressives in Federal Ship's Local 16 gained popularity. Expelling the left at Fore River amounted to a purge of some of the best organizing talent in the yard, but it checked Green's potential rivals within the IUMSWA.[9]

With the IUMSWA weakened and divided, and the Independent Union in-

[7] Arthur Boyson interview, Oct. 4, 1982; *Shipyard Worker, Fore River Edition*, Sept. 9, 1943; Fran Bollen interview, July 29, 1989; Don Bollen interview, July 29, 1989; U.S. Senate, Permanent Subcommittee on Investigations of the Committee on Government Operations, *Hearings, Subversion and Espionage in Defense Establishments and Industry*, Part 7, Jan. 3, 1955, testimony of Lawrence W. Parrish, pp. 291–96. Bilotta et al. to Gallagher, Feb. 20, 1944; Hugh Brown report on Fore River, March 16, 1944; both IUMSWA Archives, Series V, Box 21.

[8] Bilotta et al. to Gallagher, Feb. 20, 1944; Brown report, March 16, 1944. In late 1942, Gallagher began to share responsibility for national organizing with Van Gelder, and by 1943 he was promoted to the full-time post of organizational director; Mergen, "History of the Industrial Union of Marine and Shipbuilding Workers of America," p. 153. This change in the national office helped consolidate the anti-left group around Green and anti-left policies in the field.

[9] Brown report, March 16, 1944; Kaplan interview, Jan. 8, 1983; Milton Vogel, "The Fore River Strikers, a Study in Allegiance Dynamics" (MA thesis, Massachusetts Institute of Technology, 1948), pp. 114–15; Reeder interview, May 21, 1988 (for the Local 1 challenge to Green in 1944, which Reeder helped lead as its local president). Don Bollen, by this time a UE

creasingly corrupt and complacent, workers had no way to address deteriorating conditions at the yard. Wartime inflation continued, while pay remained almost the same. Extensive overtime provided some extra money for workers, but this only created more dissatisfaction over the lack of adequate vacation time. Unrest had been growing among most of the nation's shipyard workers over the issue of vacations and the strain of excessive overtime. While cost-plus contracts led to idleness among some, the vacation issue was a legitimate grievance that would have received much prompter action in peacetime.[10]

Parrish and the other left-wing activists took advantage of the Independent Union's complacency by helping to publicize their rivals' scandalous behavior and misrepresentation. Fore River Independent Union delegates, like ERP representatives before them, worked under comfortable circumstances and regularly got paid time off from their jobs in order to conduct "union business," earning the resentment of many workers. IUMSWA members maintained surveillance on these men and funneled information to organizer Jimmy Marino, who exposed their activities in his extremely popular satirical column, "Diary of an Independent Delegate," published in the Fore River edition of the *Shipyard Worker*. Arthur Boyson recalled vividly how the Independent Union delegates would come to work and then mysteriously disappear. Everyone read Marino's exposes, which used fictitious names that were quite transparent. One day Marino's union assistants located the Independents "down on Wollaston Beach in the afternoon, while your boys were dying overseas." Another time they followed them "to a ball game."[11]

In contrast to workers in shipyards like Fore River and Newport News, where company unions were in control, those in shipyards represented by the IUMSWA had a voice through the Shipbuilding Stabilization Committee and its successor, the Shipbuilding Stabilization Commission. This wartime tripartite agency regularly stalled on issues such as vacations and classification re-rating, which led to wildcat strikes at Federal Ship, New York Ship, and other major shipyards. The agency did, however, provide an official mechanism for negotiations between labor and business that eventually led to improvements for workers. The IUMSWA's representative on the Shipbuilding Stabilization Commission was Lucien Koch, the Independent Union's old enemy. Although the Independent Union belonged to a paper organization of company unions called the East Coast Alliance of Independent Ship

---

organizer, knew both Parrish and Carlson through the CIO and left-wing political activities. He told me that the *Daily Worker* was sold not by CP union activists inside the yard but by some of the shipyard workers' wives at the gates.

[10] Kimball Sturtevant (Independent Union) to W. H. Steele, Oct. 14, 1943, NA, RG 25; Don Bollen interview, Sept. 23, 1982.

[11] Don Bollen interview, July 29, 1989; Boyson interview, Oct. 4, 1982.

Yards, it was powerless in Washington compared to the IUMSWA and its CIO backers.[12]

After the IUMSWA's 1941 defeat, the Independent Union met with management to request improved vacations for workers. Although the company met intermittently with the Independent Union for the next two years to discuss the issue, it made no concessions. In June 1943 the IUMSWA invited the Independent Union to file a joint brief with the Shipbuilding Commission, but the Independent declined. When the Independent Union finally submitted its own brief to the NWLB over a year later, on September 20, 1944, it asked for improved vacation benefits, but failed to demand wage improvements as the IUMSWA had done. As a result, Fore River workers lost fifteen months in improved wages and had to wait a number of months longer than those in IUMSWA yards for better vacation benefits.[13]

Fore River exploded on October 9, 1944, when news of the Independent Union officers' gross incompetence on the wage issue reached workers in the yard. First, the pipefitters walked off the job in protest. Then Jim McGonnigal, who was sympathetic to the CIO and became chairman of the sheet metal workers committee that was formed on the spot, led his department out. The shipfitters joined in, and the next day the riggers, chippers, electricians, and cleaners stopped work. Each group that struck formed a committee to represent its own trade. The walkout continued for three days, until the Massachusetts State Board of Conciliation and Arbitration agreed to handle all grievances for the workers. Federal government officials also came to the yard to assist.[14]

At the height of the strike, about 7,000 workers, including 500 women, participated; the walkout involved over 30 percent of the 22,500 employees in the yard. It was by far the largest strike at Fore River since the end of World War I. Many IUMSWA activists opposed the walkout, even though they sympathized with the complaints of the workers, because they felt that stopping production would hurt GIs overseas and violated the CIO's no-strike pledge. At this time, the left-wingers were the most active group in the local union, even though many of them had been barred from official membership. They also were among the strongest backers of the no-strike pledge. Most strikers,

[12] Lucien Koch interview, June 7, 1983; W. H. Steele, Progress Report on Fore River, Oct. 12, 1941, NA, RG 25; *New England Shipbuilder*, April 25 and June 13, 1945; NWLB, *Termination Report*: vol. 1, *Industrial Disputes and Wage Stabilization in Wartime* (Washington, D.C.: GPO, 1947), p. 854.

[13] Koch interview, June 7, 1983; Steele, Progress Report on Fore River, Oct. 12, 1941; *New England Shipbuilder*, April 25 and June 13, 1945.

[14] "HRC" to John Sullivan and "HRC" to James McGonnigal, Oct. 10, 1944; Sullivan's Preliminary Report, Oct. 10, 1944; W. H. Collins to James Morarty, Oct. 11, 1944; Sullivan's Final Report, Oct. 12, 1944; all NA, RG 25. Vogel, "The Fore River Strikers," pp. 117–19.

on the other hand, had not been active in the IUMSWA, but now wanted some form of genuine union representation.[15]

Ernie Trueman and Larry Parrish rushed to the sheet metal shop and angrily confronted McGonnigal, whom they felt had taken reckless action on his own. Other more independent-minded leftists reluctantly supported the strike, such as Jack McGill, who had been rehired at Fore River during the wartime buildup. Veteran IUMSWA leaders Boyson and Palmer did not participate in the strike but believed it was justified, a view shared by their fellow "old-timers."[16]

Alex Turoczy and organizer Al Turner investigated the Fore River upheaval first-hand for the national IUMSWA. Turoczy, who had been a key inside organizer at Federal Ship in 1937 and later served as a Local 16 officer, was appointed as the IUMSWA's New England Regional Director after Hugh Brown was fired for failing to win drives in the region. Turoczy had experience with coalitions that encompassed all shades of political opinion and was personally sympathetic to the left, which made him well equipped for dealing with the Fore River crisis. Turner, by contrast, came from a traditional, politically moderate New England trade union background, but had no use for the divisive anticommunism of Brown and Kelleher.[17]

When Turoczy and Turner arrived at Fore River, they found an incredible scene. Turoczy reported to Gallagher that "strikers were standing before all the Gates, discussing the strike, and protesting the action that the Independent Union had taken . . . [declaring] that it was a wildcat strike." Even though the Independent Union shortly "retracted" its position and declared the strike legitimate, "the workers belonging to the Independent Union lost all faith in their delegates and were wildly roaming around. We opened the door at the CIO Headquarters and met with the . . . workers, who were volunteer organizers on the various [Quincy] drives."[18]

When government mediators arrived at the yard, Independent Union delegates tried to "represent" the workers but were not taken seriously by most of them. One company union officer involved was secretary James Hardie, the

[15] "HRC" to Sullivan and "HRC" to McGonnigal, Oct. 10, 1944; Sullivan's Preliminary Report, Oct. 10, 1944; Collins to Morarty, Oct. 11, 1944; Sullivan's Final Report, Oct. 12, 1944; all NA, RG 25. Vogel, "The Fore River Strikers," pp. 117–19. Boyson interview, Oct. 4, 1982.

[16] "HRC" to Sullivan and "HRC" to McGonnigal, Oct. 10, 1944; Sullivan's Preliminary Report, Oct. 10, 1944; Collins to Morarty, Oct. 11, 1944; Sullivan's Final Report, Oct. 12, 1944; all NA, RG 25. Vogel, "The Fore River Strikers," pp. 117–19. Boyson interview, Oct. 4, 1982.

[17] Fran Bollen interview, July 29, 1989. Alex Turoczy report to Gallagher, Oct. 12, 1944; Turner, "Proposed Organizational Plan for . . . Fore River," Oct. 13, 1944; both IUMSWA Archives, Series II, Box 21. Kaplan interviews, Jan. 8, 1983, and Aug. 1, 1989.

[18] Turoczy report to Gallagher, Oct. 12, 1944.

former Local 5 officer who had turned against the IUMSWA in 1935. Although Parrish, Trueman, and some other union activists opposed the strike, the standing of the IUMSWA and the larger CIO had become far stronger than that of the Independent Union because they were seen as effective organizations that delivered for their members.[19]

Striking workers had requested the meeting at Local 5. In contrast to former IUMSWA staffers Brown and Kelleher, Turoczy and Turner listened carefully to what each worker had to say. Charlie Palmer stated that the company had done nothing to prevent the strike from spreading. Workers in the affected departments were angry and wanted to strike, but the Independent Union delegates "had little or no control over the men." Palmer had heard that the Independent Union now wanted to have a seat on the Stabilization Commission as a way to repair its reputation and thus control workers in the yard. IUMSWA Local 5, Palmer concluded, "should start an immediate drive."[20]

McGonnigal described grievance meetings with Independent Union delegates where nothing had been accomplished. Workers in the sheet metal shop had decided they had no alternative but to strike. McGonnigal blamed the start of the strike on "some loud-mouthed boys in the department," even though Boyson and Parrish (neither of whom was present at this meeting) believed he had been the main leader.[21]

Carl Carlson, one of the left-wingers expelled from the IUMSWA but still active, observed that the workers "were backing up one another as individuals, in the various departments" and were not solidly behind the Independent Union. The strike, he believed, had discredited the Independent among many workers, including its own members. Three departments planned to "line up and demand a meeting and throw out the present officers, and also to change the by-laws."[22]

Turoczy made it clear that the IUMSWA needed more than cards to start a drive. The workers themselves would have "to share the future responsibility for organizing." At a subsequent meeting, he reported that the union activists wanted the local to "be given its autonomy back, so that workers could see democracy in our Union, in letting them run their own affairs." Turoczy was absolutely convinced of their sincerity and strongly recommended to Gallagher that their request be granted. The blame, he believed, did not rest with the workers but with the way Hugh Brown had abused his authority. Even

[19] Turoczy report to Gallagher, Oct. 12, 1944; Fran Bollen interview, July 29, 1989.
[20] Turoczy report to Gallagher, Oct. 12, 1944.
[21] Ibid.
[22] Ibid.

as Turoczy was writing, the yard appeared ready to erupt again, as Turoczy reported:

> It seems that the conduct of our past Regional Director, along with some of the organizers who have worked in Quincy, left behind them the bitterness of red-baiting individuals and smearing workers, which was resented by this group, and they requested that we send in someone who could act human and discuss the problems with which they shall be confronted in the campaign. . . . It is now 4:15 P.M., Thursday, and in talking to the boys in the Quincy office, I find that there is a threat of another walk-out so you can readily see that things are not settled yet.[23]

Turner concurred with Turoczy. Both men believed that the union should start a drive, but also that there was "a tremendous amount of work to be done." Turner emphasized the strong feeling against the Independent Union and the need to give Fore River workers complete initiative in any new campaign. Turner's analysis was a concise and powerful, diplomatically phrased summation of what had held back IUMSWA efforts to unionize Fore River: anticommunism not just among workers but within the IUMSWA leadership. It was anticommunism—both "red-baiting" and the "resentment of outsiders"—that had to be completely overcome to achieve unity among pro-union workers and ensure their active participation in a new drive. The initiative had to come from inside the yard. Turner wrote:

> At the present time, the sentiment of the shipyard workers as a whole, in Fore River Yard, is the need of a change in Unions. They are thoroughly convinced that the Union that now represents them, at least the officers and delegates, are not doing the job. The talk of CIO has been very prevalent throughout the shipyard. . . . Publicity should be kept at a minimum until such time that [the campaign director] is ready for his all out drive. *I am convinced that the work must be done by the workers themselves,* even the distribution of leaflets or any other literature in front of the gate. There is still a very strong resentment to outsiders in this area. A volunteer organizing committee has already come forth, ready, willing, and anxious to start to work. . . . *I suggest that there be no more red-baiting campaigns within the ranks of the organizing committee, that every solitary worker, regardless of his political affiliations, be utilized to the fullest extent.*[24]

---

[23] Ibid.
[24] Turner, "Proposed Organization Plan for . . . Fore River," Oct. 13, 1944 (emphasis added).

Turner's analysis followed the basic organizing perspective that led to earlier union victories at New York Ship and Federal Ship.

Both IUMSWA president John Green and organization director Tom Gallagher disregarded the two staff members' suggestions. Local 5 remained in receivership and the ostracized union activists stayed on the anticommunist blacklist. Turner was sent back to New London where he originally had been assigned, while Regional Director Turoczy was transferred and replaced by Bill Smith. Bill Hartwick, a Green loyalist from New York Ship who lacked Turner's and Turoczy's experience, took charge as the new Fore River organizer.[25]

Hartwick's organizing method was haphazard, and he failed to set priorities. He often got lost in details, wading through the enormous backlog of old membership cards, and had no program or schedule for what had to be accomplished other than building "a committee of approximately 200 or 300 people." Without assistance from Parrish and other left-wing union activists, Hartwick would have been helpless, but ironically he endorsed the expulsion of the left.[26]

Hartwick apparently received little or no assistance from IUMSWA regional director Bill Smith, his immediate superior. Smith was not much of an improvement over Hugh Brown, and to some extent shared Brown's inclination for red-baiting shipyard workers who had left-wing political views. Smith did not fulfill his professional responsibilities and seems to have been rather lazy. According to Boyson, the national office eventually decided to "transfer" Smith out of Boston after he failed to appear at a conference in Kansas City. It turned out that Smith was not in Kansas City, but was relaxing at his Boston home instead, and was caught when he answered a phone call made from the national office.[27]

In January 1945, Hartwick officially started a new organizing committee at the regular membership meeting, with only some twenty workers present. A number of workers who were nominated to head the committee declined. Ernie Trueman, who was in the hospital and not there to refuse, finally was elected, and Boyson offered to act in his place until he recuperated. Relatively few of the 15,000 workers now employed at Fore River were convinced that

[25] Kaplan interview, Jan. 8, 1983; Boyson interview, Oct. 4, 1982. William Hartwick report on Fore River to William Smith, Nov. 22, 1944; Hartwick report on Fore River, "Activity since Nov. 18, 1944," c. Dec. 1944; both IUMSWA Archives, Series V, Box 21.

[26] Hartwick to Smith, Nov. 22, 1944; Hartwick report on Fore River, "Activity since Nov. 18, 1944"; Boyson interview, Oct. 4, 1982.

[27] Boyson interview, Oct. 4, 1982.

this effort by Hartwick was serious, even with the Independent Union discredited and the CIO viewed more favorably. John Hanna, a staff organizer who assisted with the difficult consolidation of Local 16 at Federal Shipyard during 1943 and 1944, arrived several days after this meeting and brought some hope to the workers. Even after he arrived, Hanna confessed to national organization director Tom Gallagher: "The activity in the Fore River shipyard stinks. It is a little better than it has been in the past."[28]

Recognizing how difficult Fore River was to organize, Green and Gallagher assigned Lou Kaplan, perhaps the union's best organizer, to head a new drive. Kaplan had played a major role as an inside activist in consolidating the union at Federal Shipyard and later directed the 1944 organizing drive at Sun Shipbuilding in Chester, Pennsylvania. Sun Ship was notorious for its violence-prone company union, the Sun Ship Employee Association (SSEA), and its segregated, all-white and all-black yards. The yard that employed black workers was created in 1942 by Sun Ship's owner, John Pew, in response to the wartime labor shortage; black workers filled all the positions in the yard, from laborers up to foremen. In 1943 the IUMSWA barely won an election at the yard after nine long years of organizing setbacks. The results were contested, however, and another NLRB election was mandated to settle the dispute. When Kaplan was assigned to direct the new drive at Sun Ship, he adopted a strategy that was unorthodox for the national office but had worked well at Federal Ship. He brought in both white and black organizers, despite IUMSWA President John Green's doubts, and mobilized significant black community backing both in Chester and in nearby Philadelphia. He made special use of highly experienced, left-wing organizers, including those from the UE, as well as mainstream New York Ship trade union leaders, such as Andy Reeder and Pat McCann. He created a "20 Point Program" based on his assessment of what both white and black workers wanted. The program's number one demand, according to Kaplan, was the desegregation of the two shipyards. Finally, his organizing team deliberately split the company union, winning its top officer, Aggie Campbell, to the side of the IUMSWA. When the election was held in December 1944, the IUMSWA won a landslide victory with 15,597 votes out of 19,345 cast; the SSEA received only 3,274.[29]

---

[28] Hartwick report on Fore River, "Activity since Nov. 18, 1944"; Minutes of Meeting in Fore River [union] Office, Jan. 15, 1945; Smith to Gallagher, Jan. 19, 1945; Hartwick report on Fore River, Feb. 26, 1945; all IUMSWA Archives, Series V, Box 21.

[29] Kaplan interview, Jan. 8, 1983; Kaplan and Reeder joint interview, Sept. 3, 1986; Speeches by Kaplan and Reeder, First New York Ship Welders' Reunion, May 31, 1987; IUMSWA Local 2 leaflet (Sun Ship), 1945, Reeder personal papers. See also Daniel Letwin, "Industrial Unionism vs. Industrial Emancipation: Black Workers at Sun Shipyard During World War II" (unpublished paper, Yale University, 1982). Letwin's account ends with the 1943

Immediately after the Sun Ship victory, Green and Gallagher assigned Kaplan to head a new Fore River campaign. Kaplan recalled that the two national officers told him: "'There're more old time shipbuilders there than at any other place, outside of New York Ship. . . . We don't know why we can't get that place organized.'"[30]

Kaplan initially approached Quincy in the same way he had started the Sun Ship drive. When he arrived in the Boston area, he did not tell any of the regular staff that he was in town. After checking into the Manger Hotel across from the Boston Garden, he spent three days in Quincy surveying the scene at a diner opposite the main shipyard gate, where he anonymously listened to workers while having a cup of coffee. Many workers liked the CIO, he found, but they were also skeptical about its practical program. Workers also were not sure that they wanted "this bunch of radicals"—as they referred to the IUMSWA—to represent them. Their conservatism did not bother Kaplan. In his report to Regional Director Bill Smith, he summed up what he had learned:

OBSERVATIONS
1:—The Company Union was thoroughly discredited.
2:—The workers were far from sold on the C.I.O.
3:—The workers were concerned with three major problems:
   (a) Will the C.I.O. take away their bonus?
   (b) Will they be able to have jobs after the war?
   (c) Will they maintain their wage rates?[31]

Kaplan got in touch with UE leaders in the area, who introduced him to Larry Parrish. From Parrish, he heard the incredible story of how Green, with Gallagher's assistance, had expelled some of the key volunteer organizers. Kaplan then called Gallagher and said: "Are you kidding? You got 13 guys expelled and you're sending me into this god damn place? You know how I feel. There'll be no god damn red-baiting if I'm on the campaign. And if you want me to come into this campaign then these . . . guys have to be readmitted."[32]

Gallagher conferred with Green and then told Kaplan: "'Green said, don't go out on a wing now. There's going to be no political philosophy in this campaign.'" Kaplan agreed, stating he had every intention to "stick to trade union

---

drive, before Kaplan led the successful 1944 IUMSWA challenge that destroyed the segregationist policies of the company and the SSEA.
[30] Kaplan interview, Jan. 8, 1983.
[31] Kaplan interview, Jan. 8, 1983, and Aug. 1, 1989; Kaplan report to William Smith, early April 1945, IUMSWA Archives, Series V, Box 21.
[32] Kaplan interview, Jan. 8, 1983.

questions, but anybody who wants to be a member of this union *will* be a member of this union. We'll do just what the preamble of this constitution says."[33]

The national officers' decision to reinstate the thirteen blacklisted members who were still active allowed Kaplan to reunite the core leadership and instilled new confidence among those who were organizing or on the verge of getting involved. The decision also established Kaplan's authority as director of the campaign. Kaplan made it clear that unnecessary interference from the national office would not be tolerated, but he also took care that local interests not be pitted against those of the national office, which was a clear departure from the disastrous pattern of 1941.[34]

Kaplan was politically astute. He focused on uniting local activists, and did not attack Smith or others whom he considered incompetent. His main objective was to instill general confidence that this time the company union was finished and the IUMSWA would win at Fore River. He reported: "The spirit in the Yard is magnificent, the morale is high, organization is definitely on the up-swing and I feel the opportunity is present for a C.I.O. victory at Fore River." Support for the campaign was coming from all quarters. "The old-timers and the newer elements in the Yard are showing a real understanding of the C.I.O. program and the problems that the workers at Fore River face. . . . A great many individuals have come forward in the past several weeks."[35]

Kaplan worked with a small organizing staff at Fore River, but he ran a very disciplined and well-organized campaign. He dismissed several organizers sent by Gallagher, whom he considered useless and little more than mouthpieces for the national office. Bill Hartwick stayed on the drive, but Kaplan kept him "at arms length," as he believed that Hartwick was "a spy for the national union" and a red-baiter.[36]

John Hanna particularly impressed Kaplan because he drew on his radical, working-class past to educate and mobilize Fore River Workers. "I thought John Hanna was unbelievable. . . . He was one of the Protestant leaders of the Irish [1916] Rebellion. . . . He was working class [and] Irish to his toes." Hanna sang the old Clydeside revolutionary songs at IUMSWA meetings, which were especially popular with workers of Scottish and Irish descent. His non-sectarianism (a Protestant who had championed a mainly Catholic cause),

---

[33] Ibid.

[34] Kaplan interviews, Aug. 1, 1989, and Jan. 8, 1983.

[35] Kaplan interviews, Jan. 8, 1983, and Aug. 1, 1989; Kaplan report to Smith, early April 1945.

[36] Kaplan interviews, Jan. 8, 1983, and Aug. 1, 1989; Kaplan report to Smith, early April 1945; *New England Shipbuilder*, March 28, 1945; "Fore River Campaign Expenses," July 28, 1945, IUMSWA Archives, Series V, Box 21.

progressive ethnic politics (Irish but also left-wing), and appeal to many of the old-timers helped bring unity to the drive. His most important work on the campaign, once Kaplan arrived, was community outreach to churches, city government, and the local press.[37]

Organizer John McGonagle (not to be confused with Jim McGonnigal, the sheet metal worker and leader in the 1944 strike) covered the second shift. Organizer Louis Yared, a former company union member whom Kaplan recruited into the IUMSWA, proved useful in winning over more conservative workers, especially those active in the Independent Union. Yared's greatest asset was his ability to obtain confidential company information for the campaign, including a complete set of employee lists for each department.[38]

Kaplan saw that the Independent Union had been torn by factionalism and sought to exploit this division on behalf of the CIO. After the October 1944 strike, the Independent broke into three groups. The strongest faction consisted of the old hierarchy, which remained in power. The most prominent challengers to this group called themselves the Bradford Committee (after the hotel where they met) and were led by Howie King, vice president of the Independent Union. Their goal was to turn the Independent into a decent union or else destroy it. A third and much smaller faction pursued a more moderate, accommodationist program. Led by a former socialist named Fabrinzio, it urged the Independent Union to modify some of its rules.[39]

Jack McGill infiltrated the Bradford Committee on behalf of the CIO and seems to have scored some major successes for the drive. The Independent Union's leaders decided to cancel the annual election in May because of the turmoil within the organization. The Bradford Committee aligned itself with the union drive in early July. Under Howie King's leadership, it attacked the Independent Union as undemocratic and called on Fore River workers to vote for the CIO. According to Boyson, Kaplan falsely promised Bradford Committee leaders their own offices, phones, and other special privileges if the CIO won. Before Howie King came over to the CIO, Kaplan had taken a number of "honest" Independent Union members into the campaign. Kaplan had no illusions about those who held power in the company union and then professed

[37] Kaplan interviews, Jan. 8, 1983, and Aug. 1, 1989; Kaplan report to Smith, received in Camden April 27, 1945; Kaplan report to Andrew Pettis and Gallagher, May 5, 1945, IUMSWA Archives, Series V, Box 21.

[38] Kaplan report to Smith, early April 1945; Kaplan report to Smith, received in Camden April 27, 1945; Kaplan report, May 5, 1945; "Fore River Campaign Expenses," July 28, 1945; all IUMSWA Archives, Series V, Box 21.

[39] Kaplan report to Smith, early April 1945; Vogel, "The Fore River Strikers," pp. 119–20.

a change of heart at the last minute. He accepted their support, but kept them out of leadership positions.[40]

The real key to the drive's spectacular momentum was the hundreds of volunteer organizers who worked in the yard. They were mobilized mainly through a well-disciplined "special organizers committee" but also by the formally elected "steering committee," which was chaired jointly by Arthur Boyson and Ernie Trueman. With this dual committee setup, Kaplan directed his own special group of trouble-shooters while maintaining relations with the official leadership group, which administered the signing up of new members.[41]

The special organizers focused on developing new leaders where the union was not yet strong. Among these leaders, Kaplan especially valued two newcomers, Bill Percy and Tom Clancy. The official steering committee concentrated on steadily increasing membership by getting every worker involved in the drive. Its goal was to create a "Committee of 1000" under the steering committee, with each member a volunteer organizer. Second-shift activists set a similar goal, with 250 as their target for the volunteer organizing committee.[42]

In addition to developing an organizational structure and mobilizing workers, Kaplan designed a twenty-point program suited to Fore River as a way of unifying the drive. This program amounted to a briefly stated "union contract," as well as including a number of proposals dealing with larger postwar labor issues, such as a guaranteed annual wage and a shorter work week. The union's program emerged from Kaplan's first meetings with union activists in late March. He recalled how he convinced the workers that this had to be their program and their fight.

The first meeting we called there were the thirteen guys who were expelled . . . a bunch of spies from the employees' association, and maybe two neutrals [Boyson was one]. . . . And I said, "We're going to have a program [that's] going to be drawn up by the people meeting together, after we get a committee started. Once we adopt that program, that's the credo we go by. That's what we fight for. We fight for democracy within the local union, we organize everybody regardless of what his beliefs are."

[40] Vogel, "The Fore River Strikers," pp. 119–20, and leaflet reprints ("Howard King Speaking" and "The Stand of the Bradford Committee"); Kaplan report, May 5, 1945; Boyson interview, Oct. 4, 1982.

[41] Kaplan interview, Jan. 8, 1983; Kaplan report to Smith, early April 1945; Kaplan report, May 5, 1945.

[42] Kaplan interview, Jan. 8, 1983; Kaplan report to Smith, early April 1945; Kaplan report, May 5, 1945.

When the left objected to the presence of spies from the company union, Kaplan told the story of how he had won over Aggie Campbell, the head of Sun Ship's company union, and why this tactic had been critical to that drive's success.[43]

Leaflets came out daily, geared to developments in each department. The Quincy-based *New England Shipbuilder*, published weekly by the IUMSWA, focused almost exclusively on the Fore River campaign. Printed material for the new "Victory Drive" (as it was called) featured workers in each department who were organizing for the union. Kaplan brought in Ray Stetson, a capable national staffer, to head up publicity. Together they made sure that the newspaper was easy to read and lively, with photos, cartoons, and plenty of useful information, such as comparisons of Fore River's rates with those in CIO yards.[44]

Kaplan made a special effort to involve workers in the union newspaper. Wherever possible he persuaded them either to write the pieces themselves or at least to contribute ideas. "I said, 'This is what the hell we're after, and nothing is going to get us off this program, nothing. . . . If this is what you want, then that's where you draw the line and you fight. . . . You're the guy who wants this, you tell me why you want it.' That's how those departmental articles started." Even though staffers had to write many of the articles themselves, workers were given the by-lines for these departmental pieces. Most important, however, Kaplan insisted that the volunteer organizers use their articles to win over workers to the IUMSWA program. He told them, "you tell me why you want it. And when you tell me, we're going to see that you're telling it to everyone in that yard. [It's] more important [for them] to hear it from you than to hear it from me."[45]

Kaplan explained how providing this leadership assisted the growth of rank-and-file democracy. "The origin of that format [articles with worker by-lines] comes from *just* the trade union thinking that *has* to originate with rank-and-file democracy. It's just an organizational weapon. . . . The philosophy was simple. It was to try to get from them input so that that campaign was more rank-and-file. People are afraid to talk. And once you open them up, you open up other people who say, 'I'd like to have my say.'"[46]

[43] Kaplan interview, Jan. 8, 1983; Kaplan report to Smith, early April 1945; *New England Shipbuilder*, April 11, 1945.

[44] Kaplan interview, Jan. 8, 1983; *New England Shipbuilder*, April-July 1945; Kaplan report to Smith, received in Camden April 27, 1945.

[45] Kaplan interview, Jan. 8, 1983; *New England Shipbuilder*, April-July 1945; Kaplan report to Smith, received in Camden April 27, 1945.

[46] Kaplan interview, Jan. 8, 1983.

Kaplan and the other staff members maintained a low profile, rarely publicizing their own roles. No speeches by IUMSWA staff organizers were published, although their pictures occasionally appeared in the *New England Shipbuilder*. IUMSWA president John Green's visits to Quincy were prominently covered, as were the national IUMSWA officers' efforts to push reconversion in the shipbuilding industry. But Fore River's shop issues and the opinions and activities of departmental leaders received the most extensive coverage. Even the staff's personal style changed in this drive. Kaplan organized in casual clothes, wearing a leather jacket when the weather was cold, and sought numerous ways to bridge the distance between IUMSWA staff (who previously had worn suits) and the shipyard workers.[47]

In the last two months of the campaign Kaplan brought in more staff organizers, all of his own choosing, for intensive visits with workers in their homes. Al Turner, who had assisted him at Sun Ship, proved particularly valuable for reaching more conservatively oriented, "Yankee" workers.[48]

The IUMSWA organizers also convinced many people in the greater Quincy and Boston area community who did not work at Fore River to support the drive. Numerous trade union speakers, including national UE president Albert Fitzgerald from the huge GE complex in Lynn, spoke at meetings. The IUMSWA held a number of large rallies for workers, their families, and their friends, featuring national officers, such as President Green and Vice President John Grogan, and CIO leaders, such as Secretary-Treasurer James Carey. Kaplan spoke before community and church groups, and he even addressed students and faculty at Harvard University at the invitation of Professor Sumner Slichter. The IUMSWA decided to call itself the CIO during the drive, to convey the sense that a massive labor movement stood behind Fore River workers. This simple name change, for the moment, made it easier for shipyard workers and outside supporters to identify with the drive. In contrast to 1941, however, the involvement of the CIO was only supportive; the IUMSWA kept full control of the organizing.[49]

Job security became a critical issue during the campaign. Layoffs at Fore River began in late 1943 and had increased substantially by 1945. Between January and July 1945, national shipyard employment fell from 510,000 to 300,000. Workers like Boyson, who were highly skilled and had decades of seniority, were not particularly concerned with this problem, but most of the newer "war babies," as organizers called them, were alarmed by the prospect of unemployment. The IUMSWA's plans for job security and reconversion

[47] Kaplan interview, Jan. 8, 1983; *New England Shipbuilder*, April–July, 1945.
[48] Kaplan interviews, Aug. 1, 1989, and Jan. 8, 1983.
[49] Kaplan interviews, Aug. 1, 1989, and Jan. 8, 1983; *New England Shipbuilder*, April–July, 1945.

after the war were regularly highlighted in the *New England Shipbuilder*. The Independent Union and Bethlehem management offered no real alternative to the IUMSWA proposals, which gave the IUMSWA a clear edge among younger, less skilled workers.[50]

There was intense competition to sign workers into the union. Boyson, Stanley Kyler (who worked in the pipe shop and later became president of Local 5), Bill Percy (who organized outside machinists and layers-out), and Morris Sherwin (a formerly blacklisted activist who worked in the sheet metal shop) were top contenders for recruiting the highest number of members. The most successful volunteer organizer was Italian American welder Frankie Luongo, who worked on the second shift and had the advantage of belonging to the job classification that contained the largest number of workers.[51]

Luongo was a dedicated trade unionist and socialist. He had become discouraged by Hartwick's incompetence and disagreed with the blacklisting of alleged communists, but once Kaplan entered the drive, he did not hold back. Luongo's style endeared him to many workers. Boyson, who considered Luongo one of the finest union men in the yard, had not forgotten the loyalty of many Italian workers in previous years. Boyson associated these Italians with the radical spirit of Sacco and Vanzetti, the two Italian anarchists who were tried for murder in nearby Dedham some twenty years earlier; he never forgot their execution, which he considered a terrible injustice. As a second-generation Swedish American still able to speak his parents' native tongue, Boyson was acutely aware of anti-Italian prejudice at Fore River. He believed at the time that Luongo could play a critical role in lessening this type of ethnic prejudice among workers.[52]

Luongo's role in the organizing campaign was particularly important because more than 30 percent of Fore River workers were of Italian descent. Louis Cantelli, from IUMSWA Local 25 in East Boston, later joined the organizing staff to assist with the Italians. Kaplan found that workers of Irish ancestry could be the most militant but also the most anti-union, while Italians were quieter but tended to be more pro-union. Above all, he found that the Italians would stick together, a characteristic that Luongo exploited brilliantly.[53]

Luongo wrote a unique column, entitled "Under the Central Time Clock

[50] *Shipyard Worker*, July 30, 1945; Boyson interview, Oct. 4, 1982; Kaplan interview, Aug. 1, 1989; *New England Shipbuilder*, April 25, 1945.

[51] Boyson interviews, Oct. 4, 1982, and Sept. 12, 1986; Kaplan report to Smith, received in Camden April 27, 1945; *New England Shipbuilder*, May 9 and April 25, 1945.

[52] Boyson interviews, Oct. 4, 1982, and Sept. 12, 1986; Jim and Fran Bollen conversations regarding Frank Luongo. Luongo had not been blacklisted.

[53] Boyson interviews, Oct. 4, 1982, and Sept. 12, 1986; Kaplan report to Smith, received in Camden April 27, 1945; *New England Shipbuilder*, May 9 and April 25, 1945; Kaplan interview, Oct. 6, 1982.

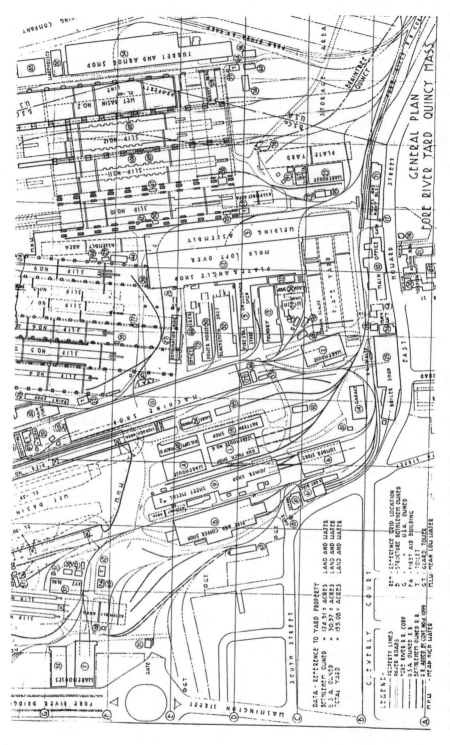

Fore River Shipyard plant layout map, 1943. Note the size of the Machine Shop and its central location in the yard. *Source:* General Plan, Fore River Yard, Bethlehem Shipbuilding Corp., in Quincy Historical Society, Massachusetts. Reprinted courtesy of The Quincy Historical Society.

New England Shipbuilder newspaper from the Fore River campaign of 1945, with photos of Tom Gallagher, Arthur Boyson, and Lou Kaplan. Meetings by shifts and departments went on constantly during the drive, with this newspaper serving as a source of department information and meeting schedules. This particular issue was the only one to carry a picture of Kaplan, in typical leather jacket. He generally preferred not to be featured over rank-and-file leaders from the yard. This issue reprinted courtesy of Carl Carlson.

with Mr. CIO," for the shipyard union newspaper. Despite the fact that Kaplan assisted him, Luongo's individualized Italian flair came through:

> It is now almost three years that I came to Fore River shipyard to do my part in the war effort to build those ships of Democracy in our fight to uphold the freedoms we hold dear. Working here at Fore River I never dreamt that the day would arrive that I, Mr. CIO, the little man with the Flat Top Hat would win fortune and achieve fame and notoriety. I am doing alright for just a *First Class Learner Mild Steel Production Welder*. My dreams are getting better all the time. Its the CIO way and come on lets make it 100 percent CIO.

Luongo's "office" under the time clock became the favorite place for dozens of other volunteer organizers to sign up new members. Luongo's success also shows that the welders were now playing a leading role.[54]

[54] *New England Shipbuilder*, April 25, 1945 (emphasis in original).

HOWARD
KING SPEAKING

To Men of Fore River:

On Monday, July 9th, I resigned as Vice President of the Independent Union. You men of Fore River know me — you know my record. You know that for over two years I have been working and fighting for Real representation for the workers. I have been fighting for a better UNION.

I'm Tired of Fighting Alone!

I am convinced that under the present set-up of the Independent, a democratic union is impossible. I know now that my efforts have been futile. This union can never operate honestly and wholly above-board.

Here's Why

Under the present constitution of the Independent Union of Fore River Workers, ALL power to function is vested in a tight little group of EIGHT men. No one else can enter this sacred circle.

★ These men have consistently refused to negotiate a written contract.

★ They have refused to amend or revise this faulty constitution.

★ They have refused to issue a monthly audit of Union finances.

★ They have refused to publish the minutes of ANY meeting of the Board of Delegates.

★ They have refused to call a public meeting for the membership.

★ Too many men have refused to stay on the job IN THE YARD and properly represent the men on vital matters of grievance, wages or working conditions.

★ Too few men are forced to carry the whole load for the Union.

★ To sum it all up, this "Union" refuses to operate as a Union!

I have labored under the delusion that the right men could remedy this situation. But I know that the right men can't get in. The whole vicious system is fundamentally wrong. The only remedy is to clean house.

If the workers of Fore River are to have their rights protected in seniority, wages, and all other basic rights of working men, they must have a far stronger, more intelligently alert and fighting union. We cannot have this with the Independent. We cannot take further chances because our jobs are placed in jeopardy by the ineptitude of the elected officers of the Union.

We Need A National Union

My decision to resign came after much hard thinking and with a troubled mind. I am convinced that only with a national Union can the rights of Fore River shipyard workers be recognized and protected.

Signed:

Howard F. King

55 Dept.

"Howard King Speaking"—leaflet by pro-CIO faction of the company union, Fore River campaign of 1945. The IUMSWA made little progress at Fore River until factionalism had a chance to erode the strength of the company's Independent Union. Kaplan and others worked actively behind the scenes to recruit disaffected company union leaders such as King. Leaflet reprinted courtesy of Carl Carlson.

VICTORY RALLY

Next Wednesday Night - July 18

Hear JOHN GREEN, CIO Shipbuilders Union

SPEAK ON

"JOBS FOR 500,000 SHIPYARD WORKERS"

Other Nationally known figures in the Labor Movement will speak on major issues confronting the shipyard workers today.

ALBERT F. FITZGERALD
President, United Electrical Workers—CIO
(OVER ONE MILLION MEMBERS)

THOMAS J. GALLAGHER
Director, CIO Shipbuilders Union
(OVER 500,000 MEMBERS)

FRANCIS F. CARMICHAEL
Director, Congress of Industrial Organizations

JAMES A. MALVEY
United Automobile Workers—CIO
(Over ONE and ONE-HALF MILLION MEMBERS

LT. FR. O'BRIEN
U. S. Navy

This pre-election rally of Fore River Shipyards will be the biggest meeting of workers in the history of New England's Industry. It will open at 8 o'clock next Wednesday night at Chamber of Commerce Hall, 1535 Hancock St., Quincy

Get The True, Factual Picture from

MEN WHO KNOW!

EVERYBODY WELCOME   Bring The Family

ARTHUR BOYSON — ERNEST TRUEMAN
Co-Chairmen, Fore River CIO — Steering Committee

"Victory Rally"—leaflet by IUMSWA, Fore River campaign of 1945. Although both the 1941 and 1945 drives at Fore River were called "Victory Campaigns," the 1945 one drew mainly on rank-and-file activity. Only at the end did it focus heavily on the IUMSWA's national strength and its connections to the CIO. Note the IUMSWA's exaggerated membership claim and the focus on job security as an organizing issue. Leaflet reprinted courtesy of Carl Carlson.

The Independent Union did not run in the election, but it engaged in a slanderous campaign against the IUMSWA and the CIO that included anti-Semitic and anticommunist attacks. For example, this diatribe was published in its newspaper:

> I would rather take a chance on men I can vote for [in the Independent] than on men the CIO appoint. I have always believed in the Church. The Church opposes Communism and I do too. I don't want to be just a number in the communistic CIO system. . . . I like my freedom. I am an American. . . . The CIO Program at Fore River: *C*ommunists' *I*nternational *O*rganization. . . .
>
> LET'S TELL THE WORKERS THE TRUTH. In order to draw a red herring across the main issues they have been spreading rumors around the yard and raising racial issues. The four main names in the CIO campaign based on their own newspapers are Andy Pettis, regional director of the CIO, Louie Kaplan, boss of Local 5, and their lawyers, Goldfant and Goldstein. We mention these names in our paper and they accuse us of Jew-Baiting. Baloney! They are the ones that are running the show. We asked the Fore River Workers if they want their lives dominated by these four. It is the old CIO propaganda to try to stir up one race against another.[55]

In fact, Pettis played a minor role in Quincy, Goldfant only represented the union when it submitted its NLRB petition for election, and national IUMSWA chief counsel Goldstein had no direct connection with the campaign. Kaplan, who directed the campaign, received the brunt of these attacks. The Independent Union made no mention of Green, Gallagher, or John Grogan, key national leaders who all had important links with the campaign and, like many Fore River workers, were of Scottish or Irish ancestry.

By June, the IUMSWA had a solid majority at Fore River and a strong leadership core in each department. Both opposition groups in the Independent Union—the Bradford Committee and the Fabrinzio faction—backed the CIO drive. The left contributed to building the union without creating political divisions. Members of all ethnic groups backed the union, including the large number of Italian-speaking workers. The few women who remained in the yard supported the effort and had their own female representative on the steering committee. Old-timers led by Boyson brought their colleagues back into Local 5, including union veterans Charlie Palmer and Johnny Hicks. Even many non-production workers (foremen, time-keepers, guards, and others) supported the union and expressed a desire to join. Church groups in the com-

---

[55] *Independent* (vol. 3, no. 2), June 6, 1945 (emphasis in original).

munity backed the campaign, and Quincy city officials no longer opposed the union. It was an astounding turnaround from 1941.

Even though some support for the IUMSWA began eroding as a result the company union's anti-CIO propaganda during the last weeks before the election, the majority held. Organizers played up the theme of patriotism without diluting the union message. The July 3 issue of *New England Shipbuilder* featured a picture of troops on parade surrounded by American flags, with the headline "July the 4th—Victory Peace Jobs," in red, white, and blue. It was an appropriate format, given that VE Day had been celebrated just two months earlier and American soldiers and sailors were still dying in the Pacific Theater. Behind the scenes, the pace of organizing increased, especially with intensive house visiting.[56]

In desperation, on the last day the Independent Union hired a band with a loud speaker system to disrupt the IUMSWA's momentum. Allowed by the company to perform on top of one of the yard buildings, the band played the Walt Disney "Seven Dwarfs" song, with the words, "Hi ho, hi ho, you'll join the CIO! You'll pay your dues, to a pack of Jews, hi ho, hi ho!" A crowd of several hundred men gathered opposite the building. Boyson recalled how Kaplan, standing between the building and the crowd, jumped onto something to make himself visible and started singing, "Hi ho, hi ho, we'll join the CIO! We'll vote today, for higher pay, hi ho, hi ho!" The crowd of workers joined in, drowning out the company union song and forcing the band to leave.[57]

On election day, union supporters marched in large groups to the polling places, many chanting CIO slogans. This time attempts at intimidation by company union delegates had no chance of succeeding. At the end of the day, when the vote was counted, the IUMSWA emerged victorious. Of 12,661 ballots cast, the union received 7,226 votes; 5,317 workers voted for no union. The IUMSWA had won with 57 percent of the vote. As a result of this victory, the union represented workers at the entire Bethlehem shipyard chain on the East Coast. The 1945 "Victory Drive" at Fore River in many ways was a return to the rank-and-file organizing strategy initiated a decade earlier by John Green at New York Ship. Local 5 workers in Quincy had participated in a renewal of democracy, however brief, within the IUMSWA. They could now join with their union brothers and sisters in seeking a new contract after years of disappointment and waiting.[58]

[56] Kaplan interview, Jan. 8, 1983; *New England Shipbuilder*, July 3, 1945.

[57] Kaplan interview, Jan. 8, 1983; Boyson interview, Dec. 22, 1982 (in this interview, Boyson sang the company and union versions of this song).

[58] *CIO News*, July 30, 1945; *Shipyard Worker*, July 30, 1945.

CONCLUSION

The many gains made by the IUMSWA during World War II, which culminated in the victory at Fore River in 1945, evaporated during the postwar era. Membership plummeted from 178,300 in 1945 to 76,800 the following year, and continued to fall throughout the 1950s. By 1962, the union could claim only 18,700 members on its rolls, fewer than it had in 1937.[1] Much of this loss can be attributed to the decline in government contracts for naval shipbuilding. Many yards were forced to close, including the Federal Shipyard in 1948. Over the following decades, naval production shifted away from the Northeast yards where the IUMSWA's membership was concentrated, while commercial shipbuilding nationally declined to new lows. By the 1960s, New York Shipbuilding had shut down, and on May 17, 1986, the last ship descended the ways at Fore River, 102 years after the company's founder, Thomas Watson, sold his first marine engine.[2]

Declining ship production and employment, however, were not the sole cause of the IUMSWA's membership loss. Dissent and anticommunism within the union became widespread during the postwar era; internal divisions led to the loss of some of the best leaders and organizers, as well as the disaffiliation of some important locals. At the 1946 IUMSWA convention at Atlantic City, former secretary-treasurer Phil Van Gelder tried to regain his national post by running against Ross Blood, whom John Green had installed temporarily while Van Gelder was serving in the U.S. Army overseas. Blood had no intention of resigning and retained Green's full support. Van Gelder was backed by

[1] Leo Troy, "Trade Union Membership, 1897–1962," Occasional Paper 92, National Bureau of Economic Research (New York: Columbia University, 1965), table A-2.

[2] *Boston Globe*, May 18, 1986.

a broad-based coalition of anti-Green delegates led by the left (but not the Communist Party). Opposition to Green's autocratic style of leadership had grown during World War II. A number of dissident locals had elected two sets of delegates in highly questionable contests. Lou Kaplan, elected from Federal Ship Local 16, was one of the key leaders of the dissidents. Green and Gallagher had refused to let Kaplan stay at Fore River after the 1945 election victory to negotiate a first contract. In protest, Kaplan went back to his old shipyard job in Kearny to fight from the inside. At the January 1946 IUMSWA convention, when Green refused to seat the challengers, Kaplan and others jumped out of the balcony onto the main floor and literally fought their way to the front stage. Green had police remove the dissidents from the hall, and the floor vote endorsed his slate of local delegates.[3]

Opposition at this convention also came from unexpected quarters, including Andy Reeder and others active in New York Ship's Local 1. Reeder had served as president of Local 1 during the war, when some 50,000 workers were employed in the yard. After the convention, he carried the fight back into Green's own local, but again the Green forces won. In disgust, Reeder simply walked out of the shipyard one afternoon and never returned.[4]

Green, Blood, and Gallagher effectively crushed both the left and democratic opposition within the IUMSWA and went on to become allies of the emerging anticommunist wing of the CIO. By the late 1940s, the IUMSWA was trying to recoup its losses in shipbuilding by conducting raids on the left-wing Mine, Mill, and Smelters Union and, with CIO approval, organizing railroad maintenance of way and shop craft workers. This shift fueled dissent in the big shipyard locals, where many workers felt they were being undercut and underrepresented. The leadership of this dissent now came from the right rather than the left. By the early 1950s, workers at both New York Ship and Sun Ship had voted to disaffiliate from the IUMSWA and joined the conservative AFL Boilermakers, which had large union locals on the West Coast.[5]

Then Green found himself challenged by his own allies in the national office. John Grogan, who began his IUMSWA career by running the Hoboken

---

[3] Phil Van Gelder and Lou Kaplan joint interview, Oct. 25, 1982; Andy Reeder and Kaplan joint interview, Sept. 3, 1986; IUMSWA, *Proceedings, 11th National Convention*, Atlantic City, N.J., Jan. 7–12, 1946.

[4] Reeder interviews.

[5] For the IUMSWA's move into railroads, see Bernard Mergen, "A History of the Industrial Union of Marine and Shipbuilding Workers of America, 1933–1951" (Ph.D. diss., University of Pennsylvania, 1968), pp. 191–205. For the disaffiliation of New York Ship Local 1 from the IUMSWA, see IUMSWA Archives, Series V, Boxes 7–12, Special Collections, University of Maryland at College Park Libraries; and Ben Maiatico interviews. By the early 1950s, there were few black workers in the Northeast shipyards; this may account for the preference of Sun Ship workers for the Boilermakers, which had a terrible record of excluding and later discriminating against black workers.

local in North Jersey, replaced Green as IUMSWA national president in 1951. The official story was that Green simply "retired," but in reality he had lost credibility after the loss of New York Ship and Sun Ship to the AFL. His domineering style and poor direction alienated even those closest to him, despite their respect for his earlier work. Grogan, however, fit the mold of the union political machine, which had become a standard feature of the New York port locals and which increasingly characterized many national CIO unions at the top.[6]

The IUMSWA finally disappeared as an independent organization in 1986, fifty-three years after its founding, when the continuing decline in its membership forced it to merge with the IAM. The IUMSWA had only been a major American trade union and a real force in the labor movement during the 1930s and 1940s. Its historic importance for American labor history lies in its pioneering role during that early period of industrial unionism.

Between 1933 and 1945, the IUMSWA developed significant breakthroughs in union organizing strategy. The history of organizing at New York Ship, Federal Ship (U.S. Steel), and Fore River (Bethlehem) reflects the union's experience in the Northeast, but it has implications beyond that region, the era, and the industry.

There were a number of factors of primary importance for shaping shipyard organizing strategy. Most important were: (1) the development of organizing in three general stages, from a single yard, to larger port regions, and finally to the national industry; (2) the development of leaders and mobilization of the rank-and-file, all within the workplace; (3) the selection of organizing staff and utilization of national officers (all operating outside the workplace) as leaders who adapt to and respect local conditions and develop local leadership; (4) the development of "active" tactics adapted to specific conditions; (5) the comprehension and exploitation of management weaknesses; and (6) the promotion of a broader view of trade unionism than just "better wages and working conditions" to motivate organizers and guide union policy.

The IUMSWA's strategy developed in three stages, initially concentrating within a single yard, then broadening to cover a major port region, and finally encompassing the national industry. The day-to-day experience of organizers, especially those inside the yards or working closely with the rank-and-file, became the basis for devising organizing strategy. For the IUMSWA, this process took considerable time and involved trial and error. The original breakthrough for the IUMSWA occurred at New York Shipbuilding in Camden from

---

[6] John Green obituary, *The Shipbuilder*, Feb. 28, 1957; interviews with Van Gelder, Reeder, and Maiatico.

1933 to 1935. Efforts to extend organizing beyond this yard—for example, to organize other Delaware River yards (Wilmington and Sun Ship) or yards elsewhere on the East Coast (in New England and Newport News)—proved fruitless without solid management recognition of Local 1 at New York Ship. Union recognition was finally achieved after the victorious 1935 Camden strike and the government-enforced arbitration process. Until this issue was settled, the IUMSWA's resources were too scarce to be used anywhere but Camden.

Once the IUMSWA had a secure base at New York Ship it could move into the second stage of organizing strategy, focusing on an entire port region from late 1935 to 1940. The union was most successful in the area around New York harbor, which included North Jersey, but again it had to secure several key yards (initially Staten Island Shipyard and later Federal Shipbuilding) to hold the port. Attempts to organize other port regions at this time were not successful, although the IUMSWA did gain representation at a number of smaller yards. Baltimore was dominated by Bethlehem, which required a national, not just regional, approach. New England, Newport News, and Sun Ship all had powerful company unions that had yet to be discredited among relatively conservative workforces and outlawed by the Supreme Court. To take on company unionism in major yards like these required a national strategy that the IUMSWA could not yet implement, as it had to devote most resources at this time to New York harbor.

Starting in 1941, the IUMSWA succeeded in implementing a strategy encompassing the national shipbuilding industry, rather than just one yard or one port. In 1933, when the union was established in Camden, this national objective had been the core of its long-term program and the basis of its "industrial union" philosophy. Not until the World War II era, however, was this approach realistic. New York harbor had to be secured first. The growth of the CIO union movement and the assistance of wartime government bodies (especially the Shipbuilding Stabilization Commission) contributed substantially to this new development. The IUMSWA national leadership failed, however, to create a viable method of defeating entrenched company unions in the big yards until the breakthrough at Sun Ship in 1943 and 1944. Fore River stands as a case study in this failure (the 1941 defeat) and subsequent partial turnaround (the 1945 victory). IUMSWA national officers John Green and Tom Gallagher, the core leaders from 1943 to the end of the decade, never fully solved this problem, which contributed to the postwar decline of the union.

A second primary factor behind organizing strategy involved the development of inside leaders and mobilization of the rank-and-file based on conditions within the yard and region targeted. The victories at New York Ship (1933, 1934, 1935), Federal Ship (1937 and 1940), and Fore River (1945) were all firmly grounded on an orientation toward rank-and-file organizing. Any organizing had to start with a core of inside leaders, such as Purkis, Green, and Gallagher at New York Ship (1933), Levin, Shapiro, and Turozcy at Federal Ship (1937), and Boyson, Hicks, and Palmer at Fore River (1937). The greater the initiative by these leaders on the inside, the better the prospects were for a more rapid organizing victory. Inside leadership had to be in place throughout the plant, including the overall yard; at division level, that is, the hull division (outside shipways) or shop areas (indoor skilled trades, and later assembly); and finally at the "shop floor" level in departments and by job classification (such as welders, machinists, or shipfitters).

Once these inside leaders had begun to emerge, the rank-and-file could be reached with one-on-one organizing, group mobilization, and recruitment into the union (as members and, for some, into leadership as well). The relationship between inside leadership and the rank-and-file became critical, and could vary by yard, company, and region. New York harbor yards, for example, proved far easier places to recruit and mobilize the rank-and-file than Quincy's Fore River yard, with its relatively conservative worker culture.

The level and involvement of inside leaders in a campaign was a measure of an organizing strategy's success. At Fore River, significant progress in organizing was not made until 1945, when leadership became unified, ideological differences and red-baiting were put aside, and workers were finally mobilized to support the union. A comparison of rank-and-file leaders who were active in the 1941 Fore River campaign with those involved in the 1945 campaign there provides a remarkable example of how important the development of such leadership was for organizing. There were sixty-five prominent activists in the yard during the 1941 campaign, in contrast to 121 in the 1945 drive. Employment levels during the two campaigns were roughly the same. Furthermore, there were only eight leaders who were active in both years. The most prominent were Arthur Boyson, Charlie Palmer, John Hicks, Harry Elliot, Ernie Trueman, and Larry Parrish. Only Parrish was new to the union in 1941; all the others were "old-timers" from the late 1930s. Just one of 121 inside leaders active in 1945 had been developed as a leader in the earlier 1941 campaign. The IUMSWA failed to retain younger organizers, such as Don Bollen and Nick Stephenson, after the 1941 defeat. When Kaplan came to Quincy in early 1945 he literally had to build the campaign from the ground up. The 1941 defeat was not simply an electoral loss for the IUMSWA but a massive organizational erosion of its local leadership base that took years to overcome.[7]

---

[7] This information about leaders comes from union activists' names that appeared in the 1941 issues of *Fore River Facts* (six months) and the 1945 issues of *New England Shipbuilder* (four months).

A third major factor for organizing strategy involved the essential role of the union organizing staff and the national office as a link between inside yard leaders and the national union. The IUMSWA, as an industrial union, had as its main objective the organization of the shipbuilding industry throughout the country. Organizing on this scale required a national institutional structure with elected officers and paid staff; a constitution and by-laws for the union's principles and rules of governance; and a national newspaper (*The Shipyard Worker*). National policy was set by the annual convention and the General Executive Board, but in practice was often shaped and directed by president John Green and secretary-treasurer Phil Van Gelder. The IUMSWA endorsed union democracy in the preamble of its constitution, but it needed centralization to implement policy on a consistent, national basis. The tension between local union democracy and national centralized direction ran through the IUMSWA from the beginning. The earliest example occurred during the 1935 New York Ship strike, when Mullin and Baker resigned from the negotiating committee in protest against the concentration of decision-making and insufficient worker involvement. Perhaps the clearest case in which centralized coordination of policy was imperative is the 1937 New York harbor strike, which could have destroyed the IUMSWA in the entire port region. The ongoing differences that arose from 1937 to 1944 between leaders of Local 16 (Federal Ship) and Local 5 (Fore River), on the one hand, and Green and the national office, on the other, are typical examples of this tension in later years.

The best staff organizers found ways to resolve this tension between the local union and the national office when they directed organizing campaigns. Mike Smith at Federal (during the spring of 1937) and Lou Kaplan at Fore River (during the spring of 1945), for example, won the confidence of local leadership and the rank-and-file but also dealt effectively with the national officers and their policies, even though they were highly independent. Both of these lead organizers embraced the "rank-and-file" strategy, developed inside leaders and then guided them in mobilizing other workers, and utilized imaginative tactics and methods of communications for reaching workers.

Other lead organizers had integrity and could work well within the union bureaucracy but lacked both the imagination and the sense of realpolitique that shipyard organizing required. Lucien Koch (at Fore River from 1937 to 1941) is representative of this type. He certainly had the confidence of both the local leadership and the national office (at least Van Gelder), but he lacked the tactical genius of Smith and Kaplan, and on a number of occasions he allowed himself to be outmaneuvered by anticommunist company unionists and a management skilled in using legal loopholes against the IUMSWA. Koch tended to trust the national office, so he was totally taken by surprise when Green and Van Gelder pushed the Bethlehem Memorandum of Understandings onto his 1941 Fore River campaign. In contrast, Smith and Kaplan not only understood how to negotiate with the national office but firmly held their ground.

Some lead organizers proved entirely ineffective. Gavin MacPherson and George Craig (at Fore River in 1941) and Francis Hunter (at Federal Ship in 1937–1938) are particularly representative. These individuals showed virtually no appreciation of local conditions or the interests of local leaders. They either failed to address the problem of red-baiting or (in MacPherson's case) actively promoted it, dividing local leadership from the workers while serving the narrowest interests of the national office.

The importance of lead staff organizers can not be underestimated. They were the main link between the national union and workers in the yard. It was they who directed and developed the campaign in the field, and who ultimately took the credit or blame for the outcome of a union organizing drive. More than any others inside a trade union, it was these organizers who devised and carried out organizing strategy.

The fourth critical ingredient in a successful organizing strategy involved developing tactics with an active character and adapting them to specific conditions. IUMSWA activists used a range of tactics in their organizing, including direct action (sit-downs, slow downs, and sabotage); subverting company structures (destroying company unions from the inside and eroding their influence on workers); legal maneuvers (court suits, labor board cases, and lobbying for direct government intervention); mass strikes; conferences, negotiations, and arbitration; creating grievance protests where no formal grievance machinery existed; and publicity (through internal union materials, city newspapers, and testimony in Congressional investigations).

The use of appropriate and well-timed tactics was essential for an effective strategy. Conversely, inappropriate tactics or bad timing could destroy what appeared to be a perfectly good organizing strategy. Tactics worked best when they were suited to conditions in particular yards and regions. For example, organizers used very different methods in New England than in New York harbor yards, for in New England the shipyard workforce was relatively homogenous and culturally conservative, while in New York the workforce was ethnically and racially diverse as well as open to change. Tactics also had to be timed properly within an overall campaign. The successful takeovers of company unions at New York Ship (1933) and Federal Ship (1937) occurred at the peak of each yard's initial organizing campaign. In contrast, the 1935 attempt to take over the Fore River company union was not conducted within the context of an organizing drive. The election of Local 5 representatives that year to minority status within the company union proved disastrous for the IUMSWA. These representatives could not carry out any pro-IUMSWA changes or reforms; they lacked power within the company union and a firm base outside it, both of which were necessary for success. In such situations, labor representatives might even be coopted. When Hardie and Mitchell turned against the IUMSWA, their actions destroyed Local 5's local leadership base and credibility for a number of years.

Effective use of direct action, too, depended on conditions within a particular yard. Don Bollen succeeded in instigating the brief wildcat strike over a firing and unsettled grievances on the *U.S.S. Massachusetts* in mid-1941 because the Vice President of the United States would be attending the launch the next day. Bollen's timing was superb; management was forced to negotiate immediately in order to avoid public embarrassment. The same dynamic operated at Federal Ship when union steward Andy Reeder and other third-shift welders used sabotage against the "counting" machines in 1938. Reeder's unauthorized actions coincided with the welders' strike on other shifts, which had national office support. Direct action was generally not a realistic tactic at Fore River, however, because most workers there were more reluctant to take risks than were workers at Federal and elsewhere. Younger, left-wing inside organizers at Fore River criticized the union for not using direct action as an organizing tool, but most workers in the Quincy yard simply would not have responded to this approach. Marty Williams's failed work stoppage and firing in May 1941 is just one example. At crucial points, however, even Fore River workers supported large-scale direct action, as with the 1944 wildcat protesting the company union. Ironically, the national IUMSWA failed to take advantage of this "tactical" upheaval by directing it into a broader organizing strategy, despite the advice of Turoczy and Turner.

Use of publicity proved an especially effective tactic at New York Ship in 1935, but this approach was possible mainly because the long strike that year tied up a strategic national defense industry and drew the interest of the national press, Congress, and even President Roosevelt. Such a scenario could not be duplicated elsewhere, which meant that publicity had to take on a different character. At Fore River in 1945, Kaplan helped redesign the *Shipyard Worker* so that it was locally based but had the image of a national CIO paper. The primary target group was Fore River workers. Articles focused not just on national IUMSWA gains but also on news from Fore River departments, including photos and names of inside organizers. The paper was entertaining, in total contrast to the generic and pedestrian IUMSWA paper put out in the fall of 1941 at Fore River.

Tactics, then, depended on the particular drive's focus, the specific yard involved, and the type of workers in that yard. Above all, tactics had to have an active character, involving as many rank-and-file workers as possible, rather than allowing most workers to remain passive while leaders or small groups carried out union activities.

A fifth factor of primary importance was understanding management weaknesses and effectively exploiting them. The best organizers at New York Ship, Federal Ship, and Fore River had a sense of workers'. experiences under a given management, the conditions specific to a yard, and probable management responses to various union tactics. In some ways the IUMSWA was fortunate that Clinton Bardo, who ran New York Ship in 1933 and 1934, was relatively unsophisticated in dealing with unions. When more conservative executives took over in late 1934, the IUMSWA had a solid base among the yard's workers, a strong group of inside leaders in every department, and a first contract, making the union very difficult to dislodge.

Organizers at Federal Ship, too, had the advantage of operating in a rather crude labor relations environment. Federal Ship's company union was more visible to workers than New York Ship's, but it was destroyed from within by IUMSWA representatives. Federal Shipbuilding president Lynn Korndorff offered no resistance through the courts, but confined his anti-union efforts to the yard itself. U.S. Steel, which owned Federal Ship but let it operate in a relatively autonomous way during the 1930s, did not offer Korndorff a larger plan for opposing the IUMSWA in Kearny.

In contrast, Fore River came under the direct oversight of Bethlehem Shipbuilding, a major division of Bethlehem Steel Corporation, and was more than just a passive subsidiary of the larger company. Bethlehem Shipbuilding had a unified national labor relations policy in place by the 1920s. Each of its shipyards had a modern personnel department, standard (though minimal) employee benefits, and a sophisticated Employee Representation Plan with uniform rules nationwide; and the shipbuilding division had its own, high-powered legal department that litigated virtually every attempt to organize.

In 1934 Van Gelder chose to challenge Fore River through the new labor relations board established under the New Deal. While this strategy made sense, Van Gelder himself admitted that he put far too much faith in the legal process, which overwhelmingly favored Bethlehem at that point. Van Gelder and Green repeated this mistake, in a different form, when they opted for the June 1941 Memorandum of Understandings that prohibited further legal action against Fore River's reorganized "Independent" company union. This time, however, it would have made sense to continue the legal fight, given that the NLRB and even the Supreme Court would have ruled against Bethlehem.

Dealing with management's sophisticated anti-union policy required worker mobilization and ongoing legal challenges, not negotiated compromises that left anti-union structures intact. In 1941, Green and Van Gelder effectively demobilized any efforts by local organizers to undermine Fore River's company union. In 1945, on the other hand, Kaplan undermined Fore River management from within by actively mobilizing IUMSWA organizers to win over company union leaders and factions, thereby splitting the "Independent" and removing it as a tool of management.

A sixth factor primary to the IUMSWA's organizing strategy was promoting a broader view of trade unionism than just "better wages and working conditions." The IUMSWA was formed, above all, to improve the lot of shipbuilding workers on the job and to give them a voice in the workplace. Leaders at all levels of the union, however, believed in and advocated more than these basic objectives. Some leaders were declared or undeclared socialists, while Communists and anarchists were further to the left. Many leaders were simply supporters of Roosevelt's New Deal coalition. Most IUMSWA leaders, however, shared the view that their union would help change the workplace, challenge the domination of the economy by big business, and reform the country at large.

In the 1930s, the IUMSWA was a relatively small operation that hardly offered "careers" for its organizers and local officers. By World War II, a number of career-oriented opportunists could be found in the union, but many leaders still held to ideals of the industrial union movement and the early CIO. Their broad social vision can be found in many IUMSWA documents, such as the preambles to the union constitution, the *Shipyard Worker*, and convention speeches. Activists eloquently articulated their hopes for a better world in interviews conducted many years later as well.

This social vision within the IUMSWA leadership came mainly from the left. Without left-wing organizers (who initially included Green and Van Gelder), the IUMSWA could not have developed such effective organizing strategies. Whenever the left was excluded or persecuted, as at Fore River from mid-1941 to 1944, division and failure followed. Left-wing activists in the shipyards were generally not openly ideological, but instead promoted a broader way of understanding basic workplace rights and advocated alternatives to capitalist ownership of industry. An alternative social and economic vision of this type was essential for motivating organizers when they faced difficult or discouraging situations.

"Pure and simple trade unionism," with its roots in the AFL of Samuel Gompers and William Green, could not provide most organizers with much inspiration. A number of staff organizers and elected officers were driven by personal ambition and the desire for power within the IUMSWA, but this type of motivation was generally not very effective for inspiring others in an organizing campaign. The IUMSWA developed in opposition to the orientation toward business unionism that characterized AFL craft unions in shipbuilding, especially the Boilermakers. When the IUMSWA succumbed to this business union outlook in the late 1940s, the union's organizing prospects receded.

A range of other secondary factors contributed to the shaping of the IUMSWA's organizing strategy. A number of nonshipbuilding union leaders and organizations assisted the IUMSWA. John L. Lewis and the UMW offered financial and moral support during the New York Ship strikes of 1934 and 1935. Their subsequent loans to the new shipyard union made it possible to hire Charlie Purkis and Mike Smith as full-time staff organizers. The ACW and its leader, Sidney Hillman, also provided help, especially in making critical government contacts in Washington during the New Deal years.

Such union solidarity, however, played a subsidiary rather than essential role in organizing at New York Ship, Federal Ship, and Fore River. Internal organizing by workers inside the yards and effective staff direction from outside proved far more critical than financial support from other unions. Solidarity *among* shipyard workers and locals, on the other hand, was very important. There were times when assistance from other unions could actually prove harmful, as was the case at Fore River in late 1941 when CIO Organizing Director Allan Haywood sent in George Craig and other UMW staffers who knew nothing about shipyard workers or New England working-class culture.

The emerging legal framework of the New Deal under which the IUMSWA operated and the positive federal government intervention that took place until the end of World War II furthered the prospects of organizing the shipyards and contributed to the shaping of union strategy. Labor law, government labor relations bodies, and the courts had a significant impact on the IUMSWA's development. Court decisions and labor board findings could help or hinder organizing, which was particularly noticeable at Fore River during the 1930s. Direct intervention by President Roosevelt, too, proved essential at times, as at New York Ship in the resolution of the 1934 and 1935 strikes. Such direct intervention, however, did not occur at Federal Ship or Fore River during the 1930s.

Organizing strategy had to take into account the "informal" and "formal" labor relations systems of different periods, from direct intervention by the Department of Labor during the early 1930s to the statute-based NLRB hearings and decisions of the late 1930s. Legislation, in particular the NLRA, and court decisions, especially *Myers v. Bethlehem Shipbuilding*, also were important factors in shaping the direction of strategy.

Overall, however, the legal framework provided the backdrop for organizing, but did not determine its success or failure. Discontinuing the legal case against the company union at Fore River in June 1941 demobilized the IUMSWA's campaign against the Independent Union and demoralized local organizers, but winning the case would not have guaranteed an election victory. In 1938 the NLRB hearings led to a Board decision against the Fore River company union, but the decision had little impact in the yard itself because of the union's inability to activate a campaign at the time. It is important to note, however, that the Roosevelt administration created a climate conducive to organizing, first through the spirit and policies of the New Deal and then under the emergency conditions of World War II.

The IUMSWA learned quite early the importance of extending organizing into the larger community beyond the families of shipyard workers, but the effectiveness of this tactic varied considerably in different Northeast ports. The commonplace view held by many progressive trade unionists today is that successful organizing requires mobilization of the community as well as the workforce. The experience in shipbuilding indicates that this outlook is valid in only some cases; conducting a broad-based campaign in the community did not ensure success within a shipyard. At New York Ship, organizing community support for the 1934 and 1935 strikes was absolutely essential, especially to gain the support of women in shipyard families; any long-term strike in Camden had to adhere to this approach.

At Federal Ship, by contrast, the community played a very minor role throughout, mainly because the shipyard was located in the middle of a vast industrial area and workers came from all over the North Jersey-New York City region. Although technically located in Kearny, Federal Ship was actually closer to residential areas in Jersey City. In such a setting, organizing strategy had to focus mainly on the workplace itself and secondarily on the industries around it, especially neighboring shipyards.

At Fore River, organizing the community was important, but it was not central to a successful organizing strategy. Here, too, workers came from all over the metropolitan area, especially during World War II at the time of the two big drives. The 1945 drive did organize within the community, giving it an edge that previous campaigns did not have. This aspect of the campaign, however, was not as critical as building internal leadership, countering management and the company union, and mobilizing workers inside the yard.

One weakness of IUMSWA organizing at all three yards during the 1930s and 1940s was the union's failure to address the exclusion of blacks and women from shipyard employment. During World War II, these two groups generally were relegated to temporary yards adjacent to the major works, or were hired in disproportionately small numbers into unskilled or lower-level skilled jobs in the main yards. As employment declined toward the end of the war, black and women workers were the first to be let go, and the IUMSWA did not support retaining their positions.

During the 1930s, however, shipyard organizing succeeded despite this weakness. New York Ship was successfully organized and consolidated by 1935, when almost none of the thousands of Camden's black residents were employed at the yard. The IUMSWA opposed racial discrimination in the preamble to its constitution, but this proclamation proved meaningless without criticism of existing shipyard hiring practices. "Organizing success" in fact may have hindered blacks' access to shipyard jobs, since positions held by white workers were protected by union seniority and traditional (white male) hiring networks.

Had the left been able to exercise more power in the IUMSWA, this pattern of acquiescence to employer discrimination probably would have been directly challenged. The actions of John Brown and other Communists at New York Ship on behalf of black and women workers during World War II ran counter to Local 1 leadership's general disinterest in the issue of discrimination. At Federal Ship during World War II, the left-wing progressives led by Nat Levin, Lou Kaplan, and others included Henry Tully, a black steward who fought on behalf of other black workers at the Kearny yard. This group consistently fought for non-discriminatory hiring and promotion policies and practices. Fran Bollen, a Communist, actively advocated the interests of women and blacks as a rank-and-file IUMSWA organizer in Bethlehem's Hingham yard, but she and others like her never had a chance to work in the permanent Fore River yard just down the road. By the late 1940s, the left had been purged from leadership at every level of the IUMSWA, and rank-and-file Communists, such as Carl Carlson at Fore River, had been completely marginalized. With the demise of the left within the IUMSWA, voices for a broader social base in shipyard employment disappeared.[8]

Arthur Boyson typifies the rank-and-file leaders who were motivated by more than just "bread and butter" unionism. Boyson was a shipyard worker his entire life. He entered Fore River in 1917, during World War I, and worked as a heater boy on a rivet gang. Later he served an apprenticeship, and he worked as a machinist until he retired in the 1960s. To reach someone like Boyson, the IUMSWA had to have a strategy that was practical but also had a social vision.

As a young shipyard worker, Boyson took fellow workers to hear Socialist Party leader Eugene Debs speak in Boston. During the First World War, he worked under Joseph P. Kennedy (father of John F. Kennedy), a Boston politician who served as a temporary manager at the Fore River yard. Boyson knew the Italian immigrants working at the Braintree rail crossing who had seen the murder there for which anarchists Sacco and Vanzetti were unjustly accused and subsequently executed. During the Great Depression he supported President Franklin D. Roosevelt and CIO head John L. Lewis, even though he remained loyal to the AFL-affiliated IAM until the mid-1930s. During the McCarthy era, he saw left-wing trade unionists, including his friend Larry Parrish, persecuted by the government and ostracized by the union. Finally, in the 1980s he witnessed the closing of the Fore River Shipyard, the only place he had ever worked.

[8] Terry Foy interview, May 20, 1988; Foy and Kaplan joint interview, April 6, 1988; Kaplan interviews, 1982–1989; Reeder interviews and correspondence, 1986–1989; Al Petit-Clair interview; Henry Tully interview; Fred Bradley interviews, June 4, 1983, and Aug. 7, 1987, Hanson, Mass.; Fran Bollen interview, July 29, 1989; Fran Bollen and Jim Bollen joint interview, Oct. 3, 1982; Don Bollen interviews, 1982–1989.

Boyson's vision was uncomplicated and direct, perhaps befitting a New Englander. He did not care much for left-wing ideology. He believed, however, that there was a potential power in the shipyard workers' movement that seemed always to revolve around the problem of organizing. Boyson took great pride in his union, the IUMSWA, even though he felt that many leaders within it had succumbed to opportunism. His perspective was deeply resonant with the ideas that had guided John Green and Phil Van Gelder when they first built the IUMSWA in Camden, New Jersey. Recall these words from the first IUMSWA constitution: "We prepare ourselves for the Workers' struggle . . . to abolish forever the system of exploitation that compels us to support with our labor an idle owning class."

In 1988, workers and others in Quincy and the surrounding communities were supporting efforts to reopen the Fore River Shipyard under worker ownership. Boyson joined the coalition. In speaking to this contemporary community issue, he echoed the IUMSWA's sentiments of a half century earlier. Boyson identified worker ownership of the yard with workers' control and the rights of American workers with the rights fought for during the American Revolution. His socialist and radical outlook was not foreign, but solidly grounded in the long history of Massachusetts. "I spoke up at the town meeting for re-opening the [Quincy] shipyard, and I said, wouldn't it be something to have the shipyard workers on the inside running things and the management on the outside. It reminded me of the [British] surrender [to the American revolutionaries] at Yorktown, when the band played 'The World Turned Upside Down'."[9]

[9] Boyson interview, Sept. 22, 1988.

SELECTED BIBLIOGRAPHY

Manuscripts: Institutional Collections

Camden County Historical Society, Camden, N.J.
    New York Shipbuilding files
The CIO Files of John L. Lewis, Part 1 (University Publications of America microfilm).
Hagley Museum and Library, Wilmington, Del.
    Steel and shipbuilding industry collections
    Bethlehem Steel and U.S. Steel collections
Hart Nautical Museum and Library, Massachusetts Institute of Technology, Cambridge, Mass.
    Bethlehem collection
IUMSWA Archives, Special Collections, University of Maryland at College Park Libraries.
    IUMSWA papers
Littauer Labor Collection, Harvard University, Cambridge, Mass.
    IUMSWA published papers, leaflets, and contracts
    Fore River newspapers
Local 5, IUMSWA, Quincy, Mass.
    Miscellaneous union documents, 1934–1950s (incomplete)
National Archives, Washington, D.C., and Suitland, Maryland.
    National Recovery Administration, RG 9
    National Labor Relations Board, RG 25
    U.S. Shipping Board, RG 32
    U.S. Department of Labor, RG 174
    National War Labor Board (World War II), RG 202
    Shipbuilding Stabilization Committee, RG 254
New Jersey Historical Society, Newark, N.J.
    Kearny files

Federal Shipbuilding company magazines
Philadelphia Maritime Museum, Philadelphia, Penn.
New York Shipbuilding papers and company magazines
Quincy Historical Society, Quincy, Mass.
Bethlehem Fore River collection

Manuscripts and Papers: Personal Collections

Arthur Boyson, Quincy, Mass.
Personal papers on Fore River Shipyard (union-related)
Carl Carlson, Scituate, Mass.
Personal papers on Fore River Shipyard (union-related)
John A. Green, Collingswood, N.J.
John Green family personal papers
Hobart Holly, Quincy, Mass.
Federal Shipbuilding and Drydock ship list (company document)
Lou Kaplan, Collingswood, N.J.
Personal papers (union-related)
Lucien Koch
Personal papers
Jack McAlack
Personal papers (IUMSWA Local 1), in possession of Eleanor Gehoosky and Janet
Friedman
Andy Reeder, Wilmington, Del.
Personal papers
Jessie Green Snyder, Collingswood, N.J.
John Green family personal papers
Phil Van Gelder
Personal papers on IUMSWA and the Socialist Party

Personal Interviews and Correspondence, Public Speeches and Forums

(Only those interviews cited in the text are listed here; all are in the possession of David
Palmer.)
Horace Bevan. See New York Ship group interview.
Don Bollen, Sept. 23, 1982. Swampscott, Mass.
——, July 29, 1989. Phone interview.
Don and Jim Bollen (joint interview), May 7, 1983. Swampscott, Mass.
Fran Bollen, July 29, 1989. Phone interview.
—— and Jim Bollen (joint interview), Oct. 3, 1982. Lynn, Mass.
Jim Bollen, Jan. 12, 1987. Phone interview.
Arthur Boyson, Oct. 4, Dec. 22, 1982; April 26, 1983; Sept. 12, 1986; Feb. 11, 1987;
June 3, Sept. 22, 1988; Aug. 8, 1989. Quincy, Mass.

Fred Bradley, June 4, 1983; Aug. 7, 1987. Hanson, Mass.

Abe Cohen, Feb. 19, 1987. Quincy, Mass.

Jack Collins, Sept. 13, 1987; May 22, 1988 (second welders' reunion). Gloucester, N.J. See also New York Ship group interview.

George "Chips" De Girolamo, June 14, 1987. Marlton, N.J.

Terry Foy, May 20, 1988. Union, N.J.

—— and Lou Kaplan (joint interview), April 6, 1988. Union, N.J.

Thomas J. Gallagher (son of Tom Gallagher), Aug. 15, 1987. Stratford, N.J.

Eleanor Gehoosky (daughter of Jack McAlack), tape-recorded interview by Janet Friedman (niece of Gehoosky), July 1988. Trenton, N.J.

Jessie Green Snyder (daughter of John Green), Sept. 13, 1987 (handwritten notes only). Cherry Hill, N.J.

Charlie Harker. See New York Ship group interview.

Vincent Hennebary, interview conducted by David Palmer and Jack Broder, Nov. 22, 1982. Norwell, Mass.

Leon "Reds" Johnson. See New York Ship group interview.

Lou Kaplan, Jan. 8, 1983. Collingswood, N.J. See also: New York Ship reunions; joint interviews with Terry Foy, Andy Reeder.

——, Oct. 6, 1982; Aug. 1, 1989. Phone interviews.

—— and Phil Van Gelder (joint interview), conducted by David Palmer and Steve Meacham, Oct. 25, 1982. Newark, Del.

Lucien Koch, interview conducted by David Palmer and Pete Hoefer, Jan. 7, 1983. Alexandria, Va.

——, June 10, 1987. Alexandria, Va.

Nat Levin, letters to David Palmer, March 11 and 31, Nov. 18, 1988; Jan. 8, 1989.

Arthur "Ott" Lynch. See New York Ship group interview.

William McCann. See New York Ship group interview.

Neil McMahon (with William Chalmers), June 26, 1987. Kearny, N.J.

Ben Maiatico, Sept. 13, 1987. Mt. Laurel, N.J. See also: New York Ship group interview; first welders' reunion.

Agnes, Alex, and Tom Mitchelson (joint interview), May 8, 1987. Quincy, Mass.

Paul Mulkern, Sept. 3, 1987. Milton, Mass.

New York Ship, IUMSWA Local 1, Reunion. Public speeches by Andy Reeder, Phil Van Gelder, Lou Kaplan, and others. Oct. 25, 1986, Rutgers University. Camden, N.J.

——, First Welders' Reunion. Public speeches by Andy Reeder, Lou Kaplan, George "Chips" De Girolamo, Ben Maiatico, and others. May 31, 1987. Gloucester, N.J.

——, Second Welders' Reunion. Public speeches by Andy Reeder and others, May 22 1988. Gloucester, N.J.

——, group interview, including Ben Maiatico, Jack Collins, Charlie Harker, Leon "Reds" Johnson, George Snyder, and others. Aug. 16, 1987. Gloucester, N.J.

Al Petit-Clair, Sept. 15, 1987. Toms River, N.J.

Andy Reeder, May 30, 1987, May 21, 1988. Wilmington, Del. Nov. 17, 1988. Cambridge, Mass. See also New York Ship reunions.

——, Letters to David Palmer, Aug. 4, 1986; Oct. 31, 1988.

—— and Lou Kaplan (joint interview), Sept. 3, 1986. Wilmington, Del.

George Snyder. See New York Ship group interview.

Henry Tully, April 4, 1988. New York City.
Phil Van Gelder, June 6, 1983; June 11, 1987. Catonsville, Md.
——, Oct. 11, 1987; Feb. 20, 1988. Phone interviews. See also: joint interview with Lou Kaplan; New York Ship reunion.
——, Letters to David Palmer, Nov. 27, 1982; Nov. 22, 1986.

Government Publications

U.S. Circuit Court of Appeals. *Bethlehem Shipbuilding v. NLRB*, 7 LRR Man. 330–341. 1940.

U.S. Circuit Court of Appeals. *Bethlehem Shipbuilding v. NLRB*, 8 LRR Man. 500–502. 1941.

U.S. *Congressional Record*. 1935.

U.S. Department of Commerce, Bureau of the Census. *Sixteenth Census of the United States: 1940, Population*, vol. 2, part 3, *Massachusetts*. Washington, D.C.: 1943.

U.S. Department of Commerce, Bureau of the Census. *Sixteenth Census of the United States: 1940, Population*, vol. 2, *Characteristics of the Population*, part 4, *New Jersey*, and vol. 3, *The Labor Force*, part 4, *New Jersey*. Washington, D.C.: 1943.

U.S. Department of Commerce, Bureau of the Census. *Seventeenth Census of the United States: 1950, Population*, vol. 2, part 21, *Massachusetts*. Washington, D.C.: 1952.

U.S. Department of Commerce. *Reports of the Commissioner of Navigation*. 1898–1926. Washington, D.C.

U.S. Department of Labor, Bureau of Labor Statistics. *Handbook of Labor Statistics*. Washington, D.C.: 1976.

U.S. Department of Labor. "Wartime Employment, Production, and Conditions of Work in Shipyards," by Edward Marsh Gordon. *Bureau of Labor Statistics Bulletin* No. 824. 1945.

U.S. House of Representatives, Subcommittee of the Committee on Labor. *Hearings Relating to Labor Practices of Employers of Labor in the Shipbuilding Industry*, 74th Cong., 1st sess. 1935.

U.S. National Labor Relations Board. *Bethlehem Hingham Shipyard and AFL*, 12 LRR Man. 97–98. 1943.

U.S. National Labor Relations Board. *Bethlehem Shipbuilding v. IUMSWA*, 3 LRR Man. 569–576. 1939.

U.S. National War Labor Board. *Bethlehem Shipbuilding v. IUMSWA*, NWLB Case No. 38 (with documents). 1942.

U.S. National War Labor Board. *Termination Report*, vol. 1, *Industrial Disputes and Wage Stabilization in Wartime*. 1947.

U.S. President Franklin D. Roosevelt. *White House Press Conferences*. 1934–1935.

U.S. Senate, Permanent Subcommittee on Investigations of the Committee on Government Operations. *Hearings, Subversion and Espionage in Defense Establishments and Industry*, 84th Cong., 1st sess. 1955, part 7. Testimony of Lawrence W. Parrish.

U.S. Senate, Special Committee Investigating the Munitions Industry. *Hearings*, 74th Cong., 1st sess. 1935.

U.S. Supreme Court. *Myers v. Bethlehem Shipbuilding*, 1A LRR Man. 575–580. 1938.
U.S. Supreme Court. *Newport News Shipbuilding v. Schauffler*, 1A LRR Man. 580–582. 1938.

Labor Publications

Amalgamated Clothing Workers of America. *Report of the General Executive Board and Proceedings of the Tenth Biennial Convention.* Rochester, N.Y. May 14–19, 1934.
Communications Workers of America (CWA). "The CWA Triangle: Organizing, Representation, Community / Political Action." Washington, D.C. Circa 1990.
IUMSWA (Phil Van Gelder). "Book of Facts for Shipyard Workers: Story of the Rise of the Industrial Union of Marine and Shipbuilding Workers of America." Camden, N.J. Oct. 1935.
IUMSWA. *Constitution.* 1934, 1936, 1941, 1966.
——, *Proceedings, 1st National Convention.* Quincy, Mass. Sept. 28–30, 1934.
——, *Proceedings, 2nd National Convention.* Camden, N.J. Aug. 20–23, 1936.
——, *Proceedings, 3rd National Convention.* Camden, N.J. Sept. 24–27, 1937.
——, *Proceedings, 4th National Convention.* Camden, N.J. Sept. 9–12, 1938.
——, *Proceedings, 5th National Convention.* Jersey City, N.J. Sept. 8–11, 1939.
——, *Proceedings, 6th National Convention.* Baltimore, Md. Sept. 13–15, 1940.
——, *Proceedings, 7th National Convention.* Sept. 23–26, 1941.
——, *Proceedings, 8th National Convention.* Sept. 1942.
——, *Proceedings, 9th National Convention.* New York City. Sept. 21–24, 1943.
——, *Proceedings, 10th National Convention.* Atlantic City, N.J. Sept. 28–Oct. 3, 1944.
——, *Proceedings, 11th National Convention.* Atlantic City, N.J. Jan. 7–12, 1946.
——, *Proceedings, 12th National Convention.* Saratoga Springs, N.Y. Sept. 23–28, 1946.

Other Published Primary Documents

American Iron and Steel Institute. "Employee Representation in the Iron and Steel Industry, As Set Forth by Men and Management before the Senate Committee on Education and Labor." New York. Circa 1934.
Bethlehem Steel Corporation. *Annual Reports.* 1941–1945.
Bureau of Vocational Guidance. Division of Education, Harvard University. *Shipyard Employment, A Place for Men to Help Win the War.* Washington, D.C.: U.S. Shipping Board. 1918.
Fifty Years: New York Shipbuilding. Camden, N.J.: New York Shipbuilding Corp. 1949.
Foster, William Z. *American Trade Unionism: Principles, Organization, Strategy, Tactics.* New York: International Publishers. 1947.
Gould, Harry E. "History of Bethlehem's Fore River Yard." Society of Naval Architects and Marine Engineers, *Historical Transactions, 1893–1943* (1945): 202–7.
Labor Research Association. *Labor Fact Book 7.* New York: International Publishers. 1945.

Lorwin, Lewis L., and Wubnig, Arthur. *Labor Relations Boards: The Regulation of Collective Bargaining under the National Recovery Act*. Washington, D.C.: Brookings Institution. 1935.

National Industrial Conference Board. *Strikes in American Industry in Wartime: April 6 to October 6, 1917*. Boston: NICB. March 1918.

New York Shipbuilding. *A Record of Ships Built*. Camden, N.J. 1921.

Perkins, Frances. *The Roosevelt I Knew*. New York: Harper and Row. 1946.

Porter, Paul R. "Labor in the Shipbuilding Industry." In *Yearbook of American Labor*, vol. 1: *War Labor Policies*, edited by Colston E. Warne, Warren B Catlin, et al. (New York: Philosophical Library, 1945), pp. 345–60.

Revolutionary Policy Committee (Socialist Party). *An Appeal to the Membership of the Socialist Party*. April 1934.

Roosevelt, Franklin D. *F.D.R.: His Personal Letters, 1928–1945*, vol. 1, edited by Elliot Roosevelt and Joseph P. Lash. New York: Duell, Sloan and Pearce. 1950.

Rowan, James A. "Mr. Koch Comes to Town." *Iron Age*. April 21, 1938, pp. 26–31, 74.

INDEX

253